T

NORTHERN HEIGHTS OF LONDON

OR

Historical Associations

of

HAMPSTEAD, HIGHGATE, MUSWELL HILL, HORNSEY, AND ISLINGTON

BY

WILLIAM HOWITT,

AUTHOR OF

"VISITS TO REMARKABLE PLACES."

LONDON:
LONGMANS, GREEN, AND Co.
1869

William Howitt

The cover shows detail of
View of Highgate from the Ponds, from a photograph of 1868

The Northern Heights of London,
first published in 1869,
is here republished by Michael Wood and FamLoc

FL

A FamLoc Book
Available in Print and eBook Format

Originally published 1869
This FamLoc Edition first published 2017
Copyright © 2017 Michael Wood
All rights reserved.

ISBN-13: 978-1544123073
ISBN-10: 1544123078

CONTENTS

PART I: HAMPSTEAD

The Manor of Hampstead
History of the grant of this Manor — Given to the Convent of
Westminster — Account of it in Doomsday Book — Manor of
Belsize granted to the Monks of Westminster by Sir Roger
Brabazon in Edward III's reign — A right of lodging his retainers
in Hampstead and Hendon granted by Henry IV to Lord Scrope of
Masham — Wolsey resting at Hendon Place on his way to York —
Hendon Place pulled down in 1756 — Hampstead Manor since the
Reformation — Granted to Sir Thomas Wroth by Edward VI —
Lady Wroth, niece of Sir Philip Sidney, and author of 'Urania' —
Sold to Sir Baptist Hickes, Viscount Campden, in 1620 —
Transferred to the Noels by marriage — The Noels Earls of
Gainsborough — The Hon. Mrs. Baptist Noel establishes The
Wells — The Manor of Hampstead sold to Sir William Langhorne
— descends to Margaret Maryon, and again to Sir Thomas Maryon
Wilson, Bart. — Procession of Horns at Charlton Manor — The
old Manor House at Hampstead

Manor of Belsize
Granted to the Waads (or Wades) after the dissolution of
Monasteries — Sir Armigell Wade, Clerk of the Council to Henry
VIII and Edward VI — sailed to America in 1536 — Sir William
Wade, Ambassador from Queen Elizabeth to Spain — his
independent conduct — employed at the Courts of France,
Portugal, and Denmark, and in treating with the Queen of Scots —
Lieutenant of the Tower, &c. — superseded by Carr, Earl of

succeeding incumbents — the present incumbent, the Rev. Charlton Lane — In the Church are monuments or memorial tablets of Dr. Anthony Askew — the wife of Lord Erskine — the mother of Mr. Tierney, M.P. — In the Churchyard are memorials of Daniel Bedingfield, Clerk of Parliament in 1637 — Lady Elizabeth Norton — Lord and Lady Delamere — Hon. Elizabeth Booth — John Harrison the chronometer-maker — Miss Joanna Baillie, her mother and sister — Sir James Mackintosh — Henry Cort — Constable the artist — In the Register are the names of Sir Arthur Athye — a son of Sir William Jones — Tyke Marrow — Thomas Jevon, actor — John Pate, actor — a Countess of Pembroke — Christopher Bullock, actor, &c. — Dr. George Sewell — the Earl of Buchan (1745) — the Countess of Buchan — Joseph Dorman, dramatic writer — James Pitt — William Popple — James MacArdell and Charles Spooner, mezzotinto engravers — Henry Barnes, legal author — Sir William Duncan, physician to George III — James Pettit Andrew, historian, and advocate of chimney-sweep reform — Remarkable cases of longevity

Countess of Huntingdon — Heath Street Chapel

Rosslyn, and named Rosslyn Lodge — since inhabited by Sir Francis Freeling — School for Soldiers' Daughters — Memoir and character of Lord Rosslyn — his violent attack on Dr. Franklin — a ruthless tool of a despotic government — the first to deny the right of the poor to glean in harvest-fields — his ostentatious style of living — violent opponent of peace with the Americans — also with France — thorough opponent of Reform — his strenuous endeavours to condemn Horne Tooke, Hardy, and Thelwall — estimates of his character by George III, and Lords Camden and Brougham it, famous for duels — Singular occurrence in 1805, near Primrose Hill

Biographical Notices   Page 199

In 1664 only one family in Hampstead who gave in a pedigree — Lord Chief Baron Wylde, who drew up the impeachment against the Bishops, resident at Hampstead — Sir Geoffrey Palmer, manager of the evidence against the Earl of Strafford, died at Hampstead in 1670 — Henry Millar murdered on the Heath — the murderer gibbeted on the spot in 1672 — one gibbet-tree remaining — The Right Hon. Lord Wharton, father of the notorious Duke of Wharton, died here in 1695-96 — Dr. Sherlock died here, 1707 — Joseph Keble, an eccentric law-reporter, lived here — William Popple, Esq., Secretary of the Board of Trade, etc., and a dramatic author, died here in 1722 — Dame Julia Blackett, a lady of much note, died here — Christopher Bullock, an actor, died here, 1722 — Robert Millingen — Sir George Sewell, translator of Ovid's 'Metamorphoses,' etc., died here in 1725 —John Gay, the poet, at Hampstead — John Merry, governor of the Hudson's Bay Company, died here — Dr. Arbuthnot at Hampstead for his health — Mr. Andrew Pitt — his curious interview with the Prince of Wales in 1736 — received a letter from Voltaire — Mark Akenside — introduced to Hampstead by the Hon. Jeremiah Dyson — Dyson and Akenside fellow-students at Leyden — settled together at North-End — haughty conduct of Akenside — removes to Bloomsbury Square — Bucke's account of Akenside — great success of his 'Pleasures of Imagination' — want of success in practice at Northampton — generous conduct of Mr. Dyson — Akenside introduced at Court — Miss Hawkins's account of Akenside — his personal appearance — his treatment of patients in the Hospital of St. Thomas — The Lords Delamere — Dr. Johnson at Hampstead — Visits his wife at Hampstead — James Pitt buried here — mentioned in the 'Dunciad' — James MacArdell and Charles Spooner, mezzotinto engravers, buried here — Richard Cromwell, a descendant of the Protector — his daughters possessed portraits and other valuables inherited from their great ancestor — James Newnham, lieutenant in Marlborough's army — fought at Blenheim — died here, 1773 — Dr. Anthony Askew, collector of classical works, died here in 1774 — John Harrison,

the Chronometer Maker Buried here, 1776 —Mr. Isaac Ware —
lived at Hampstead — translator of Palladio's 'Architecture,' etc.
— Lady Janetta de Conti died here in 1784 — Jenny Diver, the
pickpocket, died here in 1783 — an accomplice of Barrington —
her legacy   — Mr. Thomas Longman, publisher, lived at
Hampstead, and died there in 1797 — his son, Thomas Longman,
killed by a fall from his horse — Admiral Barton — his singular
history — Dr. George Armstrong, the poet, practised medicine at
Hampstead — his writings — Mrs. Mary Green — Richard Pepper
Arden, Lord Alvanley, resident at Hampstead — Sir Francis
Delaval resident at Hampstead — Lovell Edgeworth's telegraph —
Thomas Day, author of 'Sandford and Merton,' resident at
Hampstead — Romney, the painter, at Hampstead — his house
and gallery there — died in 1802 at Kendal — character of his
works — Mrs. Tierney, mother of the M.P. — Mrs. Dorothea
Baillie, mother of Dr. Matthew Baillie and Joanna Baillie, died
here, 1806 — Dame Joanna Watson and Chief Justice Watson —
William Collins, the painter — his cottage at Hampstead — his
rambles in early life about Hampstead with Morland — anecdotes
of Morland — Collins and Kirton at Highgate and Willesden —
Collins settles at Hampstead — visits Coleridge — Edward Irving
— Collins at North-End and Hampstead Green — removes nearer
to the Heath — incidents at Hampstead — removes to Bayswater
— pictures painted and money made by him — Sir David Wilkie
at Hampstead — John Constable — fond of painting Hampstead
Heath — lived in Well Walk — character of his paintings — his
tomb in Hampstead Churchyard — Sir William Beechey resident
at Hampstead — Crabbe the poet — his visits to the Hoares of
Hampstead — distinguished people met there — anecdote of the
'Black-cock' — Haydon, Leigh Hunt, and Wordsworth —
Haydon's fondness for the Heath — Joanna Baillie — Her good
and retiring character — her long life at Hampstead

Wedgwood's views of Hampstead and Highgate   Page 231
Fossils, etc. in possession of Mr. Dutton

PART II: HISTORICAL ASSOCIATIONS OF HIGHGATE

of the Sprignell, De la Warre, Mainwaring, and other families —
Robert Earl of Warwick and Ellenor Countess of Sussex — The
Blounts of Holloway — Sir Henry Blount, author of 'Travels in
Turkey,' etc. — fought at Edge-hill — Thomas Pope Blount,
author of 'Censura celebriorum auctorum,' etc. — Charles Blount,
deistical writer, committed suicide — Sir John Wollaston,
commissioner for the sale of Church lands, and also founder of
Almshouses at Highgate, buried here, 1658 — Lady Ann
Peerpoint, daughter of the Marquis of Dorchester, married here to
John La Rosse, son of the Earl of Rutland — Sir John Pettus,
cupbearer to Charles II — Charlotte, his daughter — Sir Francis
Pemberton and Dame Anne, his widow — Mr. John Shower,
Dissenting minister, author of a work on Earthquakes — Curious
memorial of Christopher Wilkinson, merchant adventurer — Sir
Jeremy Topp — Rev. Edward Yardley, author of 'Genealogy of
Christ,' etc. — Richard Browne, citizen and macon of London

Duke of Gloucester and other nobles meet in Hornsey Park in
opposition to Richard II — these nobles arraigned for high treason
— Richard II, in 1398, brought prisoner through Highgate —
Henry V met here by the Lord Mayor of London — Henry VII met
also by the Lord Mayor returning from the capture of Lambert
Simnel — Thomas Thorpe, Baron of the Exchequer, beheaded in
Highgate in 1461 — Queen Elizabeth met at Highgate on her
accession by the Lord Mayor — Venner and the 'Fifth Monarchy
Men' retreat to Caen Wood in 1661 — General Monk encamped
on Finchley Common — Trainbands encamped on Finchley
Common to resist the Pretender — Hogarth's 'March to Finchley'
— Rebel lords brought through Highgate seen by Miss Hawkins's
mother — Lord Lovat taking refreshment at the inn at the corner
— The author sees an old man who was at the Battles of
Prestonpans and Culloden — General Oglethorpe, founder of
Georgia, shot woodcocks where Regent Street now is — The 'Fox
Inn' on Highgate Hill — Rescue of the present Queen by the
landlord — Remarks of passers-by — Fine views from Highgate

— Distinguished men once resident in this vicinity — Aristocratic families who have lived in and around Highgate —John, Lord Russell, died there in 1584 — Sir Richard Baker, author of 'Baker's Chronicle,' resided there — Dr. Sacheverel died there, 1724 — Nicholas Rowe, dramatist — Mrs. Barbauld — Countess of Huntingdon — Dr. Isaac Watts — General Wade — Hogarth — Morland's visits to Highgate — Coleridge at Mr. Gilman's

and Vice-Chancellor of Cambridge — Supposed age of parish church

PART III: ISLINGTON

Islington   Page 375

Origin of the name — various theories — mentioned in the 'Tournament of Tottenham' — State of the neighbourhood at the Conquest — Famous for its open fields, frequented by shepherds and graziers — Supposed to have a church in the Saxon times — Old church pulled down in 1751 — The inhabitants of Islington broke down enclosures in 1514 — Lord Macaulay's description of the northern suburbs of London in Charles II's reign — Cowley's 'Monster London' — John Evelyn's account of the Londoners in Islington Fields at the time of the Great Fire — Queen Elizabeth crossing Islington Fields — Elizabeth beset by 'begging rogues' — Gerard the herbalist botanizing in Islington Fields — The 'Angel Inn,' in the open country — Finsbury Fields the resort of archers — Boys playing at ball there in Henry II's time — Popular sports mentioned by Fitzstephen — Ditto by Stow — Archery practised there — patronised by Henry VIII — Establishment of the City Artillery Company — Rules of the Company — King Henry's Walk at Kingsland — Henry dubs one Barlo Duke of Shoreditch, for his skill in archery — Similar titles frequent amongst the archers — In Henry VIII's time the archers broke down all encroaching enclosures — Grand shooting matches — Paul Hentzer, in Queen Elizabeth's time, notes the decline of archery — James I's endeavour to revive its use — he and Charles I keep the grounds open for archery — Shooting at 'rovers' — Markham's 'Art of Archery' — Woodcuts of archers in full costume — Engraved tickets of admission to members of Archery Societies — Charles II present at the Archery Meeting at Finsbury in 1682 — Pepys takes a walk in the Archery Fields — Sir William. Davenant describes archers in his 'Long Vacation' — Robin Hood and the King introduced in Finsbury Fields in the Ballads — The Archery Company repeatedly broke down enclosures — Distance at which an archer could hit a mark — Topham, the strong man, and the Archers — Enclosures finally drove out the archers — Odd names of citizens' summer houses — The Wells and Public Houses —

Drunken Barnaby — 'Merry Milkmaid of Islington' — Ned Ward's 'Walk to Islington' — George Colman's 'Spleen' — Sunday excursions of the citizens to Islington described by Bonnel Thornton — Goldsmith's 'Shoemakers' Holidays' at Islington and Highbury — Sir William Davenant's 'Citizen going to Islington' — The dairies and milk, cakes, syllabubs, and custards — Islington called the 'London Hospital' for resort of invalids — Anecdote of a lodging-house keeper — The citizens fortifying the roads at Islington against the Pretender — The Fields now buried under brick and mortar

Ponds, Conduits, and Rivers   Page 391

The ducking-ponds — A ducking-pond in Aldgate — one in Mayfair — one in Limehouse — a number of them about Islington — Ducking-pond House — Wheel Pond, very dangerous — Howell's description of the duck-hunting and other sports there — Pepys in the Ducking-pond Fields — The various conduits supplied by these ponds — The New River — The grand enterprise of Sir Hugh Myddelton, a native of Wales — neglected by the City, but supported by King James — The New River, for some reason, not appreciated — Liberal conduct of James I and Charles I to Sir Hugh — Original cost of the New River — Subsequent improvements — Rules and government of the Company — Descendants of Sir Hugh — Small grants to them by the Company — Extensive growth of the Company — Stow's Account of the first opening of the New River — Portrait of Sir Hugh in Goldsmiths' Hall

Remarkable Buildings and Institutions   Page 399

Districts of Islington — The Old Lazaar-house near the Whittington Stone — The Whittington Stone supposed to be the base of an ancient cross — Cromwell's House at Upper Holloway — The 'Crown' Public House, now pulled down — Sir Arthur Haselrigge assaulted — Great danger of the roads about Islington as late as 1770 — People at night only dared to pass thence to the City in company — The robber Duval — Butler's allusion to Duval — Dick Turpin near Islington — The Mother Redcaps in different places — Drunken Barnaby at the 'Mother Redcap' at Holloway — Cheesecake houses at Holloway — Cheesecakes sold by a man on horseback in London — Allusion to them in 'Jack Drum's Entertainment' — Holloway the residence of the Blount family — suicide of Charles Blount — Highbury House — Highbury famous for springs and conduits — The Corporation of London made excursions to the Springs — Gerard the herbalist's notice of plants there — Manor of Highbury formerly called Tollington — Manor House re-erected on the supposed site of a camp — probably a British barrow—Manor House of Highbury, a favourite retreat of the Priors of St. John — demolished by Jack Straw — Sir William Walworth knighted, on the sandhills near Islington, for killing Wat Tyler — Others knighted, and some ennobled there — The dagger that killed Wat Tyler long preserved in Islington —Manor of Highbury granted successively to Lord Cromwell, Queen Mary, Prince Henry of Wales — Sold by Charles I, and passed through many hands — Highbury Barn — The ancient farm to the Manor House — Barn synonymous with dairy — Barn-measure of milk — Cream Hall — Resorts of Londoners to drink milk and eat custards, &c. — Highbury Barn becomes a tavern and tea-garden — Court Baron held there — Place made very popular by Mr. Willoughby before 1785 — Great place for public dinners — Freemasons dined there, 500 in number — The Dissenters' 'Highbury Society' — their singular mode of proceeding thither — their game of hop-ball — their standing toast — Portrait of Father Ponder, Treasurer of the Society — Highbury Barn of to-day — The Eel Pie House, and Hornsey Wood House — Highbury College

Canonbury   Page 411

Former names of Canonbury — Formerly the property of the Berners Family — Granted by them to the Priory of St. Bartholomew — At the dissolution granted to Lord Cromwell — At his death Ann of Cleves dowered out of it — Granted to Dudley Earl of Warwick — Granted by Queen Mary to Lord Wentworth — Left by him to Sir John Spencer — Crosby Hall, Sir John's town-house — Canonbury Tower in its best state — The attempt to kidnap Sir John — His daughter carried off by Lord Compton — Sir John reconciled to his daughter by Queen Elizabeth — Lord Compton deranged by the vastness of his wealth — The famous letter of Lady Compton — Lodgers at Canonbury Tower —

Poole, traveller — Osborne the bookseller — Rev. John Lindsay, author of 'History of the Regal Succession' — John Hyacinth de Magelhaens — Cooke the Miser of Pentonville — Rev. John Pridden, epitomizer of the Rolls of Parliament, &c. — Mrs. Olivia Serres, *soi-disant* Duchess of Cumberland — Her daughter, Mrs. Ryves — Her trials for her supposed rights — Contradictory stories of Mrs. Serres — Exposé of her claims by Sir Robert Peel — Exposé in the 'Leeds Mercury' — Pretended Will of George III — The Duke of Kent imposed on stoker, Colonel Okey, lived at Islington — Sir Arthur Haselrigge, the friend of Cromwell, living at Holloway — Accident to General Skippon in Islington — Plot against Cromwell — Vowell the schoolmaster — Private and Public Meetings — Copenhagen House originated and frequented by Danes menaced by the Gordon rioters — Place of political meetings — frequented by Horne Tooke, Hardy, and Thelwall — Great Trades' Union meeting in 1834 — The Cattle Market — Established in Copenhagen Fields — Mr. Perkins's Cattle Market near Ball's Pond — New Prison at Pentonville — New City Prison at Holloway

Remarkable Persons who have lived in the Parish of Islington

John, second Baron Berners — Dame Juliana Berners — Lord Berners, the translator of Froissart — Manor of Barnsbury passes to the Fowler family — thence to the Wilsons — Sir Henry Yelverton, a judge under James I — Robert Brown, founder of the Brownists — his singular character — Rise of the Independents — Bishop Stillingfleet, prebendary of Islington — John Bagford, collector of books — Addison — an idea of his sojourn at Islington doubtful — Defoe educated at Islington — singular treatment of him — Halley the Astronomer resident at Islington — account of him — Topham the Strong Man — anecdotes of him — killed his wife and committed suicide — John Banks, bookseller and writer — Mrs. Forster, granddaughter of Milton — kept a chandler's shop at Lower Holloway — account of her by Dr. Johnson — Collins the Poet — some time at Islington — his fate — beauty of his Odes — Colley Cibber — lived at Islington — Mrs. Clarke, his daughter, kept a public house at Islington — Alexander Cruden, author of the 'Concordance' lived at Islington — his singular character — confined as a lunatic — his eccentric philanthropy — attempts at reform of prison discipline — the forerunner of Mrs. Fry — sound sense displayed in his literary labours — James Burgh, author — John Allingham, dramatic writer — Dr. Nicholas Robinson, medical writer — Isaac Ritson, translator of 'Homer's Hymn to Venus,' &c. —Joseph and Mary Collyer, translators from Klopstock, Gesner, &c. — their son Joseph, a celebrated engraver — Oliver Goldsmith — Arrested by his landlady at Canonbury — Dr. Richard Price — account of him — a great calculator —

zealous republican — friend of Dr. Priestley, John Howard, Franklin, &c. — The Rev. George Marriott — The Rev. John Palmer — Mary Wollstonecraft — kept a day-school at Newington Green — buried in Old St. Pancras churchyard — Baron D'Aguilar — A wealthy Portuguese Jew, developing into a most cruel miser and debauchee, living on the banks of the New River — miserable scene in his house — awful starvation of his animals — his miserable end — large amount of his property — strange enigma of such characters — Alexander Aubert — The friend and patron of Smeaton, the engineer — Abraham Newland — Celebrated manager of the Bank of England — his plodding habits — his house at Highbury — his peculiar life — his constant residence at the Bank — Dibdin's song of 'Abraham Newland' — Dr. William Hawes, founder of the Royal Humane Society — Account of him — his opposition to premature interments — Lectures on suspended animation — Benevolent exertions on behalf of the Spitalfields weavers — Great success of his Society — Humane character of his brother, Benjamin Hawes — James Elphinston — Critic and translator of Racine the younger — Joseph White — Collector of Saxon coins — Sir Brook Boothby — Tanslator of Sappho — William Huntington — Coalheaver preacher — account of him — his singular epitaph for himself — The Rev. Timothy Priestley — Brother of Dr. Priestley — Thomas Skinner Surr — Novelist — author of 'Splendid Misery,' 'George Barnwell,' &c. — John Thurston and Robert Branston — Engravers — Thomas Davison — Excellent printer of Whitefriars — Mr. and Mrs. Barbauld — John Nichols — Proprietor of the 'Gentleman's Magazine' — an account of him and his numerous and excellent works — his tomb in Islington Churchyard — Daniel Wilson — Vicar of Islington — Bishop of Calcutta — his works — Dissenting ministers — Burder, Bogue, and Clayton — The Rev. Rowland Hill in White Conduit Fields — William Woodfall, the reporter — John Thomas-Smith — Keeper of prints in the British Museum — author of the 'Life and Times of Nollekens,' and many other works — Samuel Rogers the poet — An account of him — proceeds of his books, pictures, &c. — Charles Lamb — Account of him and his sister — his friend George Dyer nearly drowned in the New River by Lamb's house — numbered all the great writers' of the time as his friends — Wainwright, the poisoner, a fellow-writer in the 'London Magazine' — his end — Lamb's last days — Sir Richard Phillips — His origin and progress — imprisoned in Leicester Jail for selling Paine's works — Daniel Lambert, of obese fame — His jailor — became a sheriff of London — started the 'Monthly Magazine' — Combated Newton's philosophy — a vegetarian — a specimen of his vegetarian habits — Sir Richard a literary curiosity — Miss Lawrence — Dr Jackson, present Bishop of London.

LIST OF ILLUSTRATIONS

PREFACE

The outskirts of London, in almost all directions, are rich in historical and biographical reminiscences. The Northern suburbs are amongst the most affluent in this respect. Before the aristocratic class acquired the tendency to spread itself over the flats of the West, the City itself and the hills which arose on its northern confines were the chosen abodes of its nobles and wealthy merchants. Hampstead and Highgate bear even today, amid all the changes of the last two centuries, the traces of this former predilection of the affluent dwellers in and frequenters of the metropolis; and Islington, if possessing fewer of the residences of the nobles of secular rank, is still more abounding in the memories of the intellectual heads of society. Its easy approach at all times from the City had made it at once the resort and the abode of a great number and a great variety of those who lived and worked there. These facts being pressed on my attention by my own residence for some years on these 'Northern Heights of London,' have led me to the attempt to bring the most prominent of the historic incidents and characters into one connected view, freed from much of the mere topographical matter which, in the local records, envelopes them. In fact, my intention has been to introduce them to the public as a third series of my 'Visits to Remarkable Places.'

In carrying out this plan I have, of course, availed myself of all existing authorities within reach, local and general; and therefore, to prevent the necessity of continual reference, here state that I have made as free use of the local historians as of the national ones, as they have made of those who went before them. I have drawn from Maitland, Norden, Stow, Park, Prickett, Nelson, Lewes, Tomlin, Lysons, etc., what was necessary for my purpose. Besides these sources, those of private societies and individuals have been very kindly opened to me. To many gentlemen, and ladies too, of the included neighbourhoods, I beg to express my grateful sense of the ready kindness with which they have responded to my enquiries, and by which they have so greatly enriched the contents of this volume. To John E. Gardner, Esq., of St. John's Wood Park, I must, in a more particular manner, express my thanks for the great trouble he has taken in searching out and selecting subjects of illustration from his most magnificent collection of original drawings, old and new prints, and photographs of the most remarkable buildings, past and present, views of streets and localities, customs and characters, of London and its neighbourhood. The use made of this most liberal and friendly opportunity will be seen in the list of the illustrations of this volume.

There must be many imperfections and little inaccuracies in a first impression of a work of this nature. The local memories of things and persons on the outlying shores of such a vast ocean of life as London, fade out of the general mind with a rapidity only equalled by that of the spread of population into the suburbs, and the consequent metamorphoses of their surface. By any correction of such accidental errors, and by any information calculated to render this work more valuable to the public, I need scarcely say that I shall be greatly obliged.

W. H.
Esher, Surrey, February, 1869.

PREFACE TO FAMLOC EDITION

For this FamLoc Edition of *The Northern Heights of London* there have been some inevitable changes to format and punctuation, especially regarding the quotations, although the prose has been faithfully retained, other than changes to one or two typographical errors and the very few instances where clarity was required.

The footnotes of the original are now endnotes contained in the *Notes to Text* chapter at the end of the book. The annoted text is underlined.

Always bear in mind the book was originally published in 1869, and all mention Howitt makes of relative dates, such as "two centuries ago", "thirty years ago", etc within the main text are with reference to that publication date. Also, Howitt often refers to Queen Elizabeth - obviously Queen Elizabeth I.

Some antiquated words and contractions used in *The Northern Heights of London*:

Viz was used for "namely", "that is to say", and "as follows". &c. is an older form of "etc."

Esq. is a contraction of Esquire, much used until fairly recently as a polite title appended to a man's name in the absence of any other title. Originally, it denoted a member of the English gentry ranking below a knight.

Currency: The currency was Pounds, Shillings and Pence, abbreviated to £. s. d. There were twenty shillings to the Pound, and 12 pence to the shilling. In old records, 3d. (for example) was written as iij^d with a "j" replacing the final i, and the "d" as a superscript. There is also the superscript ^{li} for "pounds" in some of the quotations.

l: Prior to the £ symbol, this was used to denote pounds, although a suffix rather than a prefix (20*l* = £20). We have changed Howitt's use of it to modern usage, but retained the antiquated symbol when presenting direct quotes.

Area of Land: As well as acres, there were subdivisions of the rod and pole. These three were abbreviated to a, r, p.

FamLoc Website

Those wishing to discover more about the local history and family history of can visit

www.famloc.co.uk

- and navigate to the relevant Town or Location from the menu, or navigate to the Local History Books section, where additional information on the topics included in this book can be can be found, uploaded and exchanged, and debate entered into.

Finally, we would like to give our thanks to William Howitt, without whom much of the history of Hampstead, Highgate, Muswell Hill, Hornsey and Islington would have been very difficult to collate, or indeed have been lost.

Michael Wood, FamLoc, 2017.

PART I: HAMPSTEAD

William Howitt

The Old Church
(From Park's 'History of Hampstead')

THE MANOR OF HAMPSTEAD

The first grant of this manor purports to be from the Crown under Edgar the Peaceable in 978 to his minister Mangoda. Unfortunately, Edgar the Peaceable died in 975, that is, three years before the date of the grant said to be made by him. This looks very like a forgery on the part of the monks of Westminster, to whom the manor was granted after the death of Mangoda, who it seems had no heirs, and allowed it to lapse again to the Crown. If the grant of Mangoda was a forgery by the monks of Westminster, it must have been a very clumsy and needless one, for as it did not at all affect the title, which was a subsequent grant, not from Mangoda, but from the king, the monks could have no motive for such a forgery. The real cause of the anachronism of the date was, probably, an error in the copying the 9, 8, or 3, which are figures so often confounded. This is much more likely than that the monks of Westminster should forge a charter in which they had not the smallest interest.

The extent of the manor thus granted was five cassati, or hydes, a cassatus, or hyde, being supposed to be 120 acres, which would make the five hydes just 600 acres. It is named as five hydes in Edward the Confessor's grant of other privileges, when he

3

restored the cathedral of Westminster. In the Confessor's grant it was freed from the burden of trinoda necessitas, or military duty, and from all regal or episcopal exactions whatever.

In Doomsday Book, the account is very confused. It states that the abbot had four hydes and three ploughs. But directly after it says that the demesne consisted only of three hydes and a half, and employed one plough, but villeins held part of another hyde, and there was wood for 100 Swine. The villeins had another plough; so that, after all, only two ploughs appear on the estate, and a hyde of land is missing, probably already alienated by the monks, who were much in the habit of alienating uncultivated land. The value in the Confessor's time was 100s.; in the Conqueror's only 50s., and the chief villein was a Ralph Peverel, that is, a Norman who had married Ingelrica, the Conqueror's discarded mistress. Probably, the alienation lay in this quarter.

In the reign of Edward II the convent of Westminster received by a grant from Sir Roger Brabazon, Chief Justice of the King's Bench, the manor of Belsize adjoining. It consisted of a house and fifty seven acres of land. In the twelfth year of Henry IV, the villages of Hampstead and Hendon were conferred on Sir Henry Scrope, afterwards Lord Scrope of Masham, for the lodging of his retinue, horses, &c., during his attendance on the King as royal harbinger or forager. This was, however, only a right to quarter there, during such times, as we find Hendon still the property of the convent of Westminster in Henry VIII's time; for Wolsey on his journey from Richmond in Surrey to York in his time of disgrace and banishment to his diocese, made his first resting at Hendon Place, that is, Hendon Manor House. This old building had a spacious gallery, and seems to have been long after in the hands of the Crown, passing thither at the dissolution of the monasteries; and there was a famous cedar there, said to have been planted by Queen Elizabeth. The old house was not pulled down till 1756, when it was the property of a Mr. Snow.

Hampstead Manor since the Reformation

At the dissolution of monasteries, the Manor of Hampstead was conferred on the bishopric of Westminster, established in the year after the suppression of the convent of Westminster, namely, in 1540, when Thomas Thirlby was consecrated bishop of the new see. In nine years this bishop had alienated nearly all the property of the see, and it was reduced to a deanery. The Crown, however, obtained possession of the manor of Hampstead, and Edward VI in 1551 conferred it on Sir Thomas Wroth. It was then valued at £65 15s. yearly. Sir Thomas Wroth was from the west of England. On the accession of Queen Mary he fled to Strasburg, but returned on the accession of Queen Elizabeth, and died at his manor of Durants in Enfield in 1573. His grandson, Sir Robert Wroth, married Mary, daughter of the Earl of Leicester, and niece of Sir Philip Sidney. She was a literary lady, and wrote 'Urania,' in imitation of her uncle's popular 'Arcadia.' It was called the Countess of Montgomery's 'Urania,' in compliment to the wife of Philip, Earl of Montgomery, who was their neighbour at Enfield. The poem, though praised by the adulators of the age, is not likely to win much attention from the present generation. Sir Robert Wroth, husband of the poetess, ordered in his will that the manor should be sold, and it was accordingly made over to Sir Baptist Hickes, afterwards Viscount Campden, in 1620, by his three trustees: John Wroth, his uncle; his brother, and his cousin, for the discharge of his debts and legacies.

Sir Baptist Hickes was the youngest son of Sir Michael Hickes, who was a great silk mercer and foreign merchant. He was knighted by James I on his coming to the English throne. Sir Baptist is said to have been one of the first citizens who kept shop after his knighthood, and insisted on taking precedence of the aldermen on that account. The affair led to an examination of these claims by the Court Marshall, and the decision was ultimately left to Sir Robert Cotton and other referees. From the account in the Cotton Manuscripts it appears that Sir Baptist's son-in-law, Sir Edward Noel, very unceremoniously sent Sir Robert a bribe, in the shape of a 'piece of some commodity, very extraordinary for its goodness,' and with it solicited his honourable decision. The contest had been carried on with great heat and through various suits by Hickes and Herrick, 'knights commoners of the city, and their imperious wives,' but it seems they would not, after all, venture to abide by the judgment of the lords' referees.

In 1611 Sir Baptist Hickes was himself elected an alderman, but at the express desire of the King, he paid a fine of £500, and was discharged. The following year he built at his own expense

Hickes' Hall, in St. John Street, Clerkenwell, partly for a meeting place for the magistrates, and partly for a House of Correction. He founded also at Campden, in Gloucestershire, a hospital for six poor men and six poor women. In 1620 he was named one of the Commissioners by James I to enquire into the condition of St. Paul's.

Sir Robert Noel, who married Juliana, the eldest daughter of Sir Baptist, and transferred the manor of Hampstead to the Noels, was the son of Sir Andrew Noel, of Dalby in Leicestershire, and of Brook in Rutlandshire, a gentleman who for his free expenditure obtained the distinction of an epigram by Queen Elizabeth:

> The word of denial and letter of fifty,
> Is that gentleman's name who will never be thrifty.

King James I, visiting him at Burleigh in Rutlandshire, was so charmed with his hospitality, and his great merits and abilities, that he created him a peer by the title of Lord Noel, &c. He attached himself to the cause of Charles I, and enjoyed the titles of Lord Hickes and Viscount Campden on the death of his father-in-law. He died in garrison at Oxford, in March 1643, and was buried at Campden.

His son Baptist Noel appears to have married four wives; namely, Ann Fielding, second daughter of the Earl of Denbigh; Ann Countess of Bath; Hester, daughter and co-heiress of Thomas Lord Wotton; and Elizabeth Bertie, eldest daughter of Montague Earl Lindsey, who survived him. This, the third earl, on the fall of Charles I, was severely fined, but of course, at the Restoration, he was compensated. His eldest son was created Earl of Gainsborough. The wife of his third son, Baptist Noel, founded the Wells Charity at Hampstead. The son of this Baptist Noel, who succeeded to the title, after the decease of Wriothesley Noel, his elder brother, third Earl of Gainsborough, alienated the manor of Hampstead by sale to Sir William Langhorne, Bart., in 1707.

Sir William Langhorne was a wealthy East India merchant. He had also purchased the manor of Charlton, near Woolwich, Kent, and hence the connection of these two properties still existing. Sir William married first, a daughter of the Earl of Rutland; and secondly, the daughter of Dr. Warren, rector of Charlton. Sir

William had no issue, and left his property to his nephew, William Langhorne Games, with various remainders in case of failure of heirs; hut he dying without issue, it went to Sir John Conyers, Bart., who married another sister; but Sir John Conyers dying before Mr. Games, the remainders now took effect, and the estates went to Margaret Maryon, and next to her son, the Rev. John Maryon, whose granddaughter married General Sir Thomas Spencer Wilson, Bart., and their only son, Sir Thomas Maryon Wilson, is the present proprietor. His three sisters married, the eldest, Charles George Lord Arden; the second, the Right Hon. Spencer Perceval, who was shot by Bellingham in the House of Commons in 1812; and the third, Sir John Trevelyan, of Nettlecombe, Bart.

Of the mother of the present Sir Thomas Wilson, the following curious fact is related. At the fair of Charlton, of which manor Sir Thomas's father was lord through marriage with the heiress of Charlton, there used to be a procession of horns. These horns consisted of those of sheep, goats, and smaller animals, gilt and decorated. The fair was a kind of carnival, or masquerade, in which the visitors wore masks, and where men often appeared in women's clothes. Lady Wilson was a great admirer and patroness of the fair, and even in her old age used to come down with her attendants every morning during the fair, and proceed in procession from the steps of the hall to the outside of the gates of her courtyard, where the bands of the different shows hailed her appearance as a signal to strike up their melody of discords. Richardson, the great peripatetic theatre-master, who was in high repute in his day, and in whose troop Edmund Kean made his debut, always pitched his great portable theatre in front of the house. The neighbouring gentry used to proceed to Charlton Fair in their carriages, and there was a general cry of 'Horns! Horns!' and most people purchased and placed them in their hats and bonnets; of course, Lady Wilson and her retinue honouring the custom. In 1825 Richardson was not there; the shows were few and poor, and the fair was rapidly falling into neglect.

There is a curious circumstance related of Sir William Langhorne by Park, in his 'History of Hampstead.' Dr. Warren, who resided like a domestic chaplain in the house of Sir William, and who had the character of being a 'mighty hunter,' not of foxes, but of legacies, coming, one day, into his relation's closet at Charlton, Sir William said, `I have just been making my will.' 'Have you?' cried the Doctor, 'well, what have you done for me?' `O,' replied the other very complacently, 'I have made you thirteenth in remainder in these manors.' `Thirteenth in remainder!' replied Dr. Warren, in a disappointed tone `is that all? Sir, I would not thank you for it!' Sir William, taking him at his word, dashed out the clause, and the intended devisee lived to see the eleventh, if not the twelfth, remainder expire. However, Dr. Warren appeared as the sole executor of Sir William and guardian of his nephew, W. L. Games. The Margaret Maryon to whom the estate eventually fell, is said to have been the fourteenth tenant-in-tail, so that Dr. Warren, or his heirs, would have taken precedence of her.

Such is a brief outline of the descent of the Manor of Hampstead into the present hands.

MANOR OF BELSIZE

This manor and manor house after the dissolution of the monasteries fell into the Waad or Wade family. This family is stated to be of high antiquity, as no doubt every family is if we could trace it out, the stem-father being Adam to us all; but the earliest tracing of the Wades is to one Richard Wade of the reign of Richard I. The records of the Herald's Office, however, do not ascend higher than Armigell Wade, of the Wades of Yorkshire. He was clerk to the Council under Henry VIII and Edward VI. He is asserted by Anthony à Wood to be the first Englishman who discovered America, but this cannot be the case, for he is stated to have accompanied a Mr. Hore, of London, in the `Minion,' Mr. Hore himself sailing in a ship of 140 tons, called the 'Trinity,' which sailed from Gravesend in 1536, about the end of April. They reached Cape Breton, the Penguin Isles, and Newfoundland, suffered much from famine, and arrived again in England at the end of October. Why Mr. Wade should have seen the American shore sooner than Mr. Hore does not appear. Possibly his ship sighted it first, but this, if the fact, which we are uninformed of, hardly gives him a title to be an earlier discoverer. True, the voyage of Hore and Wade was forty-two years before that of Gilbert and Raleigh to Virginia; but Englishmen sailed with Sebastian Cabot as early as 1497, and Cabot himself was an Englishman, though his father was a Venetian merchant settled in Bristol. Wade, however, and Hore, must be numbered amongst the earliest visitors and explorers of the northern coasts of America.

Armigell Wade, after his voyages, and an embassy from Queen Elizabeth to the Duke of Holstein in 1559, settled down at his Manor of Belsize, then a *retirement*, says Park, in the full sense of the word. He died there in 1568, and had a mural monument erected in the chancel of Hampstead old church.

His son, Sir William Waad, or Wade, was a still more distinguished figure in his time. James I knighted him at Greenwich in 1603. He had previously served on distinguished missions under Queen Elizabeth; to the Emperor Rodolph in 1583, and to the King of Spain in 1584. This last was a delicate business. It was to inform the monarch that his countryman Mendoza was banished from England for treasonable practices against the sovereign. The Spanish King would not admit him to his presence, but ordered him to deliver his instructions to his Minister. This, however, Wade refused to do, and returned. He was then sent to Henry III of France to lay before him an account of the conduct of the Spanish ambassador, and afterwards was employed diplomatically to the courts of Portugal and Denmark. Wade was also employed in some negotiations of Elizabeth's with her prisoner, the Queen of Scots. Sir William was Clerk of the Council, Commissary-General of England, and Inspector of the Irish Forces. He was Counsellor to James I, Muster-Master-General and Lieutenant of the Tower.

Old Belsize House
(From a print in the possession of J. E. Gardner, Esq.)

From the lieutenancy of the Tower he was removed by the notorious Carr, Earl of Somerset, in 1613, it is asserted, to put in a more pliable man, in order to the murder of Sir Thomas Overbury. In an article in 'Somers' Tracts,' called 'Truth brought to Light,' &c., it is said that one Sir Jarvis Yelwis offered a handsome sum to get him out. This article gives him the highest character for integrity and honour, though too fond of wealth; but Sir Anthony Weldon refuses this fair character by saying that all the evidence brought against Sir Walter Raleigh was matter wormed out of Cobham by Wade, and put down in writing over a signature of Cobham's obtained by unfair means. This is also made to be asserted by Cobham himself in the 'Court and Character of King James.' (London, 1650).

If these things are true, Sir William was not more immaculate than nine-tenths of the diplomatists and courtiers of those times. David Lloyd, however, in his 'Statesmen and Favorites,' defends him zealously as a most honourable man; and if we could put faith in epitaphs, so does that of Sir William at Battailes-Waade in Essex, where he died in 1623:

> You that have place and charge from princes' trust,
> Which honours may make thankful, not unjust,
> Draw neare, and set your conscience and your care
> By this true watch of state: whose minutes were
> Religious thoughts, whose howers heaven's sacred food;
> Whose hand still pointed to the kingdom's good
> And sovereigne safety; whom Ambition's key
> Never wound up to guiltiness, bribe, or fee.
> Zeale only, and a conscience cleare and even
> Raysed him on earth, and wound him up to heaven.

Sir William was author of some tracts on subjects of political interest at the time.

The manor of Belsize passed from Sir William's widow, Lady Anne Wade, daughter of Lord Wotton, and thrice married: first, to Henry de Kirkhoven, Lord of Hemfleet, in Holland; secondly, to Lord Stanhope; and thirdly, to Daniel O'Neale, Esq. She is said to have disposed of the leasehold to John Holgate, Esq., but it did not remain more than ten years in his hands, and came back to Lady Anne Wade, for in 1660 she renewed the lease to Daniel O'Neale, her third husband, who was Gentleman of the Bedchamber to Charles II. In 1667 her son Charles Henry de Kirkhoven, by her first husband, succeeded her, and, on account of his mother's lineage, was created a baron of the realm, as Lord Wotton of Wotton in Kent. He died without issue.

During the occupation of Belsize House by Lord Wotton, a

desperate attack on it was made by robbers, which is thus recorded in the 'True Protestant Mercury' of October 15-19, 1681:

> 'London, Oct. 18. Last night eleven or twelve highway robbers came on horseback to the house of Lord Wotton at Hampstead, and attempted to enter therein, knocking down part of the wall and gate; but, there being four or five within the house, they very courageously fired several musquets and a blunderbuss upon the thieves, which gave an alarm to one of the lord's tenants, a farmer, that dwelt not far off; who, therefore, went immediately into the town, and raised the inhabitants, who going toward the house, which was about half a mile off, it is thought the robbers hearing thereof, and withal finding the business difficult, they all made their escape. It is judged they had notice of my lord's absence from his house, and likewise of a great booty which was therein, which put them upon this desperate attempt.'

Lord Wotton appears to have lived at Belsize from 1673 till 1683. In 1668 Pepys visited it, and made this note:

> 'July 17,1668. To Hampstead, to speak with the Attorney-General, whom we met in the fields by his old route and home. And after a little talk about our business of Ackeworth, went and saw the Lord Wotton's house, Belsize, and garden, which is wonderful fine; too good for the house the gardens are, being, indeed, the most noble that I ever saw, and have orange-trees and lemon-trees.'

The property, on Lord Wotton's death in 1683, as leasehold, fell to his half-brother Philip, second Earl of Chesterfield, who was the son of Lady Anne Wade by her second husband, Lord Stanhope. In the Chesterfield family the estate was again granted on a lease of three lives, and in 1807 the Earl of Chesterfield sold his interest in the estate to Germain Lavie, Thomas Forsyth, Thomas Roberts, and James Abel, Esq., who divided the estate (about 234 acres) into several allotments, which obtained fresh grants. Since the death of Lord Wotton the old Belsize House had been in the occupation of under-tenants, and, during the possession of the Chesterfields, was described as in ruins. As it was sold by the Earl of Chesterfield in 1807, the house must have been rebuilt after that period, but it does not seem to be known exactly when. The former house was said to be built about the time of Charles II.

The restored house had an old look in 1852, when it was entirely pulled down, and the park wall with it.

But to return. In 1718 it was occupied by a very singular and independent sort of person: Mr. Povey, a coal merchant who, not having been brought up to the business, was very much persecuted by the trade, He was not a man, however, to sit down quietly with such attacks. He was very active with his pen, and wrote a pamphlet, called 'The Discovery of Indirect Practices in the Coal Trade,' (London 1700), exposing all the dishonest practices in that trade. He was the first institutor of the Sun Fire Office; and he followed up his expose of the coal trade by other volumes, some in quarto, some in octavo. One of them, called 'England's Inquisition,' &c., exposed the extortions and oppressions of the Excise. In this, issued from Belsize, he inveighed bitterly against the Whig Ministry. In another, 'The Unhappiness of England,' he records a lively exposition of the miseries of the poor; the pernicious consequences of wearing swords; the licentious scenes enacted in the theatres; with the proper measures for reforming those evils. He defended the government of William III; and he says that altogether his books and pamphlets amounted to more than 600 in number.

When he was the occupier of Belsize House, the French Ambassador, the Duc d'Aumont, desired to take the house and grounds at a rent of £1,000, and the Duke to put the apartments and gardens in repair. But he wanted the house on account of its having a chapel attached. Povey would not let it for the chapel to be desecrated by Popery. This piece of religious zeal he seems, however, to have thought merited reward from the Crown, and was much surprised to receive a reprimand instead of a commendation from the Privy Council, as an 'enemy to the Queen.' It was a time, he says, when there was a danger of having mass-houses set up in our universities and in London. On the arrival of the Prince of Wales - afterwards George II - he says he made him acquainted with these particulars, and offered him his house and chapel as a place of residence, and was again surprised not to receive even an answer to his offer, though 'he kept his mansion and park open for a considerable time.'

Mr. Povey evidently had an eye to self when he was pro-fessing an anxiety to benefit the nation and its princes, but does not seem to have been a very shrewd observer of the signs of the times.

BELSIZE AS A PLACE OF AMUSEMENT

In 1720 Belsize House ceased to be a private mansion, and for twenty or thirty years continued to be a place of public amusement.

> Estates are landscapes, gazed upon awhile,
> Then advertised, and auctioneered away.

According to an old 'Description of Middlesex,' formerly in the possession of John Britton, Hampstead in the reign of Henry VIII was chiefly inhabited by washerwomen; and here the clothes of the nobility, gentry, and chief citizens were brought from London to be washed. But at the commencement of the eighteenth century it had become a watering place, from the discovery of medicinal wells there; and the aristocracy and wealthy citizens of London frequenting them, carried all their follies and dissipations there.   Says Park:

> 'It was towards the commencement of the eighteenth century that Hampstead became celebrated as the resort of the wealthy, the idle, and the sickly, under the specious name of a watering-place. Houses of amusement and dissipation now started up on all sides, and the public papers teemed with advertisements of concerts at the long-rooms, raffles at the wells, races on the heath, entertainments at Belsize, and private marriages at Sion Chapel.'

Ben Jonson, in his comedy of 'A Tale of a Tub,' seemed to have an ambition to celebrate all the 'northern heights' and suburbs of London. He brings together his characters from every quarter of the district: the Vicar of Pancras, the Squire of Totten-Court, the Justice of Maribone, the High Constable of Kentish Town, the Tilemaker of Kilburn, Headborough of Islington, the Farrier of Hemsted, the Tinker of Belsize, Scriben the writer of Chalcot, and rumours, at least, from Highgate.

A comedy called 'Hampstead Heath' was acted at Drury Lane in 1706. It was altered from one called 'The Act of Oxford,' which was prohibited from appearing at that university city. It purported to be by the author of 'The Yeoman of Kent,' but was written by a Mr. Baker. A passage or two will show what sort of place Hampstead was at that period:

Act I. Scene 1. Hampstead.

Smart: Hampstead for awhile assumes the day. The lively season o' the year; the shining crowd assembled at this time, and the noble selection of the place, gives us the nearest show of Paradise.

Bloom: London now indeed has but a melancholy aspect, and a sweet rural spot seems an adjournment o' the nation, where business is laid fast asleep, variety of diversions feast our fickle fancies, and every man wears a face of pleasure. The cards fly, the bowls run, the dice rattle; some lose their money with ease and negligence, and others are well pleased to pocket it. But what fine ladies does the place afford?

Smart: Assemblies so near the town give us a sample of each degree. We have city ladies that are overdressed and no air; court ladies that are all air and no dress; and country dames with broad brown faces like a Stepney bun; besides an endless number of Fleet Street sempstresses, that dance minuets in their furbeloe scarfs, and their clothes hang as loose about them as their reputations.

[Enter Driver]

Smart: Mr. Deputy Driver, stock-jobber, state botcher, the terror of strolling women, and chief beggar-hunter, come to visit Hampstead!

Driver: And d' you think me so very shallow, Captain, to leave the good of the nation, and getting money, to muddle it away here 'mongst fops, fiddlers, and furbeloes, where everything's as dear as freeholders' votes, and a greater imposition than a Dutch reckoning. I am come hither, but 'tis to ferret out a frisking wife o' mine, one o' the giddy multitude that's rambled up to this ridiculous assembly.

Bloom: I hope, Mr. Deputy, you'll find her in good hands: coquetting at the Wells with some Covent Garden beau; or retired to piquet with some brisk young Templar.'

Belsize House and park being, as we have said, involved in this sphere of gaiety, was opened by the following advertisement in 'Mist's Journal,' of April 16, 1720:

'Whereas the ancient and noble house near Hampstead, commonly called Bellasis House, is now taken and fitted up for the entertainment of ladies and gentlemen during the whole summer season, the same will be opened on Easter Monday next, with an uncommon solemnity of music and dancing. This undertaking will exceed all of the kind that has hitherto been known near London, commencing every day at six in the morning, and continuing till eight at night, all persons being privileged to admittance without necessity of expense, &c. &c.'

By handbill it was added:

'The park, wilderness, and gardens being wonderfully improved, and filled with variety of birds, which compose a most melodious and delightful harmony. Persons inclined to walk and divert themselves may breakfast on tea or coffee as cheap as at their own chambers. Twelve stout fellows completely armed to patrol between Belsize and London,' &c. &c.

Howell, who appears to have possessed a considerable fund of low humour, and who went by the name of the Welsh ambassador, was the adventurous opener of Belsize House in this character. In the year after the opening, Howell gave a plate of six guineas to be run for by eleven footmen. The exploits of Howell, and the follies of the place, are fully treated in a satiric poem called 'Belsize House,' published in 1722, that is, when it had been open two years. From the following quotations from this poem, it appears that Howell managed to get into Newgate Prison. Whether his incarceration was for debt or offences against public morals does not appear; but the immorality of the place was enormous.

> But since he hath obtained his liberty
> By Habeas, the wicked merry be;
> Whom he by advertisements invites
> To visit him amidst his false delights:
> Assuring them that thirty men shall be
> Upon the road for their security:
> But whether one-half of this rabble guard,
> Whilst t'other half's asleep on watch and ward,
> Durst rob the people they pretend to save,
> I to the opinion of the reader leave.

In 'St. James's Journal' of May 24, 1702, it is stated that,

> 'The Court of Justices at the General Quarter Sessions at Hickes's Hall, have ordered the high constable of Holborn division to issue his precepts to the petty constables and headboroughs of the parish of Hampstead to prevent all unlawful gaming, riots, &c., at Belsize House and the Great Room at Hampstead.'

This great room was afterwards converted into a house inhabited by Charles Cooper, Esq. By another advertisement in the same Journal, we learn that

> 'on Monday, June 7, 1772, the appearance of nobility and gentry at Belsize was so great that they reckoned between three and four hundred coaches, at which time a wild deer was hunted down and killed in the park before the company, which gave three hours' diversion.'

The poem already quoted gives us a little light about the hunting in this park, said to be a mile round, or less than a quarter of a mile across.

> The Welsh ambassador has many ways
> Fools'-pence, whilst summer season holds, to raise.
> For 'tis not only chocolate and tea,
> With ratifia, brings him company:
> Nor is it claret, Rhenish-wine, or sack,
> The fond and rampant lords and ladies lack,
> Or venison pasty for a certain dish,
> With several varieties of fish:
> But hither they and other chubs resort,
> To see the Welsh ambassador make sport,
> Who, mounting on a horse rides o'er the park
> Whilst cuckholds wind the horn and beagles bark,
> And in the act of hunting has the luck
> To kill in fatal corner tired buck,
> The which he roasts and stews, and sometimes bakes,
> Whereby his excellency profit makes.
> He also on another element
> Does give his choused customers content,
> With net, or angling-rod to catch a dish
> Of trout, or carp, or other sorts of fish, &c.

The house is described in this poem, or rather volume of very wretched verse, as follows:

> This house, which is a nuisance to the land,
> Doth near the park and handsome garden stand,
> Fronting the road, betwixt a range of trees,
> Which is perfumed with a Hampstead breeze;
> And on each side the gate's a grenadier,
> Howe'er they can not speak, think, see, nor hear;
> But why they're posted there no mortal knows,
> Unless it be to fight jackdaws and crows;
> For rooks they cannot scare, who there resort
> To make of most unthoughtful bubbles sport.

This poem professed to expose: 1. The fops and beaus who daily frequent that academy. 2. The characters of the women, whether maid, wife, or widow, who make this an exchange for assignations. 3. The buffoonery of the Welsh ambassador. 4. The humours of his customers in their several capacities. It professed to be by a serious person of quality.

Belsize House was, in fact, one of the houses rightly called folly-houses, of which there was a wooden one anchored in the Thames opposite to Somerset House, another at Blackwall on shore, &c. It was also the prototype or predecessor of Ranelagh and Vauxhall, which arose about the middle of the century, and were scenes of the most disgraceful gambling, folly, and wickedness. None of the above places could exceed Belsize House.

Belsize House, we have seen, was opened in 1720. The 'Gentleman's Magazine' of 1786 says, that Vauxhall Gardens came into the hands of Mr. Tyas in 1736, who opened them with a *ridotto al fresco*, by silver tickets one guinea each. This was probably the first opening, as a jubilee was given in 1786, in commemoration of this event being fifty years before.

The house and property might have been named from the profligate family Bellasis, but does not appear to have ever had any connection with it, but rather to have taken its original name from Bel-Siége, being currently called Belseys. Thackeray seems to have named his freely spending Jack Belsize to indicate the class that he belonged to.

The evil reputation of Belsize increased so rapidly, that the highwaymen who lay in wait for the gamblers, and all who were likely to carry any considerable sums of money along with them, increased in an equal ratio, and the 'twelve stout fellows completely armed,' in less than a year had to be increased to thirty, so perilous had the journey between it and London become. Two sentinels, moreover, were regularly posted at the door of the house. In the fourth volume of Knight's 'Illustrated History of England,' p. 827, is an engraving of the house as it appeared at that time. It was not closed as a public resort till after 1745, for foot races were advertised in May of that year in the 'London M. Advertiser,' to take place there.

After it became again a private residence, it was occupied by the unfortunate Spencer Perceval from 1798 to 1807. In Lysons' time it was in the tenure of James Everett, Esq., and afterwards G. J. Wright, Esq. The last tenants were an aged gentleman and lady, Roman Catholics, and at their decease it was pulled down, and the ground disposed of for building. In 1852, when I left St. John's Wood for Australia, it was standing in its large old gardens surrounded by part of the old park wall, at the farther extremity of which, in a then lonely spot, a frightful murder had shortly before been perpetrated.

Murder of Mr. Delarue

On the 21st of February, 1845, Mr. James Delarue, a professor of music, was murdered by a young man named Thomas Henry Hooker, only twenty two years of age. This crime was perpetrated about seven o'clock in the evening, by a stile at the corner of Belsize Park, on a foot-road leading to Belsize Park from Chalk Farm. The spot, then very solitary, is now either covered with houses or is very near them. Mr. Hilton, a baker of West End, passing near there in his cart, heard repeated cries of murder, and seeing a gentleman named Kilburn about to proceed in that direction, mentioned this to him, and desired him, if he made any serious discovery, to halloo to him, and leaving his horse and cart at the Swiss Tavern, he would hurry to him with assistance. Mr. Kilburn, at the spot mentioned, found a man weltering in his blood. On the arrival of police and others, Hooker, who had proceeded coolly to the Swiss Tavern after committing the murder, and there called for brandy and water, also appeared on the spot; enquired what was amiss, and taking the dead man's hand, felt his pulse and pronounced him dead. The murder was afterwards clearly traced to Hooker; the cause of it being jealousy and revenge, so far as it appeared, for his being supplanted by Delarue in the affections of a young woman of Hampstead. On the trial Hooker read a paper endeavouring to throw the charge of the murder on a friend of his, whose name, of course, he did not disclose; and added an improbable story of the manner in which his clothes had become stained with blood. The reading of this paper only impressed the court and the crowd of spectators with an idea of Hooker's excessive hypocrisy and cold-bloodedness. He was convicted and executed.

Increase in Housing, St. John's Wood to Haverstock Hill

The lane which passed Belsize House from St. John's Wood to Haverstock Hill might still be called a rural lane in 1852; but St. John's Wood was crowding up to it. The Dissenters had already built their college within sight of it. When I returned from Australia two years afterwards, house, park, and all were gone, and a town stood in their places, still called Belsize Park, it is true, but a park of streets and human dwellings. The old elm-tree avenue leading from its ancient site to Haverstock Hill is the only thing now denoting its ancient whereabouts; and some of these fine elms are in danger of destruction, some are already killed, by the earth, in raising the road in the lower part of the avenue, being heaped about their boles above its customary level. The French display a better knowledge of natural history; and on their boulevards have grates round the stems of the trees to admit the air and rain to their roots.

THE WELLS AT HAMPSTEAD

Those who now pass through the lime avenue of Well Walk, and see the old Assembly Room, afterwards a chapel, and now the guard-room of the West Middlesex Volunteers, who see the Wells Tavern and the chalybeate well opposite, perhaps very seldom have any idea of the scenes which had taken place there at no very distant date.

The chalybeate wells on Hampstead Heath seem to have attracted attention at the commencement of the eighteenth century as of medical efficacy. Mr. Gibbons is said to have been the first physician of eminence who strongly recommended the drinking of these waters. He himself continued to drink them 'whenever business and the season permitted him to be there,' till he died in 1725. It is asserted that through his recommendations, and those of other physicians, such as Drs. Stephens, Hare, Plumtre, &c., these wells became as celebrated and much frequented as those of Tunbridge Wells. As appears by an advertisement in the 'Postman' of April 20, 1700, the Hampstead waters were carried fresh every day and sold by various persons at Holborn Bars, Charing Cross, Temple Bar, Ludgate Hill, Stock's Market, Bloomsbury, Cheapside, and King's Street near Guildhall. Mr. Richard Philps, apothecary, at the Eagle and Child, Fleet Street, not only sold them every morning fresh, at threepence per flask, but sent them out to people's own houses at a penny per flask more, the flask returned.

Dr. Gibbons played a considerable part in Garth's 'Dispensary,' under the name of Mirmillo. According to the poet, he was one of the most killing of doctors. He puts him amongst the stoutest opponents of the proposed dispensary, and makes him say:

> Oxford and all her passing bells can tell
> By this right arm what mighty numbers fell.
> Whilst others meanly asked whole months to slay
> I oft dispatched the patient in a day:
> With pen in hand I pushed to that degree,
> I scarce had left a wretch to give a fee.

Some fell by laudanum, and some by steel,
And death in ambush lay in every pill.
For save or slay, this privilege we claim,
Though credit suffers, the reward's the same.

And again:

Long have I reigned unrivalled in the town,
Oppressed with fees, and deafened with renown.
None e'er could die with due solemnity,
Unless his passport first was signed by me.
My arbitrary bounty's undenied:
I give reversions and for heirs provide.
None could the tedious nuptial state support,
But I to make it easy, make it short.
I set the discontented matrons free,
And ransom husbands from captivity.

But the fame of these waters was not very enduring. In 1734 Dr. John Soame, who lived at Hampstead, wrote a little volume to endeavour to revive their reputation. He termed his work 'Hampstead Wells; or Directions for drinking the Waters.' He gave many instances of wonderful cures effected by these waters; and made as dire an onslaught on drinking tea, as ever Cobbett did on eating potatoes. To this he added an analysis such as, perhaps, the state of chemical knowledge of the time allowed. But all did not avail to win back the departed fame of Hampstead Wells. Mr. Bliss, member of the Royal College of Surgeons in 1802, gave a much better analysis.

The fame of the waters at first brought a great concourse of people from London and other places, and Hampstead was speedily turned into as dissipated a watering-place as any in the kingdom, or any in Germany at the present moment. The Wells were furnished with a tavern, coffee room, dancing room, raffling shops, bowling green, &c. &c. Park gives numerous advertisements from the 'Postman' and the 'Tatler,' from 1701 to 1710, which show what was going on during the summer season there. People were informed that the Wells would be opened with good music for dancing all day, on May 10, to continue every Monday during the season:

'good eating and drinking, a very pleasant bowling-green, with convenience of coach-houses, and very good stables for fine horses, with good attendance, and a farther accommodation of a stage-coach and chariot from the Wells *at any time in the evening or morning.*'

It is clear, therefore, that dancing went on all night as well as all day, which the play of 'Hampstead Heath' also assures us:

'*Arabella*: Well, this Hampstead's a charming place - to dance all night at the Wells, and be treated at Mother Huff's - to have presents made us at the raffling-shops; and then take a walk in Cane Wood with a man of wit that's not over rude - but to be five or six miles from one's husband! Marriage were a happy state, could one be always five or six miles from one's husband!'

Concerts of both vocal and instrumental music were constantly advertised by the best masters. Jeremy Bowen was to give songs, or Mr. Hughes and Mr. Dean to perform on the violin. On one occasion several opera songs were to be given by a girl of nine years old, a scholar of Mr. Tenoe's. Tickets were usually only a shilling; dancing in the afternoon only sixpence; but on especial occasions tickets were as high as two-and-sixpence. The dancing took place in the great or long room, which was 75 feet long and 33 feet wide. On each side of the entrance were small rooms for tea and cards. A subscription of a guinea admitted a gentleman and two ladies every other Monday through the season.

There was another very accommodating place somewhere near, namely a private chapel, called Sion Chapel, where any couples could be married who brought a licence and five shillings; and an advertisement in 'Read's Weekly Journal' of September 8, 1716, informs us that

'Sion Chapel, being a private and pleasure place, many persons of the best fashion were married there. Now, a minister is obliged constantly to attend, and therefore notice is given that all persons, on bringing a license, and who shall have their wedding dinners in the gardens, may be married in that said chapel without giving any fee or reward whatever.'

Long Room at the Wells
(From a print by Chatelaine, in the possession of J. E. Gardner, Esq.)

Those who did not dine in the gardens were only charged the ordinary five shillings.

Thus the chapel as well as the dancing room was an appendage to the inn, and one concern. The place was the prototype of the Fleet and May Fair.

Besides these amusements and those at Belsize, Hampstead had its fairs and races on the Heath. The fair was held in the Lower Flask Tavern Walk, on the 1st of August, and lasted four days. This, too, was in the immediate vicinity of the Wells, and on the line leading out of the town to them. The races were put down, on account of the crowds of bad company that they drew together, and the mischief occurring. Probably the fairs were treated the same, from the same causes, for they appear to have long ceased. The Middlesex elections were also held on the Heath till 1701, when they were removed to Brentford.

With all these places and scenes of dissipation, Hampstead could not have been then a very desirable place of residence, nor does one wonder at the following passage in the 'Tatler':

'I am diverted from my train of discourse of the fraternity about this town by letters from Hampstead, which give me an account there is a late institution there, under the name of a raffling-shop, which is, it seems, secretly supported by a person who is a deep practitioner in the law, and, out of tenderness to conscience, has, under the name of his maid Sisly, set up this easier way of conveyancing and alienating estates from one family to another. He is so far from having an intelligence with the rest of the fraternity that all the humbler cheats who appear there are faced by the partners in the bank, and driven off by the refection of superior brass. This notice is given to all the silly faces that pass that way, that they may not be decoyed in by the soft allurement of a fine lady, who is the sign to the pageantry; and at the same time Signior Hawkesly, who is the patron of the household, is desired to leave off this interloping trade, or admit, as he ought to do, the knights of the industry to their share in the spoil.'

In 1698 the Hon. Susanna Noel, relict of the Hon. Baptist Noel, and mother of Baptist, Earl of Gainsborough, did, by consent of her son (then a minor, and lord of the manor), grant, in a court baron held for the purpose, six acres of the waste land lying about and encompassing the Wells, in trust to the poor of Hampstead. On this land the chapel and several houses in Well Walk are built. This 'Wells Charity' is still applied to apprenticing out poor children whose parents have been parishioners for three years without receiving parish relief. The boys must be fourteen, and the girls twelve years of age. The Wells estate in 1812 produced £92 per annum, and the trustees, had also £1,100 in the 3 per cents. The income must now be much larger.

The great assembly room of the tavern seems to have been converted into a chapel in or about 1733, as Dr. Soame mentions it as a chapel in 1734, and it was not so in 1732. The Rev. Charles Grant, who became rector of Hinton Parva in Dorsetshire in 1800, was some time curate at Hampstead, and was proprietor of Well Walk Chapel for upwards of thirty years.

As the wells of 'the northern heights of London' are so numerous, and in the last generation presented a peculiar characteristic of that suburban region, leaving their consequences in the theatre of Sadler's Wells to this time, we cannot select a better opportunity of introducing an account of them than here.

THE MINERAL WELLS NORTH OF LONDON

In the 'Gentleman's Magazine' there is an account of the most remarkable wells in and round London, from which we take what concerns those on the north of the metropolis. Soon after the Revolution, upon the Drama being emancipated from the shackles of the Puritans, a novel species of amusement first became general, under the name of Musick-houses. One of the earliest of these was Coleman's Musick-house near Lamb's Conduit, which soon became a place of much abandoned company. In fact, this was their general character, and, in the end, caused their putting down one after another. One of the most frequented, and one which long outlasted others, was that at Islington called Miles's Musick-house or Sadler's Wells. Epsom and Tunbridge Wells were in use before Sadler's Well acquired its modern reputation, and there was also another well at Islington near the same spot called Islington Wells or Islington Spa, to which we shall anon refer. But as to Sadler's Well, in a tract referred to by Sir John Hawkins, Lysons, and Strutt, published by Thomas Malthus at the Sun in the Poultry, 1684, we are told that

> 'the new well at Islington is a certain spring in the middle of a garden belonging to the musick-house built by Mr. Sadler on the north side of the great cistern that receives the New River water near Islington; the water whereof was, before the Reformation, much famed for several extraordinary cures performed thereby, and was thereupon accounted sacred, and called the Holy Well. The priests belonging to the Priory of Clerkenwell used to attend there, and made the people believe that the virtues of the water proceeded from the efficacy of their prayers. But upon the Reformation, the well was stopped up, on the supposition that the frequenting it was altogether superstitious; and so by degrees, it grew out of remembrance and was wholly lost. Mr. Sadler being made surveyor of the highways, and having good gravel in his garden, employed two men to dig there.'

These men rediscovered the well, a large well of stone, arched over and curiously carved. Supposing that the fame of the well formerly had proceeded from some medicinal virtue, Mr. Sadler carried some of it to a doctor, who advised him to brew beer with it, and sell it in bottles, called roundlets. Dr. Merton and others recommended their patients to drink it. And they were told in a puff, that it was well to drink a glass of Rhenish or white wine with it, and for those who smoked, to take a pipe or two whilst the water worked. In fact, it was intended as at all such places, to make it a resort for dissipation in the pretence of seeking health. The well appears to have been opened in June 1697, being recommended in the 'Post-boy' and 'Flying Post' as a powerful chalybeate spring. Sadler would seem only to have held it till 1799, for in that year it was called Miles's Musick-house, though the well continued to hold the name of Sadler's Well.

A description of the people frequenting the well and music house, which shows the rude, low, and disgusting character of the population resorting to such places at that period, is given in the 'Weekly Comedy,' a play 'then acted in the Coffee-houses of London.' Of this 'Weekly Comedy' the first number was published about May 3, 1699, and it was issued periodically in half sheets, folio, apparently with remarks and anecdotes. It was by Edward Ward; and the same piece was afterwards inserted in his Miscellaneous Works, as the 'Humours of a Coffee-house.' These works of Ned Ward present a faithful, no doubt, but a most awful and disgusting picture of coarseness, obscenity, and vile debauchery of the common people of London at that date, in language which could not be read now in any decent family. In the third number of Ward's 'Comedy,' and in 'Dowke's Protestant Mercury' of the same date, 1699, a story is related of a fellow at Sadler's Wells, who, after he had dined heartily on a buttock of beef, for the wager of five guineas eat a live cock - feathers, entrails, and all - with only a plate of oil and vinegar for sauce, and half a pint of brandy to wash it down; and offered, after an interval of two hours, to do the same thing again for five guineas more. In the same paper of January 4th following, the same monster is stated to have eaten a live cat at a music house in St. Katherine's. These horrible feats were attested by many credible people, who were eye-witnesses. According to Ward's account, not only butchers, bailiffs, prize-fighters, deer-stealers, and a world of 'vermin trained up for the gallows,' but fine ladies and gentlemen from the inns of court, from the wealthy circles, frequented the New Tunbridge and Sadler's Wells, at Islington, where they were regaled with cheese-cakes, custards, bottled ale and cider, and with singing and dancing. In this motley crowd were conspicuous numerous women of the town, and the quality of the singing and dancing was of the lowest and most sensual kind. Mimicry and pantomime, and a sort of masquerading, made up the entertainment, which was witnessed by the more select, if any attending such places could merit the name, from galleries adjoining the organ-loft.

The celebrity of the springs at Sadler's Well and the Islington New Tunbridge, did not last long, but the music halls and their attractions continued to draw crowds for several years. There is a rare tract called 'God's Judgment against Murderers, or an account of a cruel and barbarous murder, committed on Thursday night, the 14th of August, at Sadler's Musick-house, near Islington, on the body of Mr. Waite, a lieutenant of a man-of-war, by one Mr. French, a lawyer of the Temple, showing how they quarrelled about women,' &c., 1712. This tract, which calls the place Sadler's, otherwise Miles's Musick-house, gives it the character of a most abandoned resort 'of unaccountable and disorderly people.'

Sadler's music-house in his own time was a wooden building. Miles is said to have much improved and beautified the place and made it very popular. One account says that Miles was succeeded by Francis Forcer, the musician; but Sir John Hawkins, in his History of Musick, makes Francis Forcer succeed Sadler:

'One Francis Forcer, a musician, and the composer of many songs, printed in the Theatre of Musick, published by Henry Playford and John Carr, in the years 1685, 1686, and 1687, became the occupier of the Wells and Musick-house. His successor therein was a son of his, who had been bred up to the law, and, as some said, a barrister. He was the first who exhibited there the diversions of rope-dancing, tumbling, &c. He was a very gentlemanly man, remarkably tall and athletic, and died in an advanced age, about the year 1740, at the Wells, which, for many years, had been the place of his residence.'

William Garbott in his 'New River, a Poem,' praises Francis Forcer highly as a gentleman and man of education, educated at

Oxford, and a member of the Bar, and 'most obliging man,' though he confesses that 'Miles first did make the Wells known,' or, at least, 'first got it fame.' A few stanzas from Garbott's poem will give an idea of the place and its amusements:

> Through Islington then glides my best-loved theme,
> And Miles's garden washes with his stream;
> Now Forcers garden is its proper name,
> Though Miles the man was who first got it fame.
> And though it's owned Miles first did make it known,
> Forcer improves the same we all must own.
> There you may sit under the shady trees,
> And drink and smoke, fanned by the gentle breeze,
> Behold the fish, how wantonly they play,
> And catch them also, if you please, you may.
> Two noble swans swim by this garden's side,
> Of water-fowl the glory and the pride,
> Which to the garden no small beauty are;
> Were they but black, they would be much more rare:
> With ducks so tame that from your hands they feed,
> And, I believe, for that they sometimes bleed.
> A noble walk likewise adorns the place,
> To which the river adds a greater grace;
> There you can sit, or walk, do what you please,
> Which best you like, and most suits at your ease.
> Now to the show-room let's awhile repair
> To see the active feats performed there;
> How the bold Dutchman on the rope doth bound,
> With greater air than others on the ground;
> What capers does he cut! how backward leaps!
> With Merry Andrew eyeing all his steps:
> His comic humours with delight you see,
> Pleasing unto the best of company.
> The great D'Aumont has been diverted there,
> With divers others of like character;
> As by their generous gifts they make appear.
> The famous tumbler lately is come o'er,
> Who was the wonder of the other shore:
> France, Spain, and Holland, and High Germany,
> Sweden, and Denmark, and famed Italy,
> His active feats did with amazement see,
> Which done by man they thought could never be.
> Amongst the rest, he falleth from on high,

Head-foremost from the upper gallery,
And in his fall performs a somerset,
The women think in dread he'll break his neck,
And gently on his feet comes to the ground,
To the amazement of beholders round.
Black-Scaramouch and Harlequin of fame
The ladder-dance, with forty I could name,
Full as diverting, and of later date,
You may see there at a much cheaper rate
Than at The House, as well performed too:
You only pay for liquors, not the show;
Such as neat brandy, Southam cyder fine,
And grape's true juice as e'er was pressed from vine.

Francis Forcer continued lessee of the premises till the time of his death, which happened in April 1743. In his will he added the house at Sadler's Wells, with all its stock, scenery, &c., to be sold for the payment of his debts. This was done; an encouragement to a new place of the same kind opened at Clerkenwell. A view of old Sadler's Wells is engraved in a quarto volume of songs set to music, called 'Universal Harmony, or the Gentlemen and Ladies Companion,' 1745 and 1746. The Well House is seen standing detached from the Musick-house. 'A song on Sadler's Wells' in the volume says:

Herds around, on herbage green,
And bleating flocks, are sporting seen;
While Phœbus with his brightest rays
The fertile soil doth seem to praise;
And zephyrs with their gentlest gales,
Breathing more sweet than flowery vales,
Which give new health, and heat repells,
Such are the joys of Sadler's Wells.

Let us just imagine the site of Sadler's Wells now, in the heart of brick Islington!

The next proprietor was Rosoman, who in 1765 pulled down the old wooden building and erected the theatre on an enlarged scale, at a cost of £4,225. In fitting up the theatre every attention was paid to the accommodation of the audience with liquors during the performance, for which purpose the seats had backs with ledged shelves at the top, so as to secure the bottles for each row of visitors in succession, and the glasses having only short stems, were turned down over the mouths of the bottles. A bill of 1773 gives us the terms on which this theatrical system was conducted:

> 'Ticket for the boxes, 3s., which entitles the bearer to a pint of Port, Mountain, Lisbon, or Punch. Ticket for the pit, 1s. 6d. Ticket for the gallery, 1s.; either of which, with an additional sixpence, will entitle the bearer to a pint of either of the aforesaid liquors. Any person choosing a second pint may have it at 1s., the price paid at any other public place.'

At benefits, the performers relied on their popularity to fill the house, and announced, 'boxes 3s.; pit and gallery, 1s. 6d. Those who choose wine may have it at 2s. a bottle.' There was a temporary revival of this most objectionable custom during the seasons of 1803-1805; and the wine supplied at 2s. the bottle and 1s. the pint.

In 1778 the whole interior of the house was broken down and materially improved. About the same period, if not some years earlier, Dibdin composed several favourite pieces for this theatre. The music was popular, the scenes novel, and the pantomimes celebrated for their comic tricks and changes. Here Grimaldi shone in all his inimitableness. From Rosoman Sadler's Wells went to the celebrated performer, Mr. King, Serjeant the trumpeter, and Arnold, a goldsmith and jeweller. Arnold and Mr. Wroughton, of Drury Lane, purchased the place for £12,000. The Wells were afterwards the joint property of Messrs. Wroughton, Siddons (husband of the celebrated Mrs. Siddons), Hughes (proprietor of several provincial theatres), Coates (a linen-draper), and Mr. Arnold, jun. In 1802 it was purchased by Charles Dibdin, Mr. T. Dibdin (his brother), Mr. Reeve (the composer), Mr. Andrews (the scene-painter of this theatre), and two gentlemen of the City. The proximity of the New River enabled the proprietors, in Easter of 1804, to exhibit a water entertainment called *Naumachia*, in which real water was introduced, with a large basin, where the stage originally stood, with boats, ships, and huge sea monsters upon it.

The Islington Spa, or New Tunbridge Wells

This was a similar place of entertainment, as we have said, before Sadler's Wells was opened; though it does not seem to have had music until Sadler's Wells compelled it to introduce it or to fall behind in interest. In 1700 it advertised music for dancing all the day long every Monday and Thursday during the summer season. No mask admitted. In 1733 it was visited by the Princess Amelia for drinking the waters. George Colman wrote a dramatic trifle called 'The Spleen; or Islington Spa,' which was acted at Drury Lane in 1776. In the following year Mr. Holland, the proprietor, advertised that the number of patients daily receiving benefit 'was scarcely to be creditted.' Holland soon after failed, and the remainder of the lease was sold. The place continued to go down. The gardens, however, for some years opened on Mondays for drinking the waters, and on afternoons for tea. Annual subscription one guinea; visits to drink the waters, sixpence each to non-subscribers. In a volume of songs, published about 1727, there is a view of the company walking round the quadrangle enclosing the well, and others walking in the gardens. After the gardens were closed an attempt was made to re-open them again as a minor Vauxhall; but before 1812 they were broken up and a row of houses built on the spot. The well, however, continued open.

The Clerks' Well

So called from the monks of Clerkenwell Priory, and which now gives name to the populous parish of Clerkenwell, this is the most ancient of those in the vicinity of the metropolis. It was indebted for its fame to the history of the drama, and not to any medicinal virtues of the spring.

Bagnigge Wells

These were situated on a little stream called the River Bagnigge, though scarcely better than a ditch. The House of Bagnigge was at one time inhabited by Nell Gwynn. On an inscription on the front of it stood, 'T. S. This is Bagnigge House near the Pindar a Wakefeilde, 1680.' In it was a chimney-piece with a carved effigy of Nell surrounded by prints of all sorts, gilt, supposed to refer to her origin as seller of fruit at the theatres. In 1760, on discovery of the wells, it was opened for water-drinking, and for the rest of the amusements given at such places, and probably from Nell Gwynn's residence there, called, 'The Royal Bagnigge Wells.' It was a great Sunday resort. A curious mezzotint print of Bagnigge Wells was published by J. R. Smith, 1772. In 1813 the tenant, a Mr. Salter, was a bankrupt, and the furniture, fittings-up, with all the leaden figures of the garden, pumps, suckers, pipes, coppers, garden lights, shrubs, 200 drinking tables, 250 forms, 400 dozen of bottled ale, &c., were sold.

Kilburn Wells

These were not publicly known at the time of the publication of Dr. John Birkenhead's 'Outlines of Natural History,' in 1772; but in the following year they were advertised as having their gardens and great room for music, dancing, &c.

St. Chad's Well

Located near Battle Bridge, this was much resorted to by the population of the neighbourhood.

The River of Wells

This commenced at the foot of Hampstead Hills, ran between Pond Street and Kentish Town to Pancras, and then by several meanders through Battle Bridge, Black St. Mary's Hall (where also there was a spring), and thence by Turnmill Street, Field Lane, Holborn Bridge, to Fleet Ditch. Of this river tradition says, according to Norden,

> 'that it was once navigable, and that lighters and barges used to go up as far as Pancras Church, and that in digging, anchors have been found within these two hundred years.'

Hence, by the choking up of the river, it is easy to account for the decay of the town of Pancras.

Other Wells

In the neighbourhood of Clerkenwell there were several wells: *Skinner's*, *Fag's*, *Tode*, *Loder's*, and *Rodwell Wells*; and from the overflowing of these, according to Stow, this was called the *River of Wells*. All this is now covered in, and runs under houses.

KILBURN PRIORY

Old Kilburn Priory
(From an old drawing in Mr. Gardner's Collection)

This conventual property and estate having been intimately connected with the Manor of Hampstead, both under the monks of Westminster, and afterwards. It will be convenient to give a concise notice of it before entering on the details of the Village of Hampstead.

This nunnery was, it appears, originally a hermitage. One Godwin had retired thither, being in possession of certain lands there; and he built his hermitage on the banks of the little rivulet, Kule-Bourne, or the Coal Brook, synonymous with the phantom of Kuhleborn in the story of Undine. It was surrounded with wood; and was very much as Spenser describes such a place in his Faerie Queene:

A litle lowly hermitage it was,
Downe in a dale, hard by a forest's side,
Far from resort of people, that did pass
In traveill to and froe; a little wyde
There was a holy chapell edifyde
Wherein the Hermite dewly went to say
His holy things, each morne and eventyde:
Thereby a christall streame did gently play
Which from a sacred fountaine welled forth alway.

The place is a town now, but no doubt was solitary enough in the reign of Henry I in the early part of the twelfth century. Godwin, it appears, soon became weary of so much solitude as Kilburn then afforded, and made over his cell and lands to the Abbey of Westminster; and the abbot of Westminster, the Bishop of London consenting, conveyed the place to three virgins, named Emma, Gunilda, and Cristina, who had been maids of honour to Matilda, queen of Henry I. The queen was herself a most religious personage, who is stated to have gone every day in Lent to Westminster Abbey, bare-footed and bare-legged, wearing a garment of hair. She would wash and kiss the feet of the poorest people. These three maids of honour probably were inspired by their devout mistress with a desire for a religious life; and they and all others who should thereafter take up their abode in that place, under monastic regulations, were to have the guardianship of a warden of suitable age and character. Godwin received this office first, and no doubt found his solitude agreeably relieved by the society of those ladies who, as maids of honour, must have possessed whatever education court-ladies then received.

On the death of Godwin, the nuns were to elect, with the advice of the Abbot of Westminster, some senior person capable of presiding over their church, and their chaplain was not to interfere with the temporal matters of the convent, for into that it grew; neither was the Abbot of Westminster to put any one into this office without their consent; they were to enjoy all the possessions which God might please to bestow on them, 'as freely as St. Peter did his.'

Very soon, additions were made to the property by the Abbot of Westminster and others for prayers for the souls of abbots and brothers of Westminster and Feschamp. The church was dedicated to St. John the Baptist; and Herbert, the abbot, soon after gave them an estate in Knightebruga, or Knightsbridge, called the Gara, probably the Gore at Kensington. His successor, Gervase, gave them two corradies, one of bread and beer, and another of cooked meats for the kitchen, called *coquina*, and of clareto.

Abbot Walter, in 1191, gave the Manor of Paddington to the Abbey of Westminster, and on the anniversary of this gift, the nuns of Kilburn received a fresh allowance of bread and wine.

Great strife arose afterwards betwixt the Abbot of Westminster and the Bishop of London, as to right of spiritual interference in the nunnery, and the question was referred to Pope Honorius in 1225, who gave the decision as was just, according to the charter, to the Abbot of Westminster; but the Bishop of London, who had now become very powerful, resisted this, and referred the question to the Bishop of Rochester and the Prior of Dunstable, who decided in his favour. Henceforward, the bishops of London exercised ecclesiastical authority over the nunnery, consecrated the nuns, appointed the chaplain, and the prioress, for they now had one. Further benefactions were made to this nunnery of the Manor of Middleton in Surrey, by John de Somerie, and the priory was exempt from all tenths, fifteenths, and taxes and tallages whatever. In the reign of Edward III Roger de Aperdele granted the prioress and nuns the Manor of Minchin in Surrey; and, in the same reign, Thomas de Wolton and William Topcliffe granted them the advowson of the church of Codam, and an acre of land in Kent. Yet, after all, one is surprised to learn that in 1377 the nunnery was in great distress, and an enquiry being instituted by the Bishop of London, 'a wretched spectacle of distress' was exhibited to the eyes of the visitors. It is not explained how this distress came about, but it must either have arisen from mismanagement of the property of the nunnery, or from the great hospitality which the nuns had to exercise to travellers so near London, when the convents were the only or nearly only, houses for the reception of travellers.

Park gives an inventory of the goods in the nunnery at the time of the visitation in the reign of Henry VIII, in order to the suppression. Amongst the articles of daily use were '6 stone cruesys to drynke in.' The fittings-up of the church do not appear to have been very costly. The nuns were found in possession of forty acres of cultivated land in the parish of Willesden, besides the other property mentioned. The nunnery must have been of less yearly value than £200, as it was suppressed under that category.

After the dissolution, Henry VIII made over the lands of the nunnery at Kilburn, Hampstead, and Kilburn Wood, in exchange for Paris Garden and other estates, to the Knights of St. John of Jerusalem. The Knights Templars formerly owned this property, but having been dissolved in 1312, it was transferred to the Knights Hospitallers of St. John of Jerusalem; and also they, in their turn, were dissolved by Henry VIII in 1540; and the King granted the site of the Priory of Kilburn to the Earl of Sussex, and the Manor of Shuttup-Hill, called also the Manor of Hampstead, to Sir Roger Cholmeley, Chief Baron of the Exchequer. Kilburn afterwards passed through many different hands. Sir Roger Cholmeley having only two daughters, his property also passed through various hands, and in those of Sir Arthur Atye in 1564, the two estates became again united, only to be afterwards divided again. In Park's time, there remained the farm of Shuttup-Hill, which was freehold and in possession of Arthur Annesley Powell, Esq. of Devonshire Place; and a portion of the Kilburn property called the Abbey Farm, forty-six acres, copyhold, was in the possession of Mr. Richard Marsh of Simonshyde, near Hatfield. All the conventual buildings had disappeared, except a portion of the domestic buildings of which he gives an engraving.

HAMPSTEAD HEATH AND ITS ASSOCIATIONS

Before entering the village of Hampstead we may as well take one stroll on the Heath, now greatly diminished from what it once was, and greatly defaced by the destruction of trees, the uprooting of its luxuriant furze and broom, and the carting away of its heathery surface for gravel and sand. In old Gerard's time, who ranged the Heath as he did all the country round London, a most remarkable variety of plants grew upon it. But it is really amazing to see in the catalogue of Mr. Bliss, furnished to Park, such plants as the crowberry, the henbane, the lily of the valley, bilberries, the service-tree, and raspberries, were still to be found on the Heath in the present century. These are wholly exclusive of rare plants found in Caen Wood park, woods, and ponds, as furnished in the catalogue by Mr. Hunter, Lord Mansfield's steward. There probably they may yet be found, as they are protected; but to what an extent must the surface of the Heath have been ravaged and deteriorated within the last fifty years. Only, indeed, by the jealous care of its inhabitants has it been saved from the process of enclosure which has swallowed so many other of the open spaces around the metropolis and other great cities, so vitally essential to the health of their inhabitants. It is not to be wondered at that the lords of manors, tempted by the enormous value which such open expanses have acquired as building land, should have exerted all their power and influence to appropriate them. In proportion as this value increased, so did the lords of manors propound the theory that the fee simple resided in them, and that they could enclose at pleasure. But this doctrine has met with a decided check at Great Berkhampstead, at Wimbledon, and at Hampstead. At Great Berkhampstead the lord of the manor had already proceeded to enclose, and set the inhabitants and commoners at defiance. At Wimbledon, the lord of the manor had more magnanimously offered to bestow the common on the inhabitants; but in both cases the commoners and inhabitants put in a claim of rights on their part as valid as those of the lord, and their rights were allowed by the legislature or the courts of law. Hampstead Heath has been for many years menaced with enclosure by the lord of the manor, and the numerous attempts of Sir Thomas Maryon Wilson to beguile Parliament into sanctioning his desire for enclosure, is a piece of history unique and curious of its kind. Fortunately, as lords of manors rose in their claims, it became clear to the minds of the public that, if there were any truth in the maxims of common law, and any force in successive acts of parliament, in declaring the acquisition of right by the unrestricted enjoyment of a property for a certain number of years, the public enjoyment of the open grounds near particular places, by the inhabitants of those places, constituted a right of such enjoyment as strong as that of the lord of the manor; and that without their consent neither the lord of a manor, nor the lord in co-operation with the freeholders, copyholders, and those enjoying commonage, called the homage, could enclose at all. This right, too, has received the sanction of the law, as may be seen in the treatises on common rights which have lately been published. Besides this, the Act of Parliament procured by the Right Hon. William Cowper in 1866 has now for ever barred the enclosure of such lands within a circuit of fourteen miles round Charing Cross, London. These will prove serious obstacles to the inflated demands of Sir Thomas Wilson of some half million for Hampstead Heath, as advanced on the basis of building land value to Sir John Thwaites, the head of the Metropolitan Board of Works; and the enquiry in Chancery, on the part of the inhabitants of Hampstead, into Sir Thomas's real rights will, no doubt, result in a fresh confirmation of the solid and inalienable claims of the public over all such lands where they have for more than thirty years established a user. Whether the mischief done by the sale of sand can be checked is perhaps more dubious.

One of the earliest and most curious facts of history connected with Hampstead Heath is that stated by Matthew Paris, or rather by Roger of Wendover, from whom he borrows it, that so late as in the thirteenth century it was the resort of wolves, and was as dangerous to cross on that account at night as it was for ages afterwards, and, in fact, almost down to our own times, because of highwaymen.

But Matthew Paris not only says that wolves in his time abounded in this neighbourhood, but also wild boars, deer, and wild bulls, the ancient British cattle; so that neither the wolf's-head tax of King Edgar in Wales, nor the mandates of Edward I in England, had anything like accomplished the extirpation of the wolf in this island. Fitz-Stephen in his 'Survey of London,' so late as 1182, and Juliana Berners, still later, in the reign of Henry VI, in the fifteenth century, asserts in the 'Boke of St. Alban's' that the wolf and wild boar still haunted the forests north of London. Of the four 'beastes of venerie,' she says:

> The fyrste of theym is the harte; the second is the hare,
> The boore is one of tho: the wulfe and not one mo.

As late as the commencement of the present century, highway robberies were of daily occurrence within twenty miles round London. They were pretty frequent about Hampstead Heath. The following account in the 'Domestic Occurrences' in the 'Gentleman's Magazine' for July 1803 shows that there were plucky fellows amongst the London tradesmen then:

> 'This morning, June 26, as Mr. Orrell, of Winsley Street, Oxford Street, with Mrs. Orrell, were passing in their chaise over Goulder's Green, on their way to Hendon, about half-past eight, they were stopped by a single highwayman, who produced a pistol and demanded their money. Mr. Orrell declared he would not be robbed, and after the highwayman had uttered violent oaths and threats, and put his pistol several times to the head of Mr. and Mrs. Orrell, Mr. Orrell jumped out of the chaise, and seizing the highwayman, nearly pulled him off his horse, and laid hold of the pistol; on which the highwayman struggled and spurred his horse, and having extricated himself, gallopped away towards Hampstead. He afterwards stopped one of the Hampstead stages near Red Lion Hill, in which were six passengers, with two men and the coachman outside, and robbed them of upwards of 40*l*. Besides this number of persons in and on the coach, there were several persons passing at the time! He then rode coolly off.'

What a striking proof that a bold heart in a single man's breast is worth a score of men without hearts.

To what a regular profession the 'dealing with gentlemen for rings, watches, purses, canes, swords, and other commodities' on the heaths round London had become, is demonstrated by a Bill filed by a highwayman. One of the most remarkable facts in the history of highwaymen, who a century ago played a hold and very prominent part on the roads round London for a dozen miles or so, is connected with Hampstead, as it also is with Finchley, Blackheath, Hounslow Heath, and other favourite places for the kind of 'dealing' in which this gentleman and his partner were engaged. It is a

> 'Bill filed in the Court of Exchequer by William Wreathock, of Hatton Garden, attorney, between John Everet and Joseph Williams, two notorious robbers; the former of whom was afterwards executed at Tyburn, and the latter at Maidstone, in Kent; for which insult and affront on the Court, Wreathock was committed prisoner to the Fleet, where he remained six months.'

It is worth while to quote some portion of this extraordinary Bill as a curiosity.

> 'To the Right Honorable the Chancellor and Under-Treasurer, the Right Honorable the Lord Chief Baron, and the rest of the Honorable the Barons of His Majesty's Court of Exchequer:
> Humbly complaining, sheweth unto your Honours your orator, John Everet, of the parish of St. James's, Clerkenwell, in the county of Middlesex, gent., debtor and accountant to his Majesty, as by the record of this honorable court and otherwise it doth and may appear; that your orator being skilled in dealing and in buying and selling several sorts of commodities, such as corn, hay, straw, horses, cows, sheep, oxen, hogs, wool, lambs, butter, cheese, plate, rings, watches, canes, swords, and other commodities, whereby your orator had acquired to himself a very considerable sum of money, to the amount of 1,000*l* and upwards; and Joseph Williams of the parish of -----, in the said county of Middlesex, gent., being acquainted therewith, and knowing your orator's great care, diligence, and in-dustry in managing the said dealing, he, the said Joseph Williams, in or about the year of our Lord 1770, applied himself to your orator, in order to become your orator's partner therein; and after several such applications and meetings between him and your orator for that purpose . . . your orator agreed that the said Joseph Williams should become his partner.'

In the same legal style the Bill continues to the extent of several pages, but we may note its depositions much more concisely. These are, that the said Joseph Williams agreed to enter into this trade, or, in plain language, general system of robbery, and to pay half the expenses of it on the roads, at inns, alehouses, markets, and fairs, &c.; and should furnish his share of necessaries, as horses, bridles, saddles, assistants, and servants. This partnership was only for one year, and was to end at Michaelmas 1721.

This trade was to be plied on Hounslow, Hampstead, and Blackheath, at Finchley Common, Bagshot, and Wimbledon in Surrey, Salisbury in Wiltshire, and elsewhere; in which places they dealt with gentlemen for divers watches, rings, swords, canes, hats, cloaks, horses, bridles, saddles, and other things (purses, no doubt, though not mentioned). In this trade they were so successful that they soon were in possession of 2,000*l*. But when the said Everet called on the said Williams to render a full and fair account, and to divide the proceeds (for Williams is made to appear to have been 'the Judas, and carried the bag'), instead of so dividing, he made similar claims on Everet, and these being refused, commenced an action at law against him in Court of Common Pleas at Westminster, and actually obtained a verdict for 20*l*; on which account, and also because the said Joseph Williams threatened the said Everet with fresh lawsuits, and moreover. maligned his character, denied the receipts of money attributed to him, and even denied the contract of partnership (which the plaintiff confesses was not in writing, but merely verbal), this John Everet seeks redress from the Court of Exchequer, and prays that the fraudulent Joseph Williams may be cited and compelled to show a fair account, by the production of all the necessary books, papers, writings, memorandums, and accounts; that he may be compelled to make a fair division of profits on such accounts thus proved, and may be restrained from any further action at law against the said John Everet, &c.

This extraordinary Bill was filed on October 3, 1725,

'Int. Joh'em Everit . . . quer.
Josephum Williams . . . deft.
'P. Bill Anglicum.'

Immediately on the filing of this Bill, the counsel for the defendant, Mr. Serjeant Girdler, moved that it might be referred to John Harding, Esq., D.R. of the court, as scandalous and impertinent, which was done; and the Bill being pronounced by the court, on the report of the said John Harding, Esq., D.R. of the court, both scandalous and impertinent, Everit was sentenced to pay the costs in the case; and the solicitors, White and Wreathock, were summoned into court by the tipstaff, and each of them fined 50*l* or to be committed to the Fleet till the fines were paid. It appears that Wreathock was accordingly imprisoned for six months. John Collins, Esq., whose name appeared upon the Bill, was also sentenced to pay such costs as the Deputy should state. Such was the punishment inflicted by the Court of Exchequer for the indignity offered to it by the filing of this highwayman's Bill.

Everit, the plaintiff, was convicted in January 1729-30, for robbing one Martha Ellis on the highway near St. Pancras, and was executed at Tyburn on the 20th of February following. Williams, the defendant, was executed two years before Everit, namely in March 1727, at Maidstone, for a robbery committed there; and Wreathock, Everit's solicitor, was afterwards tried at the Old Bailey for being concerned with robbing Dr. Lancaster, in company with several others, and transported for life. As a proceeding at law, this Bill, filed by a highwayman, and drawn by a solicitor who also practised on the highway, is certainly unique.

Finchley Common, which, was enclosed only in 1812, and of which a large portion was obtained by the proprietors of Friars' Barnet, was perhaps more notorious for the practice of this nocturnal conveyancing than even Hampstead Heath.

By the year 1816 wonderful changes had been produced in and around the metropolis, as regarding the security of travelling. The improvement in the roads and in the system of magistracy and police had operated most beneficially. Before this the magistrates were, as they are still generally in the provinces, unpaid. They were, moreover, most unfit, and extremely corrupt. Few of them knew anything of law; many were retail tradesmen. Justice Blackborough, of Clerkenwell, for example, was an old ironmonger. They had no salaries, and therefore made what they could out of fees and bribes. Henry Fielding, it is said, had no salary, though his half-brother, Sir John Fielding, had. Hence the justices were called 'trading justices,' and 'basket justices.' The basket justices were open to bribes of good things, and had a basket into which such contributions by those called before them were not very privately thrown. The trading justices lived upon fees, which they shared with their clerks, and had the lion's share. Fielding describes one of these in his 'Amelia.' Jonathan Thrasher, Esq., one of the justices of the peace for the liberty of Westminster, he says,

> 'was utterly without knowledge of the laws of England, but was well versed in the laws of nature; that is to say, he looked after his own interest, and was never indifferent in a cause but when he could get nothing on either side.'

Fielding says that one of his own predecessors used to make a thousand a year of the place. One means was to issue orders to take up all the poor devils in the streets, and then bail them out at 2s. 4d. per head. Thus a hundred wretched girls at 2s. 4d. would make £11 13s. 4d. This all went to the magistrate - a tolerable morning's work. They sent none to jail, for bailing them was so much better.

The police of that time were not police, but constables, fellows picked up any where or how, for not everyone would have such a post; and many of them had trades of their own to look after. So magistrates, constables, and thieves all flourished together. The change into paid magistrates and regular police astonished the famous Bow Street officer, John Townsend. When he had held that post for five-and-thirty years, in giving his evidence before a committee of the House of Commons in 1816, he said:

> 'There is one thing which appears to me most extraordinary, when I remember that very likely in a single week there would be from ten to fifteen highway robberies. We have not had a man committed for highway robbery very lately. I speak of persons on horseback. Formerly there were two, three, or four highwaymen; some on Hounslow Heath, some on Wimbledon Common, some on the Romford Road. I have actually come to Bow Street in a morning, and while I have been leaning over the desk, had three or four people come in and say: "I was robbed by two highwaymen in such a place;" "I was robbed by a single highwayman in such a place." People travel more safely by means of the horse-patrol that Sir Richard Ford planned. Where are these highway robberies now? As

I was observing to the Chancellor at the time I was up at his house on the Corn Bill: he said, "Townsend, I knew you very well so many years ago." I said, "Yes, my lord, I remember you first coming to the bar, just in your plain gown, and then as King's Counsel, and now Chancellor. Now your lordship sits as Chancellor, and directs the executions on the Recorder's report, - but where are the highway robberies now?" And his lordship said, "Yes, I am astonished. There are no footpad robberies now, but merely jostling you in the streets. They used to be ready to pop at a man as soon as he let down his glass; that was by banditti." '

As to the frequency of highway robberies in the districts round London, Townsend added,

'Chief Justice Eyre once went the Home circuit, beginning at Hertford and ending at Kingston, when crimes were so desperate that in his charge to the grand jury at Hertford, he told them to be careful about what Bills they found, for he had made up his mind, whenever persons were convicted throughout the circuit for capital crimes, to hang them all. And he kept his word; he saved neither man nor woman. In one case seven people - four men and three women - were convicted of robbing a pedler in a house in Kent Street. They were all convicted, and all hanged opposite the house in Kent Street where the offence was committed; and, I think, on Kennington Common, eight more, making fifteen, all that were convicted being hung. With respect to the present time, and the early part of my time, such as 1781-1787, where one is committed now ten were then, and we never had an execution without gracing that unfortunate gibbet with from ten to twenty, and forty I once saw at twice. I have them all down at home.'

Since Townsend's time we cannot so much say that the thieves have decreased as that they have changed the theatre of their operations. Our highways are tolerably secure - railways have, for one thing, removed nocturnal travelling from them - but the streets of the metropolis can show all the robbery that the highways have lost. No part of the world displays such nightly assaults and plundering of the person as the British capital, as the police reports testify. The 'Arabian Nights ' boast of their 'forty thieves,' but our gas-lit and police-provided streets boast their forty thousand. When shall another Townsend be astonished at the disappearance of these perpetual feats of night-errantry?

THE GROVES OF HAMPSTEAD

Hone, in his 'Table Book,' p. 810, says Hampstead is 'the place of groves.' How long it may remain so is a secret in the bosom of speculators and builders. Its first grove townward is the noble private avenue from Hampstead Road to Belsize House, in the valley between Primrose Hill and the hill where the church stands, with Mr. Memory-Corner Thompson's remarkable house and lodge at the corner of the pleasant highway to the little village of West End. In the neighbourhood of Hampstead Church, and between that edifice and the Heath, are several old groves. Winding southwardly from the Heath, there is a charming little grove in Well Walk, with a bench at the end, whereon I last saw poor Keats, the poet of the 'Pot of Basil,' sitting and sobbing his dying breath into a handkerchief, glancing parting looks towards the quiet landscape he had delighted in, musing as in his 'Ode to the Nightingale':

> My heart aches, and a drowsy numbness pains
>   My sense, as though of hemlock I had drunk,
> Or emptied some dull opiate to the drains
>   One minute past, and Lethe-wards had sunk:
> 'Tis not through envy of thy happy lot,
>   But being too happy in thy happiness,—
> That thou, light-winged Dryad of the trees,
>   In some melodious plot
> Of beechen green and shadows numberless,
>   Singest of summer in full-throated ease.
> O for a draught of vintage! that hath been
>   Cooled a long age in the deep-delved earth,
> Tasting of Flora and the country green,
>   Dance and Provençal song, and sunburnt mirth!
> O for a beaker full of the warm south,
>   Full of the true, the blushful Hippocrene,
> With beaded bubbles winking at the brim,
>   And purple-stained mouth;
> That I might drink and leave the world unseen,
>   And with thee fade away into the forest dim.

This little incident of one of the farewell looks of John Keats on the earth, as he faded away, and 'left the world unseen,' will always confer an interest on the seat in the avenue at the end of Well Walk.

Well Walk
(From a photograph taken expressly for this work)

A noble avenue, not noticed by Hone, leads down through the fir-clump from near Mr. Hoare's house to North End, a quarter remarkable on many accounts.

To these William Hone might also have added the fine avenue leading from Squire's Mount up to the new church - Christ Church. A still more remarkable one is an avenue called Judges' Bench, or Judges' Avenue (mentioned anon), and facing the Heath, behind Upper Terrace. A very fine avenue is that leading from Roslyn House, particulars regarding which will be found under the heading of 'Roslyn House.' Another such avenue is Montague Grove itself. Besides these avenues or groves, every part of Old Hampstead is distinguished by rows of trees, either lime or elm trees, planted along the broad footpaths in boulevard style.

Hampstead stands on a great extent of ground, and its old narrow roads winding under tall trees, are continually conducting to fresh and secluded places that seem hidden from the world, and would lead you to suppose yourselves far away from London, and in some especially old-fashioned and old-world part of the country. Extensive old and lofty walls enclose the large old brick houses and grounds of what were once the great merchants and nobles of London; and ever and anon you are reminded of people and things which lead your recollection back to the neighbouring capital and its intruding histories. For instance, descending one of those quiet shady roads from Mr. Bickersteth's church towards Well Walk, you come to a still sort of three-cornered space, surrounded by houses of a somewhat deserted character, except at the lower side, where modern improvement has entered. The house No. 6 of this still quarter, which bears the name of Grove Place, and which is of lath and plaster, and stoops forward as if intending to fall forward ere long, is, you are assured, the one where the notorious Mary Ann Clarke lived when in the keeping of the Duke of York. It is no very princely abode, but is distinguished from the rest of the row by a somewhat ornamented doorway of carved wood. Next to it, but standing somewhat back, is a house called the 'Bath House,' probably set up as a bath-house in the days when the wells of Hampstead were frequented by the invalids and roués of London.

LORD ERSKINE AT EVERGREEN HILL, HAMPSTEAD HEATH

Passing by the 'Spaniards' public house at the eastern entrance of Hampstead Heath, on the way from Highgate, with what a different feeling do we contemplate the house next adjoining it, to what we do the abode of Lord Chancellor Wedderburn, or even the great mansion of Lord Mansfield in Caen Wood. Of this house we see little but its end, and a simple portico leading into it from the road. A high wall shuts in what little of garden it has on that side, and another high wall shuts out from view the spacious gardens and grounds formerly belonging to it on the other side of the road. There is no grace of architecture about the building; it is simply a bald square mass, shouldered up again by another house at its back. We see, however, the tall windows of its large drawing-room on the second floor, commanding a splendid view over Caen Wood and some part of Highgate. Yet this was the house inhabited by Thomas Lord Erskine, cotemporary with both the law lords, his neighbours, Mansfield and Loughborough. Here he converted the place from a spot of no account into a very charming residence, laying out with great enthusiasm its grounds, and so planting it with bays and laurels that he called it Evergreen Hill. He is said also to have planted with his own hand the extraordinarily broad holly hedge separating his kitchen garden from the Heath, opposite to the Fir-Tree Avenue.

Lord Erskine has been pronounced by other distinguished lawyers the greatest forensic orator that England has ever produced, but his fiery and electric eloquence was not more remarkable than the warm and noble impulses of his heart. They were his humanity and patriotism, his indignation against whatever was unjust and oppressive, which kindled and inspired his great intellect, and their expression carried irresistibly the souls of his hearers along with him. Under the fervid outgush of his intense love of right, his vehement hatred of human wrong, the dullest hearts caught a new life and fire, and he drew verdicts from men who, without his communicated spirit, would have never dreamed of the sublime heights of truth and justice to which he carried them. The secret of his triumphs was the possession of a noble heart, vivifying a quick and instinct-like intellect. He seemed to spring at once to the truth of the case submitted to him, and he hurried his hearers with him almost unconsciously to the same goal. It is rare to see a mind like Erskine's surviving all the cold cautions and technical sophistries of a legal education, and seeking its triumphs only in the triumphs of humanity - a mind unseduced by royal favour, or party, much less by selfish individual interests - exulting in securing the victory of truth, even at the highest peril of self sacrifice. Such men may have their weaknesses, as Erskine had his, but they have a strength to which no mere intellect or learning can ever reach. For this reason there is no life of any lawyer which I ever read with the same delight as I have read that of Thomas Erskine.

Lord Erskine's House, near 'The Spaniards'
(from a photograph taken expressly for this work)

Lord Erskine was the youngest son of Henry David, tenth Earl of Buchan, who, though a Scottish earl of long and high descent, possessed only about £200 a year, and, with a numerous family, lived in one of the upper 'flats' or storeys of a very tall house in the Old Town of Edinburgh, where, indeed, some of the houses were sixteen stories high. His mother was - as almost all the mothers of great men are - a woman of extraordinary intellect, greatly cultivated, and of equal piety - a daughter of Sir James Stewart, of Goodtrees, in the county of Mid-Lothian, baronet. Thomas Erskine was born on January 10, 1750, in that lofty, but small and ill-furnished, eyrie. At an early age he attended the High School of Edinburgh, and displayed a lively disposition, and a capacity for rapidly acquiring knowledge, being generally dux of his class. The resources of the family not allowing them to continue in Edinburgh, as all the children began to require education, Lord Buchan removed to St. Andrews, where young Erskine not only finished what education he had, but learned, he tells us, amongst other accomplishments, to dance single and double hornpipe, and *shantrews*, a peculiar Highland dance. At the age of twelve, he expressed a desire to be bred to some learned profession, but was told that the means of the family would only allow of his becoming a midshipman, and much to his discontent, though without any resistance, he was sent on board the 'Tartar' man-of-war, at the age of fourteen, under the command of Sir David Lindsay. He would much have preferred the army, but this could not be accomplished, and it is pleasant to find that Lord Mansfield, who was the uncle of Sir David, recommended him to be kind to the young middy. After his father's death, however, he quitted the navy, and managed to purchase an ensigncy in the 1st regiment of Foot, by the absorption of the whole of his little patrimony. Like too many young men of quick feelings and imaginative sentiment, he married, at the age of twenty, a young lady of good family, but with no fortune. His wife was the daughter of Daniel Moore, Esq., M.P. for Marlow, and a brother of Sir John Moore, of Coruna memory. In everything but fortune this was a happy marriage. Mrs. Erskine was a sweet and most amiable woman; and their attachment was perfect. After some sojourns in country towns, they went with the regiment to Minorca, where they remained two years. During this interval of foreign seclusion, Erskine directed himself to the study of English literature, and became an enthusiastic admirer of Milton and Shakespeare, the latter of whom he could quote at almost any part. He deeply imbued himself also with the harmonious verse of Pope and Dryden, and the noble sentiments of the greatest amongst these writers no doubt, falling on a congenial mind, refined and exalted those ideas of truth, honour, and heroic virtue which gave such a power and glory to his oratory. During the absence of the army chaplain on furlough, Erskine read the service to the men, who were chiefly Presbyterians, and soon proceeded to make them lay addresses, which were greatly liked by the soldiers, and he himself always remembered these occasions of religious oratory with peculiar satisfaction. In fact, he already felt within him the impulses of public speech which were his true inspiration, and indicated his true vocation. On his return to England he published an energetic pamphlet on the abuses of the army, 'By the Honourable ___, an Officer,' which, bold as it was, had a great success, although he lashed the vices of the aristocratic officers in a manner which appeared very hazardous. He said,

> 'So long as the battalions are encamped on native plains, or ensconced in peaceful barracks, so long these sons of riot and effeminacy maintain their posts. The brilliant orbit of Ranelagh glows with their scarlet, and the avenues of Vauxhall glitter with blades drawn against unarmed apprentices in honour of a courtezan, which rust in their scabbards when their country calls. If for a review or a muster they are obliged to loll in their vis-à-vis to the quarters of their regiment, it is but to inflame the contempt and hatred of the people of England against the defenders of their peaceable privileges. They gallop again to town after having filled the country with such horror at their debaucheries that hospitable doors are shut against officers of principle and reputation. Such are the advantages which the military profession reaps from these apes in embroidery; such are the heroes that in the event of war must lead the British troops to battle; for these men rise almost universally over the heads of officers grey with fatigues and rough with scars - whose courage and abilities yet preserve the honour of the English name - who, without money and without interest, languish in the subaltern ranks, unknown and unrespected; who, after having braved all the terrors and calamities of war, and immortalised their country, sink into obscure graves, unwept and unremembered, without a tongue to speak their worth or a stone to record their virtues.'

So far from injuring him, this daring exposé did him good, and he soon after was raised to the rank of lieutenant. But his heart was not in the army. During his visit to London he seemed naturally to seek the society of distinguished men of letters, and was on friendly terms with Dr. Johnson. An event in 1775 decided his destiny. He entered the court of assize in the town where he was quartered, and Lord Mansfield presiding, invited the young officer who had sailed with his nephew to sit on the bench by his side, and kindly explained to him the nature of the proceedings as they went forward. What struck him was that the barristers, though men of standing, and thought to have very ably discharged their duties, did not by any means urge the best points in their causes; and he then and there saw his real path in life, and resolved to go to the Bar. There were enormous difficulties in the way. The main one was the want of the necessary funds to enable him to maintain his family during the years of his preparation for a call to the Bar. The shortest time for someone without an M.A. was five years; for someone with an M.A. from one of the universities of Oxford and Cambridge, three years. He was not, however, daunted. Lord Mansfield did not discourage him, neither did his brothers; his mother encouraged him. He sold his commission, entered Lincoln's Inn as a student in April 1775, and Trinity College, Cambridge, as a gentleman commoner, in January 1776. He managed to keep his terms at both college and Lincoln's Inn, for as he was under no necessity to study, but could take his degree without examination, his chief business at Cambridge was to eat so many dinners in the Common Hall. He took his honorary degree of M.A. in June 1778, and he studied hard under Mr. Justice Buller, and then under Mr. Wood, afterwards Baron Wood of the Exchequer.

During the three necessary years of probation, he was reduced to the greatest straits to maintain his family. He had lodgings in Kentish Town, and his wife used occasionally to relieve the hard monotony of her own wretched home by a call at the house of a connection who kept a glass-shop in Fleet Ditch, or of a relative, Mr. Moore, a jeweller on Ludgate Hill. Mr. Harris, the manager, occasionally gave them free admission to Covent Garden Theatre. He also made frequent excursions to the villa of Mr. Reynolds, a solicitor, at Bromley in Kent, the father of Reynolds, the comic writer. He dressed very shabbily, and boasted that he lived on cow-heel and tripe, and thanked God that he did not know a lord out of his own family. Such are the hardships that a soul confident of its powers will sometimes struggle through with a desperate courage - the heroism of genius. Still, though he was called to the Bar in July 1778, he had a most gloomy prospect before him. He had made no acquaintance likely to bring him into practice, and that splendid oratorical talent within him lay all unknown to the race of attorneys. He felt the oppressive horrors of his situation, and began almost to despair of ever emerging from them. A fortunate accident, however, opened the door for his recognition, and he rose at one leap to the very summit of fame and emolument.

In the month of November 1778, Erskine was crossing Spa Fields with a friend, intending to spend the day with Mrs. Moore, the mother of his friend Mr. Charles Moore, and of Sir John Moore, when, in leaping over a wide ditch, he sprained his ankle, and was carried home. In the evening he was so much recovered that, finding an invitation to a dinner party on his table, he determined to join it. Here at table the conversation turned on the case of a Captain Baillie, a veteran officer and Lieutenant-Governor of Greenwich Hospital, who had found such abuses in that establishment that he repeatedly brought them under the notice of the Admiralty. No notice being taken of these statements, he published them, that public opinion might compel a reform. In this exposé he severely commented on the conduct of Lord Sandwich, the First Lord of the Admiralty, who, for electioneering purposes, had placed in the Hospital a great number of landsmen. In consequence Captain Baillie was immediately suspended from his office, and a criminal information filed against him in the name of several of the inferior agents for a libel against them, Lord Sandwich pulling the strings, but keeping in the background. Erskine, on hearing the case, broke out into vehement denunciations of this tyrannic proceeding, and declared that Lord Sandwich, instead of prosecuting this honest and patriotic man, ought to be prosecuted himself. Captain Baillie, unknown to Erskine, was himself at the table, at some distance, but hearing this bold and energetic expression of opinion on his case, asked who this young man was; and being told he was a young sailor who had turned lawyer, and had been just called to the Bar, declared that he was the man for him. Without seeking an introduction to him, however, he sent to his chambers the next day a retainer with a guinea fee. Erskine's pleasure, nevertheless, was, on the opening of Michaelmas term, greatly damped by finding upon his brief four counsel already engaged before him. On the 24th of November Erskine attended at Westminster Hall, but with no hope of being called on to open his mouth. The four senior counsel fired away the whole day on the case, and Lord Mansfield, supposing the whole of the defendant's counsel had been heard, adjourned the Court till next morning. This was just what Erskine wanted. During the night he prepared his speech, and the next morning it was supposed that the Solicitor-General would follow on the plaintiff's side, and the court was crowded with persons of rank, from the political aspect of the case, and the excitement which it had produced. 'There arose,' says Lord Campbell, 'from the back row a young gentleman whose name as well as whose face was unknown to most present, and who in a collected, firm, but sweet modest and conciliatory tone,' announced himself 'also as counsel for the defendant.' In a very few sentences he struck a profound silence of astonishment into the whole Court and crowd. It was felt that there was a new power amongst them; and, proceeding, he painted the disgraceful and oppressive nature of the case in such flashing colours that every one was held breathless. At length, saying, 'Indeed, Lord Sandwich has, in my mind, acted such a part,' Lord Mansfield reminded him that Lord Sandwich was not before the Court. 'I know,' replied Erskine,

'that he is not formally before the Court, but, for that very reason *I will bring him before the Court!* He has placed these men in the front of the battle in hopes to escape under their shelter, but I will not join in battle with them; their vices, though screwed up to the highest pitch of human depravity, are not of dignity enough to vindicate the combat with me. I will drag him to light who is the dark mover behind this scene of iniquity. I assert that the Earl of Sandwich has but one road to escape out of this business without pollution and disgrace - and that is by publicly disavowing the acts of the prosecutors, and restoring Captain Baillie to his command! If he does this, then his offence will be no more than the too common one of having suffered his own personal interests to prevail over his public duty in placing his voters in the Hospital. But if, on the contrary, he continues to protect the prosecutors, in spite of the evidence of their guilt, which has excited the abhorrence of the numerous audience of this crowded court; if he keeps this injured man suspended, or dares to turn that suspension into a removal, I shall then not scruple to declare him an accomplice in their guilt, a shameless oppressor, a disgrace to his rank, and a traitor to his trust.'

At this outburst the whole court and crowd were electrified; the case was dismissed with costs; and the young counsel was surrounded by throngs of eager people rushing forward to shake hands with and congratulate him. As he made his way through the hall, attorneys pressed round him to put briefs into his hands, and he went home with the proud and happy conviction that fame and fortune were before him. When people asked him how he dared to oppose Lord Mansfield as he had done, he replied that he thought his little children were plucking his robe, and that he heard them saying, 'Now, father, is the time to get us bread!' When he went down to the court, he had scarcely a shilling in his pocket. The guinea that he received as his first fee he always preserved, and frequently showed to his friends; probably it is still sacredly kept by his descendants. Lord Campbell pronounces the speech then delivered, the very first in his legal career, to be 'the most wonderful forensic effort of which we have any account in our annals.' It was the forerunner of the most vividly powerful, patriotic, and generous displays of true eloquence ever delivered at the Bar of any country.

From this hour Erskine's fortune was made; and, true to his noble instincts, he continued to the last to exert his amazing eloquence in the cause of oppressed liberty, and in defiance of the arbitrary and unjust, however powerful. It would be a long story to detail his labours and triumphs of this kind, but I will passingly allude to the most prominent cases. One of the first of these was to defend Admiral Keppel against a charge of incapacity and misconduct in the battle of Ushant in 1778. The fate of Admiral Byng, who had been shot on such a charge, excited a strong sympathy on his behalf. The trial lasted thirteen days, during the whole of which time Erskine exerted himself with unceasing vigilance and assiduity for his defence. He showed by evidence that not a whisper had been raised against his client till his superior officer, Sir Hugh Palliser, was himself accused of disobedience of orders. The King had personally complimented Keppel; the First Lord of the Admiralty had assured him of the satisfaction his conduct during the action had given to the Government, and the public had been equally pleased. As it was a trial by Court Martial, Erskine could not speak in his defence; but he wrote the Admiral a speech, which he delivered, and such was its effect that on its conclusion he was acquitted by acclamation. Keppel himself, delighted with the result, sent Erskine at once a cheque for £1,000. In his enthusiasm at this generous gift, Erskine not only ran off to express his grateful thanks to the Admiral, but he posted off to Bromley to his friends the Reynoldses, and, showing the money as he entered, exclaimed, 'Voilà! The non-suit of cow-beef, my good friends!'

This was in January 1779, and that spring, as he rode over a barren heath on the circuit betwixt Lewes and Guildford, he remained some time in deep silence, and then exclaimed to his companion, William Adams (afterwards Lord Chief Commissioner of the Jury Court, in Scotland), 'Willie, the time will come when I shall be invested with the robes of the Lord Chancellor, and the Star of the Thistle shall blaze on my breast;' both of which events took place about thirty years afterwards.

In May of that year he made his first speech at the bar of the House of Commons, in defence of Mr. Carnan, a bookseller of St. Paul's Churchyard, against the Universities of Oxford and Cambridge, which claimed a monopoly of printing and publishing almanacks. He succeeded in defeating the Universities, and throwing open this lucrative business to the public; but the ministers, by a disgraceful job, afterwards paid a large sum of the country's money to indemnify the Universities for their loss of this monopoly.

Erskine was next engaged by Lord George Gordon, to defend him against the charge of exciting the riots in which Lord Mansfield's house was burnt down and an immense amount of other mischief done by the mob. The trial was conducted before Lord Mansfield himself, a man so much injured by this mob, and his brother judges of the King's Bench; but notwithstanding both this and the exasperation of the public, by a masterly speech, in which he showed the folly of the indictment against the prisoner, as intending to compass the King's death and levy war against his person, he brought Lord George off triumphantly. That he had excited the mob by his cries of 'No Popery' was undeniable; but that he had attempted to levy war on the King, or to compass his death, was merely the law jargon by which the Government sought to convert into high treason instigations to awe Parliament into a continuance of the penal restrictions on Catholics. It was an attempt at that 'constructive treason' which the King said to Wedderburn had 'put the Government into the wrong box.' Lucky was it for Lord George Gordon that he was not tried, like the rioters themselves, by Wedderburn, just now made Chief Justice of the Common Pleas, and the Special Commission, or, spite of Erskine's eloquence, he would probably have suffered the same fate as they did, by shoals.

In 1783 Erskine became a member of the House of Commons, sitting for Portsmouth. Here he had to encounter Pitt in his full power, with whom he had been at the bar. He did not, however, produce the same effect as at the bar. His eloquence was of a kind addressed to the hearts and best feelings of men; but in that corrupt House of Commons there were not hearts to he touched, but hard political interests, and prejudices as impenetrable as the coat of a rhinoceros, to be combated. Still, he continued through his whole career, both in the lower and the higher House, to battle for right and liberty, for the most part alongside of Burke and Fox, and with no inconsiderable effect. In speaking on Pitt's India Bill, he foresaw and foretold that our policy towards that great Eastern dependency would produce misery, oppression, revolt, and the ruin of the East India Company; all of which we have lived to see accomplished.

In 1778 he obtained his silk gown, and in the same year defended the Dean of St. Asaph against a Government prosecution for publishing a pamphlet on Parliamentary Reform, written by Sir William Jones, called 'A Dialogue between a Gentleman and a Farmer.' After various delays and postponements, this famous trial came off at Shrewsbury in August 1784. Mr. Justice Buller presided, who held strictly Lord Mansfield's doctrine, that a jury had only to prove the fact of publication: the decision whether the matter was a libel must be left to the judge.

The case was exactly similar to that of William Penn and William Mead, tried before the Recorder of London in 1670, for a violation of the Conventicle Act, by preaching in a meeting-house in Gracechurch Street. Penn and Mead made their own defence. The Recorder told the jury that they had only to decide on the fact of preaching - the law was for his decision. Penn, on the contrary, told the jury that they were his judges, and not the Recorder. It was for them to pronounce whether he was guilty of breaking the law, or not guilty; the Recorder had only to record their verdict. After the most violent and disgraceful conduct on the part of the Recorder towards the prisoners, and dictation to the jury, the jury brought in a verdict of 'Guilty of speaking in Gracechurch Street.' 'Is that all?' asked the Recorder, in angry amazement. 'That is all!' said the foreman, coolly.

Such was the rage of the Recorder, that he menaced and abused the jury, refused the verdict, thrust the prisoners into a stinking hole in the prison, and locked up the jury for two days and nights without food, light, or any convenience whatever. When at length called up, they brought in a direct verdict of 'Not guilty.' In his fury, the Recorder, refusing to receive the verdict, committed the prisoners and their jury to Newgate, whence they were only released by the interference of the citizens in defence of their violated rights, and a re-hearing before Judge Vaughan.

Thomas Clarkson, the champion of negro freedom, says in his 'Life of Penn,' that 'this trial, proving juries to be the great palladium of our liberties, ought to be engraved on tablets of the most durable marble.' Yet the judges had continued from 1670 to 1784, or above a hundred years, to uphold and endeavour to enforce the same doctrine.

Mr. Justice Buller, having laid down this view of the law strongly to the jury, they, notwithstanding, returned a verdict of 'Guilty of publishing only,' when this remarkable scene took place:

Erskine: You find him guilty of publishing only?

Juror: Guilty only of publishing.

Mr. Justice Buller: I believe that is a verdict not quite correct. You must explain that one way or other. The indictment has stated that G means Gentleman; F, Parmer; the King, the King of Great Britain.

Juror: We have no doubt about that.

Buller: If you find him guilty of publishing, you must not say the word 'only.'

Erskine. By that they mean to find there was no sedition.

Juror: We only find him guilty of publishing. We do not find anything else.

Erskine: I beg your Lordship's pardon; with great submission, I am sure I mean nothing that is irregular. I understand them to say, they only find him guilty of publishing.

Juror: Certainly; that is what we do find.

Buller: If you only attend to what is said, there is no question or doubt.

Erskine: Gentlemen, I desire to know whether you mean the word 'only' to stand in your verdict?

Jurymen: Certainly.

Buller: Gentlemen, if you add the word 'only,' it will be negativing the innuendoes.

Erskine: I desire your Lordship, sitting here as judge, to record the verdict as given by the jury.

Buller: You say he is guilty of publishing the pamphlet, and that the meaning of the innuendoes is as stated in the indictment.

Juror: Certainly.

Erskine: Is the word 'only' to stand part of the verdict?

Juror: Certainly.

Erskine: Then I insist it shall be recorded.

Buller: Then the verdict must be misunderstood; let me understand the jury.

Erskine: The jury do understand their verdict.

Buller: Sir, I will not be interrupted.

Erskine: I stand here as an advocate for a brother citizen, and I desire that the word 'only' may be recorded.

Buller: Sit down, sir; remember your duty, or I shall be obliged to proceed in another manner.

Erskine: Your Lordship may proceed in what manner you think fit; I know my duty as well as your Lordship knows yours. I shall not alter my conduct.

The judge saw his error, and did not repeat his menace of commitment. The jury however added to their verdict, that 'they did not find whether it was a libel or not.' An attempt was made to set aside this verdict in the ensuing term, but Erskine, in a splendid speech, overruled it. Lord Mansfield, on this occasion, made his famous misquotation from a ballad composed on the trial of the 'Craftsman' prosecuted by Sir Philip Yorke:

Sir Philip well knows
That his innuendoes
Will serve him no longer
In verse or in prose;
For twelve honest men have decided the cause,

> Who are judges of facts though not judges of laws;

whereas the true reading of the final line is:

> Who are judges alike of the facts and the laws.

The noble stand made by Erskine on this occasion, raised the public spirit, and Charles James Fox soon after brought in a bill, to settle the full rights of juries in cases of libel, which was passed, though all the law lords in the House of Peers opposed and voted against it.

Well might Erskine be proud of having given the final triumph to this great question of constitutional right. The conduct of the judge, though overhearing, was very different from the vulgar violence and brutality of Sir John Robinson, Lieutenant of the Tower and Howel the Recorder of London, when Penn and Mead, and a true British-hearted jury, so bravely withstood them, and suffered so severely, in the detestable prisons of those times, for the liberty of the subject. But a long series of such battles for public liberty was yet before him. Lord Mansfield, now at an advanced age, retired from the bench, and Erskine was appointed to present him (as the leading counsel of his court) with a complimentary address. Other and more overhearing judges had to preside on some of the trials against reformers which followed. What was called the 'Reign of Terror,' succeeded; the determination of the Government being to crush by arbitrary measures all attempts at reform of Parliament, and all freedom of press or speech.

During the trial of Warren Hastings, Mr. Stockdale, a publisher in Piccadilly, issued a pamphlet in his defence. On this he was prosecuted, on the ground of the pamphlet being a libel on the managers of the trial in the House of Commons, chief among whom were Fox and Burke. Erskine made a magnificent speech in his defence, in Westminster Hall, and obtained a triumphant verdict of 'Not guilty.'

In the House of Commons he made a fierce onslaught on the Government 'Traitorous Correspondence Bill,' and immediately after he was retained in a most critical case - no other than to defend Thomas Paine against a Government prosecution on account of his 'Rights of Man.' His friends were greatly alarmed for him, and scandalised too, at his accepting such a retainer. Lord Loughborough met him one evening on Hampstead Heath, and endeavoured to persuade him to abandon the case, hut in vain. Though Erskine did not approve all that Paine had written in that work, he felt that the liberty of discussion was at stake, and contended that any man had a right to agitate freely every public topic, if he did it honestly and conscientiously. That it was by conflict of opinions that the public mind came to its matured conclusions. In this case, however, he failed to secure a verdict of acquittal, and the consequence of his advocacy to himself was the dismissal from the attorney-generalship to the Prince of Wales, which had been some time before conferred on him. This, however, did not prevent his undertaking the defence of John Frost on a charge of treason, where he also failed; of Perry and Gray, proprietors of the 'Morning Chronicle,' for complaining of the state of the representation and other abuses, where he succeeded; and a Mrs. Walker, on a charge of keeping fire-arms for treasonable purposes, which charge he made so ridiculous that the Government abandoned it.

To these succeeded the famous trials of Hardy, Horne Tooke, and Thelwall, for high treason, in which Erskine displayed the most masterly ability and undaunted conduct, bringing them all freely off. His speeches on these trials raised him to the very pinnacle of national popularity. 'He had now,' says Lord Campbell, 'gained a position as an advocate which no man before had reached, and which no man hereafter is ever likely to reach at the English bar.' Yet he describes his private life in a letter to a friend at this time, in these words:

'I am now very busy flying my boy's kite, shooting with a bow and arrow, and talking to an old Scotch gardener six hours a day about the same things, which, taken altogether, are not of the value or importance of a Birmingham halfpenny, and scarcely up to the exertion of reading the daily papers. How much happier would it be for England and the world, if the King's ministers were so employed in a course so much more innocent than theirs, and so perfectly suited to their capacities!'

In the House of Commons he denounced the Government

prosecutions, and resisted the extension of the treason law. In the court he successfully defended William Stone, a London merchant, from a charge of treason; soon after, he with equal success, and in a more doubtful case, defended the Bishop of Bangor from a charge of riot. In another prosecution of Thomas Paine, for the publication of his 'Age of Reason,' whilst attempting in vain to save Paine from the clutches of the law, he pronounced such a splendid oration on the truth of Christianity, as served not only to shield him from the reproaches of the religious, but drew a grand eulogium from Porteus, the Bishop of London, upon it. Passing over a number of other cases of less importance, in which Erskine stood as defender of the accused, we come to the remarkable one, that of Hatfield for shooting at the King. In this, Erskine so clearly laid down the diagnosis of insanity, and proved Hatfield hopelessly insane, that Lord Kenyon stopped the proceedings, and directed the jury to bring in a verdict of insanity, by which the man's life was saved, and he was consigned to safe keeping in Bedlam.

In 1806 Erskine became Lord Chancellor, seven-and-twenty years after his own prophecy of this event. In March 1807, he had the great seal again taken from him, having occupied his elevated post little more than a year.

Still Erskine (now Lord Erskine) put forth his powers and influence steadily for the promotion of human freedom, both personal and religious. He advocated concessions to the Catholics, and in 1809 did not think it beneath him to bring in a bill for the prevention of cruelty to animals. It was the day of dog-fighting, cock-fighting, bear-baiting, bull-baiting, &c., and by the influence of Wyndham - the great advocate of these things - were regarded as especially English! - it was thrown out. A second time he introduced it, and a second time it was rejected; but it was not lost. It had found a steady supporter in Martin of Galway, and in Erskine's own lifetime became the law of the land. Now we possess the active services of a Royal Society for the prevention and punishment of such cruelties, and we ought never to forget that we owe this distinction amongst the nations mainly to the eloquence of Thomas Erskine.

Thirty-six years after he had foreseen it, he received the Green Ribbon or Scottish Order of the Thistle; and five years afterwards he vehemently opposed the despotism of the ministers of the

Prince Regent, who had conferred it on him. He opposed energetically Castlereagh's notorious 'Six Acts,' and in 1820, in the House of Peers, he boldly and independently supported the persecuted Queen against the King - George IV - demanding for her a list of all the witnesses against her, and resisting at every stage the 'Bill of Pains and Penalties' against her, and had the final satisfaction to see it thrown out.

I have dwelt upon the noble career of Lord Erskine at greater length than the limits of this work properly admit, simply because it is but once in many ages that we meet with a man who possesses, with the most splendid powers of mind and expression, a soul so truly great and generous, spending his life in a long-continued course of combat, dazzling and victorious, for liberty, truth, justice, and humanity. The only occasions on which his enemies have been able to detect inconsistency or selfishness in him are but two: one, that he recommended proseeution for a libel on Parliament; and the other, that he retained the great seal for a week, by permission, after notice that it would be withdrawn from him, in order to make his son-in-law, Edward Morris, a Master in Chancery. Many anecdotes have been circulated of his vanity in his old age, and his frequent boastings of his battles for the defence of trial by jury. But the fact is that, though it was weak to show it, he had an enormous deal to be vain of; and as to his boastings, truly he had something to boast of. There are thousands who have not his weakness, but few who have his strength. His battles were the feats of a mighty man-at-arms; his flights of eloquence were eagle flights. I would rather be such a man as Thomas Erskine, with all his foibles, than the most faultless mediocrity that you can find me. We have seen him amid all his glories at the bar and in the senate; let us take just a peep at him in his private life.

During the many years that he lived on Hampstead Heath, he inhabited the house close by the 'Spaniards,' which is thus mentioned by Sir Egerton Brydges, in a new edition of Collins's 'Peerage,' ix. 273:

'Having purchased a house with a garden adjoining it, connected by a subterranean passage, upon the very top of Hampstead Hill, above Ken Wood, he set about to make it a fitting residence. At that time it was a very small place, and though commanding, from its elevation, a most extensive and splendid prospect, was entirely shut out from it by banks and hedgerow timber, so as to possess no beauty or interest whatever. The improvement and decoration of this spot has been the amusement of many years, and though attended with very considerable expense, by great additions to its extent, and by cultivation and ornament, has amply repaid its possessor, being now a most delightful retreat, though within an hour's distance of any part of London. It is so entirely shut out from the road between Hampstead and Highgate by walls and plantations, that no idea can be formed of it by a stranger to the place. Lord Erskine having ornamented it with evergreens of different descriptions, has lately given it the name of Evergreen Hill.'

Here, during the intervals of his arduous professional labours, he was zealously engaged in planning and carrying out his improvements. With his old gardener, John Barnett, he took his spade, and schemed and dug, and planted and transplanted; and no one who has not tried it can tell the immense refreshment of such an entire diversion of otherwise exhausting trains of thought. To men compelled to spend long days in crowded, ill-ventilated courts, the health and spirit given by such tastes is incalculable. No doubt from these occupations Erskine returned with tenfold vigour of body and mind to his pleadings and to his parliamentary conflicts.

From an account by Sir Samuel Romilly, we see not only what men frequented his house in those days, but some of Erskine's curious hobbies:

'Here he gave gay parties, of which he was the life by his good humour and whimsicalities. I dined there one day at what might be called a great Opposition dinner. The party consisted of the Duke of Norfolk, Lord Grenville, Lord Grey, Lord Holland, Lord Ellenborough, Lord Lauderdale, Lord Henry Petty, Thomas Grenville, Pigot, Adam, Edward Morris, Lord Erskine's son-in-law, and myself. If the most malignant enemies of Erskine had been present, they would have admitted that nothing could be more innocent than the conversation which passed. Politics were hardly mentioned. Amid the light and trifling topics of conversation after dinner, it may be worth while to mention one, as it strongly characterises Lord Erskine. He has always felt and expressed a great sympathy for animals. He has talked for years of a bill he was to bring into Parliament to prevent cruelty to them. He has always had several favourite animals to which he has been much attached, and of whom all his acquaintances have a number of anecdotes to relate. He had a favourite dog which he used to bring, when he was at the bar, to all his consultations; another favourite dog which, at the time he was Lord Chancellor, he himself rescued in the street from some boys who were about to kill it, under pretence of its being mad. A favourite goose, which followed him whenever he walked about his grounds; a favourite macaw; and other dumb favourites without number. He told us now that he had two favourite leeches. He had been blooded by them last autumn when he was taken dangerously ill at Portsmouth; they had saved his life, and he had brought them with him to town - had ever since kept them in a glass - had himself every day given them fresh water, and formed a friendship for them. He said he was sure they knew him and were grateful to him. He had given them the names of Howe and Clive, the celebrated surgeons - their dispositions being quite different. He went and fetched them for us to see; but without the vivacity, the tones, the details and gestures of Lord Erskine, it would be impossible to give an idea of this singular scene.'

Amongst his defences of animals, in one case he retorted a brutal fellow's arguments practically. On Hampstead Heath, seeing a ruffian beating unmercifully a wretched horse, and interfering, the fellow said, 'Can't I do as I like with my own?' 'Yes,' replied Erskine, 'and so can I; this stick is my own!' And he gave the scamp a good threshing.

His witty sallies gave much life to his society, and would have stocked a _Punch_. We may glance at one or two of them:

Captain Parry, saying 'that when frozen up in the Arctic regions they lived much on seals.' 'Yes,' said the ex-Chancellor, 'and very good living too, if you keep them long enough!'

The old Duke of Queensborough having a case for his opinion, he wrote, 'I am of opinion that this case will not lie unless the witnesses do!'

Polito, the keeper of the wild beasts in Exeter Change, having brought an action against the proprietor of a stagecoach for the loss of his portmanteau, which was taken from the boot of the vehicle, while he himself was riding on the box: 'Why did not he,' asked Erskine, who was counsel for the defendant, 'take a lesson from his own sagacious elephant, and travel with his trunk _before him?_'

As counsel for a gentleman who had been upset in a coach starting from the Swan-with-two-Necks, in Lad Lane, and had his arm broken: 'Gentlemen of the jury,' Erskine said, with much gravity, 'the plaintiff in this case is Mr. Beverley, a respectable merchant of Liverpool, and the defendant is Mr. Neilson, proprietor of the Swan-with-two-Necks in Lad Lane, a sign emblematical, I suppose, of the number of necks people ought to possess who ride in his vehicles.'

Being invited to attend the ministerial fish dinner at Greenwich, when he was Chancellor: 'To be sure,' he replied, 'what would your dinner be without the Great Seal?'

Lord Erskine was to some extent an author. He wrote a pamphlet on 'The Causes and Consequences of War,' which is said to have run through seven-and-thirty editions. He wrote a romance entitled 'Armata,' something in the manner of Sir Thomas More's 'Utopia.' He wrote a pamphlet in his old age, advocating the freedom of Greece, composed, according to Lady Morgan, with all the freshness of feeling and vigour of youth. He threw off many *jeux-d'esprit* in verse, which display much wit; but it is, after all, not as an author but as a great orator on the side of truth and liberty that Lord Erskine will be honoured. Lord Brougham says:

'Juries have declared that they felt it impossible to remove their looks from him when he had riveted, and, as it were, fascinated them by his first glance. Then hear his voice of surpassing sweetness, clear, flexible, though exquisitely fitted to strains of earnestness.'

His action,' says Espinasse,

'was always appropriate, chaste, easy, natural, in accordance with his slender and finely-proportioned figure and just stature. His features regular, prepossessing, as well as harmonious, bespoke him of no vulgar extraction. The tones of his voice, though sharp, were full, destitute of any tinge of Scotch accent, and adequate to any emergency, almost scientifically modulated to the occasion.'

Another barrister says,

'Adequately to estimate what Erskine was, we must forget all that the English bar has produced after him. They will afford no criterion by which he can be appreciated. They are all of inferior clay - the sweepings of the hall in comparison.'

Such was Lord Erskine in public and private life. Lord Byron,

Miss Burney, Lady Morgan, Hannah More, Miss Seward, Dr. Parr, were amongst his friends and advisers. As for Burke, they fought side by side for years, and only parted when Burke, frightened at the French Revolution, suddenly retreated into conservatism. Their last meeting and parting, described by Erskine, is affecting:

> 'What a prodigy Burke was! He came to see me not long before he died. I then lived on Hampstead Hill. "Come, Erskine," said he, holding out his hand, "let us forget all! I shall soon quit this stage, and wish to die in peace with everybody, especially you!" I reciprocated the sentiment, and we took a turn round the grounds. Suddenly he stopped. An extensive prospect over Caen Wood broke upon him. He stood wrapped in thought, gazing on the sky as the sun was setting. "Ah, Erskine!" he said, pointing towards it, "this is just the place for a reformer; all the beauties are beyond your reach - you cannot destroy them." '

Lord Erskine committed, in his later years, the mistake of selling this noble situation, and buying a barren estate in Sussex, which produced little but stunted birch trees, and where he is said to have set up a manufactory of brooms, as the only valuable produce of the property. He committed, probably, another in a Gretna Green marriage. But no follies or weaknesses could defraud his country or his name of the noble triumphs of his genius. He died in Scotland on November 17, 1823, in the seventy-third year of his age, on a visit to his relatives, and his remains lie at Uphall, a remote parish in the county of Linlithgow. At one time he had acquired a fortune of £200,000, but a great deal of this slipped away through his unworldly habits.

'This extraordinary man,' says Lord Campbell, 'will be a greater boast to his descendants, than any Earl of Buchan, or of Marr, or any royal progenitor.' By his first marriage he had eight children: Frances, married to the Rev. Dr. Holland, Prebendary of Chichester; Mary, married to Edward Morris, Esq., Master in Chancery; David Montague, the present Lord, whose son served his country as Minister of the United States of America, and at the Court of Wurtemberg; Thomas, a Judge of the Court of Common Pleas, one of the most upright and amiable of men; and Esmé Stewart, an officer in the army, who fought gallantly at Waterloo, and was killed near the end of the day by the side of the Duke of

Wellington.

A niece of Lord Erskine, Mrs. Bockett, lives, I am told, on the Heath, opposite to 'Jack Straw's Castle.'

The contemporary residence of these three great lawyers, Loughborough, Mansfield, and Erskine, in the neighbourhood of Hampstead, is one of the most remarkable associations of the place, and the residence of Erskine there will for ever remain one of its greatest glories.

On the staircase of the house possessed by Lord Erskine, and the copyhold of which he transferred to Lord Mansfield, there is a window of stained glass, in which are emblazoned Lord Erslrine's arms, with the Baron's coronet, and the motto which he assumed: 'Trial by Jury.' The tunnel under the road, which connected the premises with the pleasure-grounds on the other side, is now built up, Lord Mansfield having resumed the grounds on his side. Baron Tindal at one time lived in this house.

In the house next to that which was Lord Erskine's, and facing the Heath, a white house of a peculiar style, of which there are several in different suburbs of London, evidently of the same date, have lived successively Mr. Edward Cox, author of some poems, published in 1805; Sir Edward Parry, and Mr. Henry H. Vaughan, son of Judge Vaughan.

At the large square house facing the Scotch Fir Avenue, called the 'Firs,' now occupied by William Dugmore, Esq., once lived Mr. Serjeant Bosanquet. The house was built by Mr. Turner, a tobacconist of Fleet Street, who planted the Avenue of now venerable pine-trees, so great an ornament to the Heath, and also made the road thence to North End.

NORTH END, HAMPSTEAD HEATH

North End House
(From a photograph taken expressly for this work)

The temporary sojourn here of Lord Chatham is one of the most singular episodes of the career of that great, but self-willed statesman. In the year 1767, when Chatham was prime-minister, during a time of accumulating difficulties, when the affairs of the East Indies were deeply embarrassing, when the war with America was every day becoming more imminent, and John Wilkes was exciting the people against the Government at home; when, to add to the arduousness of the situation, Junius was beginning to pour a terrible raking fire of criticism into the ranks of diplomacy, and Chatham had rejected scornfully the aid of Burke, and made him a perpetual enemy; that great minister was seized with an extraordinary illness. This strange malady seemed at once to have reduced his master mind to imbecility, and to have placed the King and his council in the most fatal perplexity. In the Christmas recess, Chatham hastened to Bath to improve his health for the campaign of the ensuing session, and when Parliament met again in the middle of January, 1767, ministers were in consternation at his not reappearing. The news from India was continually bringing fresh proofs of the rapacity and despotism of the East India Company, which was at once invading the territories of the native princes on all hands, and curtailing the rights of all British traders but themselves. The troubles in America were hastening to a crisis, and the cabinet was composed of such discordant, and, for the most part, incapable materials, that, without its head, there was no hope of its existence. It contained not merely men feeble in ability, if strong in self-will, but men drawn directly from the quarters of his enemies; so that his best friends utterly despaired of its working without his presence. Tidings came that he was suffering from a severe attack of his old tormentor, the gout; and weeks passed on, and he still was absent. At length the administration was greatly relieved by hearing that, though still in a bad condition, he was on the way to town. The good news quickly changed. It was found that he had reached the 'Castle Inn' at Marlborough, where he lay for a fortnight in such a state that he was utterly incapacitated for business. The Dukes of Grafton and Bedford, who were his most devoted adherents, were thunderstruck. They found it impossible to keep in order the heterogeneous elements of the Cabinet; all the hostile qualities which would have lain still under the hand of the great magician, bristled up, and came boldly out. The spirit of Bedford, of Rockingham, and Newcastle, were active in their partizans, and gathered courage to do mischief. Lord Shelburne and the Duke of Grafton became estranged. Charles Townshend, who was much better calculated for a comic actor than a chancellor of the Exchequer, began to show airs, and to aim at supremacy. He proceeded to perpetrate the most disastrous political acts. Following in the steps of George Grenville, with his stamp acts, he did not stop till he had imposed duties on various articles imported into America, and amongst them, the fatal one, on tea, which produced the disastrous outbreak.

The Duke of Grafton, on whom lay the chief burden of responsibility, implored Chatham to come to town if possible, and when that was declared impracticable, to allow him to go down and consult with him in his sick chamber. But he was informed that the minister was equally unable to move or to consult.

Under these unfortunate circumstances, Charles Townshend,

as Chancellor of the Exchequer, proposed the annual rate for the land tax. He called for the amount of four shillings in the pound - the rate at which it had stood during the war; but he promised next year to reduce it to three. The country gentlemen grumbled, representing that in years of peace it was commonly reduced to three, and sometimes to two. Grenville saw his advantage: his great opponent away, the land-holders ready to rebel; and he moved an amendment that, instead of next year, the reduction should take place immediately. Dowdeswell supported him; and the amendment was carried by 206 votes against 138. The Opposition was astonished at its own success, and yet it needed not; they who had a vote were chiefly landowners, and men who did not like taxing themselves. As Lord Chesterfield observed, `All the landed gentlemen had bribed themselves with this shilling in the pound.'

The Opposition was in ecstacies; it was the first defeat of ministers on a financial question since the days of Walpole; and in our time, the ministry would have resigned. The blow seemed to rouse Chatham. Three days after this event, on March 2, he arrived in town, though swathed in flannel, and scarcely able to move hand or foot. He was in the highest state of indignation against Townshend, not only as regarding the land tax, by which half a million was struck from the revenue of the year, but because he had been listening to overtures from the Directors of the India House, calculated to damage the great scheme of Indian administration which Chatham was contemplating. He declared that the Chancellor of the Exchequer and himself could not hold office together. A few days, and Townshend would have been dismissed from office, and the country might have escaped one of its greatest shocks; but, unfortunately, the malady of Chatham returned with redoubled violence, and in a new and more terrible form. He was obliged to refuse seeing anyone on State affairs. For a time his colleagues and the King were urgent for some communication with him, supposing that his illness was merely his old enemy the gout; and there was much dissatisfaction amongst his friends, and exultation amongst his enemies, at what was deemed his crotchety humour, in so entirely shutting himself up under such critical circumstances, when his own fame, his own great plans, and the welfare of the State, were all at stake. But in time it came to be understood that this refusal to see anyone, or to comply with the repeated and earnest desires of the King, expressed in letters to him, to admit Grafton, or one of his best friends, or to examine important papers, was no voluntary matter, but the melancholy result of his ailment. It seems to have been the fact, that, anxious when at Marlborough to get to town and resume the reins of business, his physician, Dr. Addington, had given him some strong medicines to disperse the gout. These had succeeded in driving it from his extremities, but only to diffuse it all over the system, and to fix it on the nerves. The consequence was, that the physical frame, oppressed by the incubus of disease, oppressed the mighty mind of Pitt, and reduced him to a condition of nervous imbecility. Some people imagined that he had become deranged; but that was not the case: he was suffering under no imaginary terrors or delusions, but an utter prostration of his intellectual vigour. Lord Chesterfield expressed his condition, when, being told that Chatham was disabled by the gout, he replied, 'No; a good fit of the gout would cure him!' That is, one of his usual attacks of gout in his extremities, would be a proof that it had quitted its present insidious hold on his whole system.

Whately, the secretary of Grenville, thus describes his condition, as obtained from members of his family:

> 'Lord Chatham's state of health is certainly the lowest state of dejection and debility that mind and body can be in. He sits all day leaning on his hands, which he supports on the table; does not permit any person to remain in the room; knocks when he wants anything; and, having made his wants known, gives a signal without speaking to the person who answered his call, to retire.'

The account given by the Duke of Grafton, who obtained a brief interview with him in May, on the most urgent plea, is quite in accordance with this of Grenville's:

> 'Though I expected to find Lord Chatham very ill indeed, his situation was different from what I had imagined. His nerves and spirits were affected to a dreadful degree, and the sight of his great mind, bowed down and thus weakened by disorder, would have filled me with grief and concern if I had not long borne a sincere attachment to his person and character.'

At times the slightest mention of business would throw him into violent agitation; at others, when such matters were carefully kept from him, he would remain calm, and almost cheerful, but utterly incapable of exertion. In this lamentable condition he continued for upwards of a year.

During this time the public and many of his friends expressed the utmost impatience, not comprehending the nature of his case; and his enemies demanded why, being incapable or indisposed to discharge his duties, he did not resign, but continued to receive his salary. These complaints have been repeated by historians; but the simple fact was, that he was as incapable of thinking of his salary as of resigning his duties. Once, indeed, he had sufficient command of his energies to request, in January 1768, that the King would resume the Privy Seal; but His Majesty would not hear of it, saying that his name alone enabled the Government to go on better than it could without it. And as the Cid Ruy Diaz, though dead, was carried into the field of battle on his horse, and thus, by his imagined presence, put the enemy to flight, so the name of Chatham in some degree still gave force to the administration of affairs.

Such is the explanation of this episode in the life of Chatham, on account of which so much censure has been heaped upon him, as a wayward and intractable man, as if he were likely to be so regardless of his own fame, of his great designs, and of the country's prosperity, for which he had at other times made such gigantic efforts. The very circumstances of his setting out from Burton Pynsent to town when still so unfit, and of his seeking medical assistance to enable him to go on and attend to business, are of themselves sufficient proofs of his anxiety to have acted had he been able.

Such a strange calamity could not but be attended with mischievous consequences. Chatham was obliged to leave town and seek retirement and a purer air at North End, Hampstead.

Here, then, in this deplorable condition, the great orator and statesman was living, and, as it were, hiding from the importunities of the King and his nobles, and the pressing cares of a great empire; by his office called on to discharge the most important functions that could rest on human responsibility, and from the effects of his disease helpless as a child. During this melancholy time he used to be driven about the Heath and immediate neighbourhood in his carriage, with the blinds drawn closely down, and shunning the parts frequented as much as possible. How long Chatham led this melancholy life here is not exactly known, but probably about a year; for he came here some time soon after March 1767, and in October of the following year we find that he had refurnished Hayes, near Bromley in Kent, and had retired thither, but still not much better; and there, on October 12, 1768, he resigned his post as Prime Minister, amid the glooms and anxieties of the American War, already commenced in the outbreaks at Boston. He seems not to have fully recovered till the summer of 1769, when the gouty element quitted his general system, concentrated itself in his foot, and Chatham was himself again. Suddenly appearing in the House of Lords on January 6, 1770, he launched a most fiery diatribe at the Ministry for its violation of the rights of the colonists in America, and the rights of the people at home, in the person of Wilkes, whose return to Parliament by a large majority they had arbitrarily overruled; and the whole Cabinet went to pieces under the lightnings of his ire, and Lord North became for a long time the ruler of England's destinies.

The house at which Lord Chatham lived during this gloomy time is now called Wild Wood House, but, till recently, North End House. It is a large house standing at the northern foot of the declivity descending from Mr. Hoare's house, and between the Finchley Road and the Chestnut Avenue, leading down from Mr. Hoare's to Wild Wood. The gardens of Wild Wood House run up the hill, and have on the summit a fine summer-house, surmounted by a dome. These grounds are bounded by a Scots pine clump, near Mr. Hoare's house, where the two roads divide. Wild Wood House was once, it is said, occupied by Lord North, though he never was the copyhold proprietor of it. Probably it was owing to its being in Lord North's tenancy that Chatham came to sojourn in it. The Rev. Edward Taggart, Unitarian minister, was, and his widow I believe still is, the possessor of it. It is now occupied by William Haynes, Esq., who has raised it another story, and otherwise added to it.

The small room, or rather closet, in which Chatham shut himself up during his singular affliction - on the third story - still remains in the same condition. Its position from the outside may be known by an oriel window looking towards Finchley. The opening in the wall from the staircase to the room still remains, through which the unhappy man received his meals or anything else conveyed to him. It is an opening of perhaps eighteen inches square, having a door on each side of the wall. The door within had a padlock, which still hangs upon it. When anything was conveyed to him, a knock was made on the outer door, and the articles placed in the recess. When he heard the outer door again closed, the invalid opened the inner door, took what was there, again closed and locked it. When the dishes or other articles were returned, the same process was observed, so that no one could possibly catch a glimpse of him, nor need there be any exchange of words. This closet, and its little double-doored perforation, constitute one of the most remarkable monuments of the phenomena of the human system, of the domination of the physical organisation over the mind.

There is a tradition of a murder committed in or near the summer house at the top of the garden attached to this house, about ninety years ago. The summer house where the murder is said to have been perpetrated must have been an older one than the present one, but standing much in the same situation. The butler of the gentleman then living there is said to have killed the cook or one of the female servants of the family; but for the exact date and particulars of this murder I have sought in vain. A friend of mine at Hampstead inserted an inquiry regarding it in the Hampstead newspapers, but it produced no result. Still the inhabitants of North End are unanimous in their belief in the murder, and there are those who assert that the ghost of the murdered woman still walks in the garden - a belief most effective for the protection of the garden; a ghost walking at night being worth a dozen policemen with their bull's-eye lanterns, especially as ghosts eat no peaches.

A murder much better attested than that mentioned above marks the opposite side of the Finchley Road. Just over against the summer house here mentioned, there stands an elm tree, called the Gibbet tree. Between this tree and another formerly stood a gibbet on which was suspended the body of Jackson, a highwayman, for murdering Henry Miller on or near this spot in May 1673. Park says,

`In 1674 was published "Jackson's Recantation; or, the Life and Death of the notorious Highwayman now hanging in chains at Hampstead," &c., wherein is truly discovered the whole mystery of that wicked and fatal profession of padding on the road.'

Park was told that the post of this gibbet was in his time remaining as a mantle-tree over the fireplace in the kitchen of the `Castle' public house. One of the two trees betwixt which the gibbet stood was blown down a few years ago, hut its stumps are still visible.

Park also mentions the murder of a Thomas Cowley on Fortune Green, by one Martha Bradley and some female gipsies. This woman managed to escape conviction through want of evidence, and in her old age was an occupant of some almshouses in the Vale of Health, since pulled down. Over her wretched fire in the evening, or lying awake at night, she was continually heard confessing her crime, detailing the circumstances, and earnestly praying for pardon: a picture of desolate misery befitting the pen of Crabbe.

The house in possession of Mrs. Earle at North-End bears the name of Wild Wood, and appears to have the original claim to it. From an old map now before us, Wild Wood appears to be the wood just behind the `Spaniards' public house, being, no doubt, a remnant of the ancient forest of Middlesex.

Many associations of a literary and historical character are connected with North End, as you might suppose from the views of those ancient groves and the old mansion-like houses which they overshadow. The 'Bull and Bush' public house used to have, as now, a pleasant garden, to which, it is asserted, Addison and his friends were accustomed frequently to resort.

Here Akenside's friend Dyson bought a house for him, in order to introduce him to his friends resident in the neighbourhood, and thus create a medical practice for him; a generous design which Akenside's haughty temper rendered abortive.

Just on the edge of the Heath, below Wild Wood, stands a farm house, at which William Blake, the singularly imaginative artist and inspired poet, used sometimes to lodge. Mr. Linnell, the celebrated painter, frequently occupied this house in summer, and invited Blake there. It was a spot well calculated to refresh, by its silence and peaceful nature, his mind, harassed by poverty and neglect; for the independence of his character rendered him totally unfit to cope with the matter-of-fact persons with whom he had to deal in his profession, and he lived in the deepest poverty with his faithful, sympathising wife, both of them executing an amazing amount of work in their lifetime, to be disposed of at the most contemptible prices, to rise after his death into as extraordinary a value. Authors now rush in to praise him in biographies, and connoisseurs to purchase any scrap of his drawings, who, during his own existence, was complacently smiled at as a madman. In fact, with all his genius, it is not easy to exempt him from a considerable trace of insanity, nor to defend some of his theological ideas. They are extremely wild and strange. But no doubt there is a world where such spiritual and inspired souls find themselves understood and at home.

South view of 'The Spaniards.'
(From a print by Chatelaine, in the King's Library,
British Museum)

Mr. Coventry Patmore for some time lived at North End; Mrs. Craik, formerly Miss Dinah Mulock, the popular novelist, occupied, a few years ago, the house now occupied by Miss Meteyard, the author of the splendid and truly appreciative 'Life of

Wedgwood,' and many other charming works.

Sir Fowell Buxton lived some time at North End, to be near his brother-in-law, Mr. Hoare. He lived at the square brick house at the bottom of the avenue leading down from Mr. Hoare's to Wild Wood. This house is on the right hand as you descend the avenue, between the cross road leading from the 'Spaniards' to the Finchley Road, and an avenue descending from the Heath, and dividing it from a paddock. At the same time, Mrs. Charles Buxton, a widow, occupied Wild Wood, Mrs. Earle's house.

Sir Fowell Buxton married a Gurney of Norwich, and thus was closely connected with the Society of Friends. His services, both in the House of Commons and out of it, in the cause of freedom to the negroes, are too well known to need more than a reference. His name will always stand united with those of Clarkson, Wilberforce, and the noble band who effected that great act of justice to the black race, the freedom of their persons. Sir Fowell Buxton, from the Life of him published by his son, Mr. Charles Buxton M.P., appears to have been a man of a beautifully and tenderly religious spirit.

HAMPSTEAD HEATH CONTINUED

The Vale of Health

Formerly, fairs and races were held on Hampstead Heath, which drew so much dissolute company, and produced such scenes of riot and gambling, that they were prohibited. Recent times have seen Sunday dissipation reasserting itself, by the erection of a monster public house with a lofty tower and flag, to attract the attention of Sunday strollers on the Heath. Of all places, this raised its Tower of Babel bulk in that formerly quiet and favourite spot, the Vale of Health. That suitable refreshments should be attainable to the numerous visitors of the Heath on Sundays and holidays is quite right and reasonable; but that taps and gin-palaces on a Titan scale should be licensed, where people resort ostensibly for fresh air, relaxation, and exercise, is the certain mode of turning all such advantages into popular curses, and converting the very bosom of nature into a hotbed of demoralisation and crime. Anyone who has witnessed the condition of the enormous crowds who flock to the Heath on summer Sundays, as they return in the evening, needs no argument on the subject. When I lived at Highgate, I could from my garden hear the continuous hubbub of the retiring pleasure-seekers stretching all the way from the Heath itself to the bottom of Haverstock Hill. It sounded like a riotous mob on its way to exercise its mischievous vivacity in London; and a near approach to this noisy stream of life demonstrated, in its language, the worst effects of the liquors which it had imbibed for the benefit of the excise duties, and the damage to individual health.

This Vale of Health used, till of late years, to present a sight at once picturesque and pleasant. In front of a row of cottages, and under the shade of willows, were set out long tables for tea, where many hundreds, at a trifling cost, partook of a homely and exhilarating refreshment. There families could take their own tea and bread and butter, and have water boiled for them, and table accommodation found for them, for a few pence; but then came this great tavern with its towers and battlements, and cast them literally and practically into the shade. It was, however, really gratifying to see that the more imposing and dangerous place of entertainment never could compete with the more primitive tea-tables, nor banish the homely and happy groups of families, children, and humble friends.

The Vale of Health was formerly, for some time, the abode of Leigh Hunt, and the resort of his celebrated friends Shelley, Keats, Hazlitt, Haydon, &c. The house which he occupied, I am informed, was the same occupied at a later date by Mr. Matthew Davenport Hill, the well-known and public-spirited Recorder of Birmingham, a brother of Sir Rowland Hill. It was pulled down to make way for the great hotel just mentioned.

What an idea! the particular spot on which three or four of our most gifted and intellectual men used to meet, and speculate on ideal beauty, and on plans for the elevation of the race, should be the one on which the bestial Bacchus, the brutaliser and demoraliser of this nation, should select to squat himself down, as if in intense satisfaction of triumph over them. One seems to see the demon of drink and riot stamping his foot on the ground consecrated to genius and refinement, and laughing uproariously at his odious achievement. Every right mind will rejoice that the base speculation has failed, and that, at the moment at which I write, the huge abortion is in the market, and we may hope will be converted to some more honourable purpose. Let us revert to earlier days.

Yet even at the time that we refer to, the three poets were then far from happy. They were more or less martyrs to free thought and popular prejudices. Shelley had offended the moral sense of the public by his early indiscretions of opinion and of action. He had written 'Queen Mab,' and married a wife unsuited to him, and had separated from her; yet without sanctioning one act or the other, I may remark how many now daily perpetrate as much, and escape with a passing and often very slight censure. Shelley, at the age of nineteen only, was rudely, and, as competent authorities have affirmed, 'precipitately, unjustly, and illegally' expelled from University College, Oxford, for the printing and privately circulating a thesis on Atheism conjointly with a fellow student. To the authorship, or part authorship, he did not confess, when grossly and insultingly called upon to do so, and was on the spot formally expelled without further inquiry, and without the least attempt benevolently to convince him - an enthusiastic and inexperienced youth - of his error. Such conduct was the most certain to harden him in his opinions. It waa the observation of the awful extremes of human life, the oppressions and contumelies of the poor, which had swelled his heart with indignation, and made him call in question the existence of a Providence who could tolerate such things. How little do people who profess Christianity, and are promptly ready to avenge any disavowals of its principles, reflect that they themselves, and the multitudes acting with them, are the real originators of infidelity and atheism! People now-a-days who see the European nations professing Christianity - the religion of peace and love - yet steeped to the lips in hatred to each other, and armed to the teeth to destroy one another, may well, as thousands and hundreds of thousands do, lose all faith in a religion followed by such practice. To those of quick and impetuous feeling, the whole aspect of the *soi-disant* Christian world is one of the most barefaced hypocrisies. They read the New Testament, and find that it declares that every man shall love his neighbour as himself, that its Author declares himself the Prince of Peace, and his doctrine as love. They turn their glance on the nations professing to believe this Gospel, and see every nation covered with hundreds of thousands of soldiers, armed with deadly, and ever more deadly and devastating, weapons; they see every so-called Christian nation suspicious of its neighbour, and ready to carry the most terrible destruction through it. They take a closer view of the internal condition of these nations, and behold the wildest contrasts of life: pride, luxury, domination on the one hand, and ignorance, destitution, and consequent crime and misery on the other; and to what mental conclusion can they come, but that Christianity is a solemn farce, and that the bulk of modern society knows and believes it to be such? This is, and must be, the one prolific source of that infidelity which has of late years overrun the 'so-called civilised world with such rapidity. Yet, for an anonymous pamphlet only circulated amongst a few individuals, and written in the first astonishment and indignation of a noble heart at the inconsistent scenes around him, poor Shelley was expelled college, and a mark set on him for life.

At the time when these three persecuted men of genius used to meet here, chiefly in the year 1816, they were ostracised by the public, and two of them, Keats and Shelley, were made very miserable. In proportion to their genius was the intensity of the public hatred. Keats, indeed, at that time, was only just entering on that career of shameful abuse by the critics, and of ultimate glory, which was his fortune in a very short life. He had not yet written 'Endymion,' but he had become acquainted with a group of eminent men, who continued to appreciate him as he deserved. Leigh Hunt, Haydon (whose misfortunes equalled his own), Shelley, Mr. Dilke (afterwards proprietor of the 'Athenæum'), Reynolds (author of the amusing papers of 'Peter Corcoran,' &c.), Mr. Cowden Clarke, and soon after of Hazlitt, Lamb, and Barry Cornwall.

From this time till 1820, when he left - in the last stage of consumption - for Italy, he resided principally at Hampstead. During most of this time, he lived with his very dear friend Mr. Charles Brown, a Russia merchant, at Wentworth Place, Downshire Hill, by Pond Street, Hampstead. Previously, he and his brother Thomas had occupied apartments at the next house to Mr. Brown's, at a Mrs. ___'s, whose name his biographers have carefully omitted. With the daughter of this lady Keats was deeply in love, a passion which deepened to the last. Lord Houghton, in his 'Life and Letters of Keats,' merely says, on this subject,

'However sincerely the devotion of Keats may have been requited, it will be seen that his outward circumstances soon became such as to render a union very difficult, if not impossible. Thus these years were passed in a conflict in which plain poverty and mortal sickness met a radiant imagination and a redundant heart. Hope was there, with Genius, his everlasting sustainer, and Fear never approached but as the companion of Necessity. The strong power conquered the physical man, and made the very intensity of his passion, in a certain sense, accessory to his death; he might have lived longer if he had lived less. But this should be no matter of self-reproach to the object of his love, for the same may be said of the very exercise of his poetic faculty, and of all that made him what he was. It is enough that she has preserved his memory with a sacred honour, and it is no vain assumption, that to have inspired and sustained the one passion of this noble being, has been a source of grave delight and earnest thankfulness, through the changes and chances of her earthly pilgrimage.'

The story of the latter years of Keats' life is one of the most affecting that can be conceived. Whilst pouring out his exquisite poetry, whilst enriching our literature with some of its most beautiful possessions, he was in constant and dread conflict with poverty, disease, and murderous critical savagery, with hopes continually prostrated, with a love passionate, intense, and torturing from its inevitable despair of fruition. On the other hand, he had the solaces of friendships of the most ardent and disinterested nature, amongst which the self-sacrificing devotion of that of Mr. Severn, the artist, who accompanied him to Rome, and nursed him to the last moment with a most noble and rare magnanimity, is almost unexampled in human history.

By the aid of the statements of Leigh Hunt and Lord Houghton, we may trace most of the scenes in which the very finest poetry of Keats was written, for the noblest of his productions were all written at Hampstead. His 'Endymion,' 'Lamia,' 'Isabella,' 'Eve of St. Agnes,' 'Hyperion,' all were written at Hampstead. Leigh Hunt says,

> 'The poem with which his first volume begins, was suggested to him on a delightful summer day, as he stood by the gate which leads from the battery on Hampstead Heath into a field by Caen Wood; and the last poem, the one on "Sleep and Poetry," was occasioned by his sleeping in the Vale of Health.'

In fact, Keats slept at Hunt's own house in the Vale of Health. In the lane near Highgate leading from Milfield Lane to Caen Wood - and from its being often frequented by Hunt, Keats, Lamb, Hazlitt and Coleridge, called Poets' Lane - Keats with Hunt, first met Coleridge, who afterwards described Keats as 'a loose, slack, not well-dressed youth,' and after shaking hands with him, observed, 'There is death in that hand.' This was in 1817, when every one else thought Keats in good health, but when, evidently, the consumption which carried off early both himself and his brother, was already in progress in him. This disease Keats himself believed to have fixed fatally on him in riding outside a coach on a cold day from London up to Hampstead.

To 'Endymion,' written at Hampstead, he put the finishing touches at Burford Bridge, at the foot of Box Hill, Surrey, in one of those pedestrian excursions which he delighted to make, and in which he traversed several parts of the South of England, the Isle of Wight, Devonshire, and portions of Scotland, the Western Isles, with a peep at Ireland. He began his `Hyperion' in December 1818, immediately after removing to his friend Brown's house in Wentworth Place. This noble fragment remained a fragment, in consequence of the brutal attack on his 'Endymion' by the 'Quarterly Review' and 'Blackwood's' - a direct standing contradiction of the oft-asserted fallacy that no criticism ever destroyed or prevented the productions of a genuine poet. The kick of a cart-horse may kill a poet; and the base onslaught of a stupid critic can and does not unfrequently as completely annihilate the soul of poetry in a sensitive bosom as a deadly frost kills both flower and fruit. In this sense malignant critics murder the genius and blast the literature of their country. Lord Houghton says,

'In the spring of 1819, the admirable "Ode to a Nightingale" was suggested by the continual song of the bird that had built its nest close to the house, and which often threw Keats into a sort of trance of tranquil pleasure. One morning he took his chair from the breakfast table, placed it on the grass plot under a plane tree, and sat there for two or three hours with some scraps of paper in his hands. Shortly afterwards Mr. Brown saw him thrusting them away as waste paper behind some books, and had some difficulty in putting together and arranging the stanzas of the ode. Other poems, as literally "fugitive" were rescued in much the same manner, for he permitted Mr. Brown to copy what he could pick up, and sometimes assisted him.'

Soon after he repeated, or rather chanted, in a sort of recitative, this ode to Mr. Haydon, as they strolled together through Kilburn meadows - meadows now all buried in brick and mortar. We may add, that at one time Leigh Hunt had lodgings in Kentish Town, and then, probably, it was that they used to take their strolls up Milfield Lane and encountered Coleridge. These few glimpses of the spots on which Keats composed his most beautiful poems may serve to show us that many a piece of ground, very common-place in itself, has witnessed the walks and conversation of men whom we are accustomed to look for only in books, and that we often tread in the footsteps of the great when we little dream of it.

In sadness and poverty, and under loads of the world's scorn, evoked by the base Mohawks of criticism, here they often walked where we now walk. Of the sadness of Keats in his rambles about

Hampstead, we have evidence in what Leigh Hunt says:

> 'As we were sitting on the bench in Well Walk, near the Heath - the one against the wall - he told me, with unaccustomed tears in his eyes, that his heart was breaking. Then, and till his death, he believed that the Reviews had destroyed his fame.'

It is to be regretted that Wentworth Place, where Keats lodged, and wrote some of his finest poetry, either no longer exists or no longer bears that name. At the bottom of John Street, on the left hand in descending, is a villa called Wentworth House; but no Wentworth Place exists between Downshire Hill and Pond Street, the locality assigned to it. I made the most rigorous search in that quarter, inquiring of the tradesmen daily supplying the houses there, and of two residents of forty and fifty years. None of them had any knowledge or recollection of a Wentworth Place. Possibly Keats's friend, Mr. Brown, lived at Wentworth House, and that the three cottages standing in a line with it and facing South End Road, but at a little distance from the road in a garden, might then bear the name of Wentworth Place. The end cottage would then, as stated in the lines of Keats, be next door to Mr. Brown's. These cottages still have apartments to let, and in all other respects accord with the assigned locality.

In less than two years after the death of Keats, Shelley was drowned off the coast of Italy, namely, on July 8, 1822; and his ashes were laid near those of his dear friend and poet-brother in affliction, Keats, in the English burial ground at Rome, aged only thirty.

Never had men who conferred such glory on their country such hard measure dealt out to them by their contemporaries. Shelley was, in fact, morally outlawed and banned by the general voice of the country. The whole press, with the exception of the 'Examiner' - in the hands of his friend Leigh Hunt - pursued him with an inexorable and rancorous hatred. As his noble poems came out one after another, they were hissed and hooted at by the critics; fell dead from the press; and never were the effects of the deep melancholy which this treatment induced more graphically and pathetically depicted than in his 'Lines written on the Shore at Naples.':

I sit upon the sands alone -
    The lightning of the noontide ocean
Is flashing round me - and a tone
    Arises from its mingled motion.
How sweet! if any heart could share in my emotion

And in that other verse:

Yet now despair itself is mild,
Even as the winds and waters are.
I could lie down like a tired child,
And weep away this life of care,
Which I have borne and yet must bear,
Till death like sleep might steal on me,
And I might feel in the warm air,
My heart grow cold, and hear the sea
Breathe o'er my outworn brain its last monotony.

And what was the real character of the man whom critics and relatives, and the law, which stripped him of his children, and the self-righteous world, contrived to chase from society as a demon? A perfectly childlike and Christ-like creature. If Christianity is love, and love of your neighbour especially, then Shelley was in heart and soul and daily deed a perfect Christian. He lamented his early errors, but found no forgiveness. Captain Medwin, his relative, and one who knew him from childhood, says,

'He was an enemy to all sensuality. The pleasures of the table, that form the *summum bonum* of the herd, were not his pleasures. His diet was that of a hermit, his drink water, and his principal and favourite food bread. His conversation was as chaste as his morals - all grossness he abominated.'

His heart was one congeries of all noble and generous emotions. He was ready, at every information of human suffering, to stand up and try to relieve it; and in the pursuit of such divine objects he cared not for conventionalities or misrepresentation. Leigh Hunt gives us this picture of him here at Hampstead:

'Shelley often came there to see me, sometimes to stop for several days. He delighted in the natural broken ground, and in the fresh air of the place, especially when the wind set in from the north-west, which used to give him an intoxication of animal spirits. Here also he swam his paper boats on the ponds, and delighted to play with my children, especially with my eldest boy, the seriousness of whose imagination, and his susceptibility of a "grim" impression - a favourite epithet of Shelley's - highly delighted him. He would play at "frightful creatures" with him, from which the other would snatch "a fearful joy," only begging him occasionally "not to do the horn," which was a way that Shelley had of screwing up his hair in front, to imitate a weapon of that sort. This was the boy, now a man of forty, and himself a fine writer, to whom Lamb took such a liking on similar accounts, and addressed some charming verses, on his "favourite child." '

He then tells an anecdote very characteristic of Shelley, and which ought to make many of us think seriously of the way we look at things:

'I was returning home one night to Hampstead after the opera; as I approached the door, I heard strange and alarming shrieks, mixed with the voice of a man. The next day, it was reported by gossips that Mr. Shelley, "no Christian," for it was he who was there, "had brought some very strange female" into the house, no better, of course, than she ought to be. The real Christian had puzzled them. Shelley, in coming to our house that night, had found a woman lying near the top of the hill in fits. It was a fierce winter night, with snow upon the ground; and winter loses nothing of its fierceness at Hampstead. My friend, always the promptest as well as most pitying on these occasions, knocked at the first house he could reach, in order to have the woman taken in. The invariable answer was, they could not do it. He asked for an outhouse to put her in while he went for a doctor. Impossible! In vain he assured them he was no impostor. They would not dispute the point with him; but doors wrere closed, and windows were shut down. Had he hit on another, Mr. Park, the philologist, he would assuredly have come, in spite of his Calvinism. But he lived too far off. Had he hit upon my friend and neighbour, Dilke, they would either of them have jumped up from amidst their books or their bedclothes, and have gone out with him. But the paucity of Christians is astonishing, considering the number of them. Time flies; the poor woman is in convulsions, her son, a young man, lamenting over her. At last my friend sees a carriage driving up to a house at a little distance. The knock is given; the warm door opens; servants and lights pour forth. How, thought he, is the time. He puts on his best address, which anybody might recognise as that of the highest gentleman, as well as of an interesting individual, and plants himself in the way of an elderly person, who is stepping ont of his carriage with his family. He tells his story; they only press on the faster. "Will yon go and see her?" "No, sir, there is no occasion for that sort of thing, depend upon it. Impostors swarm everywhere: the thing cannot be done; sir, your conduct is extraordinary." "Sir," cried Shelley, assuming a very different manner, and forcing the flourishing householder to stop out of astonishment, "I am sorry to say that your conduct is not extraordinary; and if my own seems to amaze you, I will tell you something which may amaze you a little more, and I hope will frighten you. It is such men as you who madden the spirits and the patience of the poor and wretched; and if ever a convulsion comes in this country, which is very probable, recollect what I tell you: you will have your house, that you refuse to put this miserable woman into, burnt over your head!" "God bless me, sir! Dear me, sir!" exclaimed the poor frightened man, and fluttered into his mansion.

The woman was then brought to our house, which was at some distance, and down a bleak path; and Shelley and her son were obliged to hold her till the doctor could arrive. It appeared that she had been attending this son in London on a criminal charge made against him, the agitation of which had thrown her into the fits on her return. The doctor said that she would have perished had she lain there a short time longer. The next day my friend sent mother and son home comfortably to Hendon, where they were known, and whence they returned him thanks full of gratitude.'

When we read the parable of the Good Samaritan, we all despise the Priest and Levite who passed on the other side when they saw the wounded man lying in the road. We all applaud the Good Samaritan, and think we should have done just like him. Should we? - Ah! not so easy is the 'doing likewise.' Here we have an example of the Good Samaritan in our own day, and who was he? Exactly such a man as the Samaritan of old. A man under a ban and a stigma; a man to whom was denied the very name of Christian; a man persecuted, maligned, made utterly wretched by the revilements of critics and the 'unco guid.' He is the man who at once attempts to succour the poor fainting woman. He knocks at door after door, he stops the good Christians passing comfortably by, he grows desperate in his denials of help for the suffering, and stands before the wealthy man and his family issuing from his carriage, and only alarms him, only makes him probably think that he is a madman or a robber! Such are the difficulties of imitating the Good Samaritan in this age and country. Should we then so readily have done as the Good Samaritan did? Alas! there are ninety-nine in the hundred against it! If we were, as many of us think we are, such Good Samaritans in this country, there could not exist the astounding contrasts of luxury and splendour, starvation and desolation, as those which overspread this Christian England.

But the house of Leigh Hunt received and revived the poor woman. Leigh Hunt, the third of this remarkable trio, had also his share of persecutions. He dared to be a bold reformer in the days of rampant Toryism, and he was not only thrown into prison for calling the licentious Prince Regent an 'Adonis of fifty,' but the 'Quarterly Review,' 'Blackwood's Magazine,' and the whole herd of lesser journals and newspapers, fell upon his poetry, or treated it and him personally as if he had been a shameful malefactor, and his most charming poems and most genial essays as something worse than ratsbane.

Looking back at these things from the present time, we can scarcely believe the records of such malignity. Walking here over the Heath on a sunny day we can scarcely realise the fact of such men as John Keats, the tender-hearted Shelley, and the naturally blithesome and broad-minded Leigh Hunt, taking a stroll amongst the blooming furze and the flowers quivering in the summer breeze - three men branded as the enemies of society, because they had enriched our literature with some of its most beautiful possessions. The fact ought to be a great lesson, if we ever do profit by such lessons, of forbearance and kindliness towards those who are doing all they can, though not exactly as we may think they should, towards augmenting that pile of noble national thought which is the solace of our lonely and the guide of our active days. Here, with the rest, we may imagine the quaint-humoured and self-sacrificing Charles Lamb occasionally strolling up from the Temple, or the cottage at Islington, for a Sunday chat with Hunt, on what Wordsworth, Coleridge, nestled on the opposite hill of Highgate, what Hazlitt, Lord Byron, Scott, Southey, and the rest of the prolific souls of that day, were doing.

Heath Lodge. Mrs. Lessingham

The name of this lady has assumed a prominent place in the history of Hampstead, from a hotly litigated case of enclosure on the Heath. Everyone who sees the extensive appropriation from the Heath, surrounded by a ring-fence, including space for the house - Heath Lodge - pleasure- grounds, and gardens of David Powell, Esq., on the northwestern side of the Heath, must wonder how it came to be made. In 1775 a Mrs. Hemett, an actress of secondary parts at Covent Garden, professionally styled Lessingham, but also an actress of other parts which gave her a greater notoriety, had set her heart on a lodge on the Heath. At the time when this contest took place she was said to be under the protection of Mr. Justice Addington. The lords of the manor of Hampstead, it seems, had always claimed a right to grant portions of the waste lands, with consent of the homage, to persons already copyholders. Mrs. Lessingham applied to the lord of the manor for the grant of a permission to erect a house on the waste. No doubt the application was backed by influential friends, and the homage, having surveyed the ground, reported that it was no detriment to the lord, and gave their consent on July 6, 1775. The lord therefore granted the permission.

Now, however, some of the copyholders and commoners becoming aware that Mrs. Lessingham was no copyholder, raised a violent opposition. They entered a protest against the grant in the Manor Court, and proceeded to demolish the enclosure and destroy the buildings. Park says,

> `A battle of a very sanguinary nature is reported to have taken place between the bricklayers and the constables; and the public papers of the day teemed with communications on. the subject of "the riot on Hampstead Heath," the parties to which were attacked and defended with considerable warmth.'

George Stevens is said to have been very active in the composition and issue of these squibs; and Mrs. Lessingham herself put forth whatever powers of poetry and satire she possessed in a metrical pamphlet, entitled 'The Hampstead Contest.'

The discontented copyholders proceeded to try the case in the

Court of Common Pleas. The case came on in Easter Term, 16 George III, 1776, in the name of Folkard v. Hemett and others. Mrs. Lessingham seems to have been advised to extinguish the ostensible objection to her claim by purchasing a copyhold cottage, and thus becoming a copyholder. This seems to have altered the tactics of the opposition, who accordingly proceeded against her, not for being admitted to a copyholder's privilege, though a non-copyholder, but the charge was made for encroachment and injury to the right of pasturage existing in copyholders, &c. The judge treated the grants of this nature as 'a reserved right of the lord,' and the jury, declaring the land of no value, and, consequently, no damage having been done to the plaintiffs, found a verdict for the defendants. Mrs. Lessingham triumphed, finished her enclosure fences and her house; but the grand question of the lord's right to grant such enclosures remained untried, though evidence on the trial was produced to show that the lord had exercised this right from 1599 to the date of the trial, sometimes on ten occasions in one year. This will account for the numerous enclosures which have evidently, at one time or another, been made on the Heath.

Mysterious Death of John Sadleir

One of the most extraordinary events which have taken place on Hampstead Heath was the finding there the body of John Sadleir, M.P., representative of the borough of Sligo, on the morning of Sunday, February 17, 1856. A labourer was hunting for his donkey, to do service for the pleasure-seekers so numerous on that day, and a little way down the slope behind 'Jack Straw's Castle' he came upon the corpse of a well-dressed man. It was lying in a hollow, with the feet very near a small pool of water. The dress of the deceased was undisturbed, except that his hat had fallen off and lay at a little distance. The head of the deceased lay near a furze bush. The soles of his boots were not dirtied; so that it was evident that he had arrived near the spot in a vehicle. It was not far from the road leading from the flagstaff towards the Finchley Road. By his side lay a silver cream ewer, smelling strongly of essential oil of bitter almonds, and a bottle labelled, 'Essential oil of Almonds,' and 'Poison,' was also lying near it. The man gave the alarm at the 'Jack Straw's Castle;' and on the police proceeding thither, they found the person must have been dead the greater part of the night, for rigor mortis was completely established. It was a clear case of suicide; and in the pockets of the deceased were found a case of razors, denoting that the unhappy man had contemplated making use of them had the poison not operated speedily. There were also a £5 note, £3 in gold, some silver and halfpence, some pieces of lump-sugar, a latch-key, and a piece of paper on which the deceased had written in a clear bold hand, 'John Sadleir, Gloucester Square, Hyde Park.' This gave a clue to the identification of the suicide, which, on inquiry, proved correct.

Mr. John Sadleir had for some time occupied a position of so much importance in the public eye - having been, not long before, even in the Ministry - that his death under such circumstances excited not only surprise, but great commiseration. A little time, however, converted this feeling into indignation at the enormity of his crimes, which had conducted him to this tragic end, and plunged tens of thousands into misery and destitution. It was soon found that a long career of the most reckless and unprincipled speculation had been drawing to a crisis; and the news of his death brought forth astonished claimants, who in their turn astonished the public by their disclosures.

Let us, however, before entering on his remarkable career, state the circumstances which identified him. The body was removed to Hampstead Workhouse, where, at the coroner's inquest held upon it, the surgeon deposed that he detected a powerful odour of the essential oil of bitter almonds (which, in fact, is chiefly prussic acid) issuing from the mouth; and on examination he obtained from the stomach three ounces of this powerful poison, besides a considerable quantity of opium. It was clear that the deceased had taken the most determined measures for his destruction: prussic acid enough to kill a dozen horses, opium, and razors ready if the drugs failed him, which they were not likely to do.

The butler of this great delinquent deposed that he had returned to his house to dinner at about seven o'clock on Saturday evening. This was unusual, as he generally dined at his club. When he came in he gave the butler a letter addressed to his sister-in-law in Ireland, desiring that it should be posted, and a paper which he desired him to take to Mr. Maitland, a neighbouring chemist. It stated that the groom required a quantity of essential oil of bitter almonds, and requested that one pound's worth should be sent. At nine o'clock he enquired if it had arrived, and finding that it had not, directed it to be sent for. At about half-past nine it came, and the butler took it to his master and placed it by his side. He was then looking over some papers. The poison was in quantity about half a pint. At a later hour, the butler took up the tea-tray; the silver cream-ewer was part of the service. Some time after the butler went to remove the tray, but his master appeared not to have finished, and he left him. He saw him last about half-past eleven o'clock, and he must have left the house between that time and one o'clock, for when the butler went into the room at the latter hour, Mr. Sadleir was gone, and his hat and coat were missing. The servants went to bed, knowing that their master had a latch key.

As to the state of mind of the unhappy man on this miserable evening, Mr. Anthony Norris said,

'I reside at No. 2, Bedford Row, and am a solicitor. I was intimately acquainted with the deceased gentleman; I saw him last alive shortly before eleven o'clock on Saturday night, at his house in Gloucester Terrace. I had no appointment with him, but I went up there, and was with him about half-an-hour. I have known him since 1848, and have frequently transacted business with him.'

This witness deposed that on this last occasion he was greatly depressed by his affairs, and that on leaving him he noticed that his eyes were bloodshot, and that he was in such a state as he had never seen him in before; his manner being usually cool and collected. He appeared to have been weeping very much. He desired him to call at eleven o'clock on the following morning, respecting a letter just received from Ireland, but when he went at that time, he heard that he was dead. He said he had remarked to a friend, after learning the state of Mr. Sadleir's affairs, that he should not be surprised if Mr. Sadleir were to shoot himself. Here the coroner seemed disposed to close the enquiry; but the jury having heard that Sadleir had left three letters in the hall when he disappeared on Saturday night, demanded that they should be produced. They were accordingly produced and read. These revealed a condition of mind which might operate as a serious determent to those tempted to run a career of guilty ambition, could any warnings avail with such persons. One of the letters ran thus:

'Saturday night.

I cannot live - I have ruined too many - I could not live and see their agony - I have committed diabolical crimes unknown to any human beings. They will now appear, bringing my family and others to distress - causing to all shame and grief that they should ever have known me.

I blame no one, but attribute all to my infamous villany. Hundreds are ruined by my villany. I could go through any torture as a punishment for my crimes. No torture could be too much for such crimes; but I cannot live to see the tortures I inflict upon others.

J. Sadleir.

Telegraph to ___ and otherwise when you read this.'

Another of these letters was to Mr. Robert Keating, M.P. for Waterford:

'11 Gloucester Terrace,
16 February, 1856.

Dear Robert, - To what infamy have I come step by step - heaping crime upon crime - and now I find myself the author of numberless crimes of a diabolical character, and the cause of ruin and disgrace to thousands - ay, to tens of thousands.

Oh, how I feel for those on whom all this ruin must fall - I could bear all punishments, but I can never bear to witness the suffering of those on whom I have brought such ruin - it must be better that I should not live.

No one has been privy to my crimes - they spring from my own cursed brain alone - I have swindled and deceived without the knowledge of any one - Stevens and Norris are both innocent, and have no knowledge of the fabrication of deeds and forgeries by me, and by which I have sought to go on in the horrid hope of retrieving.

It was a sad day for all when I came to London. I can give but little aid to unravel accounts and transactions. There are serious questions as to my interest in the Grand Junction and other undertakings. Much will be lost to the creditors if these cases are not fairly treated. The Grand Junction, the East Kent, and the Swiss Railways, the Rome line, the Coal Co., are all liable to be entirely lost now - so far as my assets are concerned.

I authorise you to take possession of all my letters, papers, property, etc. etc., in this house and at Wilkinson's, and at Cannon Street.

Return my brother his letters to me and all other papers. The prayers of one so wicked could not avail, or I would seek to pray for those I leave after me, and who will have to suffer such agony, and all owing to my criminal acts.

Oh! that I had never quitted Ireland! - Oh! that I had resisted the first attempts to launch me into speculation!

If I had less talents of a worthless kind, and more firmness, I might have remained as I once was, honest and truthful - and I would have lived to see my dear father and mother in their old age. I weep and weep now, but what can that avail?

J. Sadleir.

Robert Keating, Esq., M.P.
Shamroque Lodge, Clapham.'

The ground for the self-accusation of forgery contained in this letter, the direct cause of the suicide, was soon explained. Mr. Josiah Wilkinson, of the firm of Wilkinson, Gurney, and Stevens, solicitors, of Nicolas Lane, stated that on the morning of Saturday, Mr. Sadleir had called upon him in a very excited state, proposing to him to raise a large sum in aid of the Tipperary Bank. The plans he proposed were altogether impracticable, and Mr. Wilkinson refused the transaction. The firm had frequently advanced large sums to Mr. Sadleir, but the balances had become so large that they had required security. This, about six weeks before, Mr. Sadleir had given. It purported to be a deed given on the purchase of an estate in the Encumbered Estate Court. Mr. Wilkinson was so much alarmed by the conduct of Mr. Sadleir upon this Saturday, and by the knowledge of the critical condition of the Tipperary Bank, that that very evening he despatched his partner, Mr. Stevens, to Dublin, for the purpose of registering it, which he had hitherto neglected doing. Mr. Stevens immediately discovered that the deed was a forgery. It was signed by two of the commissioners, and attested by two witnesses, in two parts of the deed. All these signatures were forgeries. The seal upon the deed was the genuine seal of the commissioners, but it had been transferred from some other document.

Rumours went forth that many other securities lodged by the

deceased were also forgeries, particularly some of those held by the London and County Bank, to which he was indebted; but on these being tested, they were found to be genuine, nor was any evidence adduced before the inquest to show what were the forgeries, and what the nature of the crimes to which the deceased alluded in his last letter. A particular enquiry was made as to what had become of a large sum of money which had been paid to Mr. Sadleir on the morning of his suicide; but no trace of its disposal could be found.

The letter which Sadleir had written on the day of his suicide exhibited intense distress and remorse, but no trace of insanity, and the jury returned a verdict of death by his own hand while in a perfectly sound state of intellect.

Of the extent of the frauds perpetrated by Mr. John Sadleir, no connected statement was published. The fraudulent transactions in respect of the Royal Swedish Railway appeared to consist in an over-issue of shares and obligations to the amount at least of £150,000. In respect of the Tipperary Bank, the manager, his brother, had permitted him to overdraw more than £200,000; and, with other fraudulent mismanagements, the deficit of the bank exceeded £400,000. The assets were stated to be £100,000, but they proved to be little more than £30,000. The misery caused by this infamous confederacy was unspeakable. Not only were the depositors in the south of Ireland - chiefly small farmers and tradesmen - defrauded of their whole savings, but the shareholders were stripped, for the most part, of every farthing they possessed. The means taken to entrap the last-named classes were most infamous. On February 1, one lunar month before the crash, Mr. Sadleir had published a balance-sheet and report, in which the concern was represented as most flourishing. A dividend at the rate of 6 per cent., with a bonus of £3 per cent., was declared, and £3,000 was carried to the reserve fund, raising that to £17,000. By means of this infamous fabrication, a considerable number of persons - most of them widows, spinsters, and half-pay officers - were induced to become shareholders, and lost their all. Endless suits were brought by attorneys who had purchased debts due by the company, against these unhappy persons. Some declared themselves insolvent, others suddenly disappeared, and fled to the United States with such of their property as they could hastily secure. Mr. James Sadleir, the brother of the deceased, and manager of the bank, absconded under circumstances which gave rise to much comment. It was asserted that the large sum of money received by John Sadleir the day before his death had gone to help him off. He was said, not long after, to be seen in the United States; and a most extraordinary story got abroad, and was extensively believed, that John Sadleir himself had, in addition to his many forged documents enacted a false suicide. That he had purchased the corpse of a man resembling himself, had him conveyed to Hampstead Heath, and was himself gone off to America with his brother. The whole of the circumstances, however, which came out on the inquest were too decisive of his identity to warrant this rumour. Not only did his friends and servants fully recognise him, but Mr. Wakley, the coroner, who knew him too well to be mistaken, perfectly identified him. Besides, the man found had actually been poisoned on the spot by the contents of the cream-ewer and bottle laid beside him, and could not have been brought there a corpse, even could Sadleir's servants and friends have entered into so wild a conspiracy to favour his absconding alive.

And who was this John Sadleir? He was an Irishman, the third son of Clement William Sadleir, Esq., of Shrone Hill near Tipperary, in which town a bank was established by his grandfather. He was born in 1814, and educated at Clongoes College. He succeeded an uncle in a very lucrative business as a solicitor in Dublin, which profession he continued to follow till 1846, having before that time become a director of the Tipperary Joint Stock Bank, established about the year 1827, and in which the private bank founded by his grandfather was merged. In July 1847 he became Member of Parliament for the borough of Carlow, and made himself conspicuous both as such and as parliamentary agent for Irish railways. He was in the House a distinguished member of the 'Irish Brigade.' He became a junior Lord of the Treasury under Lord Aberdeen, and appeared a remarkably rising man. This, however, lost him his seat for Carlow, but he was re-elected for Sligo in 1853. Some disclosures, not to his credit, again lost him his seat in the Treasury; but he still held his head aloft, and found public confidence enough to become chairman of the London and County Joint Stock Banking Company, and is said to have conducted its affairs with great ability. Had he restrained his ambition within the limits of honesty, he might have continued to pass for one of the most successful men of the time. He is said at one period to have been worth £200,000. Ceasing to be chairman of the London and County Joint Stock Bank, he became chairman of the Royal Swedish Railway Company, and the founder of the Joint Stock Bank of Tipperary, in which his brother James was manager. Here he crowned all his crimes and forgeries by the last act of detestable villany, which plunged such thousands into ruin, and consummated a fate evidently, to himself, as intense in its misery, as it was loaded with a lasting and far-blown infamy. The horrors of that night in which, in storm and darkness, he took his way to the black solitude of Hampstead Heath, bearing with him the accumulated apparatus of his own destruction, has something in it especially indicative of avenging justice; and the suicide's frightful delusion of escaping from God's conscience-torturing hand by rushing, steeped in villanies, into his presence, adds the last lurid shadow to the picture. It has been well said, that 'he was a swindler on the very grandest scale, and kept up the game to the last.'

THE PONDS

On the Heath are a prominent feature. The origin of these was the necessity, at an early period, of water supply in London. As the population extended on this side of the metropolis, the currents of the various streams descending from these 'northern heights' became at once decreased and polluted. The River of Wells, terminating in the Fleet, ceased to display its clear currents and its grassy and wooded banks, to which the citizens delighted to resort. Its clacking mills had disappeared; and the Fleet itself, the tidal portion of the stream, as its Saxon name *fleot* denotes, so far from bearing vessels of considerable burthen, as it was said to have done in the good old times, as far up as Holborn Bridge, was shrunk into the dimensions and into the name of a ditch. As early as the reign of Henry VIII, we are told that Sir William Bowyer Knt., Mayor of the city of London, turned his attention to these hills for water. The Act of 35 Henry VIII (1543-44), preserved in the British Museum, says that Sir William,

> 'calling with him as well dyvers grave and expert persons of brethrene, and other of the comminaltie of the saide city, as other persons in and aboute the conveyance of water well experienced, hath, not onely by diligent searche and exploracion, founde out dyvers great and plentyfull sprynges at Hampstede-heath, Mary- bone, Hackney, Muswell-kylle, and dyvers places within the saide citie, very mete, propise, and convenient to be brought and conveyed to the same.'

The Act just mentioned was therefore obtained 'for the conveyance thereof, by cundytes, vautes, and pipes, to the said citie.' They were empowered to search, dig for, and convey away water, and to 'make heades and vautes for the conveyance of the same water.' The Act proceeds to say that

> 'for every sprynge or sprynges within Hampsted-hethe, they, the sayd maire and cominaltie, and their successours, shall forever yelde, beare, and pay unto the Bisshopp of Westminster for the tyme being, at the Feast of St. Mychell tharchaungell, one pounde of pepper, in and for

thacknowledging hym and them for the lordes and verie owners of the said hethe.'

Except the term of 'making heades,' there is little indication of the formation of ponds. The chief idea in the commencement appears to have been to clear out the spring heads, and cut water-courses, and lay pipes to facilitate the flow of the waters towards the city, one great object of this increased and combined current being to enable the Fleet to scour itself, and to keep its estuary open to the Thames. This part of the project failed; but the works for the supply of water to the city were continued by Sir John Hart, Lord Mayor in 1589-90. The springs were then leased by the London municipality, and the lessees in 1692 were incorporated by the title of 'The Hampstead Water Company.' The London city authorities were prohibited by the Act of Henry VIII from interfering with the spring at the foot of the hill of the said Heath, which, it says, was closed in with brick for the use and convenience of the inhabitants of Hampstead. At the same time the Bishop of Westminster was authorised to search for springs on the Heath, and convey water from them to his manor of Hendon. From some cause or other, Lysons says, the water company and the people of Hampstead fell into disputes about what the Americans call their 'water privileges,' and then the inhabitants amongst themselves, even proceeding to law about the year 1700. Park found that the present ponds existed in the seventeenth century, being mentioned amongst the copyholds - the upper pond on the Heath, stated to contain three roods thirty perches; the lower pond one acre, one rood, thirty four perches. The pond in the Vale of Health was added in 1777. 'The ponds,' he adds, 'have been fatal to many incautious bathers, owing to the sudden shelving of their sides.' In the Vale of Health are visible two rows of wooden posts, probably the remains of a bridge either leading across or to some aquatic pleasure-house on the water.

THE VILLAGE OF HAMPSTEAD

This place was anciently written Hamestede, meaning simply Homestead.

Having now taken a survey of the neighbourhood of Hampstead, we may proceed to the village itself, and note its most prominent and historical sites as we pass along. The village and immediate vicinity, from their fine views towards Harrow and Windsor in one direction; in another, towards Hendon and Finchley, and far into Hertfordshire; in another, towards Highbury, Islington, and Epping Forest; in another, over London, east and west, down the Thames and up the Thames, and over to the Kent and Surrey hills beyond, from the open expanse of heath about it, has always been a favourite resort of Londoners, and a favourite abode of commercial and professional men. Lawyers and artists have shown a great preference for it. In times past a considerable number of the nobility had houses there; and we read of the gay and crowded fetes given there by Lady Crewe and others, amongst them Lords Erskine and Loughborough. There the Kit-cat Club for a time held its sittings; and literary men sought there retirement from the distractions of London. The great number of old brick houses standing in their ample grounds, and gardens enclosed by high brick walls, and shaded by large and lofty elms, show how favourite a place it has been to wealthy merchants, bankers, and others engaged in the commerce and professions of the metropolis.

Approaching the village from the north, but before arriving at it, on the left hand we have The Upper Flask.

THE UPPER FLASK

This celebrated house lies opposite to the new reservoir. The wall enclosing its garden and grounds extends down Heath Street from a lane nearly opposite to the pool along the Heath side towards the lower Heath, and the road leading from Heath Street to the new church - Christ Church. Outside the wall, the footpath is shaded by a fine row of elm trees. The house has long been a private house, and is now occupied by Mrs. Lister. Some time ago Mr. Sheppard, M.P. for Frome, lived there; but the house derives its fame from having been the Upper Flask mentioned by Richardson in his novel of 'Clarissa Harlowe,' from being the resort of the Kit-cat Club, and of many of our celebrated men of a former period, and subsequently, after it ceased to be a public house, the residence of George Steevens, the commentator of Shakespeare.

The Upper Flask
(From a photograph, taken expressly for this work)

Richardson, like so many men of reputation, seems to have had a great liking for Hampstead, and took the occasion, in 'Clarissa Harlowe,' to make it conspicuous as the ground of some of the leading events of his story. He represents the fashionable villain, Lovelace, who had managed, on the promise of marriage, to lure away Clarissa from her tyrannical family, as inducing her to take a drive with him, in company of two of the women of the sponging-house into which he had with infamous deception introduced her. In a letter to his friend Belford he says, 'The coach carried us to Hampstead, to Highgate, to Muswell Hill; back to Hampstead to the Hpper Flask. There, in compliment to the nymphs, my beloved consented to alight and take a little repast; then home early by Kentish Town.'

As soon as Clarissa discovers the real villany of Lovelace, and the foul place into which he has brought her, she sets about to escape, and seems for a moment to manage it. She does not hasten home, or to any of her friends, for she feels the sad effect of her elopement on her character and position; but she thinks of Hampstead, and endeavours, as a first step, to get there. But one of the creatures of Lovelace, who had attended them on their excursion to Hampstead, Highgate, &c., sees her escaping, and tracks her to a hackney coach, and, from her directions to the driver, instantly suspects her aim; he follows in disguise, and discovers her at the 'Flask.' The fellow writes to Lovelace,

> 'If your honner come to the Upper Flax, I will be in site all the day about the Tapp-house on the Hethe. I have borrowed another cote, instead of your honner's liferie, and a black wig; soe can not be known by my lady, if as how she should see me.'

Lovelace pursues his victim in all haste, and arrives at the Upper Flask, but finds that she has removed to lodgings near. In his letter on this occasion to Belford, Lovelace says,

> 'All Will's account, from the lady's flight to his finding her again, all the accounts of the people of the house, the coachman's information to Will, and so forth, collected together, stand thus:
> The Hampstead coach, when the dear fugitive came to it, had but two passengers in it; but she made the fellow go off directly, paying for the vacant places. The two passengers, directing the coachman to set them down at the "Upper Flask," she bid him set her down there also. They took leave of her very respectfully, no doubt, and she went into the house and asked if she could not have a dish of tea, and a room to

herself for half an hour. They showed her up to the very room where I now am. She sat at the very table I now write upon; and I believe the chair I sit upon was hers. O, Belford, if thou knowest what love is, thou wilt be able to account for these minutiæ.'

The scoundrel Lovelace immediately surrounds Clarissa with his vile tools and spies, and by disguise and bribery regains possession of her in her lodgings. The landlord of the 'Flask' has lent him his disguises, and he interests all the women of the house by representing Clarissa as his wife, who has quarrelled with and left him. The scene is then changed from the 'Flask' to the lodging house of a Mrs. Moore, where all the arts are carried on by which the poor entrapped fugitive is inveigled back to London and her ruin. Clarissa attempts to escape, and this conversation takes place between her and her landlady:

> *Clarissa*: `Let me look out. Whither does that path lead to? Is there no possibility of getting a coach? Can not I steal to a neighbouring house, where I may be concealed till I can get quite away? Oh, help me, help me, ladies, or I am ruined!' Then pausing, `Is that the way to Hendon? Is Hendon a private place? The Hampstead coach, I am told, will carry passengers thither.'
> *Mrs. Moore*: 'I have an honest friend at Mill Hill, where, if such be your determination, Madam, and if you think yourself in danger, you may be safe, I believe.'
> *Clarissa*: 'Anywhither, if I can but escape from this man. Whither does that path lead to out yonder? What is that town on the right hand called?'
> *Mrs. Moore*: 'Highgate, Madam.'
> *Miss Rawlins*: 'On the side of the Heath is a little village called North End. A kinswoman of mine lives there; but her house is small: I am not sure she could accommodate such a lady.'

Such is the part which not only the Upper Flask, but Hampstead at large, is made to play in this once immensely popular novel. Clarissa is frightened from further attempts to escape, by the story of highwaymen who infest the road, and of a dreadful robbery perpetrated 'but two days ago at the foot of Hampstead Hill.' A great part of the fourth and fifth volumes - there are seven - is occupied with these Hampstead transactions. But to proceed to other matters.

The house and grounds occupy rather more than two acres. It was once known as the Upper Bowling Green House, from its possessing a very good bowling green. It was much frequented by the celebrities of Queen Anne's time, when Pope and Steele are known to have been there. In the summer months the Kit-cat Club used to meet there, and sip their ale under the old mulberry tree, which still flourishes, though now bound together by iron bands, and showing signs of great age. Sir Richard Blackmore, in his poem, 'The Kit-cats,' thus reports this part of the history of the house:

Or when, Apollo-like, thou'rt pleased to lead
Thy sons to feast on Hampstead's airy head -
Hampstead, that, towering in superior sky,
Now with Parnassus does in honour vie.

The house has been added to and much altered since then, as the various heights of the rooms indicate. In 1709 Samuel Stanton, vintner, came into possession of it. He appears to have been the last innkeeper, as his nephew and successor in 1737, also Samuel Stanton, is styled gentleman. He left it in 1750 to his niece, Lady Charlotte Rich, only child of the Earl of Warwick, and his sister Mary, Countess of Warwick; but it is not known that she ever lived in it. In 1771, George Steevens, the annotator of Shakespeare, bought the property, and occupied it till his death in 1800. He added considerably to the house. Mr. Thomas Sheppard, M.P. for Frome, occupied it from 1804 till 1845, when he parted with it to Mrs. Raikes, a near relative of Mr. Thomas Raikes, whose memoirs were published a few years ago. At her death it was purchased by Mr. Lister, whose family still occupy it.

The annotator of Shakespeare was so extraordinary a character that his purchase and occupation of this house constitutes its chief interest, and demands a somewhat detailed memoir of the man.

George Steevens was the only son of George Steevens, Esq. of Stepney, many years an East India captain, and afterwards a Director of the East India Company, who died in 1768. He was born at Stepney, May 10, 1736, and admitted at King's College, Cambridge, about 1751 or 1752. His fame rests on his edition of Shakespeare's Plays, twenty of which he published in 1766, in five volumes.

For this great work the whole of Steevens's life seems to have been a preparation. 'The early editors of Shakespeare,' says the memoir of Steevens in the 'Gentleman's Magazine,'

> 'look to little more than verbal accuracy; and even Warburton consigned the sagacity of his mighty mind to the restoration of certain readings, and the explanation of dubious passages. Johnson, who possessed more of the knowledge necessary to an edition of Shakespeare than those who had preceded him in that character, was found wanting, and his first edition of Shakespeare's Plays, which had been expected with much impatience, brought disappointment along with it. In a subsequent edition, he accepted the assistance of Mr. Steevens, and consented that the name of that gentleman should be in editorial conjunction with his own.'

A year before the appearance of Steevens's edition, Dr. Johnson had published an edition with notes, in eight volumes. A coalition between these two editors having been negotiated, another edition, known by the name of 'Johnson's and Steevens's Edition' made its appearance in ten volumes in 1773. It was reprinted by these joint editors in the same number of volumes five years after, and again in 1785, under the care of Isaac Reed of Staples Inn, who, at the request of his friend Mr. Steevens and Dr. Farmer, undertook the office of editor.

The valuable assistance of Mr. Isaac Reed, Steevens had enjoyed before in bringing out his own first edition.

Of his qualifications for his work, the 'Gentleman's Magazine' gives these proofs:

> 'Mr. Steevens possessed that knowledge which qualified him in a superior degree for the illustration of our divine poet, and without which the most critical acumen would prove abortive. He had, in short, studied the age of Shakespeare, and had employed his persevering industry in becoming acquainted with the writings, manners, and laws of that period, as well as the provincial peculiarities, whether of language or custom, which prevailed in different parts of the kingdom, but more particularly in those where Shakespeare passed the early years of his life. This store of knowledge he was continually increasing by the acquisition of the rare and obsolete publications of a former age, which he spared no expense to obtain, while his critical sagacity and

acute observation were employed incessantly in calling forth the hidden meanings of our great dramatic bard from their covert, and consequently enlarging the display of his beauties. This advantage is evident from his last edition of Shakespeare, which contained so large a portion of new, interesting and accumulated illustration.

It is to his own indefatigable industry, and the exertions of his printer, that we are indebted for the most perfect edition of an immortal bard that ever came from the English press. In the preparation of it for the printer, he gave an instance of editorial activity and perseverance which is without example. To this work he devoted, solely and exclusively of all other attentions, a period of eighteen months, and during that time he left his house every morning at one o'clock with the Hampstead patrol, and proceeding, without any consideration of the weather or the season, called up the compositor and woke all his devils:

> Then late from Hampstead journeying to his book,
> Aurora oft for Cephalus mistook:
> What time he brushed the dew with hasty pace,
> To meet the printer's devils face to face,

at the chambers of Mr. Reed, where he was allowed to admit himself, with a sheet of the Shakespeare letter-press ready for correction, and found room to receive him; there was every book which he might wish to consult; and to Mr. Reed on his pillow he could apply, in any doubt or sudden suggestion, to a knowledge of English literature perhaps equal to his own. This nocturnal toil greatly accelerated the printing of the work, as, whilst the printers slept the editor was awake; and thus, in less than twenty months he completed his last splendid edition of Shakespeare in twenty volumes - an almost incredible labour.'

George Steevens concentrated the labour and energies of a life on this edition of Shakespeare, and certainly produced by far the most complete and correct edition of Shakespeare's plays up to that time. Besides this, he scarcely produced anything. A poem of a few stanzas, called 'The Frantic Lover,' appeared in Almon's 'New Foundling Hospital for Witt,' in 1771, and in Dodsley's 'Annual Register,' which has been highly praised; and he wrote a few other poems, amongst them 'The Miserable Lover,' as a contrast to the frantic one, which appeared in the 'St. James's Chronicle' in January 1774. He is stated to have been a fine classical scholar, and was celebrated for his brilliant wit and smart repartee in conversation, in which he was lively, varied, and eloquent, so that one of his acquaintance said that he regarded him as a speaking Hogarth. He was too apt, however, to indulge his satirical fancy, and to scatter his wit and his humour, his jibes and his jeers too freely around him, and they were not lost for want of gathering, by which he made many enemies, and provoked retaliation from those who had command of the press.

Mr. Steevens possessed a handsome fortune, which he managed, says his biographer,

> 'with discretion, and was enabled to gratify his wishes, which he did without any regard to expense, in forming his distinguished collections of classical learning, literary antiquity, and the arts connected with it. His generosity also was equal to his fortune. . . . He possessed all the grace of exterior accomplishment, acquired when civility and politeness were the characteristics of a gentleman. He received the first part of his education at Kingston-upon-Thames; he went thence to Eton, and was afterwards a fellow-commoner of King's College, Cambridge. He also accepted a commission in the Essex militia, on its first establishment. The latter years of his life he chiefly spent at Hampstead, in unvisitable retirement, and seldom mixed in society except in booksellers' shops, or the Shakespeare Gallery, or the morning conversations of Sir Joseph Banks.'

In 1780 Malone having published a supplement to Johnson and Steevens's edition of Shakespeare, excited greatly Steevens's indignation. This supplement contained the doubtful plays and the poems; the latter Steevens afterwards declared that he had not published 'because the strongest Act of Parliament that could be framed would fail to compel readers into their service,' an avowal betraying an ignorance of genuine poetry of a most extraordinary kind. Malone pursued his researches into the life and writings of Shakespeare, and a great rivalry sprung up betwixt Steevens and him. It was probably to outshine his rival that Steevens departed from his early plan of closely adhering to the text of the most ancient copies of Shakspeare's Plays, to lop off supernumerary syllables, and add others that appeared to have been omitted, giving what he was pleased to call 'a pleasant and commodious text of Shakespeare.' This is the text of his edition of 1793.

In 'St. James's Chronicle' and the 'Critical Review' he is accused of attacking severely the characters of many literary men of his time, whence Beauclerk said to Dr. Johnson that Steevens was malignant: to which Johnson replied, 'No, sir, he is not malignant; he is mischievous, if you will. He would do no man an essential injury; he may, indeed, love to make sport of people by vexing their vanity.' Which we may suppose means, that he would not stab a man with a dagger of steel, but only with one of sarcasm, often the most deadly weapon of the two. Neither Steevens nor Malone were capable of estimating the real genius of Shakespeare. Dibdin says that,

> 'the latter moments of Steevens were moments of mental anguish. He grew not only irritable but outrageous; and in full possession of his faculties, he raved in a manner which could have been expected only from a creature bred up without notions of morality or religion. Neither composure nor joyful hope soothed his bed of death. His language was often that of imprecation, and his wishes and apprehensions such as no Christian can think upon without agony of heart. Although I am not disposed to admit the whole of the testimony of the good woman who attended him at the last; although my prejudices, as they may be called, will not allow me to believe that the windows shook, and that strange noises and deep groans were heard at midnight in his room, yet no creature of common sense - and this was a woman of uncommon sense - could mistake oaths for prayers, or boisterous treatment for calm and gentle courage. Neither the sharpest wit, nor the most delicate intellectual refinement, can afford a man peace at the last.'

Steevens left the bulk of his property to his niece, Miss Steevens, and his curious and most valuable collection of books and engravings was sold by auction, except some particular copies, which he bequeathed to Earl Spencer, to Mr. Reed, and to Mr. Windham, of Fellbrig, Norfolk, ancestor of the unhappy possessor of the same property in our time, who sold it, and ruined himself by his follies in a few years. Amongst these were the second folio of Shakespeare, formerly the property of Charles I, with that monarch's name and autograph motto *Dum spiro spero*, which was purchased for the royal library; and one of the most complete sets of Hogarth's prints ever collected, with his commentary on them, now published with the quarto edition of Hogarth's works, and with Nichols's `Biographical Anecdotes.'

Probably there was insanity in Steevens, which produced his

eccentricities, and which, towards the close of his life, increased to such a degree, that he cut to pieces any portrait of himself that he could lay hold of. He destroyed a fine miniature of himself by Myers, and a full-length, in the character of Barbarossa, in which he had played in a private theatre with great éclat. Fortunately an excellent portrait of himself, by Zoffani, and sold to a Mr. Clark, of Prince's Street, escaped him. This he sought for in vain all over London, to destroy it, and an engraving was made for sale from it at the expense of Sylvestre Harding. This probable insanity would account for his violent and never-abated enmities, and his sudden dislike taken to friends whom he left the moment before in the most cordial kindness. He behaved the same to his bookseller. He discontinued his daily visits at Mr. White's after many years' attendance, for no real cause; and left Mr. Stockdale, who he took up on quitting Mr. White, all at once in the same unaccountable manner. Losing his snuff box in St. Paul's Churchyard, he never after took a pinch of snuff, though it cost him the custom of his life, a practice he was greatly addicted to, and being in the habit of making his memorandums on bits of paper which he carried in his box.

In the excess of this humour he lived at last in his house on Hampstead Hill, shut in by trees and shrubs, and surrounded by books, seeing no one, and seen by nobody, except when a company of strolling players visited the place, when he would turn out, and he observed watching their wretched performances with as much delight as though Garrick and Mrs. Siddons were acting, and would afterwards refit the wretched performers, who had often scarcely coats or gowns to their backs. His remains were interred in the chapel at Poplar, where there is a monument to his memory by Flaxman, and a poetic epitaph by Hayley. His house was paled in, and had a pleasant lawn in front, skirted with a variety of picturesque trees.

Miss Laetitia Matilda Hawkins, the daughter of Sir John Hawkins, author of the 'History of Music,' says of Steevens in her 'Anecdotes, Biographical Sketches, and Memoirs,' vol. i. p. 28:

'Steevens's intimacy at one time had become very great. My father had quitted Twickenham, yet still was accessible to Garrick; but, strange to say, after this time no advantage was made of vicinity. They seldom met, and a friendship that had stood for years mouldered away. I will not say that my father was wholly uninfluenced by Steevens's incessant ridicule, or by stories which he told with address, and which, though they magnified blemishes cruelly, might not be wholly without foundation. But an explosion took place, and an interview followed between my father and the celebrated dramatist, Arthur Murphy, in consequence of something which attacked the latter in the public papers precisely in the same manner as Garrick had been attacked in the Jubilee-business.

Steevens was strongly suspected of this, but I believe had not been supposed the author of the others, till comparison of facts and dates and circumstances, together with my father's production of the papers my brother possessed, brought out not only that fact, but that of his having been the occasion of the relaxation of correspondence between Garrick and my father.

Everything was now prepared to inflict on Steevens the punishment he merited; and I was in the act of copying a statement of grievances, when, at his usual very early hour, he entered the room where he was generally received. My father met him with the paper which he was preparing in his hand, and verbally taxed him with being the cause of hostility between him and Garrick and Murphy. I heard him, with guilt in his countenance, deny it, and offer to take the sacrament on the truth of what he asserted. I remember my father's saying, "A pretty fellow you to talk of taking the sacrament!" and then by the collar turning him out at the house door.'

For further particulars regarding George Steevens, see his life in Reed's 'Shakespeare;' the 'Monthly Mirror,' vol. x. p. 190, xii. p. 307; 'European Magazine,' June 1812;' 'Monthly Magazine,' February, 1800, p. 84; 'Gentleman's Magazine,' vol. lxx. p. 178; Dibdin's 'Bibliomania,' pp. 570 and 585; Nichols's 'Literary Anecdotes,' vol. ii. p. 656.

A writer in the 'Universal Museum,' April, 1764, p. 199, says that, going to observe an eclipse of the sun, he noticed near the Upper Flask a stone fixed, stating that this spot was as high as the cupola of St. Paul's. I believe no trace of such a stone is now remaining.

CELEBRATED MEN MENTIONED BY LYSONS
AS ONCE RESIDENT AT HAMPSTEAD

Lysons, in his 'Environs of London,' gives the following list of eminent persons who have lived in or adjoining Hampstead:

Sir Henry Vane
Bishop Butler
Chief Baron Wylde
Sir Jeffrey Palmer
Joseph Keble
William Sherlock
Thomas Rowe
Arthur Mainwayring
John Gay
Dr. Arbuthnot
Sir Richard Steele
Wilkes
Colly Cibber
Booth.
Dr. Akenside
Dr. Johnson
George Steeyens
Lord Macclesfield
Lord Loughborough
Lord Erskine

JUDGE'S BENCH OR JUDGE'S AVENUE

Turning to the right at Hampstead pool and reservoir, and immediately again to the right up a short lane, we come to an avenue at the back of Upper Terrace and facing the Heath, with a fine view towards Harrow and the Hertfordshire hills, a view which Leigh Hunt used to say reminded him of some Italian ones, and which reminds me of those of Normandy around Avranches. This avenue derives its name from the tradition that during the great plague of London the judges removed from Westminster, and held their courts in this very airy spot.

King's Bench Avenue
(From a lithograph in the possession of Miss Meteyard)

Branch Hill Lodge

Just below it, to the left, as you face the Heath, lies Branch Hill Lodge. This is a large house standing in extensive grounds, amounting almost to a small park, with fine old oaks. The house stands on a pleasant terrace looking towards Oak Hill Park, with a deep valley between it and the foot road leading by Oak Hill Park to New West End. At Branch Hill Lodge, Lord Rosslyn resided before he bought Rosslyn House, and before his elevation to the Barony of Wedderburn. Branch Hill Lodge formerly belonged to Sir Thomas Clark, Master of the Rolls, who, about the year 1745, built part of the house standing in Lord Loughborough's time, and bequeathed it to his patron, Lord Chancellor Macclesfield, who was obliged to purchase the copyhold part of the premises from Sir Thomas Clark's heirs, in consequence of his having neglected to surrender it to the uses of his will. Lord Macclesfield resided there some years. It was afterwards in the successive occupation of Thomas Walker, Esq. Master in Chancery, and then of Lord Loughborough. In 1799 Thomas, son of Sir Richard Neave, Bart., purchased it of Colonel Parker (a younger son of Lord Macclesfield), and greatly improved the house and grounds.

Mr. Neave had at this villa a very large and most valuable collection of ancient painted glass, a great part of which was procured from various convents on the Continent, immediately after the French Revolution. Amongst the most remarkable of the pieces may be mentioned the 'Nativity,' from a convent at Ghent, and a most rich and highly-prized piece from a convent at Rouen, representing Catherine of Austria, Queen of Portugal, consort of John III (its founder), and St. Anne. It contained also a fine piece of the 'Crucifixion,' upon a large scale, many Scripture subjects and figures of saints, besides some highly-finished historical pieces on a smaller scale. To Mr. Neave's collection also the portraits on glass of James I and the Duke of Buckingham, mentioned under the head of the Chicken House, were added.

Not long ago this house was occupied by Bartholomew Claypon, Esq., and since by Basil Wood Smith, Esq.

Grove Lodge

In a road a little lower than the one leading to Branch Hill Lodge, but running out also in the direction of Montagu Grove, and near what is called Crockett's Pond, is a large house recently inhabited by Gilbert Scott the architect, called Grove Lodge, which therefore deserves a passing notice, whatever may have been its previous history.

Montagu Grove

This is a house between Branch Hill and Frognal. Leaving

Branch Hill on our right, we find ourselves at the entrance of an avenue of lime trees. There is a footway through it, and at the bottom stands Montagu House. In this house, a century ago, resided Mr. Henry Flitcroft, an architect, who had a curious fact in his history. He was a journeyman carpenter, who had the misfortune to fall from a scaffold and break his leg, when engaged in repairs at Burlington House. The Earl of Burlington interested himself in his recovery, and one day observing him drawing, was struck with the merit of his performance, and got him put on the Board of Works, of which, he rose to be the Comptroller. He died in 1769.

Montagu Grove was afterwards occupied by Edward Montagu, Esq., the first patron of Hampstead Sunday School. The 'European Magazine' of June 1788, thus relates the following important anecdote of his life:

'June 10. This morning Lord Mansfield sent a servant from Caen Lodge to Mr. Montagu, the Master in Chancery, Frognal Grove, near Hampstead, requesting that gentleman's company to dinner. The answer returned was, that "Mr. Montagu had come home the preceding evening from London, ill, and remained then indisposed." The messenger returned back, pressing Mr. Montagu's attendance on his lordship, who had some material business to communicate: upon which Mr. Montagu replied, "he would wait on the Earl in the afternoon." At five the Master went to Caen Wood Lodge, where he was introduced to Earl Mansfield, who was alone. "I sent for you, Sir," said his lordship, "to receive, as well officially as my acquaintance and friend, the resignation of my office; and, in order to save trouble, I have caused the instrument to be prepared, as you here see." He then introduced the paper, which, after Mr. Montagu had perused, and found proper, the Earl signed. The Master underwrote it, and afterwards despatched it to the Lord Chancellor's house, who laid it before the King.'

Montagu Grove was afterwards the residence of Richard Richards, Esq., Chief Justice of Chester, and then of the Rev. Samuel White, D. D., minister of Hampstead.

The Old Workhouse

Opposite to Montagu Grove, on a slope descending from Mount Vernon, and now occupied as a garden, it is said that formerly stood the Old Workhouse of Hampstead. It has long disappeared. At this house, before it became the workhouse, Booth, Wilks, and Cibber the actors spent a summer.

The Old Workhouse
(From Park's 'Hampstead')

THE CHURCH AND CHURCHYARD

The Church of Hampstead was originally a chapel-of-ease to the church of Hendon. The first ascertained mention of this chapel is as late as 1461. It was only in 1561 that the chapel came under the jurisdiction of the bishop as a separate church, by the incumbent presenting himself at the primary initiation of Bishop Grindal. The old church was a very humble structure, built evidently at four or five different times, having a low wooden belfry. The present church was built in 1747, and cost £4,500. It was found damp, and the tower gave way, so that, so soon after the erection as 1772 it had to undergo a thorough repair. It is remarkable as having its belfry tower at the east end; and the reason assigned is that, that end facing the town, it was thus built for better effect.

Hampstead Old Church
(From Park's 'History of Hampstead')

Altogether, however, it is but a very plain brick church. Perhaps the most remarkable of its incumbents was the same Dr. Warren as already mentioned as incumbent of Charlton, and so curiously missing the legacy of the manors of Charlton and

Hampstead. He was a man of rather voluminous authorship, Park giving the titles of sixteen of his religious publications. His son and grandson, Dr. Langhorne Warren, and the Rev. Erasmus Warren, succeeded him as incumbents of Hampstead, the latter dying only in 1806. In 1806 the Rev. Samuel White succeeded as curate. The present incumbent is the Rev. Charlton Lane.

We are not writing a regular topography, but we may mention a few of the names of those who have monuments or tablet records in the church and churchyard, as recalling the idea of those who once lived here. In the church are monuments of Anthony Askew, M.D., F.R.S., who died February 28, 1774, aged 52; one to the wife of the celebrated Lord Erskine, which we have already mentioned; Mrs. Sabina Tierney, mother of George Thomas Tierney, M.P., as hereafter mentioned amongst our brief biographical notices, 1806, &c.

In the churchyard are tombs of Daniel Bedingfield, clerk of the Parliament, 1637; Lady Elizabeth Norton, daughter of the Earl of Gainsborough; Nathaniel Booth, Lord Delamere, 1770; Lady Delamere, 1773; Hon. Elizabeth Booth, 1765; John Harrison, the distinguished inventor of the chronometer, 1776; Mrs. Dorothy Baillie, the mother of Joanna Baillie, as will be mentioned.

Sir James Mackintosh: the tomb of Sir James is under the yew tree in the eastern part of the churchyard. The inscription states that he was born at Aldourie, Inverness-shire, in August 1765, and died in London in May 1832. In the same tomb are buried an infant son, his youngest granddaughter, and some other of his grandchildren. Lady Mackintosh, it is also recorded, died in Switzerland in 1830. Sir Janies is one of those men of a vast reputation, which, on referring to their works, causes us to wonder how it acquired such an extent. Perhaps the secret may in some degree be explained by the fact of his being a Scot, one of a nation who by their spirit and indomitable perseverance make the most of their talents and opportunities. To us, Sir James presents a man of grave, practical, useful, and moderately reforming character and talents, rather than of that broad and original stamp which marks the foremost leaders of mankind.

Attached to the account of his tomb may be preserved the following one of its cost, discovered by Miss Meteyard amongst the Wedgwood papers. It may afford some guidance in the matter of tomb-building:

Mr. Mackintosh,
                    To H. White, Jun.
1803 July 8.

	£	s.	d.
To fixing new Portland stone curb round grave in Hampstead Church, and cutting holes for iron-work, &c. complete	3	10	0
Dues charged for fixing	5	15	6
Sexton's charge for turfing, &c.	0	5	0
Bill for Bricklayers' work	1	13	0
Do. for Carpenters' work	0	12	0
Do. for Painting	0	10	6
Do. for Smiths' work .	10	0	0
	22	6	0

Wedgwood Papers, Mayer Manuscripts

Henry Cort: Near the east gate is the modest headstone of a man who in his day received the usual reward of merit. On it merely stands: 'Sacred to the memory of Mr. Henry Cort, of Devonshire Street, St. George the Martyr, Queen Square, London, who departed this life May 3, 1800, in the sixtieth year of his age.'

This inscription was a few years ago illegible, but has been recently restored by his surviving son. The headstone also records the memory of Mrs. Cort.

Henry Cort was born in Lancaster, where his father was a builder and brickmaker. Mr. Cort became a navy agent in Surrey Street, Strand, London, after a period of his life of which little is known. There he became aware of the inferiority of British to foreign iron, and set on foot a series of experiments for its improvement, taking np the manufacture at the point to which the labours of Ford, Dr. Roebuck, and Peter Onions had brought it. In 1783 and 1784 he took out patents for his processes. In these he not only introduced many improvements, but combined those of his predecessors with them, so as to establish an entire new era in the history of the iron manufacture. In 1786 Lord Suffield said of him,

'If Mr. Cort's very ingenious and meritorious improvements in the art of making and working iron, the steam-engine of Bolton and Watt, and Lord Dundonald's discovery of making coke at half the present price, should all succeed, it is not asserting too much to say, that the result will be more advantageous to Great Britain than the possession of the thirteen colonies of America, for it will give the complete command of the iron trade to this country, with its vast advantages to navigation.'

The first of Cort's patents was for a new process of converting cast into malleable iron; his next was for rolling it. In this he is said to have rediscovered the process of Payne. His improvements soon raised him to great prosperity. He took premises at Fontley and. Fareham, close to Plymouth Harbour, where he erected a forge and iron mill. His great success induced many iron-masters to work under his patents, and numerous of Cort's furnaces are still in operation. But, unfortunately, he entered into partnership with Samuel Jellicoe, the son of Adam Jellicoe, called Sellicoe by Ure in his 'Dictionary of the Manufacturing Arts.' This Adam Jellicoe was deputy paymaster of seamen's wages. They took a wharf of Adam Jellicoe at Gosport, who advanced large sums to the firm of Cort and Samuel Jellicoe, his son, on the security of their premises and trade. Had Cort steered clear of this partnership he must have made an immense fortune. According to both Ure and Fairbairn he had himself put £20,000 into the concern, and numbers of iron-masters were working his patents under condition of a handsome royalty to him.

On the death of Adam Jellicoe it was discovered that the money which he had advanced to Cort and Jellicoe, amounting to £27,000, had been embezzled by him from the Government funds in his hand for the payment of the sailors. The Government, therefore, seized on the property of the firm when it appeared that Cort had also assigned his patents to Adam Jellicoe as collateral security for the moneys advanced. Ure says that Adam Jellicoe had destroyed the patents thus deposited with him. Cort was made bankrupt. He afterwards solicited Government for the restoration of his patents, proving that he was perfectly ignorant of the source whence Adam Jellicoe derived the advances. He solicited in vain, and was additionally astonished to find that Samuel Jellicoe was put in possession of them, with the properties of Fontley and Gosport. Various appeals were made to Government for justice to Henry Cort, who had done so much for the trade of the country, and remained a ruined man with a family of twelve children. In 1794 an appeal was made to Pitt by a number of influential members of Parliament, but only with the paltry result of a pension of £200 a year. He died, as appears on his gravestone, in 1800, at the age of 60, broken in health and spirit. He had laid the foundation of many gigantic fortunes, and was himself suffered to perish in poverty. Mr. William Fairbairn, the great engineer, in his 'History of Iron and its Manufacture,' says that, some time ago, Cort's claims were called into question, but on examination, nearly all the great iron-masters and writers on iron have declared their validity. Mr. Fairbairn says that

'Henry Cort has conferred an amount of wealth on his country during the last three or four generations, equivalent to six hundred millions sterling, and given employment to six hundred thousand of the working population!'

Mr. Fairbairn expresses the utmost indignation at the treatment of Cort, and says that Government is bound in honour to do something for his family. Men are made affluent with pensions and estates, and their children ennobled for destroying their fellow-creatures. What, then, is due to a man who so illustriously augments the wealth and power of the nation, and gives the means of existence to hundreds of thousands? But alas! such appeals in this country are useless. We pay many millions annually to support a uselessly enormous army, and we are deaf to the claims of our greatest benefactors. This is but a parallel story to that of Thomas Gray, the projector and enthusiastic advocate of a national system of railways. Standing over this simple headstone, one marvels at the mere handful of earth which can hide for ever from the world the genius, the vast services, the griefs and wrongs of a grand public benefactor, and the lamentable ingratitude of his country.

Amongst the notices on the Register we may quote the following, with Lysons' remarks:

'Charles Athey, son of Arthur Athey; baptised Jan 23, 1598-99.' Sir Arthur Athey, who resided at Kilburn Priory, was principal of Alban Hall, and public orator of the University of Oxford. He was secretary also to the unfortunate Earl of Essex, in whose ruin he was nearly involved. Sir Arthur was knighted on the accession of James I, died in 1604, and was buried at Harrow.

'Charles, son of Sir William Jones; baptised Sept. 24, 1671.' This Sir William Jones, not to be confounded with the famous Sir William Jones of later date, was Attorney-general in 1674, and resided some years at Hampstead.

'Tyke Marrow, servant to Judge Dolben; buried May 26, 1679.' The Judge, his master, also lived several years at Hampstead.

'Mr. Thomas Jevon, from London; buried Dec. 24, 1688.' Jevon was an actor of low comedy, and dancing-master, and wrote some dramatic pieces, 'The Devil of a Wife,' &c. He seems to have been an occasional resident at West End. John Pate, another player, was buried here in 1703-4.

'Mary, daughter of Richard Lord Viscount Fitzwilliam, a Roman Catholic, was baptised Sept 8, 1707.' She was maid-of-honour to the Princess of Wales in 1726; in 1733 married Henry, Earl of Pembroke; and secondly, in 1751, North Ludlow Bernard, Esq.

'Christopher Bullock; buried April 8, 1722.' This Mr. Bullock was the son of an actor who resided at North End; was an actor himself, and dramatic writer, whose productions are enumerated in the 'Biographia Dramatica,' and was the husband of an actress, the daughter of Wilks, the comedian, and probably the father or brother of another actor, Hildebrand Bullock, who was buried here Oct. 21, 1733.

'Dr. George Sewell; buried Feb. 12, 1725-26.' We shall hereafter mention Dr. Sewell in the Biographical Notices.

'The Right Hon. David Erskine, Earl of Buchan; buried Oct. 17, 1745.' The fourth Earl of that family. 'Isabella, Countess of Buchan; buried May 21, 1763.' Daughter of Sir William Blackett, and second wife of the Earl of Buchan. The Scottish peerage calls her Elizabeth.

'Mr. Joseph Dorman; was buried Feb. 13, 1754, N. S.' A dramatic writer, author of the entertainment of Sir 'Roger de Coverley,' and reputed author of 'The Female Rake; or, Modern Fine Lady,' produced in 1785.

'James Pitt, Esq., from London; buried Jan. 23, 1763.' To be mentioned in Biographical Notices.

'William Popple, from London; buried Feb. 13, 1764.' See again Biographical Notices.

'James MacArdell; buried June 5, 1765.' A celebrated mezzotinto engraver, a native of Ireland; buried in the churchyard, with an inscription to his memory.

'Charles Spooner, from London; buried Dec. 6, 1767.' Another celebrated engraver in mezzotinto, fellow-pupil with MacArdell, and who desired to be buried near him in Hampstead churchyard.

'Henry Barnes; buried Jan. 20, 1773.' Secondary of the Court of Common Pleas, and author of 'Notes of Cases of Practice,' in two volumes.

'Sir William Duncan; buried Jan. 14, 1774.' Sir William was physician to George III, was created a baronet in 1764, having married in the preceding year Lady Mary, daughter of Sackville, Earl of Thanet.

'James Pettit Andrew; buried Aug. 10, 1797.' Mr. Andrew was of a good family, and devoted to literature. He deserves a cordial mention for being one of the first who took up the cause of the wretched chimney sweeps, and by his writings led to an Act of

Parliament ameliorating their condition. Besides other works, he made a continuation of Henry's excellent 'History of England,' the plan of which was judiciously adopted by Charles Knight in his 'History of England.' He died at Brompton at the age of 59, and was buried in this churchyard, by the remains of his wife. His son Joseph succeeded his uncle, Sir Joseph Andrews, in his baronetcy and estates in Berkshire.

There are entries in the Register relating to the noble families of Delaware, Ikerine, Delamere, Erskine, &c., and many others great in their time, as well as many distinguished ladies, in whom the present age takes no further interest, having passed on its attention to others.

> Great in their time,
> They float away along the great time-stream,
> And others in great numbers, great like them,
> Just for a little pleasing hour of greatness,
> Succeed them, and succeed them, and pass on.
> They are not of that greatness which stands fixed
> In the firm earth of fame - for their importance,
> Made up of wealth, and birth, and such like stuff,
> Is but a vapoury fleeting show of greatness,
> And takes no hold on Time.

In this Parish Register there are some records of longevity, which speak significantly of the healthy air of the neighbourhood:

'Richard Smith, of West-End, aged 100 years, buried Dec. 5, 1684; Elizabeth Kidd, of Hampstead, aged 105 years, buried July 24, 1685; Margaret Smith, of Hampstead, aged near 100 years, buried March 12, 1687-88; Eleanor Winbush, buried Aug. 1, 1744, aged 104 years; Susanna Horder, aged 107 years, who died at West-End, and was buried March 13, 1754, N. S.; Jane Staples, who was buried March 9, 1787, said to have been 106 years of age.'

I find mention, also, of the following persons who died at Hampstead, though their names do not occur iu the Register:

Mrs. Harrison, aged 104, Aug. 1733 ; George Eccleston, aged 103, Sept. 23, 1768; and Mrs. Foa, aged 110, Dec. 1781.

BENEFACTORS OF HAMPSTEAD

Let us commemorate here the benevolence of honest John Stock. This gentleman, in 1781, gave a sum of £1,000, which, with accumulation of interest, and some donations of the trustees, purchased £2,000 Three per Cents. This sum was devoted, according to the will of Mr. Stock, to clothing, educating, and putting out apprentice six fatherless boys and four girls, the former to receive £5 as an apprentice fee, the latter £2. The number of the recipients has been since increased, being now twenty one - seventeen boys, and four girls. The relative number of the boys and girls is said to be regulated annually, but the boys, somehow, greatly predominate. The annual income, I am informed, is about £82.

In the 'Gentleman's Magazine,' vol. lx. part 1, p. 79, we also find the following fact of Mr. Stock's further benevolence to those who have few benefactors. In the former case he had his eye on the orphans, in this case on a class about as little sympathised with in general - poor curates:

'1790. A meeting was held by the trustees of John Stock, Esq., of Hampstead, who bequeathed 200*l* per annum to be divided amongst ten curates of the Church of England whose incomes did not exceed 40*l* a-year. Thirty-eight petitions were received from poor curates whose stipends were not more than 25*l* a-year, with which they had to support large families.'

Hampstead has had other benefactors. Elizabeth, Dowager Viscountess Campden, in 1643 left the sum of £200 to purchase lauds, half the produce to be appropriated to apprenticing children, the other half to be distributed among the poor of the parish. With this money was purchased an estate at Child's Hill, in Hendon. An unknown benefactress left a sum of £40 in 1643, the same year that Lady Campden's money was left, and it was united with that money in the purchase of the estate at Child's Hill. The proceeds of this £40 were to be distributed to the poor of Hampstead in halfpenny loaves on Good Friday morning. These bequests must now have greatly increased in value.

The Hon. Susanna Noel, and her son Baptist, Earl of Gainsborough, a minor, in the year 1698 gave the site of Hampstead Wells, with certain houses adjoining, and six acres of the Heath, for the use of the parish. The interest of this charity, including the interest of £1,100 Three per Cents., is appropriated by the trustees to the apprenticing poor children, or clothing them for service, and occasionally relieving aged and infirm parishioners not receiving alms.

John Robinson, Bishop of London, happening to die at Hampstead in the year 1723, this place became entitled to £100, which he had bequeathed to the parish in which he should happen to be resident at the time of his decease.

THE OLD MANOR HOUSE

From Park's account there does not appear to be really any old Manor House. He tells us that the demesne lands anciently extended from Child's Hill north, to Belsize south; but the name Manor Farm, in his time, was confined to that portion of these lands which is situated south of West End Lane. The old Manor House stood on the north side of this lane, but a Mr. Pool, lessee of the Manor Farm, pulled down the old Manor House and built a substantial brick residence upon the place. There the manors or courts were held till Pool removed to a smaller house, which he built on the south side of the road, and the courts were removed with him. This is no doubt the house called Manor Lodge, inhabited by George Chater, Esq.; the Court Leet being still held there.

The old site of the Manor House, Park says, was in his time occupied by Sir Samuel Bentham, but that the *adjoining* residence of Thomas Norton Longman, Esq., had obtained the name of the Manor House; that in 1802 this house was occupied by the Rev. Charles Grant, who was proprietor of the chapel in Well Walk, for thirty years, and in that year 'a court of view of frankpledge and general court baron and customary court' was held. This was probably before Mr. Pool was prepared to remove the court to his new house. We may therefore presume that the Manor House is the same now hearing that name, in possession of Mr. Husband, but that the next house, the Ferns, occupies the ancient site of the old Manor House.

Henry Bradshaw Fearon

At the Ferns, the next house to the so-called Manor House, formerly lived Mr. Henry Bradshaw Fearon, wine merchant, of Holbom Hill and New Bond Street, a man of liberal opinions, and actively co-operating with the originators and founders of the London University. Mr. Fearon in 1817 went out to the United States as pioneer of a numerous body of his friends who wished to know what really were the prospects for emigrants to that country.

In 1818 his reports to these friends were published, and in 1819 reached a third edition. At that time the settlement of Messrs. Morris Birkbeck, and George Flower, in Illinois, had produced a great sensation in England through Mr. Birkbeck's 'Notes of a Journey in America,' published in 1818, and his 'Letters from Illinois' in the same year. Mr. Fearon's impression of the American people, and the prospects of emigration to the States, at that period, were by no means encouraging to his friends. With the exception of some particular businesses, which he pointed out, he thought only the very poor would mend their condition by transferring themselves to the Western World. He strongly anticipated great future troubles in the United States, both from the existence of Negro slavery, and from the predominance of mob rule. Cobbett also, then living in Long Island, in the United States, vehemently attacked, in his 'Political Register,' the glowing representations of Birkbeck, and was responded to by Mr. Richard Flower, in letters from the new settlement. Mr. Fearon and his friends remained at home and flourished there. He became a leading Liberal in the City, and died a wealthy man, about twenty five years ago.

FROGNAL HALL

This house, standing close to the west end of the church, was formerly inhabited by Mr. Isaac Ware, an architect who was patronised by the Earl of Burlington. He was the author of 'A Complete Body of Architecture.' Mr. Ware's work is a large folio, printed in 1756. Its title is 'A Complete Body of Architecture, adorned with Plans and Elevations from Original Designs. By Isaac Ware, Esq., of His Majesty's Board of Works.' It states, also, in the title-page, that it contains designs by Inigo Jones never before published.

He also translated from the Italian 'Palladio's Architecture,' and engraved the plates after tracings which he had made from the original work. He published a separate edition of the first book of 'Palladio on the Fine Arts,' Palladio being then the English standard of the art. Besides this, he translated 'Senagatti's Perspective.' Mr. Ware died at his house at Kensington Gravel Pits in depressed circumstances. After him the Guyons possessed this house. This family of eminent merchants were probably amongst the refugees from the terrible effects of the Revocation of the Edict of Nantes, and lived in Hampstead till 1805. This house, however, was sold on the death of Mr. Stephen Guyon, in 1780. Lord Alvanley, Master of the Rolls, and afterwards Chief Justice of the Common Pleas, resided some years here, and his widow, Lady Alvanley, after him. In Park's time it was occupied by Thomas Wilson, Esq., and now by T. Julius Airey, Esq.

FROGNAL PRIORY

Frognal Priory
(From an original drawing in the possession of J. E. Gardner, Esq.)

Descending towards West End on our left hand, at a paddock's distance, stands Frognal Priory. This house, now hastening fast to ruin, was built by a Mr. Thompson, best known by the name of Memory Thompson, or, as stated by others, Memory-Corner Thompson. This Mr. Thompson built the house on a lease of twenty years, subject to a fine to the lord of the manor. He appears to have been an auctioneer and public-house broker, who grew rich, and, having a peculiar taste in architecture and old furniture, built this house in an old English style approaching the Elizabethan. That the house, though now ruinous, is of modern date, is also witnessed by the trees around it being common poplar, evidently planted to run up quickly. Thompson is said to have belonged to a club of auctioneers or brokers, which met once a week, and at one of these meetings, boasting that he had a better memory than any man living, he offered to prove it by stating the name and business of every person who kept a corner shop in the city; or, as others have it, the name, number and business of every person who kept a shop in Cheapside. The former statement is the

132

one most received, and is the more probable because Thompson, being a public-house broker, was no doubt familiar with all these corner-haunting drink-houses. Having maintained his boast, he was thence called Memory, or Memory-Corner Thompson; but his general cognomen was the first. Thompson not only asserted that he built his house on the site of an ancient priory, continuing down to the Dissolution, and inhabited as a suburban house by Cardinal Wolsey, but, as an auctioneer, he had the opportunity of collecting old furniture, pieces of carving in wood, ebony, ivory, &c. With these he filled his house, dignifying his furniture (some of which had been made up from fragments), as having belonged to Cardinal Wolsey, to Queen Elizabeth, the Queen of Scots, and other historical magnates. On the marriage of Queen Victoria, he offered for sale a huge old bedstead, as Queen Elizabeth's, with chairs to match, to Her Majesty; but the Queen declined it. It is said, however, to have been purchased by Government, and to be somewhere in one of the palaces. This bedstead, and the chairs possibly, had some authentic character, as he built a wing of his house especially for their reception. Thompson had an ostensibly magnificent library, containing to all appearance most valuable works of all kinds; but, on examination, they proved to be only pasteboard bound up and labelled as books. The windows of the chief room were of stained glass, casting `a dim, religious light.' And this great warehouse of articles of furniture of real and manufactured antiquity, of coins, china, and articles of vertu, became so great a show-place, that people flocked far and near to see it. This greatly flattered Thompson, who excluded no one of tolerable appearance, nor restricted visitors to stated hours. It is said that, in his ostentation, he used to leave five guinea gold pieces about on the window-seats. I have it from a lady who visited there occasionally, that, though this delighted Thompson, it was an incessant nuisance to his family. There was no security for a moment, during daylight, from the inroads of wondering people, who took all for genuine and in perfect taste. There was, in consequence, no comfort, no one could be at ease. If the bell rang, or the knocker resounded during meal time, the dishes were hurried away that the company might come in. Thompson was always telling the ladies to put things in order. If they went upstairs to dress, they were in constant trepidation, lest people should come and walk into their rooms. This informant described the gardens as being really beautiful.

Whilst this was going on at the Priory, Thompson, who owned nearly all Crown Street, Soho, and some of the adjacent streets, with numerous houses in other parts of the town, used in the latter years of his life to be driving round from house to house in his carriage every week to collect his rents, because he could not trust an agent. He was twice married, and had a daughter by his first wife, who became paralysed by rheumatism, and when she took an airing, had to be carried from her chair to the carriage and back again. She died prior to 1818. Thompson is not renowned for his virtues either as husband or father. His daughter, it is said, being very young on her mother's death, was taken by some friends or relatives, and brought up for several years entirely at their expense. In after years, falling into difficulties, they asked Thompson for £500, which he refused, whereupon they sued him for the cost of her maintenance and education, and recovered the sum of £2,000.

Thompson is stated to have died aged 80, about 1836, when a sale took place; but most of his wealth descended to his niece, who married Bernard Gregory, the notorious proprietor of the 'Satirist.' It is some proof of the moral advance of the nation, that no such journals as the 'Satirist' and the 'Age' can now exist. We remember when these papers, which trafficked in scandal, attacked the most virtuous characters in the hope of being bribed to silence. There is an *on dit*, that Gregory, making insinuations against the character of a wealthy lady, on being remonstrated with, replied that nothing was so easy as to disperse the scandal. 'Let the lady marry me. No one would believe that I would take a wife with any spot on her reputation;' and it is said that his proposal was accepted. Gregory, it seems, on the death of his wife, did not pay the fine to the lord of the manor, and Sir Thomas Wilson recovered possession by injunction, intending to remove the offices of the manor thither. From a fear, however, of some heir of Thompson's appearing after he had repaired it, which was a possibility, Sir Thomas did not repair it, and it is now too far gone for reinstatement.

A few items regarding Gregory may be drawn from liis own 'Satirist,' and from 'The Town,' edited by a man who seems to have known him well, Renton Nicholson, better known as 'Baron

Nicholson,' the late chairman of the notorious 'Judge and Jury Club,' held at the 'Garrick's Head;' as well as from others who knew Gregory formerly. He is said to have been the son of a woman who kept a small greengrocer's shop in Goswell Street Road. She obtained him an errand-boy's place in the family of a banker of Lombard Street, for whom she washed. Gregory managed to get himself advanced from the kitchen to the bank as a clerk: thence, through the influence of his master, he went into a bank as clerk, at Brighton. His ambition, however, soared higher, and in concert with an auctioneer and brewer he set up a bank himself. This daring speculation soon brought him and his partner into the Gazette. After this, he seems to have attempted many things, amongst them the role of an amateur actor. In this he played the part of Hamlet at the Coburg Theatre. Subsequently he started the 'Satirist,' and became a trafficker in character, satirising and libelling everyone from whom he thought he could extort money. For such an attempt on Mr. James Weir Hogg, M.P. for Beverley, he was tried, pleaded guilty, offered a creeping apology, but was committed and sentenced to three months' imprisonment. Once out of prison, he displayed the spirit of vengeance which animated him against his punisher. He announced himself a candidate for Beverley, in opposition to him; but a menace of exposure on the hustings from the so-called `Baron Nicholson,' compelled him to abandon the project. It is stated that some lady, who seemed to relish his scandals, left him £2,000 a year, upon which he set up as a fine gentleman. This, however, I imagine, is but another version of his marriage with the niece of Mr. Thompson, the whole of whose wealth is stated to have fallen to her, and so to Gregory, as he lay in prison for libel. This fortune he is said entirely to have dissipated. From the number of persons maligned by him, he was constantly lain in wait for, and never could be found at his office. An irritated watcher for him followed his brougham, and, mistaking an old man in it for Gregory, gave him a terrible cudgelling. Gregory is described as a short, squat, bull-headed fellow, with a very sensual expression. The 'Satirist' was a sixpenny paper, published at 384 the Strand, and was continued from 1831 to 1841.

The place looks now as if under a curse. It is a scene of damp, dreary, and wild neglect. It seems a fit haunt for guilty ghosts rather than for men. When I visited it some time ago, parties from London had been holding their revels there on the untrimmed lawn in front; benches, beer-tables, and dirty heaps of paper were scattered about, and the turf was beaten black by the heels of riotous dancers.

OLD WEST END

As on the Heath, also at old West-End, was formerly held a sort of Bartholomew Fair, where shows, plays, and games of various kinds were carried on. The 'Cock and Hoop' was a great resort; and the same riot, dissoluteness, and gambling, as were rife on the Heath, caused this popular assembling to be put down. In the 'Gentleman's Magazine,' vol. lxxxii. part 2, p. 184, we find the following statement of what took place here:

> 'At this fair, in 1812, August 21, a circumstance occurred which had nearly a fatal termination. The clown of Saunders's corps of horsemen and tumblers, on returning to the public-house where he lodged on the night on which the fair concluded, met with a party of peace-officers, with whom he fell into some altercation, which ended in blows. Some of the peace-officers drew their cutlasses, and wounded the clown in a desperate manner; but, he is likely to recover.'

From this incident we see that the police of those days carried cutlasses so late as 1812. What occurred seven years after, however, shows that their cutlasses were of no avail against the menacing roughs of the time. At the fair on the 28th of July, 1819, 200 ruffians, armed with bludgeons, fell on the people, knocked them down, and robbed them wholesale. Not contenting themselves with their purses, they stripped them of their hats, bonnets, coats, shawls, and all descriptions of their dress. Some articles they tore, others they cut away, leaving many of them, women and children included, nearly naked. The constables had no chance with them. The next day, a great number of special constables were sworn in at Hampstead, who managed to capture about thirty of the rogues, who were hanging about. It was time not only for the suppression of these suburban fairs, but for the establishment of a more numerous arid effective police.

West-End, of late years, has ceased to be an obscure nook, with a few houses almost hidden in trees. London, as on all other sites, has thrust itself in, and planted handsome houses of merchants and professional men, and opened up the secluded scene of former rude revels into a pleasant suburb of the great Babel.

Returning to the village, we pass on the left hand, in Heath Street, the Independent Chapel, a place of worship not without its historical reminiscences.

The Independent congregation at Hampstead is supposed to owe its origin to the preaching of Whitefield there in 1739, who, in his Journal of May 17 of that year says,

'Preached, after several invitations thither, at Hampstead Heath, about five miles from London. The audience was of the politer sort, and I preached very near the horse course, which gave me occasion to speak home to their souls concerning our spiritual race. Most were attentive, but some mocked. Thus the Word of God is either a savour of life unto life, or of death unto death.'

The congregation experienced its share of the persecutions of those times. The earliest mention of the chapel is 1775. It was built on copyhold land, leased for 63 years. In 1777 the lease was assigned to Charles Chandler, of Marylebone, clerk, who assigned it, in 1780, to Selina, Countess of Huntingdon, who relinquished her right in 1782. In 1785, the premises were vested in nine trustees. This chapel, called the Heath Street Chapel, was rebuilt about six years ago, and, as I am informed, is attended by Independents and Baptists, under the ministration of the Rev. Mr. Brock.

Somewhat lower down we reach, in High Street, a passage leading to The Lower Flask and Flask Walk.

THE LOWER FLASK AND FLASK WALK

The `Lower Flask' is still a public house, a little way within the entry. Formerly, Flask Walk was open to the High Street, and was shaded with fine trees. Many of these are gone, and houses have taken their place. Formerly a fair was held in Flask Walk, noted for its riot and Bartholomew Fair character. An advertisement on the cover of the original edition of the `Spectator' is as follows:

> `This is to give notice, that Hampstead Fair is to be kept upon the Lower Flask Tavern Walk, on Friday, the first of August, and holds for four days.'

Lower down, on the same side, you come to the celebrated Chicken House. This house was formerly a brick building in the farmhouse style. In it used to be some painted glass, representing the Saviour in the arms of Simeon; and in another window small portraits of James I and the Duke of Buckingham. Under James's portrait was written, `Icy dans cette chambre coucha notre Roy Jacques, premier du nom. Le 25me août 1619.' This glass was removed to the collection of Thomas Neave, Esq., of Branch Hill Lodge.

At the Chicken House died Samuel Dale the antiquary, in 1754, and was buried in the churchyard.

In the Chicken House the Earl of Mansfield had lodgings, before he purchased Caen Wood, whither some of his law friends occasionally resorted for relaxation from the fatigues of their profession. At that time, no doubt, the Chicken House had an ample garden, and overlooked the open country, for it is described as being at the entrance of Hampstead.

In 1766, not many years after Lord Mansfield and his friends used to resort to the Chicken House, we find it fallen greatly in the world. It had become a great rendezvous of thieves and vagabonds. In that year one Francis Parsons, who had been landlord of this house, was taken up for picking pockets. He was found to be worth

£700. He used to keep good wine at the house, and the security of the thieves - his companions - was so much consulted, that five or six doors had to be passed through before they could be reached. In the meantime, they escaped out of the windows, and went off across the Heath. The constables of those days could not be very adroit, or they would have planted a proper force under these windows to intercept them.

The Chicken House
(From an old print in Mr. Gardner's Collection)

The old building at present occupies the space betwixt two narrow passages proceeding from the street, and is inhabited by several families. The front next to the street appears to be more recent, containing shops, and hiding the original buildings, which are of a very dirty and shabby stamp. An outside staircase ascends from the lower passage to the upper storey. This entry is frequently filled with the wash of the families, hung to dry. When I visited it the first time, an old man stood on the outside staircase, of whom we asked if that were the Chicken House. `Yes,' replied the old man, humorously, `and I am one of the chickens.'

CHURCHES AND CHAPELS NEAR FLASK WALK

Near the Chicken House is the site of The Old Presbyterian Chapel. This chapel - at which Mr. Barbauld was minister from 1789 to 1802 - is supposed to have been established in the reign of Charles II by one of the ejected ministers whose lives are recorded by Dr. Calamy. The first minister whose name is known was Mr. Thomas Woodcock, the son of a clergyman who was ejected from St. Andrew Undershaft. This Mr. Woodcock, minister of this chapel, was cousin to Milton's second wife. Mr. Woodcock was there in the reign of William III, and was succeeded by Zechariah Merrell, who died there in 1732. He was succeeded by Mr. John Partington, a Scot, who settled at Hampstead in 1732, and preached there about six years, when he removed to the Scots Church, Founder's Hall, Lothbury. Mr. Joseph Simmons was minister here in 1739, and died in 1754. Probably a Mr. Walton officiated at the chapel before Mr. Simmons's decease, as he was preaching there in 1753. Mr. Robert Atkinson, from Coventry, officiated for a short time, but in 1757 the pulpit was vacant. In 1758 Mr. Richard Gardner, a pupil of Dr. Doddridge, accepted the pastorship, but removed into the country in 1765. His successor was Mr. Richard Amner, who left Hampstead for Cosely, or Coselegin, in Staffordshire, his native county, in 1771, and the same year was succeeded by Mr. Lionel Brown, who resigned in 1780. Then came Mr. Edward Gibson, from the Academy at Daventry, who left Hampstead for Stannington, near Sheffield, but in what year is not stated. His successor was Mr. Fuller, who left the congregation in 1785. Mr. Rochemont Barbauld followed him, but removed in 1802 to the chapel at Newington Green, and was succeeded by Mr. Methuen, who died in 1815, and the pulpit was occupied by Mr. Joyce (author of 'Scientific Dialogues'), for about a year, and by Mr. Shields (a Scot), who returned to his own country in 1819. Mr. Catlow, from Mansfield, succeeded him, and died in 1820. For some time the services were conducted by students from the General Baptist Academy at Newington Green; afterwards by the Rev. William Wilson, from Crewkerne, and afterwards by the Rev. G. Kenrick, who resigned after a ministry of sixteen years. To him, in 1846, succeeded the present excellent minister, Dr. Thomas Sadler.

In 1828 the old chapel, said to have been built by Isaac Honeywood, Esq., who lived at the adjoining mansion, was pulled down, and another built on its site. The original chapel, however, is supposed to have been removed in 1736, and the one built which disappeared in 1828. In 1862 that was abandoned, and the present handsome one completed and entered upon, the inauguration services being conducted by Dr. Sadler and the Rev. James Martineau.

A little above the site of the old Presbyterian Chapel, at the bottom of High Street, now stands the new church of the Trinitarian Presbyterians, the old Presbyterians having, a considerable time ago, become Unitarian. The present minister is the Rev. John Matheson.

There was a Catholic Chapel in a private house at the end of Church Row, of which the Rev. J. J. Morell was minister. No doubt Mr. Morell was one of the 200 French emigrants who settled at Hampstead. Some of the Morells of Hampstead, of the last generation, had passed over to the Unitarians. A Catholic chapel now stands in the narrow road leading from Holly Bush Hill, by the new cemetery, towards the church.

Hampstead also possesses a new Church of the Establishment, called Christ Church, erected on the other side of High Street, its incumbent, the Rev. Edward H. Bickersteth; and a Wesleyan Chapel, in Little Church Lane, at the back of High Street; but these, of course, boast no extent of history.

That is not the case, however, with the origin of the Sunday School at Hampstead. The origin of the Hampstead Sunday School is rather curious. A society calling itself the Society of Philo-Investigists was established in 1781, and met at the Flask. As its somewhat fantastic name imported, it was what is now called a debating society, a society for mutual instruction. It flourished, and one of its first suggestions was a wise one - namely, to raise a fund, and found a Sunday School. In 1789 it was thought that it would stimulate parents to send their children to the School if a certain number were elected for daily education; and accordingly, twelve boys and girls were selected, and sent to a good day school - a plan which was found to answer admirably. Edward Montagu, Esq., Spencer Perceval, Esq., and Joseph Holford, Esq., were successive presidents of the Sunday School Society.

Of the various religious and philanthropical associations which Hampstead, in common with other places, possesses, it is not within my province to speak.

LEIGH HUNT AND DESCRIPTION OF HAMPSTEAD

Leigh Hunt has described the scenery of Hampstead in various poems, amongst others in two rhyming letters to Tom Moore; and in several sonnets. Perhaps the following is the most descriptive:

Description of Hampstead

A steeple issuing from a leafy rise,
With farmy fields in front, and sloping green,
Dear Hampstead, is thy southern face serene,
Silently smiling on approaching eyes.
Within, thine ever-shifting looks surprise,
Streets, hills, and dells, trees overhead now seen,
Now down below, with smoking roofs between, -
A village, revelling in varieties.
Then, northward what a range, - with heath and pond,
Nature's own ground; woods that let mansions through,
And cottaged vales, with pillowy fields beyond,
And clump of darkening pines, and prospects blue,
And that clear path through all, where daily meet
Cool cheeks, and brilliant eyes, and morn-elastic feet.

From 'Foliage,' 1818.

THE AIKIN FAMILY AND MRS. BARBAULD

In a house on the right-hand side of Church Row, in Hampstead, proceeding from the town towards the church, a house with a large iron gate, there lived for some time Mrs. Barbauld, who in the last generation enjoyed a great reputation both as a poetess and a miscellaneous prose writer. She was one of the Aikin family, various members of which have been distinguished in literature, especially Dr. Aikin, the brother of Mrs. Barbauld, and Miss Lucy Aikin, her niece, the author of 'Memoirs of the Courts of Queen Elizabeth, James I, and Charles I,' a 'Life of Addison,' a Memoir of her distinguished father, Dr. John Aikin, &c. To Miss Aikin, whose life extended to within these few years, we owe also a 'Memoir of Mrs. Barbauld.' From this it appears that Anna Letitia Aikin was born at Kibworth Harcourt, in Leicestershire, in 1748. Her father, Dr. John Aikin, was a Dissenting minister there, and had a school; her mother was the daughter of the Rev. John Jennings, of Kibworth. For some years Dr. Doddridge resided in their family. Her brother John was four years her junior, and these were the only children. In 1753 her father removed to Warrington, in Lancashire, when, of course, Miss Aikin was about fifteen. In the Dissenting Academy at Warrington, where Dr. Aikin was classical tutor, were also teachers Drs. Priestley and Enfield; and hence we trace the Unitarian connection of the Aikins with the Enfields of Nottingham, where the son of Dr. Enfield became the town clerk.

In 1773 she published a volume of poems, which were well received; and the same year she joined her brother, who was then settled in Warrington as a physician, in a volume of miscellaneous prose. In the Academy at Warrington was educated Mr. Rochemont Barbauld, the son of a descendant of a French Protestant of the time of Louis XIV, who had fled the persecutions of that bigoted monarch. Mr. Rochemont Barbauld was born at Cassell, in Germany, where his father had attended George II as chaplain; whence some of his biographers style him a German. On his marriage with Miss Aikin, Mr. Barbauld settled as Dissenting minister at Palgrave, near Diss, in Suffolk. There they commenced a boarding school, which, owing much to the reputation of Mrs. Barbauld, greatly flourished; and amongst their pupils were William Taylor, of Norwich, who became the translator of Goethe's `Iphigenia in Tauris,' Burger's 'Lenore,' &c., and the author of `English Synonyms.' In fact, Mr. Taylor was one of the first of our countrymen to draw attention to German literature, which his relative, Mrs. Austin, continued by her various translations. Another of the Barbaulds' pupils was Dr. Sayers, author of the 'Dramatic Sketches of Northern Mythology.'

Mrs. Barbauld, at the same time, received a class of little boys under her own particular tuition, and amongst these she was fortunate enough to have Thomas Denman, the son of Dr. Denman, of Middleton Dale, Derbyshire, who became the celebrated Lord Denman, the bold and eloquent defender of Queen Caroline in conjunction with Henry, afterwards Lord Brougham. Here, again, we have the Unitarian connection of the Priestleys, Enfields, Taylors, and of Lord Denman being at one time Recorder of Nottingham, no doubt through the influence of Mr. Enfield, so many years not only town clerk, but the ruling spirit of the corporation; William Gell, afterwards Sir William Gell, the antiquary and topographer of Grecian and Pompeii fame, another of her pupils. For these lucky boys she wrote her charming 'Hymns in Prose, for Children.' Other pupils of the Barbaulds' at Palgrave were the late Basil Lord Daer, and three of his brothers, including the Earl of Selkirk; two sons of Lord Templetown, Lord More, Lord Aghrim, and the Hon. Augustus Phipps.

Whilst living at Palgrave, the Barbaulds made visits during their vacations to London, where they were on terms of intimacy with Mrs. Montague, and Joseph Johnson, of St. Paul's Churchyard, Mrs. Barbauld's publisher, and at these two houses saw all the fashionable literary, or the city people of distinction.

In 1785 they quitted Palgrave, and, after a tour in Switzerland and France, settled in Church Row, Hampstead, Mr. Barbauld minister of a small congregation, and at the same time receiving a few young gentlemen as pupils; Mrs. Barbauld also gave instruction to a few young ladies. Here Mrs. Barbauld appeared as a writer on several great public questions. Besides a poetical epistle to Wilberforce, on the rejection of the Bill for the abolition of the Slave Trade, she wrote a pamphlet in advocacy of the repeal of the Test and Corporation Acts; another in criticism of Gilbert Wakefield's 'Inquiry into the Expediency of Public or Social Worship,' and a third, called 'Sins of Government, Sins of the Nation: a Discourse for the Fast.' All these manifested a strong, logical, and correctly-thinking mind; but they do not retain their interest like her contributions to one of the most delightful books for children, the 'Evenings at Home.' This was supposed to be a joint-work of her brother, Dr. Aikin, and herself; but it appears rather to have been Dr. Aikin's, with some contributions by Mrs. Barbauld. Out of ninety nine pieces of which it consisted, Mrs. Barbauld furnished only fourteen, as follows: 'The Young Mouse;' 'The Wasp and Bee;' 'Alfred: a Drama;' 'Animals and Countries;' 'Canute's Reproof;' 'The Masque of Nature;' 'Things by their Right Names;' 'The Goose and the Horse; ' 'On Manufactures;' 'The Flying Fish;' 'A Lesson in the Art of Distinguishing;' 'The Phoenix and Dove;' 'The Manufacture of Paper;' and 'The Four Sisters.' 'Live Dolls' has, I believe, since been added. Those who recall the pleasant reading of their youth will recognise amongst these articles some of their chief favourites.

This seems to have been the sum total of Mrs. Barbauld's authorship at Hampstead, except a critical essay prefixed to an illustrated edition of Akenside's 'Pleasures of Imagination,' and another to a similar one of Collins' 'Odes.'

In 1802 the Barbaulds removed to Stoke Newington, Mr. Barbauld having become the pastor of Newington Green Chapel, formerly that of Dr. Price, the friend and political coadjutor of Priestley. The motive for this change of residence was the mutual desire of Dr. Aikin and Mr. Barbauld to pass the evenings of their days near each other; Dr. Aikin being established in his practice at Stoke Newington.

The poems of Mrs. Barbauld, though greatly admired at the time, and displaying excellent sense and a noble sentiment, have been succeeded by others in our time, which throw them into the shade, and create a disappointment in us. They resemble most of the poems of the day, Cowper's, Burns's, and the earliest of Sir Walter Scott's excepted, and to us lack the genuine poetical inspiration. The subjects, as you turn over the table of contents, give you at once a true idea of them. 'The Invitation,' 'To Mrs. B .

. . ,' 'The Groans of the Tankard,' 'Verses written in an Alcove,' 'An Inventory of Dr. Priestley's Study,' 'Lines on a Chimney Piece,' 'Delia,' 'An Elegy,' &c. Yet Lord Byron manages to borrow an idea from her ; namely:

> The earth hath bubbles as the water hath,
> And this is of them.—

Mrs. Barbauld's poem on 'Washing-Day,' vol. i. p. 206:

> Earth, air and sky, and ocean has its bubbles,
> And verse is one of them - this most of all.

In editorship she performed a loving and good work. She made a pleasant selection from the 'Spectator,' 'Tatler,' 'Guardian,' and 'Freeholder,' with a preliminary essay. She edited the letters of Richardson, which disappoint us. She edited also an edition of the 'British Novelists,' with excellent notices of the writers. Amongst her own letters we find a few curious touches and glimpses of cotemporaries. This of Joanna Baillie, her neighbour:

> 'I have received great pleasure lately from the representation of "De Montfort," a tragedy which you probably read a year and half ago, in a volume entitled "A Series of Plays on the Passions." I admired it then, but little dreamed that I was indebted for my entertainment to a young lady of Hampstead whom I visited, and who came to Mr. Barbauld's meeting all the while, with as innocent a face as if she had never written a line. The play is admirably acted by Mrs. Siddons and Kemble, and is finely written, with great purity of sentiment, beauty of diction, thought, and originality of character; but it is open to criticism - I cannot believe such a hatred natural. The affection between the brother and sister is most beautifully touched, and, as far as I know, quite new. The play is somewhat too good for our present taste.'

The quiet modesty of Miss Baillie will be recognised by all who had the pleasure of her acquaintance. In another place she says: 'I spent one day at Hampstead, where I met Walter Scott, the lion of this London season.' There is no date to the letter to tell us what season, but, from the letter preceding and following, it must have been 1819. In a letter of 1787, she thus speaks of Burns:

'I have been much pleased with the poems of the Scottish ploughman, of whom you have had specimens in the "Review." His "Cottar's Saturday Night" has much the same kind of merit as the "Schoolmistress;" and the "Daisy" and the "Mouse" I think are charming. The endearing diminutives, and the Doric rusticity of the dialect, suit such subjects extremely. This is the age for self-taught genius. A subscription has been raised for a pipe-maker of Bristol, who has been discovered to have a poetical turn; and they have transplanted him to London, where they have taken him a little shop, which probably will be frequented at first, and then deserted. A most extraordinary instance is that of a common carpenter at Aberdeen, who applied to the professors to be received in the lowest mathematical class. They examined him, and found he was much beyond it; then for the next, and so on, till they found he had taught himself all they could teach him; and instead of receiving him as a student, they gave him a degree.'

Why did not Mrs. Barbauld tell us who the wonderful mathematical carpenter was? His case is similar to that of Professor Lee, Regius Professor of Hebrew at Cambridge, who was also a carpenter, and owed his rise out of obscurity to his chest of tools being burnt in a fire.

Here is a pleasant medical whim:

'I have been to Dr. Beddoes, who is a very agreeable man; his favourite prescription at present to ladies is, the inhaling the breath of cows; and as he does not, like the German doctors, send the ladies to the cow-house, the cows are brought into the lady's chamber, where they are to stand all night with their heads within the curtains. Mrs. ___, who has a good deal of humour, says the benefit cannot be mutual; and she is afraid, if the fashion takes, we shall eat diseased beef. It is fact, however, that a family have been turned out of their lodgings because the people of the house would not admit the cow; they said they had not built and furnished their rooms for the hoofs of cattle.'

On another occasion, 'We have paid a visit to Hannah More and her four sisters at Barley Wood, under the Mendip Hills, where we had a Bible meeting.'

In 1787, whilst at Hampstead, the Barbaulds received a young Spaniard, and beheld a wonder, become in our time only wonderfully too common:

'He is quite a man, of one or two-and-twenty, and rather looks like a Dutchman than a Spaniard. Did you ever see *seguars* - tobacco leaf rolled up of the length of one's finger, which they light and smoke without a pipe? He uses them. "And how does Mr. Barbauld bear that?" say you. O! the Don keeps it snug in his own room.'

In taking leave of Mrs. Barbauld we may present another domestic incident, which my friend Miss Meteyard found amongst the papers of Josiah Wedgwood - a note of Mrs. Barbauld's to the great potter, which speaks for itself - one of those little peeps behind the scenes where the author is sunk in the careful housewife:

'Mrs. Barbauld's compliments to Mr. Wedgwood; begs the things she bought may be sent to No. 8 Caroline Street, Bedford Square, to-morrow morning, by seven; if, however, that hour is too early, they may be sent this afternoon. They must be packed fit for Hampstead.'

Caroline Steeet,
March 30, 1787.'

In the house which the Barbaulds occupied in Church Row, lived afterwards, that is, June 1822 to 1830, Mrs. and Miss Aikin. Mrs. Aikin then dying, Miss Aikin removed to No. 18 on the opposite side of the street, and lived there till she removed in 1844 to London. She afterwards lived with her relative by marriage, C. H. Le Breton, Esq., of Wimbledon, and finally returned to Hampstead and lived with Mr. Le Breton's family in John Street. Miss Aikin, the niece of Mrs. Barbauld, and only daughter of Dr. John Aikin, inherited the tastes and talents of this distinguished literary family. Dr. Aikin has left a large amount of testimony at once to his talents and his noble independence of mind. His works are voluminous, but these represent only a small part of his labours. His medical works, his 'Essays on Song Writing,' his 'England Delineated,' his 'View of the Character and Public Services of John Howard,' 'Letters from a Father to his Son,' his 'Arts of Life,' his contribution of the 'Annals of the Reign of George III,' were, one would have thought, work enough for a life devoted at the same time to medical practice. But besides these, and his still popular 'Calendar of Nature,' 'Woodland Companion,' and 'Evenings at Home,' he commenced and carried on for two years a periodical called the 'Athenæum;' he compiled a biographical dictionary, in connection with several coadjutors, in ten quarto volumes, which occupied nineteen years. He edited for four years Dodsley's 'Annual Register;' and, finally, made a selection of the ' Select Works of the British Poets.'

Had he never written anything but 'Evenings at Home,' he would leave all youthful posterity greatly his debtor. It has not only continued to charm the young down to this day, but has been translated into almost every European language.

The works of Miss Aikin appear like a continuation of those of her father. His mantle seems to have fallen effectively upon her. Her principal works are: 'Epistles on the Character of Women,' 'The Life of Zuinglius the Reformer,' 'Memoir of her Father, and Selection from his Works,' in which she has repaid the care which he bestowed on her education, by erecting to the memory of his genius and his virtues, a monument of touching and enduring proof. Her next works were 'Memoirs of the Court of Queen Elizabeth,' 'Memoirs of the Court of James I,' 'Memoirs of the Court of Charles I,' and 'The Life of Joseph Addison.' This last work was rather sharply criticised regarding accuracy of dates, and some other particulars; but it has been justly remarked by an American writer, that 'the character of Addison was never before set in so favourable a light.'

Certainly the name Aikin must always stand in favourable connection with the most distinguished inhabitants of Hampstead.

Miss Aikin was born at Warrington, November 6, 1781, and died at Hampstead January 24, 1864. Her remains are interred at the east end of Joanna Baillie's tomb.

ARTISTS RESIDENT AT HAMPSTEAD

In one of the houses of Church Row on the same side as that in which Miss Aikin last lived before removing to London, lives the popular and very charming artist Miss Margaret Gillies, whose works are too well known to require more than a reference to them. With her resides also her sister, Miss Gillies well known for her various works for the young.

This quarter of Hampstead seems to have particular attractions for authors and artists. Returning to the main street, we find ourselves near the residence, for many years, of Mr. Clarkson Stanfield, which stands on the right hand in descending towards London, and his garden runs up to the footroad leading behind into the Shepherd's Fields, and towards St. John's Wood.

Mr. Stanfield, the great painter of vast heaths and seashores, of battles and sieges, lived for many years in the house next but one above the premises formerly occupied by Mr. Thomas Longman, the publisher, father of the principals in the firm of Longman and Co., Paternoster Row. In early life Mr. Stanfield was a seafarer, and in that character met with Douglas Jerrold. These two eminent men, after having both quitted the sea, met at Drury Lane Theatre, one as a dramatic author, and the other as the most wonderful scene painter that ever existed. In his scenes for the stage, Stanfield lavished genius and art sufficient to have made a princely fame on more enduring canvas. Since then, his 'Battle of Trafalgar,' 'French Troops Crossing the Magra,' 'The Castle of Ischia,' 'Wind against Tide,' 'The Victory towed into Gibraltar after the Battle of Trafalgar,' and the 'Abandoned,' representing the hull of a ship rolling in a dark, desolate, waste of sea, have shown the wide and varied extent of his genius. His 'Coast Scenery,' a series of engravings from these subjects, have made the magic of his pencil familiar to the public. His scenes in Italy, the Netherlands, Germany, France, &c., have still further manifested his magnificent genius. His eldest son inherits his talents, and has exerted them in some of his father's favourite fields, as in Italy and on the Rhine. Clarkson Stanfield died in 1867.

John Rogers Herbert, the eminent artist, was till lately also an inhabitant of Hampstead, where he lived many years. His works since 1840, when he embraced the Catholic faith, have assumed a character in accordance with his religious feeling. The works of Mr. Herbert are so familiar to the public that it is scarcely requisite even to name them; yet the naming of the principal of them will at once indicate his earnest faith, and his title to be classed as one of the most eminent and serious painters of this country: The 'Introduction of Christianity into Great Britain;' a 'Portrait of Cardinal Wiseman;' 'Christ and the Woman of Samaria;' 'Sir Thomas More and his Daughter, observing from their prison Avindow the Monks going to Execution,' produced in 1844, and now in the Vernon Gallery Collection; 'St. Gregory teaching his Chant,' 1845; a 'Portrait of his friend Welby Pugin, the Catholic architect,' 1846; 'Our Saviour subject to his Parents,' 1847; 'St. John the Baptist reproving Herod,' 1848; 'The Outcast of the People,' 1849; 'St. Mary Magdalen,' 1859; and 'The Virgin Mary,' painted for the Queen, 1860.

Mr. Herbert was for some years headmaster of the School of Design at Somerset House, and in 1846 was selected to execute one of the frescoes in the vestibule of the Houses of Parliament, and was afterwards commissioned to paint a series of nine subjects illustrating Human Justice, taken from the Old Testament, for the Peers' Robing Room. His great picture, the 'Descent of Moses from Sinai,' is executed in stereochromie, or the Wasserglas of the Germans, for so many years previously used by the great German artists, and especially the greatest of them, Kaulbach, in the open-air embellishments of Munich and Berlin. Mr. Herbert was also appointed to paint several subjects from 'King Lear,' in the Poets' Hall. In the greater part of these public works, Mr. Herbert has added substantially to his fame. He was elected a Royal Academician in 1846. His eldest son, John Arthur Herbert, was a most promising artist, but died of typhoid fever when only twenty two, at Muriae, in Auvergne.

At the large old house next but one below the house of the late Clarkson Stanfield, resided many years Thomas Horton Longman, Esq., the head of the great publishing house of this name. Mr. Longman appears to have lived previously at the Manor House, Frognal, and his father (also Thomas Longman) lived and died in

Hampstead. His death took place in 1797. Nichols, in his 'Literary Anecdotes,' says,

'He was a man of the most exemplary character, both in his profession and in private life, and as universally esteemed for his benevolence as for his integrity.'

The grounds are extensive, and are embellished by many fine large old trees. From the back of the grounds an extensive view is obtained up the vale of the Thames and over the Surrey hills. The late Lord Ashburton occupied these premises shortly before his death. At this moment a large board is up, offering them for sale, so that they may soon, probably, be broken up and covered with new houses.

Just below, with only one house intervening, lie the premises once belonging to Sir Harry Vane.

Sir Harry Vane's House
(From Park's 'Hampstead')

A large square house on the left hand of the entrance into the town of Hampstead, which Park says in his time was the residence of Charles Pilgrim, Esq., is supposed to have been built and was inhabited by Sir Harry Vane. This house, which stood in ample grounds, and of which we present an engraving, has been for some years pulled down, and its site is now occupied by the Soldiers' Orphan Asylum. Certainly no spot in Hampstead is one of greater interest, or more hallowed by all the claims of an exalted patriotism. Sir Harry Vane has been represented as a fantastic theorist, whose speculations were as visionary as his language was difficult to understand. Clarendon, who was Vane's enemy, because he was the staunch friend of liberty, describes him as a great dissimulator, and one exceeding Hampden 'in all mysterious artifices.' The simple truth is - and modern enquiries into the historic records of those times have shown it beyond dispute - that he was one of the most open, direct, and consistent lovers of freedom that ever lived. His speeches in Parliament, and his writings, especially his 'Healing Question,' 'The People's Case Stated,' 'The Retired Man's Meditations,' and his famous speech at his execution, are ample proofs of this. Vane was not only a great and undaunted advocate of constitutional liberty, but a sound and conscientious Christian, displaying both these qualities in every action of his life. He was ever ready to sacrifice himself and his property for the public good, and no temptations or persuasions of friends, far less considerations of future consequences, could ever move him from what he believed to he the right and his duty. His learning, genius, eloquence, and general ability, assisted and guided by these principles, placed him at the head of the great movement which rescued this country from the determined and incorrigible tyranny of the Stuarts, and that amid such coadjutors as Cromwell, Pym, Henry Marten, Milton, Fairfax, Scott, Bradshaw, Hampden, Algernon Sidney, and a host of others inspired with all the stoical rigour of ancient democracy. It was at this house in Hampstead that he was seized by the emissaries of Charles II and carried away to incarceration and death. A brief review of the life of such a man is necessary, to give due honour and interest to the scene of his last abode.

Harry Vane was the son of Sir Henry Vane, of Hadlow, in Kent, and was born in 1612. His family was of high and ancient degree. One of the branches of it altered the name to Fane, and were the ancestors of the present Earl of Westmorland. His father, and then himself, succeeded to the possession of Raby Castle and estate in Durham, to the manor of Hadlow and other estates in

Kent, to property at Belleau in Lincolnshire, and were the ancestors of the present Duke of Cleveland, the Marquis of Londonderry, &c. From Sir Harry's sisters are also descended the Honeywoods, Vincents, of Surrey, Lord Ravensworth, the Duke of Newcastle, the Earl of Chichester, and Lord Yarborough. In worldly rank and connection, Harry Vane stood scarcely second to any man below the position of royalty in the country; but all this weighed nothing with him in comparison with the honest discharge of his duty to God and his country. In the maintenance of the divinity of his conscience, he was ready to sacrifice everything else. Mr. John Foster, in his `Lives of Eminent British Statesmen,' has rendered a real service in clearing away many of the calumnies heaped on the name of this great patriot, and in presenting him to our view as he is - one of the proudest ornaments of our national history.

In his youth, Vane, like most young men of his rank and time, was addicted to gaiety and pleasure; and this seems to have pleased his father, who was not only a Royalist and courtier, but Comptroller of the King's Household, and Secretary to the Privy Council. A more serious mood came over him; he had been partly educated at Leyden, partly at Oxford, and, travelling on the continent, he spent some time at Genoa, where he imbibed the spirit of republican liberty, without that persecuting bigotry which Knox and others so unfortunately brought thence. On the contrary, no man was ever more thoroughly tolerant of the religious opinions of all other men. Despairing of being able to enjoy the religious freedom that he loved, amid the Church and State conservatism of England, he emigrated to the New England States of America. Thither the persecuted Puritans and Nonconformists had fled, and Vane imagined that those who had sought freedom of conscience there would be sure to allow it to others. As all the world, however, knows, they had learned only to love the rights of conscience in themselves, and had not advanced a step beyond their persecutors at home, who did the very same. Vane soon became involved in conflict with this one-sided liberty, in defending the famous Mrs. Hutchinson, who did not understand a Janus kind of liberty, which, seen on one side, showed the features of freedom, but on the other had the old lineaments of tyranny. Vane was elected Governor of Massachusetts; but the rigid Puritans were soon very glad to be quit of him. Nothing, indeed, could have been more anomalous than for a people who were for hanging and burning every man and woman who differed from them in creed, to be governed by a man who had all the tolerance of Christ, who, when those 'Pilgrim Fathers,' his disciples, would love to scorch up with thunder all who did not believe with them, said quietly, 'Let them alone.' Vane was for letting alone both so-called Christians and heathens too, of every phase of opinion. He was for universal toleration, and was, therefore, soon voted out of his governorship, and found that he might as well return to England - in fact, far better, for there he could enjoy the sympathy of great and enlightened men like himself, and not suffer all the rude savagery of a little knot of the harshest bigots in a rude and unreclaimed wilderness.

On his return to England, the spirit of the nation had driven Charles I to the calling of a Parliament, after twelve years of disuse of Parliaments, and Harry Vane was at once elected the representative of Hull, where Andrew Marvel afterwards also sat. Great was the consternation of the Court on the news of this event, and not less so that of his own father; for it was well known what were his views of government, and how inflexible he was in his nature. To draw him to the Court side, he was immediately knighted, and made joint-treasurer of the navy with Sir William Russell. This was a post of great trust and profit; but neither that, nor the fear of losing it, weighed for a moment with him. He had imbibed an utter abhorrence of the attempts then made by the Crown to erect a perfect despotism in England, and he cherished a lofty idea of the true functions of government. Ludlow, who knew him well, says on this occasion:

'In this station, he soon made appear how capable he was of managing great affairs, possessing in the highest perfection a quick and ready apprehension, a strong and tenacious memory, a profound and penetrating judgment, a just and noble eloquence, with an easy and graceful manner of speaking. To these were added a singular zeal and affection for the good of the Commonwealth, and a resolution and courage not to be shaken, or diverted from the public service.'

From this time he became the leading spirit of the great revolution already in progress. He very soon furnished evidence, which he had fallen accidentally upon, of the secret league formed between the King, Laud, and the Earl of Strafford, for what they called 'the thorough,' that is, for bringing an Irish army to completely crush the constitutional liberties of England. This evidence, produced on Strafford's trial, put the climax to his fate.

In the war which speedily broke out between the King and Parliament, Sir Harry Vane not only most ably defended the Parliament from his seat in the House of Commons, but, as treasurer to the navy - this office being conferred by the Parliament on him alone - managed so well, that he soon turned the tables on the Dutch, who, under Van Tromp, were not only chasing the English navy from the seas, but from the very Thames itself, and, by the appointment of the celebrated Blake and other able admirals, he raised the fame of England on the ocean to the highest pitch, making her, in fact, the mistress of the seas. Still more, he refused to accept the 'fees of his office,' amounting to £20,000 a year, and stipulated only that his deputy should have £1,000 a year. It is impossible to conceive a higher stretch of pure patriotism.

We cannot here follow in detail his brilliant services and counsels through the great war which dethroned and decapitated Charles, and placed Cromwell on the pinnacle from which Charles had fallen, though only under the name of Protector. It is sufficient to say that, surrounded by such men as Cromwell, Marten, Scott, Ireton, Harrison, Bradshaw, Milton, and others in and out of the House of Commons, Vane stood chief amongst them as a statesman. So soon as he discovered the treachery of Cromwell, he denounced it, and himself and Marten, who had been his closest as well as his ablest of friends, severed themselves from him. Vane refused to have anything to do with the trial and execution of Charles, retiring, during this period of what he deemed apostasy and treason to the great principles of liberty which they had advocated, and writing, in the seclusion of his estates, 'The Retired Man's Meditations.'

Well might Cromwell exclaim, when he was breaking up by military force the Long Parliament, 'Oh, Sir Harry Vane! Sir Harry Vane! the Lord preserve me from Sir Harry Vane!' For he knew that no man had so much power of exposing his usurpation, and that nothing which he could offer him could for a moment induce him to wink at, much less favour it. He kept him out of the packed

Parliament summoned by himself, and Vane employed his leisure at Raby in writing not only 'The Retired Man's Meditations,' but his great 'Healing Question,' in which he painted Oliver's violent suppression of the nation's gloriously achieved liberties in such horrid colours that the tyrant arrested and consigned him to a dungeon in Carisbrook Castle, in the Isle of Wight, the very prison in which Charles I had been confined during the last year of his life. Bills were prepared for the confiscation of his estates, and other measures of menace and harassment; whilst, on the other hand, favour and honour were secretly offered him if he would cease his opposition, and coalesce with the usurper. But no such measures, either of persecution or offers of favour, ever had the least influence on the pure and noble soul of Sir Harry Vane.

After Cromwell's death, Sir Harry resumed his public and parliamentary efforts to restore the republic; but it was too late. Cromwell had destroyed the public faith in the stability of a republican Government, and he had shown Monk the way to supersede Governments by armies. On the return of King Charles II, Vane was certain to fall a victim to his pre-eminence in opposition to his father, though he had declined to stain his hands with the dying monarch's blood. To a man like Charles II - a base sensualist - such a man as Vane was a standing reproach. With this wretched monarch, as imbecile in government as he was faithless and vindictive as a man, neither his solemn declaration, at Breda, of full indemnity to all persons regarding the past, nor his reported assurance of oblivion of all enmities, was likely to have any weight. If we needed any proof of the utter baseness, the utter worthlessness of this most contemptible man, and of the disorder to which he reduced this kingdom, we have these in the Diary of Pepys, who was a Royalist and a courtier. Such scenes of neglect of all royal duties, of licentiousness, obscenity, of profligacy, and outrage on all ideas of religion and humanity, are not to be found in any narratives like those of Pepys, Evelyn, and others who frequented the Court of this modern Sardanapalus.

When Sir Harry Vane was brought to trial on the charge of having compassed the King's death, his defence startled and confounded in no slight degree the arbitrary legal tools of the King, the judges, who were set not to try, but to condemn him; and the effect of his speech on the scaffold, which the sheriff had in vain endeavoured to drown by the noise of drums and trumpets, produced a stupendous effect throughout the whole kingdom. We cannot have better evidence of this than Pepys, a thorough-paced Royalist. In his 'Diary,' under date of May 22, 1662, he says:

'Nicolas, the Secretary of State, hath sent one Mr. Lee to see what papers in his office - the same in which Vane had so long presided, the secretaryship of the navy - would help to found a charge against Sir Harry.'

On the 7th of June, he says:

'Sir Harry was the day before condemned, after a full hearing in the King's Bench . . . Sir John Robinson, Lieutenant of the Tower, said he never heard any one plead so simply in his life. The fact was, that he pleaded most ably, although he had not been allowed to see the indictment against him till he came into Court; and when he demanded the right to have counsel, he was told by the judges that they would be his counsel - they, the King's appointed tools of his destruction. In fact, the judges, so far from saying a word in his favour, did all in their power to stop his mouth, and deprive him of all means of defence.'

The same Sir John Robinson, Pepys tells us, attended Sir Harry's execution on Tower Hill, on the 24th; and reported that 'he died in a passion, but with as much courage as never man did.' This Sir John Robinson was the same who, with the Recorder of London, presided at the trial of Penn and Mead. He was a most prejudiced and arbitrary fellow, and not likely to report favourably of Sir Harry Vane, under any circumstances. But Pepys himself attended the execution, and under same date we find this entry:

'About eleven o'clock, having a room got ready for us, we all went out to the Tower Hill, and there, over against the scaffold, made on purpose this day, saw Sir Harry Vane brought. A very great press of people. He made a long speech, many times interrupted by the sheriff and others there, and they would have taken his paper out of his hand, but he would not let it go. But they caused that all the books of those that writ after him to be given to the sheriff; and the trumpets were brought under the scaffold that he might not be heard. Then he prayed, and so fitted himself, and received the blow; but the scaffold was so crowded that we could not see it done. But Boreman, who had been upon the scaffold, told us that first he began to speak of the irregular proceeding against him. That he was, against Magna Charta, denied to have the exceptions against the indictment allowed, and that there he was stopped by the sheriff. Then he drew out his paper of notes, and began to tell them, first his life, that he was born a gentleman; he had been, till he was seventeen years old, a good fellow, but then it pleased God to lay a foundation of grace in his heart, by which he was persuaded, against his worldly interest, to leave all preferment and go abroad, where he might serve God with more freedom. Then he was called home and made a member of the Long Parliament, where he never did, to this day, anything against his conscience, but all for the glory of God. Here he would have given them an account of the proceedings of the Long Parliament, but they so often interrupted him, that at last he was forced to give over; and so fell into prayer for England in general, then for the churches in England, and then for the City of London; and so fitted himself for the block, and received the blow. He had a blister, or issue, upon his neck, which he desired them not to hurt; he changed not his colour or speech to the last, but died justifying himself and the cause he had stood for; and spoke very confidently of his being presently at the right hand of Christ; and in all things appeared the most resolved man that ever died in that manner, and showed more of heat than cowardice, but yet with all humility and gravity. One asked him why he did not pray for the King. He answered, "You shall see I can pray for the King: I pray God bless him!" The King had given his body to his friends; and therefore, he told them he hoped they would be civil to his body when dead; and desired they would let him die like a gentleman and a Christian, and not crowded and pressed as he was.'

He adds, a few days afterwards, that the courage of Sir Harry at his death was everywhere talked of as a miracle. Lord Sandwich told him that Sir Harry must be gone to heaven, for he died as much a martyr and a saint as ever man died, and that the King had lost more by that man's death than he will get again a good while. Still, at the end of the month he says,' All men do cry up the manner of Sir Harry Vane's death, and he deserves it.'

Bishop Burnet also says, 'that it was generally thought that the Government had lost more than it gained by his death.' No doubt the political murder of this eminent patriot and excellent man by the dissolute Charles was a capital mistake, and was one of the many odious things which sank deep into the public mind, and drove the detested Stuart family for ever from the throne of England.

That Charles personally urged his death remains under his

own hand. The day after the trial, he wrote from Hampton Court to Clarendon, saying, 'Certainly he is too dangerous a man to let live, if we can honestly put him out of the way. Think of this, and give me some account of it to-morrow.'

It is an interesting circumstance that it was from his house at Hampstead that this great and good man was led away to pay the penalty of his life for his exertions for the liberties of us all. It is a spot made sacred to all time by this event, and around it linger also the memories of Milton, Andrew Marvel - poor but incorruptible, the witty and staunch patriot Henry Marten, of the eloquent Scott, of Cromwell himself, before he had been drawn aside by a poor and personal ambition from the great object of a country's regeneration, and of many others of those men of iron who fought at Naseby, Dunbar, and Worcester, for the Commonwealth of England, and made the House of Commons ring with the most eloquent tones of an indignant patriotism which shook the throne, and read an eternal lesson to despotic kings. All these must at times have assembled around Sir Harry Vane here, to relax from the tension of political cares, or to plan the progress of the nation's enfranchisement.

Says Park:

'In the same house afterwards lived Dr. Joseph Butler, Bishop of Durham, the author of the "Analogy of Religion, Natural and Revealed, to the Constitution and Concerns of Nature." He lived there several years, and ornamented the windows with a considerable quantity of stained glass, which is still preserved there, and consists of a large series of scriptural subjects, in squares; some very finely executed, and two or three of them with biblical inscriptions in old English, and the date of 1571 underneath; several figures of the apostles, with their names subscribed in Latin, in smaller oblong squares. These are reported by local tradition to have been a present from the Pope to Dr. Butler; some modern pieces, of inferior execution, in small ovals - namely, landscapes, &c., and a circular piece of painted glass, containing a figure of St. Paul, seated in the centre of some rich Gothic stall-work, and circumscribed "Sigillum com'une Decani et Capituli eccl'ie Pauli Londin." '

Dr. Butler was promoted to the Deanery of St. Paul's in 1740, by George II.

Park continues:

'All the pieces above mentioned, except the modern ones, are inlaid in borders of stained glass adjusted to the panes. In the upper storey there was a very large room, now divided into several smaller ones, running along the whole back-front of the house, and containing the bishop's library. Most of the apartments were hung with tapestry when a late possessor occupied it. The house has been considerably modernised in some parts, but still retains enough of the antique hue to make it a very interesting object. The back-front entrance, with carved staircase, are in their original state. The garden is laid out in the old style, with a very large and square grass-plat, and avenue of fine elms at the end. An adjoining house, the residence of Mr. Langhorn, now completely modernised, was, I believe, formed out of the bishop's offices, and contains painted glass in almost every window, in continuation of the scriptural series before mentioned.

After the bishop's death, this house, which was his own copyhold property, was sold, together with the whole of his real estates, for the payment of his debts, as directed by his will. He had been scarcely two years in the rich see of Durham before his death; and whilst he was Bishop of Bristol, he is said to have expended more than the whole revenue of his income in repairing and improving the episcopal palace. A box containing his sermons, letters, and other papers he ordered in his will to be burnt, without any of them being read, soon after his decease, which, I suppose, was done. The mansion was divided into two by the bishop's successor, Mr. Regnier.'

So far Park. It is now pulled down, and on its site stands, as already observed, that excellent institution, the Orphan School of Soldiers' Children.

ROSSLYN HOUSE AND LORD ROSSLYN

On the hill a little below Hampstead, and nearly in an oblique line betwixt the Church and the site of the now destroyed Belsize House, the footpath proceeding from one to the other, passing the front, stands Rosslyn House, once the seat of Alexander Wedderburn, a Scottish lawyer, who worked himself up to the rank and dignity of Lord Chancellor, and to the titles of Lord Loughborough and Earl of Rosslyn. He is still remarkable as a brilliant adventurer who devoted his life simply to ambition, and succeeded, little concerned for the causes in which he appeared, and less for a fame founded on virtuous and patriotic principle.

Rosslyn House
(From a photograph taken expressly for this work)

Rosslyn House at that time, and long after, stood alone amidst the fields, commanding a vast view of the country round; of Epping Forest over Highbury, on the one hand, and of the Surrey Hills on the other; of much of London, and of the Vale of the

Thames upwards, far beyond Richmond, and of the tower of Windsor.

Lysons states Rosslyn House to have been many years 'in the occupation of the Cary family,' probably of the Hunsdons, or ancestors of the Falklands; that it was held under the Church of Westminster, and that when Lord Rosslyn bought it, it was called Shelford Lodge. It has been supposed that a family of the name of Shelford built it, and, being Catholic, planted the great avenue leading to it in the form of a cross, the head being towards the east, and leading direct to the high road. But this is very doubtful. The celebrated Lord Chesterfield is said to have lived here some years, when he held the lease of the manor of Belsize, of which it was a part, and more probably his ancestors gave it the name, from Shelford Manor, their seat in Nottinghamshire; for the Earls of Chesterfield held the estate of Belsize from 1683 till 1807, when they sold it to 'several' purchasers, who divided the lands amongst them. Whoever planted the avenue must have done it in the reign of Elizabeth, as proved by a fact hereafter given. When Lord Rosslyn purchased the place he added a large oval room, thirty four feet long, on the west side, with a spacious room over it. These spacious rooms, of a form then much in vogue, whilst they contributed greatly to the pleasantness of the house, disguised the original design of it, which was on the plan of what the French call a *maison* or *château à quatre tourelles*, four-square, with a high mansarde roof in the centre, and a square turret at each corner, with pyramidal roof. Notwithstanding various other alterations by Lord Rosslyn and his successors, part of this original structure is visible, including two at least of the turrets.

Before purchasing Shelford House, Wedderbum resided at Branch Hill Lodge, Hampstead, which had been the abode of a succession of lawyers. Shelford Lodge, to which he gave the name Rosslyn House, in Lord Rosslyn's time occupied as fine a situation as can well be imagined, surrounded by its gardens, groves, and fields, with no neighbour much nearer than the village of Hampstead above, and Belsize House below, to disturb the feeling of ample and aristocratic isolation. Having thus located this lucky lawyer in so fair a spot, we may in some detail contemplate him in his career.

Lord Loughborough was one of that group of great lawyers

who, about the same time, planted themselves on the heights of Hampstead, but with very different characters and aims: Mansfield, Loughborough, and Erskine. Lord Loughborough was, in simple fact, a legal adventurer of Consummate powers, which he unscrupulously and unblushingly employed for the purposes of his own soaring and successful ambition. He stood in strange contrast to the nice honour of Mansfield, the eloquent enthusiasm of Erskine, and the glowing, impulsive patriotism of Chatham, who, for a short time also, as noticed, was resident on these hills. Junius, whom some people simply enough have supposed Loughborough to be, has finely characterised him as 'Wedderburn the wary, who has something about him that even treachery cannot trust.' It is perhaps more instructive to trace the career of such a man than that of a more upright one, for we are more often moved with indignation at unprincipled deeds of selfishness than stimulated by the examples of the generous and the great.

Alexander Wedderburn was the son of Peter Wedderbum, the owner of a small estate in East Lothian, practising with considerable success as an advocate at Edinburgh. Like many poor Scots, the Wedderburns boasted of a long aristocratic descent; and his grandfather was made a judge of the Court of Session; and his father, Peter Wedderbum, was also - but only shortly before his death - raised to the Scottish Bench by the title of Lord Chesterhall, the name of his estate. When a boy, young Wedderburn had nearly been extinguished by a turkey-cock. The anecdote is amusing:

'When he was between three and four years old, having provoked a fierce turkey-cock by hallooing to him -

Bubbly Jock, your wife is a witch,
And she is going to be burnt with a barrel of pitch,

the animal flew at the child, laid him flat on the ground, and seemed disposed to peck his eyes out, when he was saved by his nurse, who rushed in to the rescue with a broom in ber hand. A young lad, then acting in the family as assistant to the gardener, witnessed this scene, and many years afterwards, when passing through London, having been carried into tbe Court of Chancery to see Lord Loughborough in all his glory, instead of being, as was expected, overwhelmed with awe and admiration, after he had coolly contemplated him for some time, at length exclaimed, "Weel, weel! he may be a great man noo; but I mind fine he was aince sair hadden doon by bis mither's bubbly-jock." '

After being educated at Dalkeith, in his fourteenth year be was sent to tbe University of Edinburgh, where he made the acquaintance, young as he was, of Robertson the historian, Adam Smith, and David Hume. He was destined to the bar, and seems very early to have contemplated practising at the English bar, as the only sphere ample enough for his ambition. Mr. Yorke was already practising there with great eclat, and William Murray, afterwards Lord Mansfield, was already Attorney-General. His father, on hearing of these vaulting ideas, took him to Hugh Campbell, brother of the Earl of Marchmont, who was also practising at the English bar; but there he received a great and almost fatal blow, for Campbell pronounced him 'a hopeless dunce,' an opinion which he afterwards savagely revenged. Undaunted, however, by this rebuff, he made a journey to London in his twentieth year, with a letter in his pocket from David Hume to Dr. Clephane. He then and there entered himself as student of the Inner Temple, though intending to return and practise at the Scottish bar till he had raised money enough to take his chance in London. In the same year he obtained his call to the Scottish bar, where he practised for three years, slipping away to London each year for a sufficient time to eat the number of dinners in the Inner Temple Hall, the only thing then required for a call to practise English law in the Courts. He managed to improve his oratory and power of disputation by becoming an elder of the Scottish Church, and taking a prominent part in the debates in the General Assembly, where he defended David Hume and Lord Kames against the charge of infidelity presented against them, in which, being supported by Dr. Robertson, he was successful. Soon after, a proposal of excommunication was laid against John Home, who, being a clergyman, had committed the awful offence of writing a play - namely, his very popular tragedy of 'Douglas.' In this defence young Wedderburn was less successful. He was, in fact, much more in his element in the Poker Club, than as an elder of twenty one in the church. This club, originally of a political character, became a very jolly convivial one; and though it enumerated amongst its members Allan Ramsay, its projector; David Hume; Home, author of 'Douglas;' Dr. Robertson, Hugh Blair, Adam Smith, Sir David Dalrymple, Drs. Monro and Hope, and afterwards Lord Kames, Lord Elibank, the Earls of Glasgow, Lauderdale, and Bute, and the Duke of Hamilton, Wedderburn was elected its first president.

One of the objects of this club was to cultivate the true pronunciation of the English language, under the instruction of Dr. Sheridan, father of the famous Sheridan, who spoke in a broad Irish brogue; and they also started an 'Edinburgh Review' - but not the enduring 'Edinburgh Review' - which was to appear twice a year! These club affairs and Review affairs not being attended with much practice at the bar, an incident suddenly brought Wedderburn's connection with it to an end. Being insulted by the judge, Lockhart, Dean of Faculty, and afterwards Lord Covington, a man of learning, but rude and overbearing, Wedderburn stripped off his gown at the bar, and vowed never to enter the Parliament House again. Forthwith he started for London, protesting that he would never again enter Scotland - a resolution which he faithfully kept.

In London, almost a total stranger, and with very little money in his pocket, he set himself zealously to study the English pronunciation under Sheridan, and afterwards under Macklin the actor; but his remaining term at the Inner Temple obtained his call to the bar, and then he sought for practice in the Court of King's Bench. His success there was, however, by no means encouraging; and for three years, that is, during the remainder of the reign of George II, he was in very low water. With true Scottish perseverance, however, he went into society, and assiduously cultivated the good graces of men capable of giving a young aspirant a lift. Amongst these was Lord Bute, who had been a member of the Poker Club; and Wedderburn so successfully renewed his acquaintance with him, that on the accession of George III, when Bute became Minister, Wedderburn was brought into Parliament by his influence, for the Rothesay and Inverary burghs. Once in Parliament, such a man as Wedderburn was sure to work himself upward; for a man of his stamp is like an Indian bat - every extremity has a hook or a tooth by which he can catch and cling; mouth, legs, wings, tail, every joint of him, can catch, and seize, and hold. His character at this period is thus sketched by Churchill in the 'Rosciad':

> To mischief trained, even from his mother's womb,
> Grown old in fraud, though yet in manhood's bloom;
> Adopting arts by which gay villains rise,
> And reach the heights which honest men despise;
> Mute at the bar, and in the senate loud,
> Dull 'mongst the dullest, proudest of the proud;
> A pert, prim prater of the northern race,
> Guilt in his heart, and famine in his face.

Having now obtained a silk gown, he grew more daring at the bar. He had already violated recklessly the etiquette of his profession by canvassing for practice; and he even made an unprecedented inroad in the Northern circuit, it being contrary to all custom for a barrister, after obtaining a silk gown, to select his circuit, as it is equally contrary to it to change from one circuit to another. But he chose this circuit with the hope of suddenly stepping into the practice of Sir Fletcher Norton, who was made Attorney-General. Of course he was cut by the whole of the barristers of that circuit, and his bold adventure proved a failure. In the Court of Chancery his success was greater; but when Bute was driven by public opinion from the Ministry, Wedderburn suddenly shifted his politics, and from a staunch Tory appeared as staunch a Whig; nay, he became a flaming patriot, and defended what he called that injured brother-patriot, John Wilkes. Carrying his patriotism a little too far in support of Wilkes, he lost his seat for the borough of Richmond, which had returned him as a Tory, and was feted as a martyr at a dinner at the Thatched House Tavern by the leading patriots of the day, amongst them George Grenville, Burke, Lord Clive, Lord George Sackville, Alderman Beckford, and Colonel Barré.

In the next session he was returned by Clive for his pocket borough of Bishops Castle, and he proceeded to attack Lord North's policy vehemently, panegyrised the liberty of the press, sympathised with the Americans, asserted the rights of juries, and stood forth as a patriot of the first degree. In the very next session he ratted openly and shamefully; and it was on this occasion that Junius branded him with the words, that 'there was something about him that even treachery could not trust.' For this, which Lord Campbell calls `one of the most flagrant cases of ratting in our party annals,' he was made Solicitor-General; and his own saying, applied to another, was now in everybody's mouth `Bit by the tarantula of Opposition, he is cured by the ermine of the Court.' The Secretary of the Treasury, John Robinson, was believed to have brought Wedderburn thus suddenly over; and Sheridan alluding to the circumstance vaguely, there was a cry of 'Name him! name him!' on which he said, 'I *could* name him as easily as say *Jack Robinson*.' Thurlow being Attorney-General, Horne Tooke observed that Lord North now sat secure to guard the Treasury Bench, between his two brazen pillars - Jachin and Boaz.

On the occasion of his crossing the floor of the House on this sudden change of party, even the brazen assurance of Wedderburn broke down: he appeared for some time after embarrassed; and Junius said, 'We have seen him in the House of Commons overwhelmed with confusion, and almost bereft of his faculties.'

In order to recover his popularity, he now seized on several occasions to display great liberality. He behaved with remarkable moderation in the great question which arose betwixt the City and the House of Commons regarding the publication of its proceedings, in the course of which Crosby, the Lord Mayor, and Alderman Oliver were committed to the Tower for protecting the reporters, and which ended in the establishment of the right of reporting the Parliamentary debates: members of the present day being as eager to have their speeches reported as those of that day were averse.

Wedderburn patronised literature, and defended the propriety of Dr. Johnson's pension. He advocated the right of laymen to study in the Universities without subscribing to the Thirty Nine Articles. He strongly argued for the copyright of an author in his works; he showed a considerable bearing towards Woodfall, the printer, when prosecuted for publishing the letters of Junius; and in all these cases his speeches were as able as they were just.

About this time he defended the Indian policy of Lord Clive, and recommended Clive to allow Voltaire to write the history of his conquests in India, as he wished to do. In 1773 he married a rich heiress of Yorkshire, and lived in a style, with one house at Mitcham and another in Lincoln's Inn Fields, near the Duke of

Newcastle's, equalling that of the nobility. Clive had given him the house at Mitcham, and some lacs of rupees, for his defence of him in Parliament; and in horses and equipages he was quite princely. He told Lord Haddington that on being made Solicitor-General, he immediately ordered a service of plate at a cost of £8,000. The son of the little Scottish lawyer now seemed in the element, if not on the summit, of his ambition - that of mere social distinction.

But now came an event, in which he indulged his powers of vituperation to his country's loss of a great dependency. In 1774, Benjamin Franklin, then political agent of the American colonies in England, came into possession of certain letters written by Governor Hutchinson of Massachusetts, and Mr. Oliver, Lieutenant-Governor of that province, to Mr. Whateley, who had been private secretary to George Grenville, the originator of the tax on tea imported into the American colonies. These letters, which, however, were not official, but written as from one friend to another, recommended the employment of a military force to suppress the discontents there. Franklin, it has since appeared by a Memoir of Dr. Williamson, by Dr. Hosack, of New York, had procured them from this Dr. Williamson, who, having been employed in Mr. Whateley's office, had purloined these letters, and sold them to Franklin, who transmitted them at once to the Speaker of the House of Assembly, who read them publicly. The exasperation occasioned by this discovery was intense; and Franklin was instructed to demand the recall of Governor Hutchinson and the Lieutenant. But before this was done, it had led to a duel betwixt Mr. Whateley, banker in Lombard Street, and brother to the late Secretary Whateley, and Mr. Temple, Lieutenant-Governor of New Hampshire, whom Whateiey suspected of having some concern in the purloining of the letters. Gordon, author of 'History of America,' very partial to the American side, seems to support this view. Franklin, however, on the duel taking place, wrote and published a letter, declaring that he alone was responsible for obtaining and transmitting the letters, and excusing both Whateley, who was severely wounded, and Mr. Temple. He then applied to the Privy Council, by petition, for the removal of the Governor and Lieutenant-Governor of Massachusetts, Dunning being his leading counsel.

It is said that no juridical proceedings had excited so much interest and expectation since the trial of Sacheverell. The case came on in the Council Chamber, at the Cock Pit, Whitehall. Thirty five privy councillors attended, with Earl Gower, the Lord President, at their head. Burke, Priestley, Jeremy Bentham, and other distinguished strangers, were accommodated with places near the bar, and a dense throng filled the adjoining rooms and passages. According to Bentham's account,

> 'the president's chair was with the back parallel to and not far distant from the fire; the chimney-piece, projecting a foot or two, formed a recess on each side; alone, in the recess on the left hand of the president, stood Benjamin Franklin, in such a position as not to be visible from the situation of the president, remaining the whole time like a rock, in the same posture, his head resting on his left hand, and in that attitude abiding the pelting of the pitiless storm.'

Dunning and Lee, as counsel for the petitioners, stated their case, and supported the prayer of the petitioners, but feebly, as if ashamed of the manner in which the letters had been procured. On the other hand, Wedderburn, as assessor of the Privy Council, made a trenchant speech against the purloiners of the letters. He highly praised the Governor and Lieutenant-Governor of Massachusetts as most honourable and accomplished men, and meritorious public officers; declared that there was no charge against them, no accusers, no proof. The petitioners only simply said these officers had forfeited their confidence. As to the letters, they were simply private letters, and therefore could not be made the ground of a charge against them.

Wedderburn said:

> 'How these letters came into the possession of any one but the right owners, it was a mystery for Dr. Franklin to explain. He was not the rightful owner, and they could not have come into his hands by fair means. Nothing will acquit Dr. Franklin of the charge of obtaining them by fraudulent or corrupt means, for the most malignant of purposes - unless he stole them from the person who stole them. This argument is irrefragable. I hope, my lords, you will mark and brand the man, for the honour of this country, of Europe, and of mankind. Private correspondence has hitherto been held sacred, in times of the greatest party rage, not only in politics but in religion. The betrayer of it has forfeited all the respect of the great, and of his own associates. Into

what companies will the fabricator of this iniquity hereafter go with an unembarrassed face, or with any semblance of the honest intrepidity of virtue? Men will watch him with a jealous eye; they will hide their papers from him, and lock up their escritoires. Having hitherto aspired after fame by his writings, he will henceforth esteem it a libel to be called *a man of letters - homo trium literarum* (Fur, a thief). But he not only took away these papers from one brother, he kept himself concealed till he had nearly occasioned the murder of another. It is impossible to read his account, expressive of the coolest and most deliberate malice, without horror. Amid these tragical events - of one person nearly murdered, of another answerable for the issue, of a worthy governor hurt in the dearest interests, the fate of America in suspense - here is a man who, with the utmost insensibility of remorse, stands up and avows himself the author of all! I can compare him only to Zanga, in Dr. Young's "Revenue:

Know then 'twas I.
I forged the letter - I disposed the picture -
I hated, I despised - and I destroy.

I ask, my lords, whether the revengeful temper attributed by poetic fiction only to the bloody-minded African, is not surpassed by the coolness and apathy of the wily New Englander.'

The effect of these scathing words was tremendous at the moment, and still more so ultimately. Charles Fox, in a debate in 1803, warning the House against the delusive eloquence of Pitt, bade them remember,

'how all men tossed up their hats, and clapped their hands in boundless delight, at Mr. Wedderburn's speech against Dr. Franklin, without reckoning the cost it was to entail upon them.'

Bentham, who was present, professed himself not only 'astonished at the brilliancy of Wedderburn's lightning, but astounded by the thunder which accompanied it.' Dr. Priestley, also present, declared that 'at the sallies of his wit, all the members of the cabinet, the president himself, Lord Gower, not excepted, frequently laughed outright.' No person belonging to the council behaved with decent gravity except Lord North: and Lord Shelburne, in a letter to Lord Chatham, wrote that 'the indecency of their behaviour exceeded, as it was agreed on all hands, that of any committee of election.'

And how did the victim of this terrible fulmination of legal license, accompanied by the unrestrained ridicule of the Privy Council of England, bear it? With the outward composure of a stoic or a Red Indian, but with an inward rage of revenge that no time and no success of retaliation could burn out. In that moment Franklin vowed eternal hatred to England, and the separation of the North American colonies at any cost and by any means. He retired to his lodgings, took off the suit of Manchester velvet which he wore on this occasion, locked it up in a box, and never wore it again till the day on which he signed the articles of peace, recognising the independence of the United States, at Paris in 1783, nine years afterwards. He had accomplished his vow, and the suit of Manchester velvet was returned to its chest, never to be worn again by him. Franklin's resolve of vengeance had been deepened by the Privy Council voting the petition which he had presented, 'false, groundless, vexatious, and scandalous,' thus dismissing it, and a few days afterwards dismissing him from his office of Deputy Postmaster General in America. Still further, Wedderburn filed a bill in Chancery against Franklin, to compel him to discover the means by which he had obtained these letters, and this prosecution was only interrupted by news of open hostilities having broken out in America. From this time forward Wedderburn showed himself on all occasions one of the most furious and inveterate of the urgers on of the war against the Americans, and no man was more responsible for the alienation of these colonies than he.

Having thus done the worst work of the infatuated and despotic Government of that time, and defended the worst abuses of the pension-list, Wedderburn was made Chief Justice of the Common Pleas, and a peer, with the title of Lord Loughborough, in 1780. In that year he had to judge the rioters of the Gordon riots, and no Jeffreys could have done his work more relentlessly. A great example was deemed necessary, and the rioters were executed by the score. Burke, in the 'Annual Register,' says that Wedderburn's address to the grand jury was generally spoken of in terms of indignation, as calculated to inflame the passions of the jurymen, and prejudge the case. Lord Brougham, in his 'Statesmen,' condemns Wedderburn's address on this occasion with equal severity; saying 'It consisted of a solemn and stately lecture upon the enormity of the offence, and a denial of whatever could he alleged in extenuation of the offender's conduct.'

Lord Loughborough was the first to deny the right of the poor to glean in corn fields after the harvest - a custom, if language can establish any right, existing from all time. The law of Moses was more benevolent than Loughborough law.

In 1782 he made a second marriage, with the sister of Lord Courtenay, and in the same year became Commissioner of the Great Seal. In 1788, on the first occasion of the King's insanity, he advocated the taking possession of the regency by the Prince of Wales as of right, but was defeated by Pitt's Government, and then became a flaming Liberal and voted for Catholic Emancipation. Soon after, however, Pitt found means to bring him over from Fox and what were called the Alarmist Whigs, and in 1793 he was rewarded by being made Lord Chancellor of England, the grand aim of his ambition. He carried the Great Seal home in his coach, and exultingly showed it to Lady Loughborough, though he confessed that he was afraid, on awaking in the morning, he should find it only a pleasing dream.

He now gave way fully to his unbounded love of making a great figure in the public eye. 'His style of living,' says Lord Campbell,

'was most splendid. Ever indifferent about money, instead of showing mean contrivances to save a shilling, he spent the whole of his official income in official splendour. Though himself very temperate, his banquets were princely; he maintained an immense retinue of servants, and, not dreaming that his successor would walk through the mud to Westminster, sending the Great Seal thither in a hackney coach, he never stirred about without his two splendid carriages, exactly alike, drawn by the most beautiful horses, one for himself, and another for his attendants. Though of low stature and slender frame, his features were well chiselled, his countenance was marked by strong lines of intelligence, his eye was piercing, his appearance was dignified, and his manners were noble.'

Thus we may see him parading with his grand equipages up Hampstead Hill to Rosslyn House, and there, his people all in a bustle with the attendance on such guests as the Prince of Wales, the Duke of Portland, Edmund Burke, Gibbon, Lord Spencer, Windham, Fox, and afterwards Pitt, &c.

From this time forward Wedderburn continued one of the most inflammatory promoters of the war against the American colonies, and to the last the most dogged opponent of a peace with them. In the great war with France, we owe to him the fatal scheme of subsidising the continental kings, which cost us hundreds of millions, and which makes continental Governments still so clamorous to draw us into their quarrels. They denounce our non-intervention because they long once more to be pulling at our purse-strings. We are told by Lord Malmesbury that this proposition of Wedderburn's was at first opposed by Pitt and Grenville.

In the Reign of Terror which arose here in fear of the revolutionary principles of France, Lord Chancellor Wedderburn advocated the most arbitrary measures. He opposed any idea of reform of Parliament, and supported the most rigid prosecutions of reformers. He introduced to the Cabinet the idea of the Traitorous Correspondence Bill, by which correspondence with any Frenchman was made high treason, with all the ancient terrors of hanging, drawing, and quartering. He supported the Bill for the suspension of the Habeas Corpus, in 1794; the Bill against seditious meetings, and the policy of employing spies and informers; he approved and confirmed, on appeal to the House of Lords, the infamous sentence of transportation of Muir, Palmer, and the rest of the patriots, for merely advocating Parliamentary Reform. He disgusted even George III by endeavouring to condemn Horne Tooke, Hardy, and Thelwall, by the invention of a new crime - constructive treason. The King said to him, 'You have got us into a wrong box, my lord, you have got us into a wrong box. Constructive treason won't do, my lord, constructive treason won't do.' Amongst the judgments he gave was one, that the famous Thelluson property should go on accumulating for three generations, according to the will, the family being deprived of it for that time. But, as Lord Campbell observes, the Court of Chancery conveniently ate up nearly all the rents and profits, and then an Act of Parliament was readily obtained to let the estates go to the family. Another, was that the old law of burning alive women guilty of coining should not be mitigated into hanging. He opposed all peace with France, and when Mr. Pitt would have carried Catholic Emancipation, in 1795, Wedderhurn, who was now as much opposed to freedom of religion as he had been formerly zealous for it, defeated him, and threw him out of office. He is said, moreover, to have confirmed, if not originated, the King's obstinacy on this head, by frightening him about his coronation oath. His manoeuvres against Pitt and the Catholics, however, did not benefit him. In 1801 the King dismissed him, and gave the Great Seal to Lord Eldon.

After this his influence wholly declined. He seemed to retain only the ambition of being about the person of the King, and he hired a villa at Baylis, near Slough, to be near the Court; yet, so little confidence had he inspired in the monarch, with all his assiduous attentions, that when the news of his death was brought to King George III, who had seen him the day before - for he went off in a fit of gout in the stomach - George cautiously asked if the news were really true; and being assured that it was, said, as if with a sense of relief, 'Then he has not left a greater knave behind him in my dominions!'

Lord Brougham's estimate of this splendid adventurer is equally severe. He treats him as a

'man of shining but superficial talents, supported by no fixed principles, embellished by no feats of patriotism, nor made memorable by any monuments of national utility; whose life being at length closed in the disappointment of mean and unworthy desires, and amidst universal neglect, left behind it no claim to the respect or gratitude of mankind, though it may have excited the admiration or envy of the contemporary vulgar.'

We cannot, indeed, look on Rosslyn House without reflecting how much of the disastrous politics of the reign of George III originated in it, how much of the mischievous war against America and France; and what a riding and driving to and fro there must have been, of the great movers of these events, where Rosslyn House now stands, no longer amid its solitary fields, but shouldered up by a multitude of new villas, and overlooking the advancing tide of brick and mortar from St. John's Wood, and all the vast expanse of miles of dense town, where only ten years ago spread a green expanse of fields and dividing hawthorn hedges.

Still, the situation of Rosslyn House enables it to preserve within its grounds an air of retirement and even of solitude. These grounds are spacious; below it yet remain well- wooded fields, and the fields westward remain unbuilt upon.

After passing through several hands after the death of Lord Rosslyn, it was inhabited by Robert Milligan, the projector of the West India Docks. Mr. Milligan was a great West India merchant, and in honour of his services a statue was erected to him at the entrance of the Dockyard, executed by Westmacott. Subsequently Sir Francis Freeling, secretary of the General Post Office, occupied it, and had there a very fine library. To him succeeded Admiral Sir Moore Disney, and then Mr. Davidson, senior. At his decease the house was rented for some fourteen years by the late Earl of Galloway, and there his grandson, the present Duke of Marlborough, passed, with his mother, much of his early boyhood. It was then again occupied by the Davidson family (of Tulloch), until it passed into the hands of a speculative builder, who happily failed before the old house was destroyed or all the old trees were cut down, though it was shorn of much of its beauty and adjoining lands, now covered with numerous but handsome villas, and streets of houses. During this luckless period the myrtles of forty years' growth perished; the orangery fell into decay, and it became the Home of the Soldiers' Daughters for four years. In 1860 Prince Albert led these children in procession to their present Home, built on the site of the old Vane House.

In 1861 Charles H. L. Woodd, Esq. purchased the place, and as a descendant of John Evelyn of the 'Sylva,' and of Dr. Basil Woodd, Chancellor of Rochester, who fought under Charles I at Edge Hill, has naturally a pleasure in maintaining it as much as possible in its historic integrity. His predecessor, Mr. Davidson, a wealthy West India merchant, is stated to have expended £10,000 on the house, and Mr. Woodd has evidently expended additional money and taste upon it. In the course of the alterations which he made seven years ago, several coins of Elizabeth, Charles II, and William III were found under the flooring; and upon the old panellings, when the canvas covering was removed, were seen the words written 'Tomorrow last day of Hollidays!!! 1769.' At first it was supposed that Lord Chesterfield's natural son, to whom the

'Letters' were addressed, might have inscribed this pathetic sentence; but the date shuts out the possibility. Lord Chesterfield died in 1773, and this his only son five years before him.

The main body of the avenue still exists, and amongst its trees are some very fine Spanish chestnuts, one of which measures full eighteen feet in girth. On one of these venerable trees being, from necessity, cut down, the present proprietor counted above 180 rings of annual growth, besides which a central portion representing another 100 years, almost obliterated by decay. Two hundred and eighty years - this would bring the planting of the avenue up to the latter end of the reign of Elizabeth, and the age of the trees to 1588, the year of the Spanish Armada. A clematis vitalba, also in the gardens, is worthy of notice from the size of its trunk, and the extent to which it has run over a covered way, and over the neighbouring trees, being probably one of the oldest and largest of these lianos in the kingdom.

OTHER OLD HOUSES AT HAMPSTEAD

Besides those whose inhabitants we have noticed, there are many other fine old houses in and about Hampstead, which could render up to us curious and very interesting histories, if we had the means of commanding them; but little care seems to have been exercised in preserving the memory of the former residents of many of them. Some of these residents were, no doubt, for long terms, others were temporary. John Wylde, Lord Chief Baron of the Exchequer during the Civil War, who drew up the impeachment against the bishops, resided there some time, and died there about nine years after the Restoration. Thomas Rowe, author of 'Lives of Illustrious Persons,' and husband of Mrs. Elizabeth Rowe, once a very popular poetess, whose versified 'History of Joseph' in our boyish days we greatly admired, as many persons do still her 'Devout Exercises of the Heart,' died at Hampstead in 1715, and after his decease Mrs. Rowe retired to Frome, where, with occasional visits to her dear friend the Countess of Hertford, she resided many years.

At the bottom of the town there used to be a house called 'Queen Elizabeth's House,' but evidently without a just claim, the architecture being of a later date.

The Conduit, a spring which is situated at a short distance, in Shepherd's Fields, to the west of Rosslyn House, formerly supplied the greater part of Hampstead with water of excellent quality, which was fetched thence by water-carriers, and sold by the bucket. Since the supply of the place by the New River Water Company, it has fallen into total neglect. There used to be a handsome arch over it, as may be seen from the wood-cut in 'Hone's Table Book,' p. 381. The arch is now built up. The supply of water is scanty, and only serves to make a boggy place below it. The posts and rails round are, for the most part, destroyed, and the whole spot is filthy and disreputable.

Passing the little world of new houses that have sprung up between Shepherd's Fields and the Hampstead Road, in one of which, in Haverstock Place, the late Robert Stephenson lived -

where also Charles Knight the publisher, and other men of note reside - we come to a green lying betwixt the road and Pond Street. This is called Hampstead Green, and is where Wilkie tells us that Collins the painter lived at one time. Great alterations on this Green have recently taken place. The houses and gardens on the side nearest to Hampstead have vanished, and a large hotel and a row of shops, and sundry villas, have taken their place. On the top of the Green a Church is about to be erected. A little beyond this Green, and facing Belsize Lane, is the large square brick house inhabited by Sir Rowland Hill, the great reformer of our postal system.

We now proceed further down Haverstock Hill, reminding the reader that Nichols, in his 'Literary Anecdotes,' says Grose the antiquary - commemorated by Burns for his

> Fouth o' auld nick-naekets:
> Rusty airn caps and jinglin jackets,
> Wad haud the Lothians three in tackets,
>   A towmont gude;
> And parritch-pats, and auld saut-backets,
>   Before the Flood -

was killed by a fall from his horse on Haverstock Hill, as the late Mr. Longman was on the same road to Hampstead.

Somewhere in this direction also lived a person notorious in her day, and made a permanent character by the pencil of Hogarth: Moll King. Hogarth has introduced her in his 'Four Times of Day,' in the painting of 'Morning.' She was the proprietor of 'Tom King's Coffee House,' in front of which Hogarth sketches a prim old lady, who, it is said, struck him out of her will for this piece of distinction. Mrs. Moll King, the proprietor of this house, the relict of Thomas, was well acquainted with the magistrates, and suffered in purse, as well as in person, for keeping a disorderly house. Retiring from business, and that bad eminence, the pillory, to the Hill of Hampstead, she lived on her early gains, paid for a pew in church, was charitable at appointed seasons, and died in peace in 1747. In Nichols's 'Anecdotes of Hogarth,' it is said that she built on Haverstock Hill three houses, in one of which lived the equally celebrated Nancy Dawson.

We may as well, too, imagine Dick Turpin, the famous highwayman, riding his tall black horse up and down this road; for, amongst other famous men, he had a house once at Hampstead, where the vicinity to the Heath and to Finchley Common might be a convenience; but where this abode was, I know not.

STEELE'S COTTAGE

Steele's Cottage, Haverstock Hill
(From a print in Mr. Gardner's Collection)

Still descending Haverstock Hill, we arrive at the site of what was called Steele's Cottage. This cottage stood on the right-hand side of the road, in a garden opposite to the public-house called 'The Load of Hay,' now modernised, and having much the air of a gin-palace. The cottage called Steele's Cottage, after Sir Richard Steele, was of late years divided into two dwellings, and had the name 'Steele's Cottage' painted on the front. When I visited it in 1866, the building which (as everywhere all round London) was going on there, was fast encroaching on the cottage. The long line of the new street called Adelaide Road, bounded the open ground at the back, at no great distance; other houses were fast rising still nearer; and, at the end nearest to London, new houses crowded up close to it, and it was then evidently destined at no distant date to fall, and give way to more ambitious structures. The tenants informed me that they had notice to quit, and that, in about another year, it would be swept away. This was verified in the spring of 1867, and Steele's Cottage now only exists in engravings.

I have heard it said that this was not really the cottage in which Steele once sojourned; but there can be no doubt about its identity. Engravings of it exist, some of them dating from Steele's own time, when all the country round was open. The engravings of it, in Park's 'Hampstead' and in the 'Gentleman's Magazine,' are correct, and agree with a number of such in the possession of John Gardner, Esq., of St. John's Wood Park, the proprietor of, I suppose, by far the most valuable private collection of the drawings, engravings, and photographs of scenes and buildings in and around London in existence. Amongst the many places of historical interest which the growth of London is continually sweeping away, the destruction of Steele's Cottage is a matter of general regret.

Before Steele lodged in it, however, it had been the occasional retirement of another man of historical and literary note, whom we must in order of time first note. Sir Charles Sedley was one of the most profligate men of Charles II's Court. He was author of several plays, and was the father of James II's mistress, created Countess of Dorchester. He died 1701. Pepys, vol. ii. p. 63, says he was tried in June of 1663 for debaucheries at Oxford too indecent to print; that Lord Chief Justice Foster, and the whole Bench, spoke to him in the severest manner, and told him that it was such wicked wretches as he who brought the judgments of God on the nation, calling him sirrah many times. Lord Buckhurst being present, the judge asked if it was that Buckhurst who was lately tried for robbery, and gave him also a stern reproof. It is pleasant to see judges in so corrupt an age, so boldly condemning titled offenders to their faces.

Of the character of Sedley for licentiousness, we have a pretty good idea, from his name being used as a sort of standard for judging degrees of vice. Pepys says, 'Lord Vaughan is one of the lewdest fellows of the age, worse than Sir Charles Sedley.'

In Pepys's fourth volume, page 185, we have Sedley again, and that king of debauchees, Charles II:

'Pierce, do tell me, among other news, of the late frolic and debauchery of Sir Charles Sedley and Buckhurst, running up and down all the night, almost naked, through the streets, and at last fighting, and being beaten by the watch, and clapped up all night; and how the King takes their parts; and my Lord Chief Justice Keeling hath laid the constable by the heels, to answer it next sessions, which is a horrid shame. How the king and these gentlemen did make the fiddlers of Thetford, this last progress to sing them all the obscene songs they could think of.'

Again, page 186: 'The King was drunk at Saxam (near Newmarket), with Sedley, Buckhurst,' &c.; and 'The King was so drunk, he could give not audience to Lord Arlington on pressing business.' What a charming king and charming times!

Bad as Sedley was, however, he was, like many other profligates, not without a sound place in his nature. This profligate companion of Charles II had been very properly prosecuted for offences *contra bonos mores*, and, as Anthony Wood says, 'took up and grew very serious.' It is certain that, in the first year of the reign of William III, he uttered some pithy remarks in Parliament on the Bill for raising money for the Civil List:

'Mr. Speaker: We have provided for the army, we have provided for the navy; and now at last a new reckoning is brought in. We must provide likewise for the Civil List. Truly, Mr. Speaker, it is a sad reflection that some men should wallow in wealth and plenty, whilst others pay away in taxes the fourth part of their yearly revenue for the support of the same Government. We are not upon equal terms for His Majesty's service. The courtiers and great officers charge, as it were, in armour: they feel not the taxes, by reason of their places, whilst the country gentlemen are shot through and through by them.

The King is pleased to lay his wants before us, and, I am confident, expects our advice upon it. We ought, therefore, to tell him what pensions are too great, what places may be extinguished during the time of the war and public calamity His Majesty is encompassed with. His Majesty sees nothing but coaches and six, great tables, &c., and therefore cannot imagine the want and misery of the rest of his subjects. He is a brave and generous prince; but he is a young king, encompassed and hemmed in by a company of crafty old courtiers.

To say no more: some have places of 2,000*l*, some of 6,000*l*, and others of 6,800*l* per annum a-piece. Certainly public pensions, whatever they have been formerly, are too great for the present want and calamity that reigns everywhere else. And it is a general scandal that a Government so sick at heart as ours is, should look so well in the face.

We must save the King money wherever we can; for I am afraid the war is too great for our purses, if things be not managed with all imaginable thrift. When the people of England see everything saved that can be saved; that there are no exorbitant pensions nor unnecessary salaries, and all is applied to the uses to which they are given, we shall give, and they shall cheerfully pay, whatever His Majesty can want to secure the Protestant religion, and to keep out King James too - whom, by the way, I have not heard named this session, whether out of fear, discretion, or respect, I cannot tell. I conclude, Mr. Speaker - Let us save the King what we can, and then let us proceed to give him what we are able.'

This is certainly one of the most sensible speeches ever made in the British Parliament. If our present members would study the concise and clear style of Sir Charles Sedley, and to put as much sound advice into the same compass, they would save both themselves and hearers a great deal of unnecessary waste of patience and time. What they say could at least be read, which one quarter of the immensely wordy speeches of the present day are not; whilst, from the weight and pertinence of the matter, it would be remembered, which very little of the present verbose speechification is.

Sir Charles Sedley died in August 1701 - that is, about eleven years before Steele lived in this house. In his youth he seems to have lived, during the Commonwealth, in the country, at his father's seat at Aylesford, in Kent. Thither he went from Wadham College, Oxford, where he took no degree, in his seventeenth year. On the restoration of Charles II he appeared at Court, and was one of the gayest attendants on that dissipated monarch. He was a satirical wit, poet, and comedian. According to Anthony Wood, he was in 1663 fined very heavily for a drunken frolic, of which Wood gives the particulars. Soon after this, he represented New Romney in Parliament. He seems not to have affected Court life under James II, but reappeared on the accession of William and Mary. The licentiousness of Sedley's poems is not so gross as that of many of his contemporaries. His works, with a memoir, were published in 1722, and consist chiefly of short amatory poems, his few speeches in Parliament, and the following plays: 'The Mulberry Garden,' a comedy; 'Antony and Cleopatra,' a tragedy; 'Bellamira the Mistress,' a comedy; 'Tunbridge Wells; or, a Day's Courtship,' a comedy; 'The Tyrant King of Crete,' a tragedy; and 'The Grumbler,' a comedy, have also been attributed to him. His poems are superior to his plays, and the best of them have been reprinted in 'Ellis's Early English Poets.' The verses on him, quoted by Steele (below) are from Rochester.

The descendants of Sir Charles became possessed of an estate at Oxton in Nottinghamshire. His grandson married a Miss Freeth, of Nottingham, grand-daughter and co-heiress of Richard Slater, late of Nuthall, Nottinghamshire. I remember a Sedley living at Nuthall Temple in my youth.

Drake, in his 'Essays illustrative of the Tatler, Spectator, and Guardian,' says of Sir Richard Steele,

'During part of the year 1712, it appears from our author's correspondence, that, either from necessity or choice, either with a view of escaping the importunities of his creditors, or for the mere purpose of privacy and seclusion, he removed, for a short period, to a house situated between Hampstead and London.'

It is from the following passage, in a letter from Sir Richard Steele to Mr. Pope, dated June 1, 1712, that we learn this incident in his eventful life.

'I am at a solitude, an house between Hampstead and London, where Sir Charles Sedley died. This circumstance set me thinking and ruminating upon the employments in which men of wit exercise themselves. It was said of Sir Charles, who breathed his last in this room:

Sedley had that prevailing, gentle art
Which can with a resistless charm impart
The loosest wishes to the chastest heart:
Raise such a conflict, kindle such a fire,
Between declining virtue and desire,
Till the poor vanquished maid dissolves away
In dreams all night, in sighs and tears all day.

This was a happy talent to a man of the town; but, I dare say, without presuming to make uncharitable conjectures on the author's present condition, he would rather have had it said of him that he prayed

Oh, thou, my voice inspire.
Who touched Isaiah's hallowed lips with fire.

Mr. Nichols thinks that there were too many pecuniary reasons for this temporary solitude. The editor of the 'Biographia Dramatica' observes,

'Sir Richard retired to a small house on Haverstock Hill, on the road to Hampstead. Part of this building remains, and is now a cottage. Here Mr. Pope, and other members of the Kit-Cat Club, which, during the summer, was held at the "Upper Flask," on Hampstead Heath, used to call on him, and take him in their carriages to the place of rendezvous.'

Here Steele spent the summer days of 1712, in the composition of many of his 'Spectators,' returning generally to town at night, and to the society of his wife, who at this time had lodgings in Berry Street. That he left the cottage in the autumn is probable from the circumstance of his taking a house for Mrs. Steele at the close of this summer, in Bloomsbury Square; and from his correspondence we learn that he was actually in this house on September 3, 1712.

Sir Richard Steele is one of the writers of the age of Pope, Addison, and Swift, to whom our literature owes almost incalculable benefits. He was not only a writer of a most liberal and patriotic spirit, but he was the originator of our periodical literature, and in no small degree of our newspaper press. The publication of the 'Tatler' by Steele, which appeared on April 12, 1709, was the birthday of that periodical press of England, which has now acquired such an extent and pre-eminence. What a multitude of writers owe their existence and reputation to that event, and what an incalculably vaster number of readers, a daily source of delight and information. The father of the periodical press of England ought to take his stand amongst the greatest benefactors and elevators of his race; for it was not merely that Steele thus created a new organ of amusement - it was a new and potent organ of social and moral improvement. Steele, with his great coadjutor Addison, who became an occasional contributor to the 'Tatler' soon after its publication, and from its eighteenth number a regular one, at once introduced a purer and more elegant style of writing; a style which has been studied, and which has influenced many of our best writers from that time to the present. Amongst the most avowed adopters of this style was Washington Irving. But the improvement of style was the least of the reforms aimed at or achieved by Steele, Addison, and their co-workers: they set themselves earnestly to correct the violent and morally low character of their age. Mr. Montgomery, the biographer of Steele, has traced the effects of a century and a half of bad government under the Stuarts, the destruction of morals, and the debasement of manners: 'Amid this furious strife of parties, the tottering of thrones, and the rise and fall of dynasties, the arts of peace were necessarily retarded; the little glimpses of science which appeared under the auspices of Boyle, after a few feeble flickerings, expired. A general ignorance and licentiousness, both in principle and practice, prevailed. The streams of public amusement were polluted at their source, for the writers of the drama pandered shamelessly to the popular taste; and it was customary for ladies who had regard to reputation to frequent the theatres in masks, and to attend the public performance of any new piece before they could be supposed to be aware of the prurient jest or indecent allusion. All decorum was a jest - the most sacred social institutions considered a subject of polite raillery. Gambling and duelling were the pursuits of those styling themselves men of honour.

'But in addition to the general levity and frivolity in which life was spent amongst the most refined, the amusements indulged in by some of the very highest rank, as well as the populace, were of the most brutal and savage description. Prize-fighting, bull-baiting, and bear-baiting were prevalent diversions, and were not only attended, as we are informed by an annotator of the "Tatter" (edit. 1797), by butchers, drovers, and great crowds of all sorts of mobs, but likewise by dukes, lords, knights, and squires. There were seats particularly set apart for the quality, ornamented by old tapestry hangings, &c. It was a time when duelling was extensively prevalent, and Captain Hill, in company with Lord Mohun, murdered Mountford, the actor, in the open street, in cold blood, and without provocation. Clubs of wild young bucks, under a variety of names, particularly that of Mohawks, infested the streets, and rendered them dangerous after nightfall, by savage and barbarous pranks worthy of the name they adopted, insulting, wounding, and maiming passengers in a variety of ingenious methods, for they possessed a sort of wit and drollery in their diabolical pranks. It seems utterly incredible that in addition to slashing, maiming, and wounding their victims, we have it on the authority of Gay, that they actually would thrust women into barrels, and roll them down Ludgate or Snow Hill. Another and more harmless sort of these bloods went by the name of Nickers, whose delight was to break windows with showers of halfpence, to whom Steele wittily alludes in the 'Tatler,' No. 77, on finding his floor strewed with coppers, "I have not yet a full light into this new way, but am apt to think that it is a generous piece of wit that some of my contemporaries make use of, to break windows and leave money to pay for them." '

All these barbarities, Steele and his coadjutors attacked in the 'Tatler,' and in its successors, the `Spectator,' 'Guardian,' `The Lover,' `The Reader,' `Town-Talk,' `Tea-Table Chit-chat,' &c., with the weapons of a delicate raillery, and those of sound and earnest argument. Through a period of six years did Steele, with the assistance of Addison, Pope, Swift, Parnell, Congreve, Tickell, Dr. Watts, and most of the wits and literati of the time, contrive to make war on the rudeness, cruelties, and follies of the age, and to inculcate the highest morals and the soundest and most attractive views of religion. Many of the rude and barbarous sports - such as bear- and bull-baiting, cock- and dog-fighting, and throwing at cocks on Shrove Tuesday - were so deeply rooted in the spirit of the nation, that it required until our own time to thoroughly restrain them; and cock-fighting and prizefighting, notwithstanding the injunctions of the law, and the vigilance of the police, are still struggling for a continued existence. Railway companies are still found to prepare clandestine trains to conduct the offenders of the law, in the case of prize-fighting, to some unlooked-for spot, for the commission of this brutal crime; and gentlemen and even clergymen have within these few years been found making part of these disgraceful expeditions. From these facts it may be conceived how daring and arduous was the enterprise of Steele and his fellow-writers to discountenance these practices, and how much we owe them on that account. Duelling died as reluctantly, having reached its close only in our own time. In the general refinement of manners, in the elevation of morals, and in the spread of science and general intelligence from the days of Steele to our own, with all the mighty power into which the press has grown, we see with wonder, and we ought to perceive with gratitude, the vast obligations under which we are to the writers who put this work of reform into motion, and gave, by a ten years' labour at it, an impetus which insured its ultimate triumph.

Sir Richard Steele was a warm-hearted and impulsive

Irishman, who, in his zeal to accomplish his plans and efforts for the good of society, never put his own interests into the balance, but continually ran counter to them. Hence, whilst his more phlegmatic and calculating friends, Addison and Swift, won promotion and wealth, he himself was continually victimised by Government for his hold and patriotic avowals of the truth, and demands for justice towards the public. In 1710, he lost his post of State Gazetteer for his plain speaking in the 'Tatler,' and in 1714 he was expelled from Parliament when he represented Stockbridge, in Hampshire, for his exposure of the conduct of the Ministry with regard to the treaty of Utrecht, and for their neglect of that part of it concerning the port of Dunkirk. These damaging statements he had made in his pamphlets 'The Englishman' and ' The Crisis.'

Steele married a lady of some fortune, named Scurlock, of Llangunnor, near Carmarthen, in Wales; but from his bold and independent mode of acting and writing, he was often in great pecuniary difficulties, which were, no doubt, much increased by his desire to maintain a social position which his precarious income did not warrant; and by a failing, too common in that age, of indulging in too much wine. Whatever were Steele's faults, however, they were against himself, and not against others or the public. He was warmhearted, generous, always ready to help others to the extent of and often beyond his means; and his endeavours aimed to promote the good of the nation, of literature, and of the drama, being for some years Governor of the Royal Company of Comedians. This office, with a salary of £600 a year, was taken from him by the grasping and despotic Duke of Newcastle, the Lord Chamberlain, in 1720. During his patriotic labours in the public cause, Sir Richard was attacked with the utmost scurrility and insult by his quondam friend, Dean Swift, who was as cold-blooded and cantankerous as Steele was generous and high-minded.

So much was he reduced at times, whilst maintaining this warfare for right and liberty, that in one of his letters to his wife, who was gone for her health to her native place in Wales, he says: 'We had not, when you left us, an inch of candle, a pound of coal, or a bit of meat in the house; but we do not want now.' To such extremity had he been reduced in order to raise enough to carry his wife into Wales; and when she wanted to return, she was compelled to remain there some time longer from the same cause. Steele lost his wife, a handsome and clever woman, of whom he was dotingly fond, in 1718, at the age of 40. Of four children, two boys and two girls, the only one who survived him was his daughter Elizabeth, who was married to the Hon. John Trevor, one of the Welsh Judges, afterwards Lord Trevor, of Bromham. With their only daughter, who, like Addison's, though beautiful, was of weak intellect, the race of Steele seems to have ended.

For himself, hunted down by the undying malice of the Tory party, amongst whom Swift was the most truculent and base; left solitary by the death of his wife and all his children but one, and his health undermined, he retired to the estate of his late wife at Llangunnor in Wales. Even there, the diabolical spite of Swift followed him in the distich, in which he says Steele

> From perils of a hundred jails,
> Withdrew to starve and die in Wales.

This was, however, far from the truth, a thing which Swift paid little regard to. Sir Richard left a clear balance, when all his debts were paid, of £1,400. He appears to have retired into Wales about 1725, and he lived a life of quiet serenity there, greatly enjoying the beauty of the country, till 1729, when he died at Carmarthen, aged 58, and his remains, at his own request, were buried in the town chancel. 'I was told,' says Mr. Victor, in his 'Original Letters, &c.,'

> 'that he retained to the last his cheerful sweetness of temper, and would often be carried out of a summer's evening, where the country lads and lasses were assembled at their country sports, and with his pencil gave an order to his agent, the mercer, for a new gown to the best dancer.'

This is a characteristic trait of the hand which drew the inimitable 'Roger de Coverley,' and which brought the fame of Shakespeare again to light, when it had been so unaccountably and generally obscured; which sketched the touching story of 'Inkle and Yarico,' and the 'Adventures of Alexander Selkirk,' thus laying for the immortal pen of De Foe the foundation of 'Robinson Crusoe.' The builder has wiped out the visible trace of the memory of Richard Steele on Haverstock Hill, but his memory itself is sustained in the deathless monument of the British language, and the great march of civilisation and moral greatness to which he gave so grand an impulse.

There is an engraving of Sir Richard Steele's house at Llangunnor, the hereditary property of Lady Steele, to which, as observed, he retired to end his days, given in the 'Gentleman's Magazine,' vol. lxvii., part I., p. 457. The house is not much superior to the cottage on Haverstoek Hill, and in the view appears considerably dilapidated.

PRIMROSE HILL

We may close our survey in this direction with this celebrated suburban elevation, so called from the abundance of primroses once to be found there, no doubt when Holborn had its botanic gardens, and all between London and Westminster and the present West End were solitary, and in a great degree open fields. An adjoining lane is, or was, called Primrose Lane before the 'Buy my fine beau-pot ' boys and other Londoners had grubbed them all up.

The place is notorious in history for the murder of Sir Edmond Bury Godfrey, a mystery of the reign of Charles II, which has never been thoroughly cleared up, and probably never will. It occurred in 1678, a period when the country was agitated by the pretended Popish plots of the infamous Titus Oates, and the real one of Coleman, secretary to the Duchess of York. The public had become aware in some degree of the infamous bargain by which Charles II had sold himself to the French king for a pension, and was thus allowing Louis XIV to act against the Protestantism of the Continent without check. There was a strong Protestant party in England, at the head of which were the Earls of Shaftesbury and Buckingham, and the Whigs generally. An attempt was made by this party to pass an Act of Parliament to exclude James, afterwards James II, from the throne, on account of his avowed Popery. To fan the flame of the public hatred of Papacy, all sorts of plots were declared in existence, and in the midst of these came forth the creature Titus Oates, abetted by a Dr. Tongue, the rector of St. Michael's, in Wood Street, London, and others. It was declared that the King was to be murdered to make way for James, and a ministry of Catholic noblemen, Lords Powis, Stafford, Arundel, Peters, Bellassis, and others, was to be set up, a rebellion in Ireland excited, and thus Popery to come in with all its ancient terrors. Informers swarmed in the rear of Oates, and in the midst of their inventions a real plot was discovered in a traitorous correspondence of Coleman with France. Everything, however improbable, was then believed to be true; Coleman fled, though he was afterwards captured and executed; and Sir Edmond Bury

Godfrey, an active magistrate of Westminster, who had taken the depositions of Oates, and a friend of Coleman's, was found murdered in the fields between Primrose Hill and old St. Pancras Church. Godfrey was a man of a melancholy and sensitive temperament, and seemed sometimes on the very verge of insanity. On the apprehension of Coleman, Godfrey had been seized with great alarm, and expressed his conviction that he should be the first martyr of this plot. On October 12, he burnt a large quantity of papers, and that day he was seen hurrying about the town in a state of great abstraction of mind. From that time he was missing, and it was not till the sixth day that his body was found. He lay forward, resting on his knees, his breast, and the left side of his face. His sword was thrust through his heart with such violence that it appeared at his back. His cane stood upright in the bank, for he himself sat in a dry ditch; his gloves lay near his cane on the grass, and his rings were on his fingers, and his money in his purse. All these circumstances seemed to indicate suicide, and to confirm it, it was reported that when the sword was withdrawn, it was followed by a rush of blood. This, however, the doctors denied, and after six days it was not possible in any case, whether of suicide or murder. It was declared that there were marks round his neck, showing him to have been strangled, and that he had been thrust through, and the cane and gloves so disposed as to give the idea of his having killed himself. On the other hand, it was affirmed that the marks on the neck were faint and dubious. That Godfrey had committed suicide really appeared the most probable conjecture. His great alarm at the discovery of Coleman's guilt; his burning large quantities of papers, showed that he was deeper in these popish schemes than he dared let come to the light; his rushing about town in great distraction the day before his disappearance, all confirmed this idea. He had warned Coleman to fly; he had always been a partisan of the Catholics. Coleman was now in custody, and though Godfrey had burnt the dangerous papers, something might be drawn out on Coleman's trial which might commit him fatally. The balance of evidence was certainly in favour of suicide. But if he were murdered, who were his murderers? Soon a fellow of the name of Bedloe turned up, and declared that Godfrey had been murdered at Somerset House, the Queen's palace, by the Jesuits, her attendants; that Le Fevre, the Jesuit, told him that he and

Walsh, another Jesuit, a servant of Lord Bellassis, and a waiter in the Queen's chapel, had smothered him betwixt two pillows, and had offered him two thousand pounds to take the body away in a cart. But Bedloe had made a fatal blunder in laying the scene of Godfrey's murder in a room always occupied by the Queen's footmen, and at the very time that the King was there, and not only a throng of persons all over the palace, but a sentinel posted at every door, and a detachment of guards drawn out in the court. The next day he contradicted himself worse. Though he declared that he himself had seen the body at Somerset House, yet, as the state of the body when found did not favour the smothering theory, he now dismissed the two pillows, and said that he was strangled with a cravat. Anon he pitched on one Prance, a silversmith, who had worked at the Queen's chapel, as one of the murderers, and Prance was so pressed and badgered that he lost his head, and confessed, but again recalled his confession, and charged three others with being the murderers: namely, Green, Hill, and Berry, three servants at Somerset House; that Green strangled him with a handkerchief, and punched him on the breast with his knee, but finding him not dead, wrung his neck; that on the following Wednesday night, about twelve o'clock, the body was put into a sedan chair and taken to the Soho, and then conveyed on horseback, before Hill, to the place in the fields where he was found, and where they thrust his sword through him. These men stoutly denied the whole affair; but they were hanged for it, and the Court and country proceeded to fresh plots and rumours, which implicated many other lives, and some of them men of the most exalted rank and character, as Lord Stafford, Lord William Russell, Algernon Sidney, and others. As regarded the fate of Godfrey, however, the various depositions made by such wretches as Bedloe and Oates only involved it in fresh confusion, a confusion likely to continue for ever, though perhaps suicide appears the most probable solution. On the other hand, in a little volume published by John Hancock at the 'Three Bibles, over against the Royal Exchange,' in 1682, entitled, 'Memoirs of the Life and Death of Sir Edmond Bury Godfrey, late Justice of Peace for Middlesex, who was barbarously murdered by the Papists, upon the first Discovery of the Plot,' &c., the reader has a distinct narrative of this strange event, according to the views of those who attributed his death to the Catholics.

As to the place where Sir Edmond Bury Godfrey's body was found, it is stated in a letter to Mr. Miles Prance, 1681:

'that it was a ditch on the south side of Primrose Hill, surrounded by divers closes, fenced with high mounds and ditches; no road near, only some deep, dirty lanes, not coming near 500 yards of the place, and impossible for any man on horseback, with a dead corpse before him, at midnight to approach, unless gaps were made in the mounds, as the constable and his assistants found from experience when they came on horseback thither.'

This does not favour Prance's story of Hill carrying the corpse before him in the night to such a place.

Primrose Hill has also been called Barrow Hill, and an adjoining farm, Barrow Farm, leading to the supposition that it had been the scene of a battle, as Chalk Farm, just by, has been of many a duel, and one of the latest and most sorrowful, that of Christie and Scott, in which John Scott, the editor of the then celebrated 'London Magazine,' was killed. Chalk Farm, by the bye, is probably a corruption of Chalcote Farm, the Chalcote estate extending thence to Belsize Lane. There is no chalk in the neighbourhood to originate the name.

Old Chalk Farm
From a print in Mr. Gardner's Collection)

The 'Gentleman's Magazine,' vol. lxxv., part II., p. 967, relates the following extraordinary circumstance as occurring in this vicinity:

'As a gentleman and lady, in September 16, 1805, were walking across the fields from Hampstead Road turnpike to Primrose Hill, they met a person of gentlemanly appearance, who rushed on the lady, and grasped her round the neck. The gentleman was astonished at the stranger's conduct, and concluded that he was a lunatic; but, when in the act of attempting to disengage him, the unfortunate man fell, and expired in a fit.'

BIOGRAPHICAL NOTICES

In the heraldic visitation of Middlesex, in 1664, by Ryley (Lancaster) and Dethicke (Rouge Croix), there was only one family at Hampstead, that of Woodward, which gave in a pedigree.

John Wylde, who had been Lord Chief Baron of the Exchequer during the Civil War, and drew up the impeachment against the Bishops, led a retired life at his house at Hampstead, and died there about nine years after the Restoration, or about 1669. His daughter married Lord Delaware.

Sir Geoffrey Palmer, Knt. and Bart., manager of the evidence against the Earl of Strafford, was a prisoner in the Tower, for loyalty, Attorney-General for Charles II, and Chief Justice of Chester. He was author of various law reports. He died at Hampstead, May 5, 1670, aged 72 years. He was buried at Carleton, in Northamptonshire, the ancient seat of his family.

Henry Miller was murdered by a man named Jackson, who was gibbeted for it between two trees, on the side of the North End Road, near Heath Lodge. Miller was buried March 20, 1672. The post of the gibbet of Jackson was said to remain on a mantel-tree over the fireplace of the kitchen of the 'Castle' public house.

The Right Hon. Philip Lord Wharton died at Hampstead, where he had been some time for the air, February 1695-96, being about 80 years of age. He was the grandfather of the notorious Duke of Wharton. The character of Lord Wharton, though highly eulogised in the 'Flying Post,' Feb. 4, 1695-96, is not so estimated by Grainger, vol. ii. p. 143.

Dr. Sherlock died at Hampstead, June 19, 1707, aged 67, and was buried in St. Paul's Cathedral. His chief work was his 'Practical Treatise of Death.' See Grainger's 'Biographical History,' vol. iv. p. 299.

Joseph Keble was one of the singularities of Hampstead. He was a voluminous law reporter, who had a small estate at North End, where he lived during- the vacation. He usually walked to Hampstead; and a Mr. Keble, a bookseller in Fleet Street, a relative, reported of him that 'he generally performed the walk in the same number of steps, which he often counted.' He died suddenly in Holborn Gate, Gray's Inn, as he was about to take the coach for Hampstead, aged 68.

William Popple, Esq., Secretary of the Board of Trade, is buried in a vault in the churchyard. He died in 1722, aged 56. His wife lies also in the same vault, with several children, one of them also William Popple, Governor of Bermuda in 1745. There was also an Allured Popple, Governor of Bermuda in 1737. Mr. Popple was also an author of some note. He wrote two comedies, 'The Ladies' Revenge,' and the 'Double Deceit,' as well as a volume of poems, edited by Richard Savage, in 1736, and a translation of Horace's 'Art of Poetry.' He was concerned jointly with Aaron Hill in 'The Prompter.'

Dame Julia Blackett has a slab in the churchyard with this inscription:

> 'Here lies the body of Dame Julia, relict of Sir William Blackett, of Newcastle-on-Tyne, Bart.; afterwards wife of Sir William Thomson, Knt., Recorder of the City of London. She died the 16th of August, 1722.'

Dame Julia was the daughter of Sir Christopher Conyers, Bart., by Julia, daughter of Sir Richard Lumley, Viscount Waterford. By Sir William Blackett, Dame Julia had two sons, one of whom married, at Hampstead, Lady Barbara Villiers, daughter of the Earl of Jersey; Christopher, who died young; and eight daughters, of whom Isabella was the second wife of David, fourth Earl of Buchan. Both the Earl and his wife Isabella were buried at Hampstead, the Earl October 17, 1745; and his wife May 21, 1763.

Christopher Bullock, a comedian of some note, and the son of William Bullock, of North End, also a distinguished comedian, was buried in Hampstead churchyard in 1722, his funeral being accompanied by a great number of actors. His wife was a natural daughter of Wilks, the comedian, and was also on the stage.

Robeet Millingen, Esq., died at Rosslyn House, May 21, 1809, and was buried at Hampstead. He was not only the projector, but the completer, of the West India Docks; assisted, it is true, by other public-spirited men. We have named his services under the head of Rosslyn House. A tomb in the churchyard bears a grateful record of his memory.

Dr. Geokge Sewell died at Hampstead, and was interred there on February 12, 1725. Dr. Sewell had no house at Hampstead, but only lodgings. He seems to have been a regular man-of-all-work to the publishers; edited their reprints of the poets, was a considerable contributor to the supplemental volumes of the 'Tatler' and 'Spectator,' and had the principal share in a translation of Ovid's 'Metamorphoses.' His chief work, however, was the tragedy of 'Sir Walter Raleigh,' which was successfully performed at the theatre in Lincoln's Inn Fields. He was familiarly acquainted with Pope and Addison; but it was his fate, whatever his merits, to be in a condition of extremest indigence, neglected by all his friends, and by those who used to invite him to help to dissipate the dulness of their dinner tables. His remains were consigned to a coffin little better than those allotted to workhouse paupers, and no stone marked the spot where he lay. A holly tree, one forming part of a hedgerow formerly the boundary of the churchyard, was said to indicate the vicinity of his grave; but that has long disappeared.

John Gay, the celebrated poet and fabulist, lost his fortune by the South Sea Bubble, and, suffering severely in his health, went to Hampstead for some time in 1722, for the benefit of the air and water, where, by the care of his friends, and especially of Pope and Arbuthnot, he was restored. As the South Sea Bubble burst in 1720, this visit of Gay's was about two years after that time.

John Merry, a governor of the Hudson's Bay Company, has a tombstone in the churchyard, where his remains lay. He raised the Company's fortunes from a low to a very high and wealthy condition.

Dr. Arbuthnot, the friend of Pope, Gay, and Swift, appears to have visited Hampstead first on account of Gay, as just stated, but having fallen into a dropsy himself, he went there in 1734 for the recovery of his own health, in which object he to a degree succeeded. He seems to have led a rather gay life at the Wells, for an invalid. Pope, in one of his letters to Martha Blount, says:

'I saw Arbuthnot, who was very cheerful. I passed a whole day with him at Hampstead. He is in the Long Room half the morning, and has parties at cards every night. Mrs. Lepell and Mrs. Saggioni, and her sons and his two daughters are all with him.'

Arhuthnot joined Pope and Swift in many of their literary schemes, particularly in the satire of 'Martinus Scriblerus.' He wrote two works on 'Aliments,' and on the 'Effect of Air on Human Bodies,' which might dispose him to try the value of his hygienic theories at Hampstead. Swift describes him thus: 'He has more wit than all his race, and his humanity is equal to his wit.' He was just the man to find amusement in this then fashionable resort. He died in 1735.

Mr. Andrew Pitt is said to have been 'an eminent Quaker,' who died at Hampstead of gout in the stomach. Voltaire, in his letters concerning the English nation, says,

'he was one of the most eminent Quakers in England, who, after having traded thirty years, had the wisdom to prescribe limits to his fortune and his desires, and settled in a little solitude in Hampstead. He was of a hale, ruddy complexion, and had never been afflicted with sickness, because he had always been insensible to passions, and a perfect stranger to intemperance.'

Some of our newspapers added, 'He inherited many virtues, and wanted every vice.'

On Sunday, April 4, 1736, he waited on the then Prince of Wales, to solicit his favour in relation to the Quakers' Tithe Bill, when his Royal Highness answered to this effect:

'As I am a friend to liberty in general, and to toleration in particular, I wish you may meet with all proper favour; but for myself, I never gave my vote in Parliament; and to influence my friends, or direct my servants in theirs, does not become my station. To leave them entirely to their own conscience and understanding is a rule I have hitherto prescribed to myself, and purposed throughout life to observe.'

Mr. Pitt, overcome with this conduct, replied:

'May it please the Prince of Wales! I am greatly affected with thy excellent notions of liberty, and am more pleased with the answer thou hast given me, than if thou hadst granted my request.'

In Howard's 'Collection of Letters,' p. 604, see 'A Letter from Voltaire to Mr. Alex. Pitt, a Quaker, at Hampstead, and a very orthodox Believer, concerning "Alciphron; or, the Minute Philosopher;" ' a treatise then lately published.

Mark Akenside was introduced to Hampstead by the Hon. Jeremiah Dyson, Clerk of the House of Commons. Dyson and Akenside were fellow students at the University of Leyden. On Akenside coming to London, Mr. Dyson endeavoured to introduce him as physician. As Hampstead was then much frequented, and was inhabited by many wealthy people, Mr. Dyson purchased a house at North End, where he and Akenside lived together in the summer months, frequenting the Long Room, the clubs, and assemblies of the inhabitants. Sir John Hawkins says that Akenside defeated the efforts of his friend Dyson to establish him at Hampstead, by his vanity and love of display. He seemed resolved to take the lead there, as he had done in other places, but this did not succeed. His endeavours led him into disputes, and he suffered himself to betray a contempt of those who differed from him. This, certainly, was not the way 'to make his way' as a physician. It was soon discovered that he was a man of low birth, and dependent on Mr. Dyson, and this was naturally made full use of by those whose resentment he had aroused. When he contended that he was a gentleman, this was thrown in his teeth.

Mr. Mark Noble, in a letter to Mr. Park, August 22, 1811, says:

'Akenside, of humble origin, wished to have his birth a secret, and was certainly ashamed of his relations. I was at the trouble of asking a friend at Newcastle, the place of his nativity, concerning the Akensides, and I found that his kindred were inferior persons: his father a butcher; and that, when one of his near relations called upon him in his prosperity - namely, his aunt - he would not so much as acknowledge her. This gave me a very mean opinion of his heart.'

As these circumstances totally prevented Akenside succeeding at Hampstead, his generous friend, Mr. Dyson, parted with his villa at North End, and settled him in a small house in Bloomsbury Square, assigning him £300 a year, which enabled him to keep a chariot, and make a proper appearance in the world.

Akenside alludes to his residence at Hampstead in an 'Ode to Caleb Hardinge, M.D':

From Hampstead's airy summit, me,
Her guest, the city shall behold, &c.

See Brand's 'Observations upon Popular Antiquities,' 1778, pp. 113, 800; Dr. Anderson's 'Life of Akenside,' Edinburgh edition of 'British Poets,' &c. This account (pp. 52-54) agrees to a certain extent with that of Bucke, the author of 'The Beauties, Harmonies, and Sublimities of Nature,' in his 'Life and Writings of Aikenside.' Bucke tells us that Mark Akenside was born at Newcastle-upon-Tyne on the 9th of November, 1721; that his father, indeed, was a butcher, but a respectable one; and that he and his wife were very strict in their religious observances, and were Dissenters; that the name had always been spelt Akinside, and so by the poet himself in his Dedication of his poems to his friend Dyson. It was thus spelt in all Dodsley's editions of his 'Pleasures of Imagination,' till the sixth. Akenside, like Burns, altered his name, and improved it more than Burns did.

Akenside's friends, the Dissenters, sent him to Edinburgh at the age of seventeen, to study in preparation to becoming a Dissenting minister; but he soon changed his views, and after one year he began to study medicine. During the three years' residence at Edinburgh, he made the acquaintance of Dr. John Gregory and Dr. Robertson. After this he went to Leyden, where he studied three years, and obtained his diploma as Doctor of Physic in 1744. There he made the acquaintance of Jeremiah Dyson, a young man of fortune, and one of the truest and most generous friends that any man could possibly meet with. The two young men quitted Leyden together, and on arriving in London, Dyson went to the bar, and Akenside cast about for a medical practice. At the same time, having completed his great poem, 'The Pleasures of Imagination,' he obtained £120 for the copyright of it, of Robert Dodsley, the poem having been by Dodsley submitted to Pope, who said, 'Make no niggardly bargain - this is no every-day writer.' The work was printed by Richardson, the great novelist. It at once became popular, and speedily ran through many editions, and was translated into Italian and French - in the latter language in prose.

Akenside endeavoured to obtain a practice in Northampton, but did not succeed; but he there made the acquaintance of Dr.

Doddridge and Dr. Kippis. On quitting Northampton, after a year's abortive trial, his friend Dyson thought Hampstead would be a likely place for a physician to succeed in. It was a place of fashionable summer resort - had its chalybeate wells, its long-room, clubs, and assemblies. Dyson, therefore, bought a house at North End, where he established Akenside, and resided there himself, to introduce the poetical physician to the opulent inhabitants and visitors. To put him at his ease, he allowed him £300 a year. This was friendship in its noblest and most ideal sense. Says Bucke:

> 'But Hampstead was not suited to a man like Akenside. The inhabitants were respectable and rich; but many of them were not only respectable and rich, but purse-proud, and therefore supercilious. They required to be sought; their wives and daughters expected to be escorted and flattered, and their sons to be treated with an air of obligation.'

Akenside was a man already famous through the nation, and sensible of it, and was therefore not likely to play the courtier in a corner. Besides, according to a man of great repute, Mr. Meyrick, he was 'stiff and set,' which, indeed, is the fault of his chief poem, and the great drawback from its merits. Meyrick adds that 'he could not bear to see any one smile in the presence of an invalid, and, I think, lost much practice by the solemn sententiousness of his air and manners.' The result was that, after a residence of a year and a half at Hampstead, he returned to London, and took up his abode in Bloomsbury Square, where he continued to live for the rest of his life.

The generous Mr. Dyson, who himself rose to be one of the Lords of the Treasury, and had the honour of pretty sharp flagellation by Junius for his connection with Lord North and the Earl of Bute, continued his allowance of £300 a year to Akenside, who never married. He attained to considerable medical eminence in London; received a Doctor's degree from Cambridge; was elected a Fellow of the Royal College of Physicians; a Fellow of the Royal Society; and he appears, through the influence of Dyson with Lord Bute, to have been introduced to notice at Court, and was accused of some change in his political principles through that circumstance.

Bucke observed:

'The features of Akenside were expressive and manly in a very high degree, but his complexion was pale, and his deportment solemn. He dressed, too, in a very precise manner, and wore a powdered wig in stiff curl. In respect to disposition, he is said to have been irritable, and to have had little restraint upon his temper before strangers, with whom he was precise and ceremonious, stiff, and occasionally sententious and dictatorial.'

In this character of the man, we have the exact character of his poetry; and the whole is in perfect accordance with the causes said to have made so brief his sojourn at Hampstead. He died in Bloomsbury Square in June, 1770, in the 49th year of his age; and his books, furniture, and other property, passed to his great friend, Mr. Dyson.

Miss Hawkins's description of Dr. Akenside, or rather Dr. Lettsom's, is not very favourable. Dr. Lettsom says, great was his disappointment at finding Akenside, when visiting St. Thomas's Hospital, supercilious and unfeeling. If the affrighted patients did not return an exact answer to his questions, he would discharge them. He showed particular disgust and harshness to females. This was imputed to a disappointment in love. He ordered one patient bark in boluses: he could not swallow them; Dr. Akenside ordered the nurse of the ward to discharge him, saying, 'He shall not die under *my* care.' In removing, the man expired.

'One of Dr. Akenside's legs was shorter than the other; to remedy this he wore a false heel. He had a pale, strumous countenance, but was always neat and elegant. He wore a large white wig, and a long sword. He would sometimes make some of the patients precede him with brooms, to clear the way. Richard Chester, one of the governors, upbraided him with his cruelty, saying, 'Know, thou art a servant of the charity.'

There are on the four sides of an elegant altar-tomb in the church, memorials of the Booths and of the Delameres, to whom they succeeded. The verses on some of the children of the Right Hon. Nathaniel Booth and his wife Margaret have been attributed to Gilbert Cooper, the biographer of Socrates. The title of

Delamere became extinct at the death of this Nathaniel Booth, Lord Delamere, and was granted, with that of Warrington, to the Earl of Stamford April 22, 1796.

Boswell, in Vol. I of the illustrated edition of 'Johnson's Life,' p. 134, says:

> 'In January 1749, Johnson published "The Vanity of Human Wishes," being the tenth satire of Juvenal imitated. He, I believe, composed it in the preceding year. Mrs. Johnson, for the sake of the country air, had lodgings in Hampstead, to which he resorted occasionally; and there the greater part, if not the whole, of this "Imitation" was written. The fervid rapidity with which it was composed is scarcely credible. I have heard him say that he composed seventy lines of it in one day, without putting one of them upon paper till they were finished.'

At p. 163 of the same volume, Boswell adds:

> 'I have been told by Mrs. Desmoulins, who, before her marriage, lived for some time with Mrs. Johnson at Hampstead, that she indulged herself in country air and nice living at an unsuitable expense, while her husband was drudging in the smoke of London, and that she by no means treated him with that complacency which is the most engaging quality in a wife. But this is perfectly compatible with his fondness for her, especially when it is remembered that he had a high opinion of her understanding, and that the impressions which her beauty (real or imaginary) had originally made upon his fancy, being continued by habit, had not been effaced, though she herself was much altered for the worse.'

She was much beyond his own age. He married her in 1736, when he was 27 years of age, and when she was 48, or only within two years of 50 ; consequently, at her death, in 1752, when he was 43, she was 64.

Park says the house at which Dr. Johnson used to lodge, as mentioned above, was the last house in Frognal, southward, occupied in Park's time by Benjamin Charles Stephenson, Esq., F.S.A.

James Pitt, Esq. lived in London, but was buried here. He had a periodical paper in favour of Sir Robert Walpole, and is supposed to be the person alluded to in the 'Dunciad' as 'Mather Osborne,' from his signature of Osborne in the 'London Journal.' He was appointed Surveyor of Tobacco in 1731. Some letters of his are printed in Dr. Howard's `Collection.'

James MacArdell, a mezzotint engraver of great excellence, had a memorial stone in the churchyard at one time. He undertook to engrave the Gallery of Beauties at Windsor, but only executed those of the Countess of Grammont and Mrs. Middleton. His numerous works were chiefly portraits. Charles Spooner, a fellow pupil of MacArdell, and also an excellent mezzotint engraver, was buried by him.

Richard Cromwell, Esq. was a lawyer in Chancery Lane, who died at Hampstead December 1,1759. He was a direct descendant of the Protector, being the ninth son of Major Henry Cromwell, and grandson of Henry, Lord Lieutenant of Ireland. He was born at Hackney, May 11, 1695. He had several children, but his two sons dying without heirs, his daughters became wealthy, and two of them, Eliza and Letitia, possessed the manor of Theobalds, in Hertfordshire, formerly the property of Cecil, Lord Salisbury, Minister to James I, and where James was fond of staying.

These ladies possessed the armour, medicine chest, and many other valuables and curious things of their great ancestor, the Protector, with portraits of many of the family. They were much esteemed by those who had the honour of their friendship. They were both buried at Hampstead, Letitia in November, 1789, and Eliza in October, 1792. The rest of the family were interred in the Bunhill Fields Cemetery.

James Newnham, a lieutenant in the Duke of Marlborough's own regiment, and who had a ball through his thigh at the Battle of Blenheim, was buried at Hampstead in 1773, aged 102 years.

Dr. Anthony Askew was one of the many men of merit who have resided, more or less, in Hampstead. He died there on the 27th of February, 1774, aged 52 years. Dr. Askew was the son of Dr. Adam Askew, who enjoyed a great reputation as a physician at Newcastle-on-Tyne. He was bom at Kendal, in Westmoreland, commenced his education at Sedbergh School, and completed it at Cambridge and Leyden. He practised originally at Cambridge, but seems to have been introduced to London, and zealously recommended there, by Dr. Mead. He had been at Constantinople in attendance on the British Ambassador. He was chiefly noted for his collection of classical works, which were sold at his death.

Nichols says that his collection of Greek and Latin works was one of the best, rarest, and most valuable ever sold in Great Britain, containing many noble volumes from the libraries of De Boze, Gaignat, Mead, Folkes, and the Harleian.

The tombstone of John Harrison, the chronometer maker, reads:

'In memory of Mr. John Harrison, late of Red Lion Square, London, inventor of the time-keeper for ascertaining the longitude at sea.'

He was born at Foulby, in the county of York, and was the son of a builder at that place, who brought him up to the same profession. Before he attained to the age of 21, he, without any instruction, employed himself in cleaning and repairing clocks and watches, and made a few of the former, chiefly of wood. At the age of 25, he employed the whole of his time in chronometrical improvements. He was the inventor of the gridiron pendulum, and the method of preventing the effects of heat and cold upon time-keepers, by two bars fixed together. He introduced the secondary spring, to keep them going while winding-up, and was the inventor of most or all the improvements in clocks and watches during his time. In the year 1735 his first time-keeper was sent to Lisbon; and in 1764 his then much-improved fourth time-keeper, having been sent to Barbadoes, the Commissioners of Longitude certified that it had determined the longitude within one-third of half a degree of a great circle, not having erred more than forty seconds in time. After 60 years' close application to the above pursuit, he departed this life on the 24th day of March, 1776, aged 73 years.

Park says that Mr. Isaac Ware, the architect, as already observed, lived at the house called Frognal Hall, on the west side of Hampstead Church. Mr. Ware translated 'Palladio's Architecture' from the Italian, and 'Senagatti's Perspective.' He also published a `Complete Body of Architecture,' which we shall see that Thomas Day, author of 'Sandford and Merton,' studied to his cost. He translated and edited 'Palladio's First Book on the Five Orders.'

Lady Janetta de Conti's tomb in the churchyard bears this inscription:

'To the memory of the Right Hon. Lady Janetta de Conti, eldest daughter of the Right Hon. Cosimo Conti de Conti, a noble Tuscan by birth, and Knight of the Holy Roman Empire, by Janetta his wife, the only daughter of the late Robert White, Esq., of the family of Lord Rollo, and His Majesty's agent at the city and kingdom of Tripoli in Africa, by Jean Mackenzie, his wife, of the families of the Earls of Ross and Seaforth. This young lady was born in the city and kingdom of Tripoli, in Africa, on the 8th of January 1759, and died at Hampstead, in the county of Middlesex, in Great Britain, the 18th of July 1780. Mild in her temper, gentle in her manner, in public company easy, polite, and reserved; with her friends open, cheerful, and gay; highly accomplished in music, strongly attached to the improvement of her mind by reading, and mistress in speech and writing of the Italian, English, and French. This truly accomplished and amiable young lady died in her 21st year, and this monument is erected by her affectionate parents and inconsolable grandmother, the 30th of April, 1784.'

The pickpocket Miss West died in Hampstead:

'March . . . 1783, died at Hampstead, Miss West, the notorious female pickpocket, and accomplice of Barrington; for many years celebrated by the appellation of the Modern Jenny Diver. She was said to have bequeathed nearly 2,000*l* to her two children, the eldest of whom was born in Clerkenwell Bridewell, previous to her mother's being removed to Newgate under sentence of a year's imprisonment for picking a pocket in a room over Exeter Change, while the body of Lord Baltimore was lying there in state.'

Mr. Thomas Longman, bookseller and publisher, of Paternoster Row, died at Hampstead February 5, 1797, and was buried at Barnet. Nichols, in his 'Literary Anecdotes,' vi. 439, gives him this character:

'He was a man of the most exemplary character, both in his professional and private life, and universally esteemed for his benevolence as for his integrity.'

His son, Thomas Longman, Esq., was the father of the present publishers of that name. He was killed by a fall from his horse in returning from London one evening.

In June 1756 Admiral Barton was captain of the 'Lichfield,' and captured the Arc-en-ciel, a French ship of fifty tons, off

Louisburgh. In November 1758, he was Admiral in Keppel's squadron ordered against Goree. He was wrecked on the coast of Barbary, and managed to live, though he and his crew were quite naked, on a few drowned sheep that were driven ashore. After enduring eighteen months' slavery, he was ransomed by Government. In 1760 he commanded the 'Téméraire,' in Admiral Keppel's squadron sent against Belleisle, and successfully commanded the flat-bottomed boats at the landing. He became Rear-Admiral of the Blue in 1777, in 1778 of the same rank in the White. He was afterwards appointed Vice-Admiral, and finally, Admiral of the Blue and the White. See an engraving of his house in Malcolm's 'Illustrations of Lysons' "Environs." '

Dr. George Armstrong, the poet, practised medicine for some years at Hampstead. Armstrong is best known by his poem, 'The Art of Preserving Health,' the principles of which the wealthy members of the present luxurious style of society might adopt with great advantage. He made the tour of Italy with Fuseli, the painter, and finally settled in London, where he associated with the chief wits and poets of the age. He contributed to Thomson's 'Castle of Indolence' the beautiful stanzas descriptive of the diseases resulting from indolence. He died in 1779.

Mrs. Mary Green, a descendant of the founders of Wadham College, has a flat gravestone in the churchyard, with the date 1789. Her husband, Valentine Green, was keeper of the British Institution in Pall Mall, and author of 'History of Worcester,' and 'Review of the Polite Arts in France,' 1782. He was an eminent mezzotinto engraver.

Richard Pepper Arden, Lord Alvanley, lived at Frognal Hall, the large house immediately west of Hampstead Church, afterwards inhabited by Mr. Ware the architect and Mr. Thomas Wilson. Lord Alvanley was descended from a Cheshire family, an ancient one of the Ardennes. He was Chief Justice of the Common Pleas. He died March 19, 1804, and was buried at London in the Rolls Chapel.

Sir Francis Blake Delaval, of Seaton Delaval, in Northumberland, had a house at Hampstead. Sir Francis was the last but one male individual of that distinguished family who had been remarkable for the gaiety and freedom of their lives for generations. The last Lord Delaval had a large family of sons and daughters, yet, by many of the sons not marrying, and, as it were, by a fatality, the family became extinct in the last generation, in the male line, in the person of Edward Hussey Delaval. After Lord Delaval, his brother Sir Francis succeeded to the estate, but leaving no heir, it went to Edward Hussey Delaval, and thence into the female line. The daughters of Lord Delaval were very handsome, very gay, and fond not only of theatricals, but of all sorts of disguises and extraordinary frolics. One of them married Lord Tyrconnel, and their only daughter was the mother of the late Marquis of Waterford, from which source we directly trace the fondness for such escapades which distinguished his lordship. At Ford Castle, in Northumberland, belonging to the Waterford family, there is a portrait of Lady Tyrconnel, which shows what an arch and lovely creature she must have been. She had hair of such rich luxuriance that when she rode it floated on the saddle. The Delavals were so fond of theatricals that once, by permission of Garrick, the whole family acted on the boards of Drury Lane.

Sir Francis, during his possession of the estate, kept up the character of the race for gaiety and frolic. He was remarkably handsome, and possessed abilities which, had they been seriously applied, would have given him a better distinction. He was in Parliament, and so great an authority in all racing matters, that the Duke of Queensberry, Lords Eglinton and Effingham, Mr. Thynne, Colonel Breton, and other leading members of the Turf Club, consulted him on their betting speculations, and never were deceived.

At Seaton Delaval, during his time, all sorts of fetes, jollifications, theatricals, and dissipated life went on. Sam Foote was a great companion of Sir Francis, and assisted him in many tricks and follies. On one occasion they set up as conjurors in Leicester Fields, with the design of catching, for Sir Francis, Lady Nassau Paulet, a widow with £90,000, amongst the silly moths of fashion who would be drawn to their web of mystery. In this they succeeded; and Sir Francis, though he did not live long, yet lived long enough to spend the whole of her fortune.

Amongst Sir Francis's acquaintances was Bichard Lovell Edgeworth, the father of Maria Edgeworth. Lovell Edgeworth was, as his Life by his daughter shows, very fond of mechanics, and was a great friend of Watt, Boulton, Wedgwood, and Dr. Darwin.

Amongst his mechanical hobbies was an improved system of telegraphing. This he strongly urged on the Government during the great French war, but without receiving much encouragement. In Ireland, however, he was permitted partially to try it, and, according to his account, with great success. He proposed to Sir Francis, at whose house, he says, he saw more of the world in six weeks than he could possibly have seen elsewhere in as many years, a plan by which, through telegraphing, they could, if they pleased, fleece the betters of Newmarket to a vast extent. Sir Francis was delighted with the scheme, and, had it extended no further than a capital joke, would have gone into it heart and soul.

One telegraphic experiment they however carried out, the occasion of it mentioned here. They set up a night telegraph, with illuminated figures or signals, between Sir Francis's house at Hampstead and one which Mr. Edgeworth frequented in Great Russell Street. This nocturnal telegraph, Edgeworth reports to have answered well, but was too expensive for common use. Which was the house occupied or possessed by Sir Francis Delaval at Hampstead I have not been able to ascertain.

Thomas Day, Author of 'Sandford and Merton,' was an eccentric but noble-minded man, whose story of 'Sandford and Merton' has charmed successive generations of youth, and it is to be hoped has infused into their minds some of his pure and correct modes of thinking, occupied a house somewhere at Hampstead for a time. His friend Lovell Edgeworth says, on his marriage with Miss Milnes, a lady of large fortune of Yorkshire, they retired to a small lodging at Hampstead, where he determined to reside till he should find a house suited to his taste. Mr. Day was himself a man of fortune, but, as is well known, he had views of human life and its duties, which made him less regardful of wealth and station than of the exercise of independent and liberal principles. Determined not to marry a mere woman of fashion, he educated two poor girls, in the hope of finding in one of them a consort suited to his ideas of what a woman should be. The experiment was a failure, and Mr. Day continued to middle life a bachelor. He hesitated to unite himself to Miss Milnes for some time, on account of her fortune, but his friend Dr. Small advised him to despise the fortune and take the lady, and he adopted this wise recommendation, much to his own happiness.

His taking the small house at Hampstead was in order to be at some distance from his friends, and also to avoid being drawn into the usual modes of life followed by people of his wealth and standing. The readers of 'Sandford and Merton' can imagine what were his reasonings. Miss Milnes, who was not only rich but highly accomplished, fell with the utmost readiness into his notions and plans. Mr. Edgeworth says, 'My wife,' - the celebrated Honora Sneyd, to whom the unfortunate Major Andre had been attached -

'and I went to see the new married couple at Hampstead. It was the depth of winter; the ground was covered with snow, and to our great surprise we found Mrs. Day walking with her husband on the Heath, wrapped up in a frieze cloak, and her feet well fortified with thick shoes. We had always heard that Mrs. Day was particularly delicate; but now she gloried in rude health, or rather was proud of having followed her husband's advice about her health - advice which, in this respect, was undoubtedly excellent.

I never saw any woman so entirely intent upon accommodating herself to the sentiments and wishes and will of a husband. Notwithstanding this disposition, there was still a never-failing flow of discussion between them. From the deepest political investigation, to the most frivolous circumstance of daily life, Mr. Day found something to descant upon; and Mrs. Day was nothing loath to support, upon every subject, an opinion of her own; thus combining, in an unusual manner, independence of sentiment and the most complete matrimonial obedience. In all this there may be something at which even a friend might smile; but in the whole of their conduct there was nothing which the most malignant enemy could condemn.

Mr. Day remained some time at Hampstead, being in no haste to purchase a house; as he thought that by living in inconvenient lodgings, where he was not known, and consequently not visited by anybody except his chosen few, he should accustom his bride to those modes of life which he conceived to be essential to his happiness.'

He afterwards bought a house and small estate, called Stapleford-Abbot, near Alridge, in Essex, to which he proceeded to make additions. He bought at a stall 'Ware's Architecture,' the work of the Mr. Ware who, Park says, lived at Frognal Hall. This he read with persevering industry for three or four weeks before he began his operations; and, though he had now left Hampstead, we may as well see the result, as characteristic of the man:

'Masons calling for supplies of various sorts, which had not been suggested in the great "Body of Architecture," Ware's work, that he had procured with so much care, annoyed the young builder exceedingly. Sills, lintels, door and window-cases, were wanting before they had been thought of; and the carpenter, to whose presence he had looked forward, but at a distant period, was now summoned, and hastily set to work to keep the masons a-going. Mr. Day was deep in a treatise, written by some French agriculturist, to prove that any soil may be rendered fertile by sufficient ploughing, when the mason desired to know where he would have the window of the new room on the first floor. I was present at the question, and offered to assist my friend. No; he sat immovable in his chair, and gravely demanded of the mason whether the wall might not be built first, and a place for the window cut out afterwards. The mason stared at Mr. Day with an expression of the most unfeigned surprise. "Why, Sir, to be sure, it is very possible; but I believe, Sir, it is more common to put in the window-cases while the house is building, and not afterwards."

Mr. Day, however, with great coolness, ordered the wall to be built without any openings for windows, which was done accordingly; and the addition which was made to the house was actually finished, leaving the room, which was intended as a dressing-room for Mrs. Day, without any window whatsoever. When it was sufficiently dry, the room was papered; and for some time candles were lighted in it whenever it was used. So it remained for two or three years; afterwards, Mr. Day used it as a lumber-room; and at last the house was sold, without any window having been opened in this apartment.'

This remarkable but eccentric man was killed a few years after this date in following out one of his humane ideas. He had observed that horses were often treated with much brutality by common horse-breakers. He therefore undertook the breaking of one himself. It took fright at someone winnowing corn near the road, plunged, threw him on his head, and killed him instantly.

Romney, the celebrated portrait, ideal, and historic painter, lived some years at Hampstead; but it was not till he began to feel the approaches of old age, and the satiety of his miscellaneous labours on the portraits of the aristocracy, and the scenes of Milton and Shakespeare. His house, in Cavendish Square, had been crowded with fashionable sitters and loungers; he had there painted over and over the peerless beauty of the time - Emma Lyon, the more celebrated Lady Hamilton, and fascinator of Nelson. He had made his summer flights to Eartham, and conversed at the house of Hayley with the poet Cowper, Miss Seward, Charlotte Smith, and others of that time. Amongst his sitters he had seen Flaxman, Warren Hastings, Mrs. Eitzherbert, Lord Thurlow, and most of the ministers of State; the archbishops, and many dukes and nobles; John Wesley, Mrs. Tighe, Mrs. Jordan, Chatham, Bishop Porteus, Paley, Dr. Parr, Bishop Watson, and Thomas Paine - certainly a grand variety of characters. His house was now crowded with finished, and, still more, with unfinished paintings; but, though thus full of his works, was uncheered by the presence of his excellent and affectionate wife, whom, from his first coming to London from his native north (he was a native of Beckside, near Dalton, Lancashire), he had never invited to join him. In this condition, full of fame and wealth, but not of self-satisfaction, he fancied that what he needed was an ample gallery for his paintings in a quieter scene. `This structure,' says Allan Cunningham,

'he determined to build within a few miles of London; and, true to the character assigned him by Hayley, of obeying impulses, he forthwith purchased the ground, lined out the site, and began to draw the plans. He was not the first nor the last of our eminent artists whose love of brick and mortar proved a source of amusement to their friends, and disquietude to themselves.'

Romney was now 60 years of age, and evidently not the man he had been. Old friends were dying off, and leaving the shadows of their memory on his sensitive mind. Yet this same mind was teeming with magnificent designs. Writing to Hayley, he says:

'I have formed a plan of painting the "Seven Ages;" and also the visions of Adam with the angel; to bring in the Flood, and the opening of the Ark, which would make six large pictures. Indeed, to tell you the truth, I have made designs for all the pictures; and very grand subjects they are. My plan is, if I live, and retain my senses and sight, to paint six other subjects from Milton - three where Satan is the hero, and three from Adam and Eve - perhaps six of each. I have ideas of them all, and, I may say, sketches; but, alas! I cannot begin them for a year or two; and if my name was mentioned, I should hear nothing but abuse, and that I cannot bear. Fear has always been my enemy; my nerves are now too weak for supporting anything in public.'

And now several events occurred which shook still more his shattered nerves. Gibbon, the historian, whom he knew and esteemed, died unexpectedly, exclaiming, 'Mon Dieu! - bon Dieu!' and Cowper, whom he loved next to Hayley, had fallen once more into his most melancholy and despairing insanity. He sought relief from his own feelings under these losses in the Isle of Wight, and in Hampshire; and the meeting with Warton, the poet, who praised warmly his cartoons in chalk, illustrating the 'Persians' of Æschylus, and the return of Flaxman from Rome, greatly restored his spirits for a time. Hayley had also discovered a 'Correggio' and a 'Salvator Rosa' at Teddington, and drove him out to see them; and the view of them seemed to act as a cordial to him. But there were causes, I imagine, in his constitution at this period, which soon overpowered these temporary amenities. We find Allan Cunningham thus speaking of him in 1797:

'The strange new studio and dwelling-house, which he had planned and raised at Hampstead, had an influence on his studies, his temper, and his health. He had expended a year, and a sum of 2,733*l* on an odd and whimsical structure, in which there was nothing like domestic accommodation, though there was a wooden arcade for a riding-house in the garden, and a very extensive picture and statue gallery. The moment the plasterers and joiners had ceased working, before the walls were even half dry, this impatient man of genius had bade farewell to Cavendish Square, after a residence there of 21 years; and, arranging his pictures and statues in his new gallery, and setting up his easels for commencing the historical compositions for which all this travail had been undergone, imagined that a new hour of glory was come.

A new hour had indeed come; but it was of a darker kind. To those not intimate with Romney he still appeared vigorous in frame, and strong in mind, and likely to reach an advanced age in full possession of all his faculties. He was now some sixty-four years old, and had acquired a high name; was rich enough to please himself in his mode of life, and master of his own time, and of a gallery which combined the treasures of ancient art with some of the best of the modem. All that seemed wanting now was for the painter to dip his brush in historical colours, and give a visible existence to some of those magnificent pictures with which his imagination teemed. He set up his easels, put his colours in order, and then, stretching himself on a sofa, gazed down upon London, which, with its extensive roofs and numerous domes and spires, lay far and wide before him. The old demon of nervous dejection had waited for the moment of apparent satisfaction and opening glory, to stoop once more on his prey. Hayley heard of his condition, and, though needing consolation himself, from the illness of a promising son, he hastened to see him. `I found Romney,' says the poet,

> `much dejected in his new mansion on the hill of Hampstead, for want of occupation and society; I advised him to employ himself a little with his pencil, and offered to sit with him merely for his amusement. He began a head - the first attempted in his new painting-room - and, though his hand shook a little, yet he made a very creditable beginning, and thus pleased himself. The next morning he advanced his sketch more happily, as the very effort of beginning to work again, under the encouragement of an old friend, seemed to have done him great good.'

But the effect was only temporary. Hayley, after several visits, and much laudable exertion to cheer his friend, found that his constitution and his mind were really sinking together. In another visit by Hayley, in April of 1799, the ravages of the internal enemy were much more sadly apparent on the painter. In the summer of that year, Romney could neither enjoy the face of nature, nor feel pleasure in his studio and gallery; he had made a grand mistake in thus quitting London, with its society and excitements, as a solitary man. The approaches to Hampstead were then very different from what they are in these omnibus and railway days. His old associates failed to reach him, and the man who had so coolly left behind in his youth an amiable and affectionate wife, found himself a neglected and dejected hermit amid his artistic grandeur. His biographer says,

> `A visible mental languor sat upon his brow, not diminishing but increasing. He had laid aside his pencils; his swarms of titled sitters, whose smiles in other days rendered passing time so agreeable, had moved off to a Lawrence, a Shee, or a Beeehey; and, thus left lonely and disconsolate, among whole cart-loads of paintings, which he had not the power to complete, his gloom and his weakness gathered upon him. Hayley was at a distance, and came not; and as the sinking man was considered a sort of enemy or rival to the Royal Academy, few of

its members appeared to soothe or cheer him. In these moments his heart and his eye turned towards the north, where his son, a man affectionate and kind, resided; and where his wife, surviving the cold neglect and long estrangement of her husband, lived yet to prove the depth of woman's love, and show to the world that she would have been more than worthy of appearing at his side, even when earls sat for their pictures, and Lady Hamilton was enabling him to fascinate princes, with his Calypsos and Cassandras. Romney, without disclosing his intentions to any one, departed from Hampstead, and, taking the northern coach, arrived among his friends at Kendal in the summer of 1799. The exertion of travelling, and the presence of her whom he once had warmly loved, overpowered him; he grew more languid and more weak, and, finding fireside happiness - to which all other human joy is but casual or weak - he resolved to remain where he was, purchased a house, and authorised the sale of that on Hampstead Hill, which had cost him so much in peace and purse.'

Such is the melancholy narrative of George Romney's five years' residence at Hampstead. It was as happy as that of a man deserved to be, who deserted a wife whom he professed warmly to love, in the early years of their marriage, paid her only two visits in thirty years, and then fled to her for comfort when the rest of the world, amid fame and riches, could afford him none. The house which he built, and thus inhabited, I am informed, stood on Windmill Hill, but the gallery has been pulled down. It is most probably the house standing in a garden just behind Bolton House, the one inhabited by Joanna Baillie.

The story of his after-life is soon told. His admirable wife received him without a reproach, and nursed him with tender assiduity. In his letters he spoke of her attentions in terms of the tenderest gratitude. In the soothing care of this noble consort, and the affection of their son, Romney continued to sink. In 1800 his brother, Colonel Romney, to whom he was much attached, arrived from abroad; but he scarcely recognised him, burst into a flood of tears, and then forgot both him and all else that he loved in the world. He died on November 15, 1802, when nearly sixty-eight years of age, at Kendal, but was buried at Dalton, his native place.

The works of Romney, finished and unfinished, are extremely numerous. His portraits of distinguished persons alone amount to nearly forty. He painted Lady Hamilton fourteen times, in various characters - Iphigenia, St. Cecilia, Cassandra, Calypso, Joan of

Arc, a Pythian princess, &c. Of unfinished subjects from Milton, Shakespeare, Spenser, classical mythology and common life, the list is thirty eight. Part of these were presented by his son to the Fitzwilliam Museum at Cambridge, and the rest to the Liverpool Institution. Of the character of his paintings we cannot give a more correct or just idea than that drawn of it by Flaxman:

> `His compositions, like those of the ancient pictures and basso-rilievos, told their story by a single group of figures in the front; while the background is made the simplest possible, rejecting all unnecessary episode and trivial ornament, either of secondary groups or architectural subdivision. In his compositions the beholder was forcibly struck by the sentiment at the first glance, the gradations and varieties of which he traced through several characters, all conceived in an elevated spirit of dignity and beauty, with a lively expression of nature in all the parts. His heads were various: the male were decided and grand, the female lovely; his figures resembled the antique: the limbs were elegant and finely formed; his drapery was well understood, either forming the figure into a mass, with one or two deep folds only, or, by its adhesion and transparency, discovering the form of the figure, the lines of which were finely varied with the union of spiral or cascade folds, composing with, or contrasting, the outline and chiaro-oscuro. Few artists since the fifteenth century have been able to do so much in so many different branches; for besides his beautiful compositions and pictures, which have added to the knowledge and celebrity of the English school, he modelled like a sculptor, carved ornaments in wood with great delicacy, and could make an ornamental design in a fine taste, as well as construct every part of the building.'

Mrs. Tierney, the mother of the once popular member of Parliament, the Hon. George Tierney, has a tablet to her memory in the south aisle of the church. Probably this tablet was erected by her daughter, who married Abraham Robarts, Esq., of North End, partner in the house of Robarts, Curtis, Robarts, and Curtis, bankers. Date 1806.

Mrs. Dorothea Baillie, widow of the Rev. James Baillie, Professor of Divinity at Glasgow, and mother of Dr. Matthew Baillie and of Joanna Baillie, the poetess, died at Hampstead September 29, 1806.

Dame Joanna Watson and Chief Justice Watson: Dame Joanna Watson was the relict of Sir James Watson, who succeeded Sir

William Jones as Chief Justice of India. Dame Watson died at Hampstead, May 7, 1811. The fortunes of Chief Justice Watson are worth recording. He was the son of a Dissenting minister in Southwark, and was educated for the same profession. He became pastor of a little Dissenting flock at Gosport, but grievously offended their sanctity by handing a young lady across the street, who was not one of his congregation. Probably this was the lady whom he afterwards married, a Miss Burgess, for we are told that his father-in-law insisted that he should leave so fanatical a flock, and devote himself to the law, which he did with such success that, through the influence of his father-in-law with Lord Mansfield, he rose rapidly, became M.P. for Bedford, greatly distinguished himself on the board of directors of the India House, and finally succeeded to the judicial seat of the celebrated Sir William Jones, as Chief Justice of India. The little rigid flock of Gosport Dissenters must have gazed in wonder at the soaring rise of their snubbed and catechised young pastor.

William Collins, the Painter: Amongst the various eminent artists who have added to the historic interest of Hampstead by residing in it, we find the celebrated William Collins, the painter of 'The Sale of the Pet Lamb,' 'May Day,' 'The Bird Catchers,' 'The Fisherman's Departure,' 'The Prawn Fisher,' and a host of inimitable sea-side and rural pictures; the friend of Sir David Wilkie, and the father of the present great novelist - in whose name those of the two famous painter-friends unite - Wilkie Collins.

Collins, according to family tradition, descended from the same stock as Collins the poet. His father was a picture-dealer. One of Collins's earlier pictures was 'The Bird Catchers,' and we are told that he used to go out into the fields, sometimes into the Regent's Park, to study the London bird catchers and all their apparatus; and that he finished the landscape of the piece by study of Hampstead Heath. As fame and interruptions grew upon him, he took a cottage at Hampstead in 1823, when he was about thirty five, living quietly there with his wife, and studying the scenery of the neighbourhood to his heart's content. In earlier life he had rambled about this neighbourhood and Highgate with George Morland, and this, no doubt, had given him a great liking for it. In fact, we find, when commencing his career, as a boy, he would fly off to Hampstead in any artistic difficulty, and conquer it by a close and mechanical delineation of grass, trees, leaves, or whatever was the subject which puzzled him. His first introduction to Morland is thus related by his son, Mr. Wilkie Collins:

> 'On being told by his father that Morland was in the house, he opened the kitchen door by a sort of instinct, and looked cautiously in. On two old chairs, placed by the smouldering fire, sat, or rather lolled, two men, both sunk in the heavy sleep of intoxication. The only light in the room was a small rush candle, which imperfectly displayed the forms of the visitors. One, in spite of the ravages of dissipation, was still a remarkably handsome man, both in figure and face. The other was of immense stature and strength, coarse, and almost brutal in appearance. The first was George Morland; the second, a celebrated prize-fighter of the day, who was the painter's chosen companion at the time.'

We shall soon see Morland at the 'Bull' inn at Highgate, selling there his pictures for his entertainment; and his habits of life - rambling, painting, and drinking - are well known. Notwithstanding, William Collins had such a reverence for the man, on account of his genius, that when Morland died, in 1804, and Collins was consequently sixteen, he attended his funeral in the burial ground of St. James's Chapel, Hampstead Road; and after the people were gone, he thrust his stick into the wet earth as far as it would go, carried it carefully home, and when it was dry, varnished it. 'He kept it,' says Mr. Kirton, one of his friends, 'as long as I knew him, and had much veneration for it.'

With this John Kirton, as a youth, he used to ramble, accompanied often by his father and his brother, Francis Collins, from Highgate to Willesden; and Collins was always looking out for bits of scenery à la Morland. When the others were ahead, they would call out, `Bill, here's another sketch for Morland,' which was sure to bring him up. They went to the public house where Morland painted the sign, to eat bread and cheese, and drink porter; and they clambered over hedges, ditches, and brick-fields, to look at the yard where Morland used to keep his pigs, rabbits, &c., and where Morland used to give him lessons.

When Collins settled at Hampstead he was in the zenith of his fame, and acquainted with nearly all the eminent painters of the time, as well as the great patrons of Art. Leslie, Howard, Wilkie, Danby, Sir Thomas Lawrence, Washington Allston, were amongst his intimate friends; amongst literary men, James Smith, of the 'Rejected Addresses,' Bernard Barton, Coleridge, Wordsworth, Southey; amongst his earnest patrons were Sir Thomas Heathcote, his earliest and best; Sir George Beaumont, Lords Liverpool, Lansdowne, De Tabley, Sir Robert Peel, the Duke of Newcastle, the Prince Regent, &e. He had already visited Devonshire, the Lakes, Scotland, so that he had seen a considerable variety of scenery. Before settling at Hampstead he had spent the summers there, and at Hendon, whence he used to run over to Highgate to see Coleridge, whose gifted daughter, Sara, he had made a charming portrait of at Southey's, and where he found continually some of the famous men of the time, who assembled there to hear the poet's wonderful talk. Amongst these was Edward Irving. Great, and deservedly great, as was Coleridge's reputation, we find him complaining, like Beethoven, that in the midst of his fame he was solitary. 'God knows,' he says, in a letter to Collins,

'I have so few friends, that it would he unpardonable in me not to feel proportionably grateful towards those who do not think the time wasted in which they interest themselves on my behalf. There is an old Latin adage, "Vis videri pauper, et pauper es" - Poor you profess yourself to be, and poor, therefore, you are, and will remain. The prosperous feel only with the prosperous; and if you subtract from the whole sum of their feeling for all the gratifications of vanity, and all their calculations of lending to the Lord, both of which are best answered by conferring of their superfluities on advertised and advertisable distress, - or on such as are known to be in all respects their inferiors, - you will have, I fear, but a scanty remainder.'

All this is too true; but then, what is that man to do whom no distress can bribe to swindle or deceive, who cannot reply, as Theophilus Cibber did to his father, Colley Cibber, who, seeing him in a rich suit of clothes, whispered to him as he passed, 'Thee, Thee, I pity thee!' 'Pity me! pity my tailor!'

Collins dates from North End, Hampstead, where Wilkie describes his house as a beautiful cottage, and from Hampstead Green. He afterwards removed to another house, a large one near the Heath. During his residence at Hampstead, he made excursions to Boulogne, and into Belgium and Holland. Amongst the pictures painted here, the chief were 'Stirling Castle;' 'The Cherry Seller;'

'Scene at Tuvy Castle;' 'Buckland, on the River Dart;' 'Kitly, Devon;' 'Fishermen getting out their Nets;' 'Buying Fish on the Beach;' 'Prawn Fishers at Hastings;' 'The Fisherman's Departure;' 'Young Shrimp Catchers;' the celebrated 'Frost Scene,' painted for Sir Robert Peel; 'Morning after a Storm;' 'Summer Moonlight;' 'Fisher Children.' After his visit to Boulogne, 'Les Causeuses;' 'Waiting the Arrival of Fishing Boats;' 'Coast of France,' and 'Mussel Gatherers.'

His biographer says,

'Amongst his difficulties in prosecuting his art here was that of obtaining a sight of a real pillion. Among the figures introduced in his composition of the "Frost Scene," were a man and woman mounted on a pillion (or rather, I should imagine, a saddle and pillion). All Hampstead was ransacked without success for this old-fashioned article of travelling equipment; and the painter - determined, even in the minor accessories of his picture, to trust to nothing but nature - had begun to despair of finishing his group, when a lady volunteered to hunt out a pillion for him, in the neighbourhood of Hackney, where she lived. Nor, when she had procured it, did she remain satisfied with simply obtaining the model. When the painter arrived to see it, he found her ready to demonstrate its use. Her gardener hired an old horse, strapped on the pillion, and mounted it. [Mounted into the saddle, no doubt, in front of the pillion. It is clear that the biographer never saw the saddle and pillion, as I remember them well in use, having often ridden with a lady behind me on a pillion.] His mistress placed herself in the proper position, behind; the complete series of models, however, animal and mechanical, remaining at the painter's disposal until he had made a careful study of the whole. The group thus completed, was one of the most admired in the picture for its fidelity to nature.'

At Hampstead his two sons were born. The after-life of Collins does not belong to Hampstead, which he quitted in 1830, taking a house at Bayswater. I may close my notice of this great artist and genuine lover of nature, by observing, that from the list of his works given by his son at the end of his Life, Collins, in the course of forty years, produced 220 pictures, which sold for about £35,000, besides water-colour pieces, and between seven and eight hundred drawings, studies, and sketches, which were sold by auction by Christie and Manson after his death. Probably he made in all about £40,000, or about £1,500 a year for that time. Those paintings would now fetch double the price, I should imagine.

Sir David Wilkie was not a resident in Hampstead, but on one occasion a visitor there in search of health. We must not, therefore, say more about him, or his well-known works, further than the mere record of this little episode in his life demands. In September, 1810, Sir David, having been much out of health, was recommended by his physician, Dr. Matthew Baillie, to take lodgings in the clear air of Hampstead for a while. As Dr. Baillie's mother and sisters had resided there many years, he was well acquainted with the healthy character of this retreat. Joanna Baillie and her sister Agnes, with their usual kindness, offered Sir David the use of their house during a proposed absence of three months. This offer was accepted by him. But as the house of his friends was not at liberty so soon as he wished to get there, he went into lodgings, and during that time, no doubt, it was that he had lodgings on Hampstead Green. On the 12th of September, we find Sir David entering on the Misses Baillie's house on Windmill Hill, which he says was provided with every comfort, and was in a pleasant part of the town; that they had left their servants to attend him, a number of books to read, and had not forgotten, besides, some jelly, marmalade, and Scottish cheese. With all these, he says,

> 'I have such open fields to walk in, and fresh air to breathe, that I have improved in health most wonderfully since I came here; and I have not only the prospect of getting rid of my complaint, but of establishing a stock of strength for the time to come.'

Sir David lived more than thirty years after this, and died, and was buried the same day, at sea, on his return from Constantinople, in Gibraltar Bay, on June 11, 1841.

John Constable, a disciple of Gainsborough and Wilson, was fond of Hampstead, and one of his paintings of the Heath is considered by Pilkington to be the loveliest that he ever executed. A thunderstorm is rushing over it, and driving a group of gipsies, with their asses and panniers, and tawny children, to the rough shelter of a gravel-pit. Constable, according to the inscription on his tomb, at the bottom south-east corner of Hampstead Churchyard, was born in 1776, at East Berghold, in Suffolk, and not at Farringdon, as stated in the memoir of him in Bryan's 'Dictionary of Painters.' He lived, at the latter part of his life, at No. 6 Well Walk, according to Leslie, but by others at No. 5. Whichever was the exact house, it is one of the row between the Wells Tavern and the Assembly House.

Constable's mode of painting was peculiar, and his landscapes have a curious spotty appearance. He neither imitated the ancient nor the modern masters, notwithstanding his being said to be a disciple of Wilson and Gainsborough. His belief was that he copied only nature, but certainly he did not do this in the peculiarity which I have mentioned. This singularity, however, makes his pictures striking, and marks them from all others. His skies are cloudy, and his clouds turbulent. They are charged with thunder, lightning, and rain; and when the shower falls, instead of verdant freshness, his trees and meadows are covered with flakes of snow. These traits have both their admirers and censurers. His favourite subjects were views of water-mills, landscapes after a shower, boats threading locks, lake scenery, moonlights, views of Hampstead Heath, with impending storms and heavy showers of rain.

Constable was a Royal Academician, and in private life was much esteemed for the good qualities of his head and heart. He died suddenly in London, without pain, March 31, 1837. On his tomb it is stated that his wife and two children are also interred there; and that his eldest son died at Jesus College, Cambridge, at the age of twenty three, and lies buried in the chapel of that college. Several of his paintings are in South Kensington Museum, and one, purchased by some students in honour of his memory, was presented to the National Gallery.

Sir William Beechey, says Pilkington's 'Dictionary,' 'had a house at Hampstead, and died and was buried there.' Sir William lived some time at the house on the Upper Terrace, formerly occupied by Mr. John Jackson, and now by Mr. Johnson, of the firm of Jean and Johnson, London. At another time he lived at the house of Mrs. Innes, his daughter, on Red Lion Hill, Hampstead, now occupied by Messrs. Cock and Co., surgeons.

Sir William was a portrait painter, a native of Burford in Oxfordshire, born there in 1753. He became an academician, and was patronised by George III, and shared also in the favour of the nobility, with the most eminent of his contemporaries in the same branch of art. He painted, in 1798, a review of the Horse Guards, in which the portraits of George III and the Prince of Wales were introduced, and for which he was knighted. He at one time attempted fancy subjects; but whether he found his mind not suited to the regions of poetry, or that the painting of good likenesses was more profitable, he did not pursue it with any great ardour. He died in 1839. This is about all that appears known of him, beyond incidental mentions in the memoirs of contemporary artists; and I regret not to be able to make this notice more complete.

Crabbe the Poet: Hampstead Heath was for many years a great resort of this most descriptive of all English poets. Whenever he came to London from Trowbridge, he took up his quarters at Mr. Samuel Hoare's, the banker. Campbell the poet, writing to Crabbe's son and biographer, says,

> 'The last time I saw Crabbe was when I dined with him at Mr. Hoare's at Hampstead. He very kindly came with me to the coach, to see me off, and I never pass that spot on the top of Hampstead Heath without thinking of him.'

From Mr. Hoare's hospitable mansion Crabbe used to drop down conveniently to London, and circulate amongst his great aristocratic acquaintance, amongst whom he enumerates the Duke and Duchess of Rutland, Earl and Countess Spencer, the Lansdownes, Lords Strangford, Dundas, Lord and Lady Besborough, Lord and Lady Holland, Duke and Duchess of Cumberland, Lord and Lady Binning, Lord and Lady Errol, Sir Harry Englefield, Canning, Moore, Freere, Brougham, and a vast many more of the magnates of both rank and literature. Sometimes he stayed to sleep at Holland House, sometimes to breakfast with Rogers. Bowles the poet, in a letter to Crabbe's son, claims the introduction of Crabbe to the 'Hoares of Hampstead,' with whom he was subsequently so intimate, and who contributed so much to the happiness of all his later days. The Rev. George Crabbe, junior, says,

> 'During his first and second visits to London, my father spent a good deal of his time beneath the hospitable roof of the late Samuel Hoare,

Esq., on Hampstead Heath. He owed his introduction to this respectable family to his friend Mr. Bowles, and the author of the delightful "Excursions in the West," Mr. Warner; and though Mr. Hoare was an invalid, and little disposed to form new connections, he was so much gratified with Mr. Crabbe's manners and conversation, that their acquaintance soon grew into an affectionate and lasting intimacy. Mr. Crabbe in subsequent years made Hampstead his headquarters on his spring visits, and only repaired thence occasionally to the brilliant circles of the metropolis.'

After the death of Mr. Hoare, Crabbe became still more attached to Mrs. Hoare and the other members of the family, and we find him travelling with them to the Isle of Wight, Hastings, Ilfracombe, or Clifton. At Clifton the Hoares had a house, and there Crabbe used to domesticate himself occasionally. At Hampstead he used to see Coleridge, a frequent guest at Mr. Hoare's, Joanna Baillie, Wilberforce, Miss Edgeworth, and Mrs. Siddons, and, dining in turn at Rogers's, Mr. Murray's, his publisher, or at Holland House, could meet Wordsworth and Southey; on another occasion he met Horace Smith, of the 'Rejected Addresses' who dubbed him 'Pope in worsted stockings.' In one of his letters, dated from Hampstead, June 1825, he says,

> 'My time passes I cannot tell how pleasantly. To-day I read one of my long stories to my friends, and Mrs. Joanna Baillie and her sister. It was a task, but they encouraged me, and were, or seemed, gratified. I rhyme at Hampstead with a great deal of facility, for nothing interrupts me but kind calls, or something pleasant.'

The simplicity of Crabbe's character is amusingly shown in a letter from Joanna Baillie:

> 'While he was staying with Mrs. Hoare a few years since, I sent him one day the present of a blackcock, and a message with it, that Mr. Crabbe should look at the bird before it was delivered to the cook, or something to that purpose. He looked at the bird, as desired, and then went to Mrs. Hoare, in some perplexity, to ask whether he ought not to have it stuffed, instead of eating it. She could not, in her own house, tell him that it was simply intended for the larder, and he was at the trouble and expense of having it stuffed, lest I should think proper respect had

not been paid to my present. This both vexed and amused me at the time, and was remembered as a pleasing and peculiar trait of his character.'

In closing this notice of Crabbe at Hampstead, I may remark how many people of note we find recording, or having recorded for them, the pleasure they enjoyed in rambling on Hampstead Heath. Haydon relates calling on Leigh Hunt, with Wordsworth, in May 1815, and afterwards strolling on the Heath with the poet of Cumberland:

`I sauntered on to West-End Lane, and so on to Hampstead, with great delight. Never did any man beguile the time as Wordsworth. His purity of heart, his kindness, his soundness of principle, his information, and the intense and eager feelings with which he pours forth all he knows, affect, interest, and enchant me.'

Haydon, in fact, was fond of endeavouring to escape from the weight of cares which continually oppressed him, by a ramble on the Heath, where the face of uncultured nature, the verdurous avenues, the far views over the country, and the vast stretch of the metropolis below, with its clouds of rolling smoke, presented him with grand pictorial effects. In July of 1830, he writes in his diary:

'Walked to Hampstead with dear Frank, and enjoyed the air and sweet-scented meadows. Thought of the poor prisoners in the Bench, B___ and others, who would have liked this rural stroll. The thought of what I have seen, and what I have suffered, always gives a touch of melancholy to my enjoyments.'

Joanna Baillie, the powerful dramatic writer, graceful and witty lyrist, and sweet and gentle woman, lived many years at Hampstead, in Bolton House, on Windmill Hill, a little below the Clock House, the residence of the late Miss Montgomery. Perhaps no person of literary distinction ever led a more secluded and unambitious life so near the metropolis. In the society of her sister, Miss Agnes Baillie, she seemed to care little whether the world forgot her or not. But of this forgetfulness there was no danger. Every man of pre-eminent genius delighted to do her honour, and to commemorate in their works the name of Joanna Baillie. She was, as already observed, the sister of the amiable and excellent Dr. Matthew Baillie, and was born at the pretty manse of Bothwell, near Bothwell Brig, in the fertile vale of the Clyde, and amid scenes famous in the history and the romance of Scotland. The manse of Bothwell looks directly down upon the scene of the battle of Bothwell Brig. Hear Bothwell lies also Bothwell Castle, equally poetical in the works of Scottish poets, and in its own charming situation. About a mile farther, across the Brig, stands the ducal palace of Hamilton in its beautiful park. Miss Baillie, however, only lived four years of her infancy at Bothwell. After the death of her father, who had removed to Glasgow to occupy the chair of divinity, she lived with her family in the moorlands of Kilbride, and then came to England. For many years she lived at Hampstead, visited by nearly all the great writers of the age. Sir Walter Scott, as may be seen in his letters addressed to her, delighted to make himself her guest; and on her visit to Edinburgh, in 1806, she spent some time at his house there. Sir Walter planted a bower of pineasters at Abbotsford in honour of her, from seed which she furnished, and raised Joanna's Bower. Through his means her drama, the 'Family Legend,' was brought out at Edinburgh by Mr. Henry Siddons. The last time that I saw the poet Rogers he was returning from a call on Joanna Baillie. This novel-reading age, I believe, is almost a stranger to her dramas, but they will still continue to charm such poetical readers as can appreciate vigour of conception, healthy nobility of sentiment, and a clear and masterly style. Joanna Baillie died February 23, 1851, and is interred in Hampstead Churchyard beside her mother, who had also reached the venerable age of 86.

The tomb of Joanna Baillie is one of those altar-tombs standing in a row near the east end of the churchyard, and not far below the gate. It records that the mother, Dorothy Baillie, widow of the Rev. James Baillie, above mentioned, died at Hampstead in 1806, aged 86 years. Joanna Baillie, her daughter, born in 1762, died February 23, 1851, aged 89. Agnes Baillie, the elder sister of Joanna, is buried in the same tomb. She was born September 24, 1760, and died at Hampstead, April 27, 1861, aged 100 years and 7 months. The Baillies were clearly a remarkably long-lived family.

THE WEDGWOOD VIEWS OF
HAMPSTEAD AND HIGHGATE

In 1773, Wedgwood, the great potter of Etruria, in Staffordshire, and a great improver of the English taste in pottery, executed a grand dinner and dessert service for the notorious Catherine, Empress of Russia. The account of this important work is found in Miss Meteyard's 'Life of Wedgwood,' vol. ii. p. 273. Before Wedgwood's time Russia had been chiefly supplied with porcelain from France and Saxony, but Lord Cathcart introduced to the notice of the Empress the beautiful works of Wedgwood, and she not only adorned her palace with the finest vases, bas-reliefs, and gems, which Wedgwood and Bentley had yet produced, but through the British consul she ordered these magnificent services. As the King of Prussia was having two services of Dresden china executed, one of which he intended as a present to the Czarina, and which was, therefore, to be embellished by battle-scenes betwixt the Russians and Turks, and the other for himself, to exhibit the most remarkable views and landscapes in his own dominions, the Empress proposed that these services by Wedgwood should be enriched with English scenes. For this purpose, not only were copies made of paintings of English mansions, castles, gardens, and landscapes already existing in the galleries of the royal family, of nobles and gentry, but artists were employed to make designs of the most remarkable places in the kingdom. The services were completed in the most costly and perfect style, and were for some time publicly exhibited at the rooms of Wedgwood and Bentley, in Greek Street, Soho, where they were seen by Queen Charlotte and crowds of the nobility, and thus added greatly to the fame of the potter. Amongst the views given, no fewer than twenty seven were from the vicinity of Hampstead and Highgate - the majority from Hampstead. The individual articles in the services amounted to upwards of 1,100 pieces, and the cost was £3,000. Each piece was numbered, and a catalogue, now rare, of the whole, drawn up in French. From this we take the account of the views of Hampstead and Highgate literally, as given there:

492. Vue de la Grande Salle à Hampstead, dans le Comté de Middlesex.
493. Autre vue de la même salle.
494. Autre vue du même endroit.
495. Vue d'une partie d'Hampstead, du haut de la Bruyère.
496. Vue de la Promenade du Puits à Hampstead.
497. Vue du marais qui est au bas de la Bruyère à Hampstead.
498. Vue du même objet.
499. Vue d'une partie de Highgate, auprès de Londres.
622. Vue d'une partie d'Hampstead, depuis la rue du Marais.
623. Autre vue d'Hampstead.
624. Autre vue d'Hampstead.
625. Autre vue d'Hampstead.
626. Vue d'un gros village auprès de Highgate.
627. Vue d'Hampstead, du jardin de M. Holford.
628. Autre vue d'Hampstead.
629. Autre vue d'Hampstead.
834. Vue de Pancras et d'une partie de Hampstead.
854. Vue d'une partie de Hampstead.
855. Vue de la grande Salle à Hampstead.
856. Autre vue de Hampstead.
858. Vue de Highgate.
859. Autre vue du même endroit.
862. Vue de la route de Hampstead.
956. Vue auprès de Hampstead.
958. Vue auprès de Hampstead.
959. Autre vue du même endroit.
116. Vue auprès de Highgate.

In this catalogue, the 'marais au has de la Bruyère' is, no doubt, the pond in the Vale of Health; the 'Promenade du Puits' is Well Walk; and the 'rue du Marais 'Pond Street; but we query whether the 'gros village auprès de Highgate' should not be 'Highgate, gros village auprès de Hampstead.' If not, how did the cataloguer happen not to know the name of the 'gros village,' which must he Holloway, Hornsey, or Kentish Town?

In concluding our notices of Hampstead, we ought also to inform the naturalist and archaeologist, that in the possession of Mr. Dutton, the steward of Sir Thomas Maryon Wilson, at the office of the estate, are a number of curious relics of the past, which were found in digging out the foundations of the aqueduct on Sir Thomas's property on the north-east side of the Heath. Amongst these are several celts, some of stone, others of bronze; a number of fine large agates; part of a large antler of a deer; part of a wild boar's tusk; a number of rusty keys - some of mediaeval form, others apparently picklocks; a considerable number of coins - the greater part of them of modern date - as halfpence, and even a crooked sixpence; a fleam for bleeding cattle; a fish's tooth - apparently a shark's; old rings; a human skull with two holes knocked into it - one in front, one at the back - but whether by the bludgeon of an assassin or the pick of the navvy, there is no means of knowing. The place where the skull was found, however, indicates a murder or a suicide. A careful and scientific examination of these remains might give some interesting results; but many of them, as the modern halfpence, would seem to have been slung into the water in idle pastime.

Whilst this is passing through the press, the following appears in the Times:

'The other day, while engaged in digging the foundations of the new Home for Sailors' Orphans between Church Row and High Street, Hampstead, a working man came upon a leaden coin, about two feet below the surface, in a bed of loam and clay. It is about an inch and a half in diameter, and on inspection it turns out to be a "bull" of Pope Innocent IV, one of the well-known family of Fiesco, who sat in the chair of St. Peter from A.D. 1243 to 1254. The "bull" bears on the reverse the figures of St. Peter and St. Paul, and is in a tolerable state of preservation; and we understand that it is likely to be secured for the British Museum.'

PART II

HISTORICAL ASSOCIATIONS OF HIGHGATE

View of Highgate from the Ponds
(From a photograph taken expressly in November, 1868)

ALL-DEVOURING LONDON

There is no spot in the world more thickly sown with historic memories than London and its environs. If anyone were to set himself to relate the striking incidents attached to the objects which present themselves only from the top of the house which I occupied at Highgate, he would have to write one of the most stirring and extensive narratives that the earth could present. Below, south-eastward, stretches this mighty metropolis, a breathing mass of life, composed of nearly three millions of souls. Far south-westward, up the Thames valley, runs the dense mass of houses; all in the foreground expands the wondrous province of buildings: churches and palaces, domes, and those modern monuments, railway-stations, lift their heads above the brick-and-mortar wilderness. St. Paul's looks out grandly sombre through the rolling sea of smoke, the mingled upcast of domestic fires and of the sooty breath of manufacture. The ancient minster and the modern legislative palace of Westminster tower on his lordly right hand, and around him spire up a host of lesser ecclesiastical dignitaries. On his left hand, but in the background, blazes forth in one great flame, in the afternoon sun, the Crystal Palace; nearer stand up, eastward, the New Cattle Market Tower, and the donjons of Pentonville and Holloway. Far eastward stretches this Titanic London, by Islington, Highbury, Hackney, Tottenham, and still onwards. Over this stupendous expanse of the work of the coral insects of the earth, the housification animals, called builders and bricklayers, still greet us the remains of Epping Forest, but seem to wave us a sorrowful farewell; for Lords of Manors, and Enclosure Commissioners and builders, have long been conspiring its absorption. Here at our feet rises the green swell of Traitor's Hill, where Guy Fawks's comrades stood to see his match send Parliament House, and Parliament, and, if possible, King James, into the air. And there lies Caen Wood, into which they fled when the non-explosion showed the explosion of their own design. The whole of this vast panorama is studded and clustered with the trophies of those great deeds that have made us a great nation; but how many more have been swept away by the rapid advance of this monster development of burnt clay, and buried for ever beneath its dingy piles! Look along the feet of these yet green and smiling hills - east and west, far and wide, comes up, as it were, a giant army to desolate and trample them down. See that front rank of the great house-army far as the eye can reach before you, and on either hand, coming on with a step 'steady as time and inexorable as death.' Already it has covered, with its hosts standing close serried, all the fields south of the Thames - St. George's Fields, Kennington and Vauxhall Fields, and the rest of them; already it has climbed the Surrey Hills, and Brixton and Norwood and Lewisham are one town. Already - but why proceed? - on every side the tide of population has rolled on with brick and mortar in its rear. Our ancestors lamented once the swallowing up of the pleasant villages of Holborn and Charing, and St. Giles-in-the-Fields, and many another rustic little isolation now only a dingy district, in the monotonous province of streets and shops. They lamented in vain. They saw the irresistible progress of wealth and commerce extinguish nature, and tell them to seek their compensation in society and art. Growing pollutions drove the quiet anglers from the pleasant banks of the oak-shadowed Fleet, as they have since from those of the great Thamesis itself.

It is now difficult to imagine that all where this enormous London stands was once the quiet Forest of Middlesex. Yet such was the fact, long after the Norman Conquest. FitzStephen, one of the oldest of our topographers, in his `Survey of the Metroplolis,' written between 1170 and 1182, thus describes its suburbs:

> `There are cornfields, pastures, and delightful meadows, intermixed with pleasant streams, on which stands many a mill whose clack is grateful to the ear. Beyond them, a forest extends itself, beautified with woods and groves, and full of the lairs and coverts of beasts and game, stags, bucks, boars, and wild bulls. These wild bulls were probably buffaloes, or like the beasts of Andalusia, in Spain, which, I presume, are small.'

More probably they were of the same kind as the ancient British race, which Walter Scott, in the `Bride of Lammermoor,' tells us ranged the old Caledonian Forest, and of which herds still remain in the parks of Chartley, in Staffordshire, and of Chillingham, in Northumberland - splendid, though small, white cattle, with black ears and muzzles.

But the Forest of Middlesex, in the heart of which nestled the yet infant London, FitzStephen tells us also,

> ` . . . was full of yew-trees, the growth of which was particularly encouraged in those days, and for many succeeding ages, because the wood of them was esteemed the best for making hows.'

Thus, from the ground over which now tramps the people of London, over which the crowding wagons and omnibuses roll, and under which the railway pours its vital stream, the hardy warriors of Hastings, and probably of Cressy and Agincourt, cut their bows, the death-warrants of French and Franco-Norman.

This charming old forest was, according to Maitland's `History of London,' deforested A.D. 1218, in the reign of Henry III. Already the conqueror, population, more imperious than William of Normandy, began to find itself cramped by boles of trees, and too much in company with game. No doubt, in those days primroses actually grew on Primrose Hill; and flower-girls cried, `Cowslips! sweet cowslips!' gathered on the slopes of Holborn, and 'Beaupots! pretty beaupots!' of blue-bells, wallflowers, and sweet brier, plucked from the thickets of the Strand, or in the meadows of St. Pancras.

Deforested might be the Forest of London; but those fiery times of the Crusades, and the wars of the Barons, were wondrously small times, with all their martial din, if we are to believe the statements of the chroniclers of those days. It was 'the day of small things,' truly, in England, notwithstanding the brave noise that our ancestors made. At the Conquest, the whole population of England was calculated at 2,000,000. In 1377, the last year of the great victor, King Edward III, who conquered Calais, and made France tremble, the population, as ascertained by the capitation tax, had only advanced to 2,290,000 - an increase of not 300,000 people, that is, from 1066, the era of the Conquest, or more than three centuries. Including Wales, the population only reached 2,500,000; so that Wales itself only numbered, towards the end of the fifteenth century, about 200,000 souls. And what was the superb Augusta, the glorious London, at this same time? It boasted 35,000 inhabitants!

No wonder, then, that bluff Henry VIII, though the Forest of Middlesex was deforested, retained a tolerable piece of hunting-ground, and looked after it with all his own mastership of imperial will. Here is one of his proclamations:

'Rex majori et vice-comitibus, London. Vobis mandamus, etc.
Forasmuch as the King's most royall ma^{tie} is much desirous to have the game of hare, partridge, pheasant, and heron, preserved in and about his honor, att his palace of Westm^r for his own disport and pastime; that is to saye, from his said palace of Westm^r to St. Gyles-in-the-Fields, and from thence to Islington, to our Lady of the Oke, to Highgate, to Hornsey Parke, to Hampstead Heath, and from thence to his said palace of Westm^r, to be preserved for his owne disport, pleasure, and recreac'on,' &c.

And he proceeds to denounce the penalties of imprisonment, and further punishment at his will and pleasure, against all who by any means presume to kill game within these precincts.

Thus Henry Tudor sported all over Westminster, and over all London, west and north of the city, including the then solitary and woodland districts of Highgate, Hampstead, Islington, &c. We may suppose, however, that the wolves, wild bulls, boars, and stags had retired further off, for he does not mention them.

His daughter Elizabeth used to frequent Islington and Highgate to hunt and hawk in the vast woods around. She took up her quarters at Canonbury Tower, and her courtiers had houses around it, amid woods and gardens. The residence of Sir Walter Raleigh still remains as the 'Pied Bull' public house, Islington, not very far from the Tower. During her reign, too, Sir John Spencer, Lord Mayor of London, and said to be the richest commoner of England, was lain in wait for by Dunkirk pirates, on the moors betwixt his place of business, St. Helen's Place, in Bishopsgate Street, and Canonbury Tower, to kidnap him for his ransom. They had learned that he rode daily over these moors - now one solid town - to and fro; but a storm keeping him that day in town, they became noticed, and hastened to make off.

Now, in 1575, the latter end of the reign of the great queen, who made Europe tremble, and triumphed over the great Armada, the population of these realms, according to Harrison's 'Description of England,' appears to have been only about 5,000,000; and if we quadruple the population of London from 1377, when it was only 35,000 - a period of less than two hundred years - the metropolis of her powerful kingdom would not exceed 140,000! Yet a terrible fear of its becoming an overgrown, unwieldy, and unmanageable capital,

Moved the stout heart of England's queen,
Though Pope and Spaniard could not trouble it.

What appears to us such a snail's progress was to her and her wise counsellors most alarming. In 1580, only eight years before the appearance of the Armada, she issued her proclamation for stopping the extension of London by new buildings. This proclamation, dated at Nonsuch on the 7th July of that year, sets forth that great inconveniences having arisen from the vast congregations of people in London, and greater being likely to follow - namely, want of victuals, danger of plagues, and other injuries to health - she orders that no further buildings shall be erected, by any class of people, within the limits of the said city, or within three miles from any of its gates; that not more than one family should live in one house, and that such families shall not take inmates. The mayor and corporation are called upon to disperse all such, and to send them away down to their proper places in the country. And any persons violating any of these orders - that is, by building new houses, or even laying down materials for building, or by living more than one family in one house, or by taking inmates - were to be committed to prison, there to remain without bail till they found good security for keeping these regulations. The roads were then in such a state, that there was a reasonable fear of scarcity of provisions; and great stress was laid on the mischief of heaping up many families with children in one house - 'smothered,' says the proclamation, 'with crowds of children and servants in one small tenement.' The majority feared that this wonderful attraction to the capital would cause the decay of the country, and of 'divers auncient good boroughs and towns.' Amongst other mischiefs, her Majesty considered the spirit of gain generated by such a great city one of the most serious, and declared that `all particular persons are bound by God's lawes and man's to forbeare from their particular and extraordinarie lucre.'

The Stuarts were equally haunted by the terrors of the growth of London, and issued repeated and most stringent orders for resisting it. James I had scarcely come to the throne when he ordered all such houses as had been erected contrary to Elizabeth's proclamation to be pulled down and demolished. In one of these proclamations, in 1617, James, the wonderful Scottish Solomon, ordered all noblemen, knights, and gentlemen to go hence with their wives and families to their country houses, and to remain there till they were called again to Parliament. This order he repeated in 1622, and moreover, that when the noblemen and gentlemen, and others who had business in town came up, they should leave their wives and children in the country. The proclamations and orders in council of the Stuarts to this end were numerous, the last being supposed to be that of Charles II in 1674. In one of James I's proclamations he calls the flocking of people to London 'a ricketty distemper in the head of the kingdom which occasioneth a flux of humours to approach the Court.'

Nor was Cromwell a whit the wiser in this respect. In 1656, after many more prohibitions of building in London had been treated with contempt, he ordered a fine of one year's rent against any offender who had erected a house having less than four acres of land attached to it, and of £100 against anyone who had erected a house without land. None of these proclamations were taken the least notice of, and they were looked on as merely a means for the extortion of bribes by the favourites about the Court.

Yet so small was London, and the locomotion in it, that in 1625 there were only twenty hackney coaches in all London and Westminster; but these having increased in 1635, Charles I ordered that no hackney coach should be used for anything but to carry people into and out of London at least three miles - not from one part of town to another, 'because they obstructed the streets and rendered them dangerous to his Majesty, his beloved consort, and the nobility;' as well as rendering hay and provender dear. No more than fifty hackney coachmen were ever allowed; but Cromwell extended them to 200.

During all this time the same war was going on in the city against hawkers and stalls as there is at this day. In 1631, in the time of Charles I, hawkers, stalls, and stands were, however, found to be more numerous than ever. Bakers, butchers, poulterers, chandlers, fruiterers, sempsters, grocers, oyster, herb and tripe women thronged the streets, so that a penalty of 20s. for the first offence, 40s. for the second, and £4 for the third, and for every after offence to be doubled, was decreed. William III continued this war so late as 1695.

Through all these times we find no accurate data for determining the real population of the kingdom or the capital. In 1662 and 1665 the population of England and Wales was calculated by the hearth tax at 6,500,000. In 1670 Sir Matthew Hale calculated it at 7,000,000; yet Haydn, in his 'Dictionary of Dates,' says that in 1700 it was found by official returns to be only 5,475,000. The population of London and its suburbs was calculated by Sir William Petty, in 1687, to be 696,000; and Gregory King, in 1697, by the hearth-money, made it 530,000; and yet by actual census in 1801, including Westminster, Southwark, and the adjacent bills, it proved to be only 864,845.

Our ancestors seemed to have been occasionally close on the idea of a census, but never to have arrived at the full idea. Elizabeth, in 1580, eight years before the Armada, had a census of all the foreigners in London, as a measure of precaution, but the full idea of a national numbering on accurate principles was reserved for our time, and the year 1801. Since then a census has been regularly taken every ten years, and by this means we can see to a nicety a progress of population in London that must have driven our Tudor and Stuart kings out of their senses, but which we contemplate with as wonderful an equanimity. From 1801 to 1841 - that is, in forty years - the population of London advanced from 864,000 to 1,873,000. In forty years the metropolis had increased above a million, or more than through all the previous history of the kingdom. In ten years more it had swelled to 2,361,640, or nearly half a million more. Again, in the last census, 1861, it had risen to 2,803,034, or an increase in ten years of 441,394 souls! Very soon we shall have London increasing at the rate of half a million every ten years, an amount of population which it did not reach from the Conquest till the end of the seventeenth century.

Since our colonies, our commerce, and manufactures have expanded into importance, London and the whole population and wealth of the country have expanded and must expand with them. This was the invincible force which first raised the alarm of our kings and queens and then set them at defiance. It was a vain and even a laughable struggle of royal short-sightedness against the vigour of humanity, against the prolific vitality of human enterprise, genius, and indefatigable exertion. Now we see this gigantic power of life revealed before us in its full Titan stature and measureless energy, we no longer wonder that the metropolis spreads itself in every direction like an ocean tide, swallowing fields and meadows, woods and streams, with a voracity that makes old landmarks disappear as mere scratches on the sands of a tidal beach.

Who shall limit this life? Every wind that blows from north or south, east or west, from India, China, America, or Australia, feeds it; every wheel that turns at home, every colonist who digs or watches his flocks at the antipodes, intensifies it. The marrow of London is in the backbone of the world; its blood is the blood of myriad kindred populations; its million hands seize upon the fruits, the corn, the gold, the oil, and wine of every zone. Shall we, like the wise-foolish rulers of our fathers, endeavour to stop it? Shall we stop the sun? All we can do is to exclaim every now and then, 'What will this London grow to!' and make haste to note with a loving glance the old historic footsteps that are about to disappear for ever under the ponderous surge of brick and mortar. Our business in these pages will be, in the first place, to do this for the yet green Highgate Hill. Already the engineer is laying out and planning tunnels to bore it; already the builder is climbing its grassy slopes, and the army of life shows its vast phalanx at its foot with a mien that is unmistakable.

OLD AND NEW ASPECTS

Many an age Highgate, though situated on a conspicuous hill 400 feet above the level of the sea, and within a few miles of the metropolis, continued a mere hamlet of houses, scattered here and there amid the forests. People fond of seclusion located themselves there in profound peace, for no road led through it to anywhere beyond. It was not till the fourteenth century that the Bishop of London allowed a highway to be cut through his park and woods of Harringay, the hare-inge-hagh, or meadow and wood of hares, now condensed into Hornsey. The road used to pass from London northward through Gray's Inn, then called Portepoole, Tallingdone Lane, now Tollington, Crouche Ende, Coanie Hatch, Fryarne Barnet, to Whetstone; but the carriers and wayfarers having worn out that road, and sticking fast in the deep ruts of day, and Macadam not being yet due for some 500 years, they clomb the steep of Highgate, by leave of the Bishop, who, however, had enough of the bishop in him to erect a gate and take his toll. This gate was hung in a stout-built archway, abutting on one hand on an old chapel wall, and on the other on the gatekeeper's house, so that there was no escaping it. This originated, it is said, the name of the place - High-gate. Yet, if Highgate existed before, as some suppose it must have done, what was its name? It has been suggested that Highgate was so called long before the bishop's time, in the fourteenth century, from its being on a road, often anciently called a gate. In the Northern and Midland counties roads are often called gates, but this does not appear to have been the case about London, except where the road or street proceeded from a gate, as Ludgate, Bishopsgate, &c.; and probably, where roads are called gates in other parts of the country, this originates from gates to check the straying of cattle, having stood on them.

We are told that the tall loads of the carriers often could not pass under the Bishop's archway, and so had to take their way through the gatekeeper's yard. The bishopric of London had extensive woods and demesnes beyond this gate, reaching to the gate of Hampstead Heath, now the 'Spaniards Tavern,' right back to Finchley, where the Bishop had a goodly palace or lodge on Lodge Hill, and so down to Hornsey. Many a fat slice has been carved away from this episcopal property, one of which we shall soon note; but some noble fragments of woods, Bishop's Wood and Hornsey Wood, and a broad expanse of rich lands which the Ecclesiastical Commissioners - that modern race of church economists - are about converting into a town, still remain.

A hermit was one of the earliest inhabitants of this place. He had a cell or hermitage, where pilgrims to the holy well, formerly Mouse Well, or Muswell, giving the name to Muswell Hill, used to seek his prayers, and perhaps refreshments of a more mundane stamp. This cell gradually expanded into a chapel of ease dedicated to St. Michael. Mousewell Hill had also its ancient chapel. The chapel of Highgate was granted by Bishop Grindal, afterwards Archbishop of Canterbury, in 1565, to a new grammar school erected and endowed the year before by Sir Roger Cholmeley, late Lord Chief Justice, with gardens, orchards, and two acres of land. Bishops in those church-reforming days, thinking more of promoting the public good than of maintaining a pompous rivalry with the temporal aristocracy and laying the foundations of great families, founded churches and schools - a thing little heard of amongst bishops now-a-days, who have enough to do to protest against spiritual corruptions.

The very hermits of those days seem to have been stirring and public-spirited fellows, for which we now give them little credit. Here was one William Lichfield, according to Norden, a poor, infirm hermit, who dug and carried gravel from the top of the hill, and raised the road, then very properly called Hollow-way, it having become impassable. By this means the holy anchorite at once made a good highway and a capital pond of water, which remained till 1865 a prominent feature of the village. The hermit's chapel was enlarged at a subsequent period, and took a new lease of life along with the school erected by Sir Roger Cholmeley.

The chapel was pulled down many years ago, and the church was built in another part of the village. Till 1866, however, the graveyard remained as it was; and in it stood, among other tombs, that of Coleridge, the poet and philosopher. It was covered with a large slab, and you descended by several steps to it. There you saw a board, or shutter, on which were painted, 'S. T. C.,' the initials of the poet; those also of his wife; of his daughter, Sara, and of Henry Nelson Coleridge, her husband. The sexton, removing this, showed you the coffins themselves, often much to the surprise of visitors. At the time of the rebuilding of the Grammar school, in 1866, a new chapel was also erected, in the crypt of which the tomb of Coleridge is enclosed.

HIGHGATE GRAMMAR SCHOOL

This school was founded, in 1562, by Sir Roger Cholmeley, Chief Justice of the Queen's Bench, for a general education of the children of the place and neighbourhood, such as was given at that day, and not exclusively for a grammar-school, as we shall see.

This Sir Roger Cholmeley was the natural son of Sir Richard Cholmeley, of Goldston, in Yorkshire, Knight, Lieutenant of the Tower of London, who died in 1521 without legitimate issue. He appears to have turned his attention to the profession of law in the lifetime of his reputed father, at whose death he was already entered at Lincoln's Inn. He pursued his studies so effectually, that his rise to legal honours was gradual, but rapid; for we find him to have been successively Reader in Lincoln's Inn at different periods; a Bencher of that society; Serjeant-at-law; King's Serjeant; Chief Baron of the Exchequer; and, finally, Chief Justice of the King's Bench.

Upon his removal from his high office, in the reign of Mary, he settled at Hornsey, in Middlesex, in which county, as well as in Essex and London, he possessed lands, bequeathed to him by his father; and, after an active life passed amidst the anxious and eventful scenes of that turbulent period, he appears to have spent the evening of his days in the calm delights of literary retirement. *Jucunda oblivia vitæ.*

A few years before his death, he entertained the desire, participated by many other pious and distinguished Protestants, of erecting and endowing a public grammar-school, for the diffusion of knowledge and the maintenance of the true religion; and, having accomplished his laudable purpose in the foundation of a school at Highgate, he died in June, 1565, the very month in which his seal was put to his last public act, by which he conveyed estates for the support of the establishment.

Probably Sir Roger Cholmeley held the site of the Hermitage by a grant from the Crown. By an inscription, formerly on the west end of the old chapel, it appeared that in the year above mentioned, 1562, when Chief Justice to Edward VI, he 'did institute and erect at his own charge a public and free grammar-school, and procured the same to he established and confirmed by the letters patent of Queen Elizabeth, he endowing the same with yearly maintenance.'

Lysons, in his 'Environs of London,' 1810, vol. i. p. 432, has condensed the chief particulars regarding this school and chapel, of which I now avail myself. There are two charters, one dated January 29, the other April 6, 7 Elizabeth. These charters give license to Sir Roger Cholmeley to found a grammar school *for the education of poor boys* living in Highgate and the neighbouring parts; and to provide a fund for the relief of certain poor persons in the village or hamlet of Highgate. For carrying this into effect, Sir William Hewett, and Roger Martin, Esq., aldermen of the City of London; Roger Carew, Esq., Richard Heywood, Esq., Richard Hodges, Esq., and Jasper Cholmeley, Esq., were constituted governors, and made a body corporate, with license to possess lands in mortmain, to use a common seal, &c. On a vacancy amongst the governors, by death or resignation, the remaining governors were to elect a new one. Sir Roger Cholmeley was to nominate the master during his life, to fix his stipend, and to make such statutes as he should think fit for the regulation of the school. By the first charter it was directed that after his death the appointment of the master should be vested in his heirs, and on their failing to appoint within two months, the governors, with the advice and consent of the Bishop of London, were to appoint: his heirs and the governors jointly were empowered to make statutes. All the revenues then belonging to the institution, together with all future benefactions, were directed to be appropriated solely to the maintenance of a master, and the relief of the poor. By the second charter it is provided that after the founder's death the governors should elect the master, whose place must be always supplied within a month after vacancy, otherwise the appointment lapses to the Bishop of London. The governors are empowered to make any regulations relating to the school, or the master's salary, provided that they are not contrary to the founder's statutes.

The ordinances of 1571 direct that the schoolmaster shall be 'a graduate of good, sober, and honest conversation, and no light person;' and that

> 'he shall teach and instruct young children their *A B C, and other English books*, and write, and also the grammar, as they shall grow up thereto, and that without taking any money or other reward for the same, other than as hereafter is expressed; that is, 4d. at the admission of each child into the school, and 4d. for books.'

This, in 1712, was increased to 12d. The schoolmaster's office is also to read morning and evening prayers at the chapel on Sundays (except on the first Sunday in each month, when the inhabitants are to repair to their respective parish churches), morning prayers on Wednesdays and Fridays, and evening prayers on Saturdays, and on the vigils of all festivals. He must not serve, nor take any cure elsewhere, nor must he be absent above ten days in the year, and that not without urgent cause.

The master's salary was fixed by the said ordinances at £10 per annum, besides a house rent free, and kept in repair, a garden, an orchard, two acres of land enclosed out of Highgate Common, and eight loads of fuel out of the Bishop of London's woods at Hornsey. In 1712 this annual gift of wood had long been discontinued. The master was bound in a penalty of £20 to observe the above-mentioned ordinances; and it was further provided, that if he should infringe them, having been thrice warned by the governors, he should be expelled.

In 1681, the salary was £28; in 1698, £30; in 1762, £100; besides £10 as Reader, left by the will of Edward Paunceford, Esq., in 1748. In Lysons' time, 1810, the master's salary was £140 per annum, and, no doubt, is very much more at present, the value of everything having risen so much of late years. Mr. Lysons was furnished with the account of the lands and moneys vested in the governors of Highgate School, with their produce, in the year 1672. This being supplied by the treasurer, Thomas Bromwich, Esq., of course was correct. They will be found, stated at large, in 'Lysons,' vol. i. p. 433, and consist of lands, and rent-charges on lands and tenements in Highgate, St. Martin's, Ludgate, and St. Martin's, Crooked Lane, London; in Stoke Newington, Hendon, and Kentish Town; bequeathed by Sir Roger Cholmeley, John Dudley, Esq., Jasper Cholmeley, Esq., and William Platt, Esq. This property, in 1762, produced an income of upwards of £152, which must now be vastly increased in value. Besides, fifteen different items of money were invested in the funds, amounting to £4,260. Thus, independent of anything which may have been conferred on this school since, it was very handsomely endowed.

By an ancient order of the governors, the number of scholars is limited to 40, to be chosen from Highgate, Holloway, Hornsey, Finchley, and Kentish Town, if there shall be so many in those places; otherwise, they are to be elsewhere elected, at the discretion of the governors for the time being. Sir Roger Cholmeley's endowment produced, in 1794, £166 per annum. The governors pay the master's and preacher's salaries out of this endowment, aided by some subsequent benefactions; and the pew-rents, when there were such, went to the same purpose.

So far from there being now any want of boys in the places included within the limits of the endowment, candidates for education in the school - a great number more than can get upon the foundation - avail themselves of the institution. People go and live within the prescribed district to have a claim on the privilege, and numbers of supernumeraries are admitted on payment. Since the able management of the present master, the Rev. Dr. Dyne, the school has rapidly risen from a very low condition to one of great repute. Unfortunately, with the great tendency of modern education, the chief attention has been paid to carrying proficiency in Latin and Greek to a great, and, in the majority of cases, an unnecessary length. As in all such schools, what was intended for the poor has been usurped by the rich, and so far from the children of the poor receiving any benefit from this substantial endowment, those of the respectable tradesmen of the place have been excluded by the pressure of wealth and the spirit of caste. A wealthy retailer assured me that he had asked the master whether he could send his son to the school, and was answered, 'Of course; but I do not advise it.' Of course not, for the poor lad would have found himself like a pigeon in a throng of hawks, amongst the sons of wealthy merchants and professional men.

It is to be hoped, now there is appearing a wholesome perception of the folly of devoting time to classics, which could be so much more profitably devoted to other branches of practical modern sciences; and now that the spirit of reform is abroad in this direction, as it regards the 3,000 endowed grammar schools of England, that a due portion of the funds of this school will be set aside for the education of the poorer and retail trading classes. One of the great reforms needed in England, in regard to all kinds of endowed institutions, is that of a resuscitated conscience in such matters.

THE OLD CHAPEL

Old Chapel and Gateway
(From Tomline's ' Perambulation of Islington')

The old chapel adjoining the school was originally built by Sir Roger Cholmeley, on the site of a former one, which had stood from the earliest times of the Highgate hermits. Sir Roger's chapel, which had been enlarged by other benefactors, had, as we have said, been pulled down many years ago; and in 1866 both school and chapel were rebuilt in a much ampler and finer style, and now form, perhaps, the most distinguished group of buildings in Highgate.

Memorials of Persons of Distinction in the Old Chapel
Dr. Lewis Atterbury, Rector of Hornsey, and thirty six years preacher at this chapel, a brother of Bishop Atterbury, and one in the six preachers to Queen Anne at St. James's and Whitehall, was buried here in 1731.

Sir Francis Pemberton, Chief Justice of the King's Bench, under Charles II, had a monument here.

In the Register we find the following notice:

'Nathaniel f. Dni. Nathanielis Hobart, ex Annâ 27 Sep, 1636.'

This was a son of Sir Henry Hobart, Chief Justice of the Common Pleas, who had a house at Highgate, and his descendants after him for many years.

'Hon Dna Judith Platt, uxor Hugonis Platt, militis sepult. Jan. 28, 1635.'

This was the relict of Sir Hugh Platt, author of 'The Garden of Eden,' 'The Jewell-house of Art and Nature,' and other curious works. It is supposed that Sir Hugh, who died in 1605, was buried here also, but there is no register extant of so early a date.

There are entries regarding members of Sprignell, the De la Warre, Mainwaring or Manneringe, and other families of note.

'Robert Earl of Warwick and Ellenor Countess of Sussex, married Mar. 80, 1646.'

The Earl of Warwick was admiral for the Long Parliament. This marriage is not mentioned by Dugdale, nor does he speak of any Ellenor Countess of Sussex.

'Charles, son of Sir Henry, and Hester Lady Blunt, of Holloway, was baptised May 10, 1654.'

The Blount family was of Tettenhanger, in Bedfordshire, and the first in their pedigree was Sir Walter Blount, the standard-bearer of Henry IV, who was killed at the battle of Shrewsbury. The family was greatly distinguished in the time of Charles I and the Commonwealth, both in arms and letters. Sir Henry published 'Travels in Turkey and other Countries;' a satire called the 'Exchange Walk;' and an epistle in praise of coffee and tobacco. He was editor also of Lilley's 'Comedies.' He fought at Edge Hill on the royal side, but afterwards quitted the King's service for that of the Commonwealth, and on various occasions rendered great service to his country. He sat on the celebrated trial of Don Pantaleon Saa, the Portuguese ambassador, and was one of the commissioners for promoting trade and navigation. Sir Henry married the widow of Sir William Mainwaring, by which means he became possessed of the house at Upper Holloway, where he resided several years. He died in 1682. His son, Thomas Pope, so called from his relation Sir Thomas Pope, founder of Trinity College, in Oxford, was born at Upper Holloway, September 12, 1649. He published a critique in Latin on the most eminent writers of all ages - 'Censura celebriorum auctorum,' &c., a work in considerable esteem; and various essays, remarks on poetry, and a volume of natural history. He was created a baronet in 1679, and died in 1697. Charles, his younger brother, whose baptism is here recorded, was a celebrated deistical writer; he published also a pamphlet in defence of Dryden, when he was only nineteen years of age; an introduction to polite literature; and a treatise on the liberty of the press. He put an end to his life in a fit of frenzy, occasioned by the sister of his deceased wife declining his hand, she having scruples as to the legality of such a marriage. His miscellaneous works were published after his death.

'Sir John Wollaston, buried in the chancel, April 29, 1658.'

Sir John Wollaston was an alderman of London; treasurer-at-war, and one of the committee for the sale of church lands. His wife was also buried here, June 1, 1660.

Sir John Wollaston is still better known in Highgate by being the founder of the almshouses for poor widows in Southwood Lane. These houses being decayed in the year 1722, Edward Paunceford, Esq., pulled them down and built twelve others on their site, with a schoolhouse in the centre for charity girls. This excellent charity has been much augmented by property left by Messrs. Foster, Edwards, Bromwich, and Kleinert. Twenty children are clothed, and a number of poor widows made comfortable.

'The Lady Anne Peerpoint, daughter to the Honourable the Marquis of Dorchester, and John La Rosse, sonne of the Right Honourable the Earle of Rutland, were married July 15, 1658.'

The Marquis of Dorchester, a nobleman of good learning, who is remarkable for having been a Bencher of Gray's Inn, and a Fellow of the College of Physicians, had a mansion at Highgate. The marriage here recorded was dissolved by Act of Parliament in

1666.

'Charlotte, daughter of Sir John Pettus, buried May 28, 1678.'

Sir John Pettus, Bart., was cupbearer to Charles II and William III. He published 'Fodinæ Regales,' or a history of the Chief Mines and Minerals in England, Wales, and Ireland; 'Fleta Minor,' or the Art of Assaying Metals, and a hook entitled, 'England's Independency of the Papal Power,' abridged from Sir John Darril and Sir Edward Coke.

'Sir Francis Pemberton, buried June 15, 1699. Dame Anne, his relict, April 15, 1731.'

We have already mentioned Sir Francis as a resident in Highgate.

'Mr. John Shower, of the parish of Stoke Newington, a dissenting minister, buried July 5,1765.'

Mr. Shower was author of a work on earthquakes, and of various religious treatises.
There is also the following curious entry:

'Christopher Wilkinson, Merchant, Adventurer, and Alderman, 1676, and though interred far from his native land - Leeds, Yorkshire - yet hath he left there a Monument engraven in the heart of all good men.'

In the adjoining cemetery are the tombs of Sir Jeremy Topp, Bart., of Bremore, Hants, 1733; the Rev. Edward Yardley, author of 'Discourses on the Genealogy of Christ,' &c., &c., Archdeacon of Cardigan, preacher at the chapel from 1731 till his death, 1769; and this:

'Underneath lyes the body of Richard Browne, late Citizen and Macon of London, who departed this life the 21st day of March, 1720, in the 47th year of his age. He was a very ingenious Artist in his way, and a zealous son of the Church of England.'

HIGHGATE CHURCH

This church, dedicated to St. Michael, was built in 1832 on a new site, in the parish of St. Pancras. It cost nearly £10,000, of which £5,000 was contributed by the Church Commissioners, and the remainder raised by subscription amongst the inhabitants. Some delay in the consecration was occasioned by the ancient chapelry of Highgate being an ecclesiastical peculiar, situated in the three parishes of Hornsey, St. Pancras, and Islington, and, though surrounded by the diocese of London, not included in it. Claims of jurisdiction were also set up by the parish of St. Pancras, on the ground of the church having been built within its boundary. But the difficulties were set at rest by the passing of an amendment to the Act by virtue of which the edifice had been erected, and Highgate is now a district of itself, paying no ecclesiastical dues to any parish.

A number of memorial tablets were removed from the old chapel to this church. The most noteworthy is that to the memory of the poet Coleridge, whose tomb, as observed, is in the resuscitated chapel by the grammar school. The present vicar of Highgate is the Rev. Charles Dalton, a canon of St. Paul's.

HISTORICAL EVENTS AT HIGHGATE

Having thus noted the ancient, age-long condition of this fair hilltop overlooking the city, yet itself a woodland haunt rather than a haunt of men, we will take a rapid glance at the fragments of history that, nevertheless, caught like locks of wool in its thickets, from the passing flocks of mankind; for the ambitious conflict of life was always going on below.

> There would a splendid city rise to view,
> With carts, and cars, and coaches roaring all;
> Wide poured abroad behold the giddy crew -
> See how they dash along from wall to wall!
> At every door, hark how they thundering call!
> Good Lord! what can this giddy rout excite?
> Why on each other with fell tooth to fall:
> A neighbour's fortune, fame, or peace to blight,
> And make new tiresome parties for the coming night?

In the unhappy reign of Richard II we find the Duke of Gloucester, with various other nobles, meeting in Harringay, that is, Hornsey Park, to call poor Richard to account for his favouritism to Robert de Vere, Earl of Oxford. They had 4,000 men with them, and they overawed the King. In the following year these nobles were called to account themselves for their treason, at Nottingham; but the end of these troubles saw the unfortunate Richard conveyed through Highgate, in 1398, on his way from the North, by bis haughty rival Bolingbroke, mounted on a sorry steed, and hooted by the fickle rabble all the way through Islington and to the Tower of London. Henry V, a very different monarch, had a meeting with the Lord Mayor of London and 500 citizens on the same ground; and Henry VII met the Lord Mayor of 1487 here on his return from his successful pursuit of Lambert Simnel.

Thomas Thorpe, Baron of the Exchequer, was beheaded by the insurgents in Highgate in 1461.

Queen Elizabeth, on her accession to the throne, was met by the Lord Mayor and Corporation of London at Highgate, on her way from Hatfield House, and conducted into the city.

Venner and the Fifth Monarchy Men, in their riot in 1661, retreated into Caen Wood.

These seem far-off events, but much nearer to our time General Monk encamped his army on Finchley Common, just by, when planning the restoration of the ribald king, Charles II. Little more than a century ago, that is, in 1745, the London Train Bands and other troops marched through Highgate to encamp on this same common to defend the metropolis against Prince Charles and his Scots, who were already at Derby; and Hogarth was watching to sketch his immortal 'March to Finchley.' Soon after the rebel lords Lovat, Kilmarnock, Cromartie, and Balmerino were seen escorted through the village under guard, on their way to the Tower, three of them to lose their heads there.

How far removed from this present England of ours, appear Londoners marching out against rebels and a pretender to the throne; and yet, but the other day, men were living who saw this rebellion. The celebrated novelist, Miss Letitia Hawkins, daughter of Sir John Hawkins, author of the 'History of Music,' and who was living in 1824, says in her 'Memoirs,' that her mother, in 1745, saw the troops march past their house to Finchley Common to meet the rebels.

Their house was the one now occupied by Mr. Daniels, the statuary, in full view of the London Road; and that she afterwards saw the rebel lords brought in prisoners through Highgate. She had a particular view of old Lord Lovat, who stopped to take refreshments, probably at the inn at the corner, his carriage being thrown open; and she bore testimony to the faithfulness of the likeness as given by Hogarth's portrait of him. I myself have seen a man, then 112 years old, who as a boy witnessed the battles of Preston-pans and Culloden. I knew another who, being a farmer in Staffordshire, was visited by the rebels in their progress southward, and who often used to describe with much gusto these free-and-easy Scots slicing up his cheeses the whole breadth of the surface, and toasting them in huge discs on their dirks. General Oglethorpe, who was the founder of Georgia, and who used to relate that he shot woodcocks in the reign of Queen Anne where Regent Street now is, died only in 1785, and was well known to our immediate fathers. Such are the extraordinary human links that make the far past seem almost present.

Only one event of national importance has, according to my recollection, taken place during our time here, but it is one that is already making us sensible how fast the present happy reign is running away, for it occurred upwards of thirty one years ago.

A remarkable object on West Hill is the tavern of the 'Fox and Crown.' Only sixteen days after our present excellent Queen had succeeded to the throne, Monday, July 6, 1837, descending the hill in a carriage with her mother, the Duchess of Kent, the horses took fright, and dashed forward at a furious rate. Mr. Turner, the landlord, seeing the imminent danger, sprang bravely forward, made a desperate clutch at the reins, and succeeded in arresting the frightened animals.

The bold landlord probably arrested at the same time a change in the succession to the throne; and without his saving hand, we might at this moment be the subjects of we don't know who. Her Majesty, besides a handsome present, in acknowledgment, granted Turner a license to mount the royal arms; and there they stand now over the door, accompanied by an inscription recording the circumstance. On Sundays and holidays, groups of Londoners may be continually seen pointing out the royal escutcheon, and talking of the Court. As you go up and down, you may hear, too, occasionally, very curious remarks. Once, about a dozen men and women were listening to a knowing-looking commentator on the subject. 'But,' said one man, 'what is that fox doing there on the pole, above the crown?' 'Aha!' said the politician, laughing, and shaking his black shiny locks that fell from under a very little hat that seemed to have stood many a brushing and ironing,

'Aha! the fellow who put that up was a wag, and no mistake. Why, Jem, the fox always does get above the crown. As the old farmer said, "The turkey-cock is master here; I am master o' the men; wife is master o' me; Tommy is master o' wife; but the turkey-cock is master o' Tommy," Aha! that's it. I say, did you never read the story of "Reynard the Fox?" They tell me it's almost as old as Noah's Ark; but the man as writ it was no fool. Don't you know how Foxy talked old King Lion over; and though they had got him up to the gallows, and were just going to swing him off, he begged a moment to tell King Lion a secret about a treasure, and once down again, was made Lord Chancellor? That's it! I tell you the fox will always get above the crown. Crown thinks it rules us; but there's always some deep fox at hand - Pitt, or Pam., or somebody else, as says: "Let me just go up to the top of the pole, and tell your Majesty which way the wind blows." Up he goes; but the wind may blow twenty ways before you'll get him down again. Look there now. The crown has got up on a pretty high pole, above us; but fox is twiddling and grinning above it. Now you see his whiskers, and now you see his brush; but for coming down again, trust old Foxy.'

Here there was a hearty laugh from the listeners; but the politician, shaking his black locks, said gravely, 'A deep chap that was that put the fox up there.'

But if not history itself, there are testimonies of history scattered all over Highgate, in its old mansions. From the time of Elizabeth, and downwards, till lately, the aristocracy had a particular liking to this northern ridge of hills, overlooking the metropolis, and many a far scene besides. Many of the views into Kent, with glimpses of the winding Thames, into Essex, Hertfordshire, and Surrey, remind you of those from some of the hills of Normandy and Brittany. Accordingly, from Muswell Hill to Hampstead, we find the scenery studded with the residences, or the remembrances of them, of many noble and historic men and women. Around Hampstead, as we have seen, linger the memories of Sir Harry Vane; Butler, the author of 'The Analogy of Revealed Religion;' Lord Hotham, Lord Erskine, Richardson, the novelist; of Joanna Baillie, Shelley, Keats, Leigh Hunt; of Herbert and Stanfield, in art, and many others.

In and around Highgate many aristocratic families have resided, as those of Dorchester, Arundel, Cholmeley, Pemberton, St. Albans, Lauderdale, Argyll, Bute, Mansfield, Southampton, Russell, Cornwallis, Hobart, Huntingdon, &c. Amongst the chief benefactors to the poor of Highgate, besides Archbishop Grindal and Sir Roger Cholmeley, already mentioned, Sir John Wollaston founded a number of almshouses for men and women; and Dick Whittington, through the trustees of his estate, has erected a whole set of alms-houses for single women at the age of 55. These noble men go on for ever making happy a number of their unfortunate fellow-creatures. Why do not the wealthy people of our day leave such perpetual blessings behind them?

Amongst the names here mentioned, we shall speak more

particularly of the Cornwallises; John, Lord Russell, son of Francis, Earl of Bedford, who died here in 1584; and add those of Sir Richard Baker, author of 'Baker's Chronicle,' who resided here about 1603, and the celebrated Dr. Sacheverell, who died at his house here on the 6th of June, 1724.

Amongst those of more than mere aristocratic distinction, whose memories reflect honour on this ancient hill, are Nicholas Rowe, the commentator on Shakespeare, and author of seven tragedies of his own; Mrs. Barbauld, whose husband was some time minister of the Presbyterian chapel here; Sir Richard Baker, author of 'The Chronicles of England; ' the celebrated Countess of Huntingdon, the great supporter of Whitefield, and the first to commence a restoration of the abused charities of England. Dr. Isaac Watts is said to have visited here sometimes his great patron Sir Thomas Abney, and afterwards removed with him to Stoke Newington, where he died. The noisy and troublesome Dr. Sacheverell brought his busy, fussy soul into this quiet place in Queen Anne's time. General Wade, famous in the following distich for opening up the highlands of Scotland by military roads, had a house here:

O! had you seen these roads before they were made,
You would have lifted your hands and blessed General Wade.

Hogarth used to make excursions in his youthful days with his companions to Highgate. Morland was a constant guest at the 'Bull Inn,' where he sold his paintings to support himself. He knew the driver of every coach, and the pedigree of the horses, and, taking his stand at Bob Bellamy's Inn, in the village, would halloo to the gentlemen of the whip, as they made their appearance, and treat them to gin and brandy. Frequently he would parade with a pipe in his mouth before the door of the house, and hail the carriages as they passed in succession before him, and, from being so well known, was generally greeted by a familiar salute from the postilion. The consequence that he attached to this species of homage was almost beyond belief.

Here the famous Jacobite and polemic, Bishop Atterbury, used to visit his brother, Dr. Atterbury, the preacher of Highgate Chapel. Here the wealthy Sir John Hawkins - not Queen Elizabeth's Sir

John, the great slave-trade admiral, but the historian of music - used to live facing the pond, and daily set forth in his coach-and-four to discharge his magisterial functions at Hicks's Hall. And, more truly distinguished than all the rest, Coleridge lived, slily swallowed opium, and talked wondrous talk at Mr. Gilman's, the surgeon, in the Grove; the most extraordinary thing being that the literati who used to flock up from London to hear him never committed one of these wonderful harangues to paper.

COLERIDGE AT HIGHGATE

Something more must be said of Coleridge than in the above brief paragraph. His residence here was an event in the history of the place. Few of our countrymen have exceeded Coleridge in amount or variety of genius. As a poet, a metaphysician, and a theologian, he stands pre-eminent, and has produced a greater effect on our literature and modes of thinking than most people are sensible of. He was one of that illustrious band of men who hate the artificial trammels of our literature, and led us back to nature, inaugurating a new and nobler era of thought, and of the modes of expressing it. His earliest friends and coadjutors were Wordsworth and Southey, Charles Lloyd, Robert Lovell, and kind, helpful, pedantic Joseph Cottle, first his publisher, and afterwards his biographer. His early life was full of change and restlessness. At one time a Unitarian preacher, at another a light dragoon, then a journalist, and newspaper editor. He was one of the first to introduce to us the poets and literature of Germany, having visited that country with Wordsworth and his sister Dorothy, and Henry Crabbe Robinson. There he made the acquaintance of Klopstock and others, and with the works, if not the persons, of Schiller, Lessing, Gellert, Ramler, and Kant. He studied at Gottingen, applying himself to physiology and natural history, under Blumenbach, and had Eichhorn's 'Lectures on the New Testament' repeated to him by a student from Ratzeburg. 'But my chief efforts,' he says,

'were directed towards a grounded knowledge of the German language and literature. From Professor Tychsen I received as many lessons in the Gothic of Ulphilas as were sufficient to make one acquainted with its grammar, and the radical words of the most frequent occurrence; and with the occasional assistance of the same philosophical linguist, I read through Otfried's metrical paraphrase of the Gospels, and the most important remains of the Theotiscan, or the transitional state of the Teutonic language, from the Gothic to the old German of the Swabian period. Of this period I read with sedulous accuracy the *Minnesinger*, or singers of love, the provençal poets of the Swabian court, and the metrical romances; and then laboured through sufficient specimens of the *master singers*, their degenerate successors; not, however, without occasional pleasure from the rude yet interesting strains of Hans Sachs, the cobbler of Nuremberg.'

This was a vigorous introduction into the vast field of German knowledge, and the fruits of it were soon seen in his enthusiasm for Schiller, and his indoctrination by Kant. He proposed at once to translate the whole of the works of Schiller, but the English public was not then prepared for the importation of so much German poetry, and he contented himself with translating the 'Piccolomini' and 'The Heath of Wallenstein,' which, with some mistakes, showing a not sufficient familiarity with the conversational phraseology of Germany, is a masterly work. Of the part of his life chiefly spent at Highgate, I will avail myself of the narrative of my friend Freiligrath, the German poet, a man as distinguished for his knowledge of English, as for his genius:

'The next eighteen years of his life were agitated and unsettled. We find him at London, connected with Daniel Stuart and the "Morning Post," and writing a series of letters for that paper, which, by their anti-Gallican tendency, made him obnoxious to the First Consul; at the Lakes, where Southey, recently returned from Portugal, and Wordsworth, had established themselves; at Malta, in 1804, whither he had just repaired for the benefit of his health, and where he officiated for some months as secretary to the governor of that island, Sir Alexander Ball; at Rome, where he made the acquaintance of Ludwig Tieck; was painted by Washington Allston, and had to thank Wilhelm von Humboldt for a warning which enabled him to escape from the snares of Buonaparte. Again at the Lakes, planning a new periodical, the "Friend." Again at London, writing for the "Courier," lecturing on Shakespeare and Milton, visiting Lord Byron, then one of the managing committee of Drury Lane Theatre, and, through the influence of this generous friend, seeing his tragedy of "Remorse" successfully brought upon the stage. At Calne, in Wiltshire, occupied with the "Biographia Literaria," and arranging and publishing a part of his lyrics under the title of "Sibylline Leaves," until, in 1816, we see him settling, for the rest of his life, at Highgate, in the house of Mr. James Gillman, surgeon.
The motive for this removal was a sad one. To seek relief from bodily suffering, Coleridge had at an early period begun the use of opium. He continued it for the same reason, till he had acquired the habit of

opium-eating, and felt it beyond his power to shake off his unhappy bondage to the baleful drug. The consequences were such as might be expected. His physical strength gave way; his mind, at no time energetic and resolute, became utterly unstrung. A voluntary exile from his family, whom he left to the care of Southey, the kindest of friends and relatives, he was preyed upon by remorse and self-reproach. The firmness with which he resolved at last to cut down the use of the root, and for that purpose to place himself under the charge of a physician, shows the fundamental worth and soundness of his character. Mr. Gillman was the physician chosen for the difficult and delicate task; and under his roof, in the bosom of his affectionate family, who had sense and kindness enough to know that they did themselves honour by looking after the comfort of such a man, the last years of the poet's life were quietly spent. A cool and peaceful evening, after the storm of a hot and feverish day. Here, on the brow of Highgate Hill, to quote Carlyle, "he sate looking down on London and its smoke-tumult, like a sage escaped from the inanity of life's battle, attracting towards him the thoughts of innumerable brave souls still engaged there - heavy-laden, high-aspiring, and surely much-suffering man."

Still his aspirings proved stronger than his sufferings. This period was also one of unabated intellectual activity with Coleridge. He continued his literary exertions - the fragments of "Christabel," composed in 1797 and 1800, appeared in 1816; the "Biographia Literaria," in 1817; "Zapolya, a Christmas Tale," in the same year; the two "Lay Sermons," in 1816 and 1817; the "Aids to Reflection," in 1825; and the little work, "On the Construction of Church and State," in 1830. But mostly during this epoch, it was by means of oral communication that he exercised a bad and wide-operating influence. At no other time, per-haps, his extraordinary conversational powers, always the joy and wonderment of enraptured hearers - witness the enthusiastic reports of Lamb, Talfourd, De Quincy, Hazlitt, and others - proved themselves more fascinating and effective. His voice, indeed, had now grown feeble; it had lost the deep and full tone, which once reverberated from the ferny slopes of the Quantocks; but it never tired in the utterance, in copious and eloquent talk, of all the wisdom, the bright fancies, the sad experience stored up under that broad and pensive forehead.

A large circle of friends and disciples gathered round him; and he taught and talked amongst his trees and flowers, like Plato in the garden of Academus. What men entered Mr. Gillman's humble porch in those days !—Lamb and Wordsworth, Southey and Leigh Hunt, Hazlitt and Talfourd, John Stirling and Thomas Carlyle - a hero worshipped, and sometimes, we feel bound to add, reverentially censured by heroes. Ludwig Tieck, too, we are agreeably surprised to meet amongst his Highgate visitors. He, however, did not come to listen, but to be listened to. At the request of Coleridge, Tieck, in a long midnight discourse, developed to him his views of Shakespeare, concerning whom, and his English commentators, the two friends were at variance. In this way eighteen years passed by: he dreamt and he talked, he cultivated his flowers, and fed his little pensioners, the birds, until, on July 25, 1834, death gently took him away. Three months more, and he would have completed his sixty-second year.

Coleridge, with all his errors and shortcomings, is yet a name never to be omitted in a history of the march of the English mind - not so much for what he has actually performed, as for the stimulating impulses given by him. His gifts were of the richest and highest order; yet, however powerful as a critic, however profound as a metaphysician, however melodious and imaginative as a poet, he, from an innate want of courage and energy of character, had it not in his power to give to his faculties that development which, if it had been attained, would have entitled him to one of the very highest places in English literature. But what he has done amongst the poets and philosophers of his country is this: thirsting after truth, longing for the good and beautiful, "an inquiring spirit," indeed, he was the first to venture into intellectual regions far apart from the track hitherto beaten by English thinkers. The experiment, for himself, may have been to little purpose, but he at all events has opened up the road. Here lies his merit - it is that of the pilot and pioneer. It is the merit of being one of the first, if not the very first, of those who have brought about that all-important exchange of ideas between two great kindred nations, which at present, stirring and humanising, fluctuates to and fro across the German Ocean. What he did for Schiller we have mentioned already. But it was Coleridge who first introduced Kant; it was he who first introduced Fichte and Schelling to the English nation; and, although he did not carry on or diffuse their systems, nay, although towards the close of his life he even disclaimed them, and returned, a strict Trinitarian, into the bosom of the Church of England, yet, what he has written upon metaphysical subjects, has proved highly suggestive to "inquiring spirits" of a later generation. Much of the ferment in theology and philosophy, at present going on in England and America, originates in Coleridge.'

Amongst the frequent visitors of Coleridge was Edward Irving, who, himself a great preacher and teacher of religion, used to sit at the feet of Coleridge as at those of Gamaliel, meekly listening. Amongst all his admiring auditors, Coleridge never had a nobler and more Christian one than Edward Irving. Whatever may be thought of his belief of the continuance of Christian miracles and preternatural gifts to the present day, and his participation in the too eager faith in the personal appearance of Christ on earth, there can be but one opinion of his perfectly Christ-like spirit. Repeatedly thwarted, snubbed, and turned out of the chapels and associations of those whom his inspired eloquence had drawn together, though these harsh trials broke his heart, and sent him to an early grave, he never for a moment harboured any resentment. He continued persecuted, meek, loving, and forgiving to the last. Since the days of his great prototype and Saviour, we know of no man who so much resembled him in patient, loving, and unresentful faith.

The house which Coleridge inhabited in the Grove, Highgate - the third from the high-road - has recently been much altered, and may be known by its modern aspect in the row of the old Grove houses. In America the reputation of Coleridge is far more properly appreciated than in England. Some of his works are class-books in the colleges of the United States, and his `Aids to Reflection' has, perhaps more than any other production, formed the minds of the studious young men there. Such is the enthusiasm for the memory of Coleridge in the States, that numbers of Americans visit his last residence at Highgate, and one of them offered a large price for the very doors of his room, that he might set them up in his own house across the Atlantic.

Long will the pleasant walks round Highgate be connected with the memory of Coleridge. The woodland seclusion of Milford Lane, and the fields lying between them and Hampstead, will, to the lovers of genuine poetry and broadly discursive minds, revive the image of the 'old man eloquent' taking his daily stroll, with his black coat and white locks, a hook in his hand, and, probably, a group of curious children around him, whose acquaintance he was fond of making.

OTHER FAMOUS RESIDENTS OF HIGHGATE

Amongst persons born at Highgate may he mentioned Mr. John Taylor, author of 'Monsieur Tonson,' and who has written his own life in two volumes octavo, published by Bull, in Holles Street, in 1832 - a work which abounds with anecdotes of theatrical notabilities.

In the last house on Holly Terrace, farthest from the road, lived also for some years, in the latter part of Coleridge's time, and with whom he was familiar, Thomas Pringle, the first editor, and one of the projectors of 'Blackwood's Magazine.' He also wrote a very interesting work, 'A Narrative of a Residence in South Africa,' a volume of superior power; and edited the annual, 'Friendship's Offering.' But perhaps the most extraordinary part of Mr. Pringle's history was that, with a full-sized and strong body, but with scarcely any legs, owing to an accident in childhood, he used to ride enthusiastically after lions and elephants in the Cape country.

One of the most distinguished of the inhabitants of Highgate is Mr. MacDowell, the sculptor, equally remarkable for his talent and the unassuming modesty of his character. From a memoir of Mr. MacDowell in 'Portraits of Men of Eminence in Literature, Science, and Art,' published by Mr. Alfred Bennett, of Bishopsgate, in 1866, we learn that, having worked himself up to noticeable eminence by unremitting industry, his statue of 'A Girl Reading' established his fame. The progress of the artist since then is delineated in the following paragraphs:

'A most generously intended commission from Mr. Wentworth Beaumont, of Yorkshire, at this time considerably embarrassed the operations of Mr. MacDowell. This gentleman commissioned from him two large groups, stipulating, however, that he should, during three years, undertake no other work. This caused Mr. MacDowell to lose many orders which the beauty and success of his statue of "A Girl Reading" would otherwise have brought him. The works executed for Mr. Wentworth Beaumont greatly increased Mr. MacDowell's reputation, and led to his being elected an A.R.A. Through Mr.

Beaumont's friendly offer and suggestion, he visited and spent eight months in Italy. On his return, he finished for him his "Love Triumphant." A second group, executed by him for Mr. Beaumont, was the "Death of Virginia." In 1816, Mr. MacDowell was elected an R.A. In the same year he was entrusted by Sir Robert Peel to execute a figure of Lord Exmouth, one of the national statues of British admirals destined for Greenwich Hospital.

Visitors to the Great Exhibition of 1851 will recollect, as amongst the most graceful of the works of English sculptors, "Love Triumphant," "A Girl at Prayer," "Cupid," "Early Sorrow," "Psyche," "The Death of Virginia," and "Eve." His subsequent works comprise a statue in marble of Sir Michael O'Loghlen, for the Four Courts, Dublin; statues of Pitt and Chatham, for the House of Lords; a statue in bronze for the late Earl of Belfast; a statue in bronze, for Limerick, of the late Lord Fitzgibbon; a statue in marble, "The Day Dream;" a group in marble for T. Baring, Esq., M.P.; "The First Thorn in Life;" statue for the Mansion House, from "Moore's Loves of the Angels;" statue of J. M. W. Turner, the celebrated painter, for St. Paul's Cathedral, the competition for which was confined to members of the Royal Academy; a statue in marble of the late Lord Plunkett, for Dublin; and a statue in bronze of Lord Eglinton, for Dublin also.

Mr. MacDowell has since been engaged upon a monumental group in marble, for the Marquis of Donegal, to be erected in Belfast; and upon a group in marble of "Europe," for the Albert Memorial erecting in Hyde Park, a commission received from Her Majesty.'

Mr. MacDowell has one son, Mr. R. C. MacDowell, whose name is already favourably known to the public as a young sculptor of promise. He has exhibited at the Royal Academy several statues and statuettes.

CEREMONIES OF THE HORNS AT HIGHGATE

Ceremony of Being 'Sworn at Highgate'
(From Woodward's `Excentric Excursions,' in the British Museum)

In the mind of the ordinary public, however, Highgate is more famous for its former nonsensical practice of swearing travellers on the horns, than for its distinguished men. The whole particulars of the ceremony may be found in Hone's 'Every Day Book.' In the great coaching days, when the travellers to London from the North stopped at Highgate, at whichever of its nineteen public houses it might be, out came the horns fixed on a pole, and the passengers were sworn to eat no brown bread when they could get white, unless they liked it better, and not to kiss the maid when they could kiss the mistress, unless they liked her better. They were then inducted into all the liberties of the place. If they saw a swine lying in the gutter, they were free to lie down by it if they chose; and much more such nonsense, no doubt thought very droll by the poor freezing coach travellers, who, with stamping toes and blue noses, had been facing the icy blast for days and nights together.

The Horns at Hornchurch, the Horns at Kennington, the Horn Fair at Charlton, and the Horns at Highgate, all evidently have reference to an ancient passage-toll levied on horned cattle, and gathered by some park-keeper, or manor bailiff, who showed his authority by a staff mounted with a sign not to be misunderstood.

But I have promised to say something of more serious matters. Formerly there stood an old Southampton House at Highgate. It is gone long ago, and instead of it and its grounds, expand the pleasant Fitzroy Park and its pleasant villas. This and the pretty little property, now almost one solid town, stretching down to Oxford Street, is one of those nice things which the aristocracy, who say the Radicals want to pull down the Church, have filched from that amiable mother. In 1837, a writer in the 'Morning Chronicle' made public this fact:

'In the year 1768, the Duke of Grafton was Prime Minister. His brother, Mr. Fitzroy, was lessee of the manor and lordship of Tattenhall, the property of the Dean and Chapter of St. Paul's, London. Dr. Richard Brown, the then prebendary of the stall of Tattenhall, having pocketed the emolument attending the renewal of the lease, and there being little chance of any further advantages to him from the estate, readily listened to a proposal of Mr. Fitzroy for the purchase of the estate. The thing was agreed, and the Duke of Grafton, with his great standing majority, quickly passed an Act through Parliament, in March 1768, diverting the estate, with all its rights, privileges, and emoluments from the prebend, and conveyed the fee-simple entire, and without reserve, to Mr. Charles Fitzroy and his heirs for ever. The Act states it to be with the consent of Richard, Lord Bishop of London, and the privity of the Dean and Chapter of St. Paul's.

Now what was, and where lay this estate, so readily detached from the Church? It commences at St. Giles' parish, extends some distance on the north side of Oxford Street, and in other directions embraces a large part of St. Pancras parish, Camden Town, and up to Highgate, including copses, woods, and grounds lying beside Highgate of great extent, and from its situation equal in value to any land round the metropolis. Very considerable buildings were at that time erected upon it, the ground was in great request for building on, and could thus be disposed of in leases at a considerable rate per foot. Mr. Fitzroy immediately settled £400 a year on Mrs. Fitzroy, secured on only twenty three acres of this land, the estate consisting of some thousands of acres. Anyone knowing the extent and situation of the property, now that a vast town of more than three miles in length exists upon it, must be aware of the astounding value of it at present.

The full equivalent and compensation given to the Church for this princely estate was a rent-charge on it of £300 per annum, which, as £46 of it was receivable under the lease, makes the amount given for the fee simple £254 per annum! The estate being thus secured, on the strength of it Mr. Fitzroy was raised to the peerage in 1780 by the title of Lord Southampton, by which the estate is now known. Tattenhall is kept out of view, and this Church plunder is probably all the title possesses.'

The writer added that at that time, on a moderate calculation, the Southampton family had received a million and a half sterling from the estate, the full equivalent paid being then only £17,784! He intimated also that in the library at Lambeth Palace, a set of Parliamentary surveys of church lands records many similar transactions.

O! noble conservators of the `Poor Man's Church!'

FITZROY PARK

Dr. Southwood Smith

This pleasant outskirt of Highgate, deriving its name from the Southampton family, and on part of which the old Southampton House formerly stood, had as a resident for several years Dr. Southwood Smith, one of the most modest and benevolent of the men of science and genius whom this country has produced. Of his labours we have a condensed statement in the 'Men of the Time,' which, as it appears correct, we cannot do better than quote:

'Thomas Southwood Smith, author and physician, was born about 1790. He first attracted attention to himself by a work entitled "The Divine Government," written in 1814. Of this Wordsworth, in a letter, says, "The view Dr. Smith takes is so consonant with the ideas we entertain of Divine goodness, that were it not for some Scriptural difficulties, I should give this hook my unqualified approbation."
The argument is, that it seems probable, judging by analogy, that pain is a correcting process, whether physical, mental, or spiritual, and that the whole human race will be finally saved. Dr. Southwood Smith spent several years in the practice of his profession in the West of England, where he married. On the death of his wife he came to London with his son and two daughters, and attached himself to one of the metropolitan hospitals. He was soon after appointed physician to the London Fever Hospital, and continued connected with it to a late period of his life. He employed his leisure in the composition of "A Treatise on Fever," which at once took its position as a standard medical work. He assisted in the promotion of the "Westminster Review," and wrote the article on Bentham's System of Education in the first number. To this review he became a regular contributor; and it was his papers on the anatomical schools which brought the abuses of the old system of surgery so prominently before the public. He reprinted the main part of these articles under the title of "The Use of the Dead to the Living;" and his arguments, it is well known, prepared the way for the passing of the present law, which has extinguished the horrible traffic of the resurrection-men. His next scientific labours were some articles on physiology and medicine for the "Cyclopædia," and soon after he finished his celebrated treatise on "Animal Physiology" for the "Society for the Diffusion of Useful Knowledge." The success

of this work suggested the idea of treating the subject in a still more comprehensive manner, and hence, in 1834, his "Physiology of Health." Dr. S. Smith had long been the disciple and physician of Jeremy Bentham, and attended him in his last illness. A characteristic anecdote is related of the expiring philanthropist. During his last illness, he asked his medical attendant to tell him candidly if there was any prospect of recovery. On being informed that nature was too exhausted to allow of such a hope, he said, with his usual serenity, "Very well, be it so; then minimise pain."

In order to show the world his superiority to the common prejudices of mankind, Bentham left his body, by will, to Dr. Smith for anatomical purposes, and requested that, after dissection, his skeleton should be preserved. The Doctor fulfilled his desire, and delivered a lecture over the dead body of his friend in the West Street School of Anatomy, on June 9, 1832. "There, on the dissecting table," says a writer we have before quoted,

"lay the frame of that acute and benevolent man; before it stood the lecturer, pale as the corpse, yet self-possessed and reverent; around were seated most of the disciples and friends of the deceased. During the address there was a violent thunderstorm, which threw an indescribable awe over the whole scene. Every now and then the countenances of the dead and the living were lit up by the flashes of lightning; still the speaker proceeded, interrupted now and then by the thunder-crash, until at length it died away, and seemed to give up quiet possession to the lecturer's voice. In this address was given a brief but eloquent abstract of the life and writings of Jeremy Bentham."

In 1837, Dr. Smith was appointed by the Government to enquire into the state of the poor, with a view to see how far diseases and misery were produced by unhealthy dwellings and habits. His enquiries led to the passing of the Act for procuring improved drainage, and ultimately to the establishment of the Public Board of Health, of which Dr. Southwood Smith became a leading member.'

Thus Dr. Smith was the father of all those great sanitary reforms, which have now assumed national proportions, and which in the metropolis exhibit their effects in the gigantic scheme of drainage, and pursue their active enquiries into all causes of destruction of health and social decency into the remotest and most obscure corners of the United Kingdom.

The skeleton of the great legal and social reformer Bentham was preserved by Dr. Smith for many years in his house - not in its naked osseous condition, but clothed in the philosopher's own raiment, wearing his own hat, and with a waxen mask, representing him as much as possible in his living image. Many persons will recollect the start which was given them when a sort of large cheffonier was opened, and the figure of the philosopher was presented sitting before them.

Dr. Southwood Smith died at Florence on the 10th of December, 1861, a hale old man, from a sudden chill from the Tramontane wind. He was buried in the beautiful Protestant cemetery there, and a handsome marble obelisk has been erected to his memory by his family and friends, with a medallion profile, executed by Mr. Hart, the sculptor, of Florence.

Dufferin Lodge

Adjoining Fitzroy Park, on a pleasant eminence, stands Dufferin Lodge, the suburban residence of Lord Dufferin, one of our most rising and respected statesmen, and equally distinguished in literature for his lively 'Letters from High Latitudes.' As a descendant of Richard Brinsley Sheridan, Lord Dufferin inherits a large portion of the family genius and spirit of liberal reform. Before him, his mother, Lady Gifford, lived in the same house. As one of the three granddaughters of Sheridan - herself, the Duchess of Somerset, and the Hon. Mrs. Norton - distinguished equally for their personal and intellectual attractions, Lady Gifford, as Lady Dufferin, will he long remembered by her touching song of 'I am sitting on the stile, Mary,' a composition unsurpassed for genuine pathos.

CAEN WOOD AND LORD MANSFIELD

Highgate, by the difficulty of its hills, and by the estates of the church, of Lord Mansfield, and Miss Coutts, lying in front and rear of it, has retained to this hour more of a rural character than any village in the immediate suburbs of London. Unlike Hampstead, to which London has pushed forward its bricklayers' arms, both from St. John's Wood and Haverstock Hill, it yet, on its western side, stands in union with the country. London has, indeed, followed Dick Whittington up Holloway Hill, but as yet only in a slender line. The old green of Highgate yet boasts its old buildings, its old elm and lime-tree avenue, and has an air of quiet and of the past. Around stretch fields, and hills, and glades that possess an eminent beauty, which on Sundays and holidays suddenly make the Londoner think himself a countryman, and almost poetical. Especially crossing by the footpath to Hampstead, with those green undulating fields, the noble forest-look of Caen Wood, the chain of five ponds, and the far-opening views, there is little English pastoral scenery to excel it. Turning back to look at Highgate itself, the aspect of it is singularly beautiful and picturesque. The white villas, amid their trees and pleasant grounds running up the hill, are finely terminated by the tall spire of the church. On either hand, green uplands and noble scattered trees, with the waters flashing at their feet, compose a picture that has no peer anywhere immediately round London, and reminds one rather of a foreign than an English suburb. As for those fields themselves, with their green swells and slopes, and their trees dispersed in park-like order, they remind me of hundreds of miles of such lands that I have traversed in Australia, as park-like, as fertile, as green in spring, and having an air of centuries of the polishing touch of human hands, though no hands save those of God have touched them, and no feet but those of the savage and his kangaroo have, till lately, traversed them.

I have already adverted to the splendid landscape, and the vast expanse of London lying under the eye of the spectator from Highgate Hill; and I shall not soon forget the astonishment of the

Danish poet, Andersen, on his first visit to England, as we drove at night over Highgate Archway, and he saw the great world metropolis mapped out in fire below him.

Kenwood House
(From an original drawing in the possession of J. E. Gardner, Esq.)

The house and estate of Caen, or Ken Wood, however, are the finest feature, next to London itself, of the immediate vicinity of the village. The house is a large and massive building of yellow stone, impressive from its bulk and its commanding situation rather than from its architecture, which is that of Robert Adam, who was very fashionable in the early part of the reign of George III. Adam had two brothers, both architects also; and he, generally assisted by his brother James, erected Luton House, Gosford House, the Register Office in Edinburgh, as well as various buildings in London (the Adelphi, Portland Place, &c.), of which the screen at the Admiralty is by far the finest. Caen Wood House has two fronts, one facing the north, with projecting wings, the other facing the south, extending along a noble terrace, and has its facade elongated by a one-storied wing at each side. The basement story of the main body of the house is of rustic work, surmounted by a pediment supported by Ionic pilasters, the columns of the wings being of the same order. Within, Adam, as was usual with him, was more successful than without. The rooms are spacious, lofty, and finely proportioned. They contain a few good paintings, among which are some of Claude's; a portrait of Pope, the poet,

279

with whom the first Earl was very intimate; and a full-length one of the great law lord himself, as well as a bust of him by Nollekens. The portrait of Pope is said to be by himself, as well as one of Betterton, the tragedian, for he had studied painting with his friend Jervas.

The park in front, of fifty acres, is arranged to give a feeling of seclusion in a spot so near to London. The ground descends to some sheets of water forming a continuation of the Highgate Ponds, lying amid trees; and a belt of fine, well-grown wood cuts off the broad open view of the metropolis. Here you have all the sylvan seclusion of a remote country mansion; and charming walks, said to be nearly two miles in extent, conduct you round the park, and through the woods, where stand some trees of huge growth and grandeur, especially cedars of Lebanon and beeches. A good deal of this planting - especially some fine cedars yet near the house - was done under the direction of the first lord himself. A custom is kept up here which smacks of the old feudal times. Every morning, when the night-watchman goes off duty at six o'clock, he fires a gun, and immediately three long winds are given on a horn to call the servants, gardeners, and labourers to their employment. The horn is blown again at breakfast and dinner hours, and at six in the evening for their dismissal.

No doubt in the old times Caen Wood, as part of the forest of Middlesex, was a very wild and darkling region, a fit place for criminals to seek concealment in. So, as we have seen, the Fifth Monarchy men fled there with Venner, in January 1661. So the confederates of Guido Fawks fled there on the failure of the Gunpowder Plot. The hill at some distance in front of it, still called Traitor's Hill, is a bare green eminence, something resembling Primrose Hill, and giving a fine view of the Parliament House, the old predecessor of which they hoped to see start into the air. In Miss Coutts's grounds there is also a hill which bears the same name, and probably may have been the stand-point of some of the traitors; but the more western hill has the more general title to the tradition. Betwixt this hill and the woods of Lord Mansfield, on the rising ground, stands a mound or ancient barrow marked by a few Scots pine trees, making it a quickly recognisable object. The tradition connected with this barrow is, that in very early times the inhabitants of St. Alban's, who aspired to mate that town the capital of this part of England, finding London growing a vigorous rival, set out to attack and destroy it; but that the Londoners turning out, met and defeated their enemies of St. Alban's on this spot, and that this mound contains the dust of the slain.

Another association of a much more recent date which I may mention before entering on the main object of this paper, is that of the name of William Paterson, the founder of the Bank of England. Paterson was a clever Scot, whose head was as full of mercantile speculations as a hive is of bees, and he was supported by such men as Mr. Coutts, Sir John Trenchard, Sir Thomas Dalby, &c. It was the same Paterson who originated the celebrated Darien scheme in the reign of William III, a scheme which ended most disastrously - not from any folly in the scheme itself, for had it succeeded it would have established for us a passage across the Isthmus of Panama, and a short cut into the Pacific Ocean, and to China and the East Indies, more than a century and a half ago. But Paterson by his daring plan had raised the fierce opposition of the Dutch and English East India Companies, and of Dutch William at their instigation; and William crushed the enterprise by his proclamation, and by prohibiting any supply of necessaries from the West India Islands. Paterson was entirely and splendidly successful in the establishment of the Bank of England, of which he was for some time a director, and of his humble but still most useful scheme of water supply for the north of London. It is true that Paterson's water company was only established in 1690, whilst Sir Hugh Middleton had brought the New River to London in 1614 - that is, seventy six years before. But Middleton had ruined himself by his grand enterprise; and so little was it appreciated, that for above thirty years the seventy two shares into which it was divided netted only £5 a share, though they now sell at £15,000 or £20,000 each. Paterson's plan of collecting the springs of Caen Wood into ponds or reservoirs succeeded, and supplied Hampstead and Kentish Town and their vicinity till the growing power of the New River Company pushed it from the field. The ponds still remain - a fine, fresh chain of water, giving life to the scene, and highly delighted in by the summer strollers from London. But on them, too, the speculators in endless railroads, and their great devastators, the engineers, have cast murderous eyes, are yearning to let them all off, run a line along their bed, and tunnel under Caen Wood itself. Then adieu to the peaceful beauty of Highgate; it will be followed quickly by all-devouring London.

As Caen Wood yet exists, it is an example of the magnificent rewards of the law in this country. We look about in vain in England for the palaces and great estates achieved by the poets and authors in general in this book-loving England; but everywhere we run against the broad lands and aristocratic abodes of the lawyers in this law-loving England. Literati and artists in general may inherit large fortunes, but lawyers are every day creating them out of nothing. Lord Mansfield won Caen Wood, and infinitely more, out of nothing.

This charming place had been in the hands of a succession of proprietors. In 1661 it was the property of a John Bill, Esq., who married a Lady Pelham, supposed to be the widow of Sir Thomas Pelham, and a daughter of Sir Henry Vane. It must afterwards have belonged to one Dale, an upholsterer, whom Mackay, in his 'Tour through England,' says, 'had bought it out of the Bubbles,' - the South Sea affair. This was in 1720. This Dale, unlike the majority of speculators, must have been a fortunate one. It then became the property of the Dukes of Argyll; and the great and good Duke John, whom Sir Walter Scott introduces so nobly in the scene with Jeanie Deans and Queen Caroline in 'The Heart of Midlothian,' and who had lived in the reigns of Anne and Georges I and II; who had fought bravely at Ramillies, Malplaquet, and Oudenarde, and who afterwards beat the rebel Earl of Mar and drove the Pretender from Scotland, resided here when called to London. The property was then devised by the Duke of Argyll to his nephew John, third Earl of Bute, who is only too well remembered in the opening of the reign of George III for his unpopularity. Bute was one of those men of outward grace and figure who attract the eyes of women, but who, having little or nothing in their heads, are only rendered ridiculous by being put into positions of eminence and responsibility. Bute was the favourite of the widow of Frederick Prince of Wales, mother of George III, a connection of public scandal. By this influence made minister of the young King, he soon showed himself so incapable that he was compelled by universal opinion to resign. Bute married the only daughter of the celebrated Lady Mary Wortley Montagu, who, of course, resided much here as Countess of Bute. It is curious that in Lady Mary's letters to her daughter she always spells the name of the place 'Caen.' The earlier possessors spelt it 'Ken,' and it is curious, too, that though in the patent of the earldom to Lord Mansfield it is spelt 'Caen,' Lord Mansfield himself, in his letters, to the end of his life spelt it 'Ken.' The word would seem to have originated in 'ken,' a view; but there was a very early Dean of St. Paul's, named Reginald de Kentewode, from whom it and Kentish Town may have derived their appellation; for, as I have shown, much property in that direction formerly belonged to the cathedral of St. Paul.

Lord Bute, though so very unpopular as a minister, as the close friend of the Princess of Wales must have had some very good qualities as a man. He appears to have been very amiable in his family, and to have lived on the best of terms with his wife. Lady Mary Wortley Montagu, in her letters to her sister, the Countess of Mar, and her daughter, Lady Bute, always spoke of him with great respect and esteem. A good trait of Lord Bute is mentioned by Mrs. Piozzi. Dr. Johnson having said that 'knowledge was divided amongst the Scots like bread in a besieged town, to every man a mouthful, and to no man a bellyful,' and some officious fellow having carried this to Lord Bute when he was minister, he only replied, 'Well, well, never mind what he says; he will have the pension for all that.'

In the second volume of 'Lady Mary Wortley Montagu's Letters,' p. 407, she says,

> 'I well remember Caen Wood House, and cannot wish you a more agreeable place. It would be a great pleasure to me to see my grandchildren run about the gardens. I do not question Lord Bute's good taste in the improvements round it, or yours in the choice of furniture. I have heard the fame of the paper-hangings, and had some thoughts of sending for a suite, but was informed that they were as dear as damask is here, which put an end to my curiosity.'

This was written from Louvere, in Italy. In another letter from the same place, p. 415, she congratulates her daughter on the comparative leisure that she enjoys at Caen Wood.

A large fortune fell to Lord Bute from the will of Mr. Edward Wortley Montagu, his wife's father, who diverted it from his only son, whose extraordinary conduct had alienated both his parents. This most eccentric man had from a boy run away from his tutors, or from the school where he was placed. He disappeared from Westminster School, and could not be discovered for more than a year, when he was accidentally found crying fish at Blackwall, where he had apprenticed himself to a fisherman. A second time he absconded, and could not he traced for two or three years, when he was recognised as a muleteer who had brought down fruit from the interior of Portugal to an English vessel at Oporto. A third time he went off, and entered himself as a foremastman in a vessel bound for the Mediterranean. After this he was sent with a learned tutor to the West Indies, and on his return became a member of Parliament; hut his extravagances soon drove him from England, and in Paris he got into very dubious matters with Lord Southwell and a Mr. Taafe, for which he was thrown into prison, at the suit of a Spanish Jew of the name of Payba. After the death of his father, having a certain amount of income, he lived chiefly in the East, dressing like a Turk, and affecting to believe entirely in the Koran; or in Italy, where he maintained the same character. He advertised for a wife already *enceinte*, that if she had a son he might inherit a large property, left conditionally by his father; and a candidate for such a wifeship being found, the marriage was only prevented by his choking himself with a partridge bone and dying. His mother, Lady Mary, left him one guinea, which on receiving he gave away laughing to a Mr. Davison, who was his companion in his Eastern travels. This Mr. Montagu was the first child on whom his mother tried the effect of inoculation. Did she inoculate him with all this passion for Eastern life and vagabondism from the blood of some Turk, having his descent from Arabian and Ishmaelitish stock? Diseases are said to be frequently inoculated, and even insanity; why not idiosyncrasies too? It is to the honour of Lord Bute that he gave up to this strange brother-in-law voluntarily a handsome quota of the property thus left away from him by his father for his follies. We are glad to think of Caen Wood as the place where so honourable a thing was done, and to find Lord Bute in private life showing qualities so unexpected from his public and political reputation.

The Earl of Bute sold Caen Wood in 1755 to Lord Mansfield, who, on his death, devised it to go with the title to his nephew,

Lord Stormont, whose descendants now possess it. Lady Mary Wortley Montagu's daughter brought Lord Bute seven sons and six daughters, so at that time the house and grounds of Caen Wood resounded with life enough. It is now very little occupied, its proprietor being much fonder of Scone Palace, his Scottish residence. In fact, this is one of the worst features of the continued feudal system, and of enormous properties in land in England. In this little populous island thousands of the most beautiful parts of it, which God created for general pleasure, are, in a dog-in-the-manger style, shut up for the greater part of the year, and seen only by a few bailiffs and labourers. Our aristocracy too often only live themselves in the country to kill game. At the 12th of August away they scud to shoot grouse, or whatever national business demands their attention; and in February, the moment the game season expires, they hurry up to town again. During six months of spring and summer, their houses and grounds are closed to human enjoyment; in many cases where they have various houses this non-residence is the prevailing fact. If there be any truth in the gospels about doing as you would be done by, there is something grossly out of joint here. It is a condition of exclusiveness that exists in no other country of the world besides, and if there be, as Christians suppose, a state of recompense in the next world, I fear many of our shutters up of God's and nature's paradises will find themselves committed to a very high-walled pinfold there for a considerable time of expiation. But this *en passant*.

Before the Earl of Bute, however, inherited Caen Wood, there was a little boy already riding up from Scotland, on his pony, with a little meal-sack hung from its neck, in order to take possession of it. This was William Murray, the eleventh child and fourth son of Viscount Stormont, of the Castle of Scone, which, says Lord Campbell, 'in a dilapidated condition, frowned over the Tay in the midst of scenery which, for the combination of richness and picturesqueness of beauty, is unsurpassed.' Lord Stormont had married a lady of the ominous name of Scott of Scotstarvet, who brought him so many children that they were in danger of being, in Scottish phrase, 'starvet' altogether. 'To add to the difficulties of the poverty-stricken viscount,' says Lord Chancellor Campbell,

'his wife, although of small fortune was of wonderful fecundity, and she brought him no fewer than fourteen children. For these high-born imps oatmeal porridge was the principal food which he could provide, except during the season for catching salmon, of which a fishery near his house, belonging to his estate, brought them a plentiful supply.'

Willie, the fourth son, showed symptoms of great talent, and therefore much care was taken of his education - that is, so far as the scanty means of his father would allow. He was sent to the grammar school at Perth till he was fourteen; and there is a tradition that he was so short of money that he and two other boys used to join at one candle in preparing their lessons overnight for the next day. As the family was out-and-out Jacobite, and his second brother, James, had actually joined the Pretender, there was little hope of assistance from the nobles who supported the reigning family, and law seemed the only profession for the lad to succeed in. It was resolved to send him up to Westminster School, where, by the influence of Bishop Atterbury, a thorough Jacobite too, it was hoped he would be admitted and well looked after. But how was he to get there? A coach ran once a week from the Black Bull, in Canongate, Edinburgh, to the Bull and Mouth, St. Martin's-le-Grand, London, performing the journey in ten days. But the fares were excessive, and beyond reach of the Stormont purse; it was therefore resolved that the boy should travel up on his pony. On this most formidable journey for a boy of fourteen at that time, to run the gauntlet of highwaymen, and cheats and expenses at wayside inns, William Murray set off from Scone, like Gil Blas from Oviedo to Pegnaflor, on March 17, 1718. Making some stay with relatives in Edinburgh, he jogged along southward. He could draw on the contents of his meal-sack at noon by some brookside, and extemporise crowdy, whilst his pony grazed, and thus in two months, short of one week, that is, on May 8, he arrived in London. Here he was consigned to the care of one John Wemyss, who had been born on his father's estate, and now practised as an apothecary in the metropolis. Being entered of Westminster School, he made good use of his time and aptitude for learning, and acquired a wonderful passion for the higher practice of law by listening to the pleadings in Westminster Hall. Like other aspirants for legal fame, Murray had his early difficulties; but he had a Scot's indomitable perseverance, and a mild and pliant manner, that worked his way. Moreover, all his contemporaries attribute to him a silvery-toned voice exquisitely modulated, which influenced almost irresistibly his hearers. We need not say more than that in 1742 he became Solicitor-General, had distinguished himself both at the bar and in Parliament in the highest degree, and in 1745 found himself called upon to appear as Government prosecutor against the Scottish rebel lords, Kilmarnock, Cromarty, Balmerino, and Lovat. This must have been a crucifying business for him. They were martyrs to the cause which had been the enthusiasm of his youth - the cause in which his parents and all his family were engaged heart and soul. His second brother, James, had early and openly gone over to the Pretender, and had been created Earl of Dunbar by him in anticipation of success. Yet Murray went through the trial and condemnation of the rebel lords with great self-command. Only once was he seen to flinch when old Lord Lovat complimented him on his speech against him, adding, 'But I do not know what the good lady your mother will say to it, for she was very kind to my clan as we marched through Perth to join the Prince!'

And, spite of his conduct on this occasion, he afterwards experienced much trouble from this cause. As a Westminster boy, he used to go often with another boy, named Vernon, in company with three others, Stone, Johnson, and Fawcett., to dine at Vernon's father's, a draper in Cheapside, a desperate Jacobite. There the lads, in their zeal for the Pretender, drank his health on their knees. When Murray had thus become Solicitor-General, and through his good offices Johnson was made Bishop of Gloucester, and Stone sub-preceptor to the Prince of Wales, afterwards George III, this story was carried to Court, and an alarm was raised, not only that Murray was a traitor, but that he had insinuated another into the high places of the Church, and a third into the still more serious post of forming the political principles of the heir apparent to the throne. The accused were called on to answer it to the Privy Council, and though they were eventually acquitted, suspicion still clung to Murray; and Pitt, afterwards Chatham, used to make him shrink and tremble by his terrible allusions to this tender place. `Colours, much less words,' says Horace Walpole, 'could not paint the confusion and agitation of Murray's face during such an attack.'

Yet such was Murray's eloquence and profound knowledge of law, that he surmounted all this and became not only member of successive administrations, but Lord Chief Justice of the King's Bench, and Chancellor of the Exchequer, with the title of the Earl of Mansfield. His brother lawyers and countrymen, his biographers, Lords Brougham and Campbell, have not only eulogised him as the greatest lawyer, but almost the greatest man, of his time. He was a most illustrious lawyer, but by no means a great man, if we include moral greatness as the essential to such a man. As a lawyer he had a wonderful clearness of vision; he saw the true bearings of a case through any amount of enravelment; and where his personal ambition was not concerned, he was strictly and eminently just. He advocated free-trade principles, and did much to establish better forms of procedure in courts of law; in deciding the true principles of mercantile transactions, and fixing those of colonial judicature. He had the honour first to decide that no slave can remain a slave in England. He was a friend to religious toleration; but on the other hand he was a strenuous supporter of pressing seamen, of hanging all forgers, and of the destruction of the liberty of the press. These features were conspicuous in the trials of Dr. Dodd, of 'Junius' for libel, and of John Wilkes for publishing the famous No. 45 of the 'North Briton.' Whenever he was concerned for the Government, whether in Parliament or on the Bench, he was the organ of despotism in that most despotic of times. In the treatment of the American Colonies he sanctioned and advocated all the policy which outraged that people and lost that country. His biographers have egregiously erred in venturing to draw a parallel betwixt him and Lord Chatham. In eloquence, the one was a softly flowing stream; the other a consuming fire. Murray quailed and trembled when Chatham's thunder rolled over his head, and his lightnings flashed around him. Chatham was for full-grown liberty, and he saw how countries were to be won, whilst his humbler rival only saw how to lose them. Chatham instinctively saw genius wherever it existed; he chose Wolfe for America and Clive for India; and he drove the French not only from Canada but from the American colonies. Under his auspices Clive laid the foundation of our great Indian empire.

It has been said that Lord Mansfield became a victim to the Gordon riots because he had ventured to do justice to a Catholic priest on his trial. But it is probable that had he not shown himself so long the enemy of political freedom, and the instrument of a most unpopular, despotic government, his house and books would not have been burned in Bloomsbury Square on that occasion - an event commemorated by Cowper in a few stanzas.

Lord Mansfield was a brilliant orator and sagacious lawyer, disposed to be just when justice did not stand in the way of his ambition. He had his virtues and his vices. Those who would see the one may read the lives of him by Brougham and Campbell; those who would see him severely castigated for his sins against public liberty may read 'Junius's' letters to him. Lord Campbell has spoiled his intended deification of him by letting out the fact that he had no heart. A hero without a heart is but a sorry hero. `A more serious defect,' says Lord Campbell,

'was his want of heart. No one had a right to complain of him; he disappointed no just expectation of favour; and he behaved with kindness to all within the sphere of his action; but all that he did might have been done from a refined, calculating selfishness, with a view to his own credit. He had no warmth of affection; he formed no friendships; and he neither made exertions nor submitted to sacrifices purely for the good of others.'

But the great position which Lord Mansfield occupied for more than half a century in the public eye - that is, from his successful defeat of the attempt to disfranchise the city of Edinburgh, on account of the murder of Captain Porteous, in 1737, to the resignation of his office of Lord Chief Justice of the King's Bench in 1788 - demands a fuller notice of the leading incidents of his professional and parliamentary career than I have given in this brief outline of his life.

Lord Campbell, in his fair and impartial 'Life' of him, notices at the outset something of that personal vanity from which even the greatest men are rarely perfectly free. An author proposed to become his biographer, and applied to him for the necessary materials. He replied:

'My success in life is not very remarkable. My father was a man of rank and fashion. Early in life I was introduced into the best company, and my circumstances enabled me to support the character of a man of fortune. To these advantages I chiefly owe my success.'

He then advises the applicant to write the life of Lord Hardwicke, who became Chief Justice of England and Lord Chancellor, though his father was a peasant. If our sketch of his early life and origin be correct, this account of them by himself must be very incorrect; and Lord Campbell says,

'His circumstances did *not* enable him to support the character of a man of fortune; and he did *not* owe his success to the advantages which he then enumerated; and it must he curious to trace the steps by which, after riding on a wretched pony from Perth to London, he "drank champagne with the wits;" he became the most distinguished advocate in England; he prosecuted Scotch peers, his cousins, for treason against King George; he was the rival of the elder Pitt, the greatest parliamentary orator England has ever produced; he was raised to be the highest criminal judge of the realm; he repeatedly refused the still more splendid office of Lord Chancellor; he, without political office, directed the measures of successive cabinets; and, what was far truer glory, he framed the commercial code of his country.'

Campbell adds that he was the first Scot who ever gained distinction in the profession of the law in England; and, on the other hand, the father of Lord Hardwicke was not a peasant, but an eminent solicitor in England.

From these statements it would appear that Lord Mansfield really attached more value to being the son of a very poor Scottish lord than to his own talents and ennobling exertions. Lord Brougham says that Murray was removed from Scotland at the tender age of three years, and educated in England, and from that cause had contracted no peculiarity of dialect. This story was originated by Halliday, Lord Mansfield's earliest biographer, and copied by all who followed. Even Dr. Johnson, speaking of Lord Mansfield, said, 'Much may be made of a Scotchman, if he be caught young.' But Lord Campbell proves, from family documents, and the statements of his near relatives, that, as already stated, he was in his fourteenth year when he rode his pony up to Westminster, and he never revisited his native land, though his parents lived many years, and his native scenes must have awakened many tender recollections in his heart, if he fortunately had had such a heart. Speaking of the humble manner in which Lord Mansfield, after being called to the bar, lived, Lord Campbell says he occupied very small chambers, three storeys high (No. 1, Old Square, then called Gate House Court), and that these were pointed out to himself when he began his own career, at the next door, No. 2. Yet at this time, after finishing eight or ten hours' hard study, he used to spend his evenings amongst the wits, and had Alexander Pope, then in his full fame, as his intimate friend. Murray had frequent invitations to Twickenham; and Pope, coming to Lincoln's Inn, would spend hours in instructing him in the most graceful attitudes and intonations of an orator. One day the pupil was surprised by a gay Templar, who could take the liberty of entering his rooms without ceremony, in the act of practising the graces of a speaker at a glass, while Pope sat in the character of a preceptor. Bishop Warburton also testifies to the warmth of friendship which Pope entertained for the young lawyer. After the death of Pope, he never seems to have courted the society of literary men, not even of his countryman Thomson, or of the great literary dictator Johnson. But it is to his great honour that he especially patronised Blackstone, the author of the immortal 'Commentaries.' He had recommended Blackstone to fill the vacant professorship of Civil Law in the University of Oxford; but the then Prime Minister, the Duke of Newcastle, always eager to do a little bit of dirty political jobbery, gave Blackstone to understand that, in return for the office, he expected a ready compliance with any Government demands of service in the University. Blackstone demurred, and the place was given to another, namely, Jenner, utterly ignorant of law civil, canon, and common. Murray advised Blackstone, notwithstanding, to settle at Oxford, and to read law lectures to such students as were disposed to attend them. The plan was splendidly successful, and suggested to Mr. Viner to establish a professorship of the Common Law of England in the University of Oxford, and to this we owe the immortal 'Commentaries' of Blackstone. Besides this, Mr. Murray, when he became Chief Justice, continued to recommend to noblemen and gentlemen the reading of the 'Commentaries' as the best work calculated to instil into the minds of their sons the great principles of English law, and the best way of becoming acquainted with the crabbed author, Coke upon Littleton, which, he said, had disgusted and disheartened many a tyro.

Lord Campbell tells us that, owing to the intense interest in his expositions of the law, and in his decisions, when Chief Justice,

> 'the unknown practice began of reporting in newspapers his addresses to juries; and all suitors, sanguine in their belief of being entitled to succeed, brought their causes to be tried before him; so that the business of the King's Bench increased amazingly, and that of the other courts of common law dwindled away almost to nothing.'

But not content with endeavouring to dispense strict justice to the public, he was equally anxious to extend the same to the barristers practising in his court. He broke up the monopoly of the bar. Before his time, the leading counsel engrossed the whole hearing of the cases:

> 'Day by day, during the term, each counsel, when called upon, had been accustomed to make as many motions successively and continuously as he pleased. The consequence was, that by the time the attorney and solicitor-general, and two or three other dons, had exhausted their motions, the hour had arrived for the adjournment; and, as the counsel of highest rank was again called at the sitting of the court next morning, juniors had no opportunity of making any motion with which they might be entrusted, till the last day of term, when it was usual, as a fruitless compliment to them, to begin with the back row, after the time had passed by when their motions could be made of any use to their clients.'

Of course, under such a practice, people were not likely to trust their causes to juniors; and yet the leaders had so many, that they could do no sort of justice to the bulk of them. Many of these leaders were in the House of Commons, busy in political affairs, instead of carefully studying their briefs in their chambers; and thus the public business was damaged every way.

> 'To remedy these evils, Lord Mansfield made a rule that counsel should only make each one motion in rotation; and that if by chance the court rose before the whole bar had been gone through, the motion should begin next morning with him whose turn it was to move at the adjournment. The business was thus both more equally distributed and much better done.'

Another bad practice, that of questions which turned upon points of law being argued two or three, and even four times over in successive terms, though not attended with any real difficulty, but with immense expense and vexation to the clients, Lord Mansfield stoutly discouraged, always refusing a second argument, unless the court entertained serious doubts. There was another habit of the judges, that of not deciding at the close of the argument, but making an entry of *curia advisari vult*, a fearful cause of increased cost and delayed judgment, which he as strenuously opposed, seeing that judgment was often so long postponed that judges had frequently forgotten the reasons and authorities brought forward at the bar before publicly declaring their opinion. Equally was he averse to the delays occasioned by the laziness or pugnacity of counsel, when a special case or statement of facts in evidence was to be prepared for the opinion of the judges. He himself dictated such statements in open court, and saw them signed by the counsel, before the jury was discharged. He made, moreover, an order that no cases should be postponed, even with consent of the parties, without the express authority of the court; and that such postponed cases should come on *peremptorily* at the beginning of the next term.

In *Nisi Prius* causes, he put an end to much irregularity in the routine of counsel addressing juries, and in examining and cross-questioning witnesses. 'By his care,' says Lord Campbell, 'the system which we now follow was gradually matured.' According to this, the junior counsel for the plaintiff having opened the pleadings, or stated the issues, or questions of fact, raised by the record for decision, the leading counsel for the plaintiff alone addresses the jury; the plaintiff's evidence follows; the defendant's leading counsel then addresses the jury, and if he gives no evidence, the debates at the bar here close; but, if there be evidence given, the plaintiff's leading counsel addresses the jury by way of reply. The judge then sums up, and the jury pronounces the verdict.

Besides mere matters of procedure, Lord Campbell says that Lord Mansfield had a great work to perform in educing and establishing the great principles of the Common Law of England. He found this system well adapted to the condition of this country during the feudal ages, but a perfect chaos as regarded the new condition of things which had sprung up with extending commercial, manufacturing, and colonial interests of the nation. The common law judges had been too timid, or destitute of legislative genius, to decide on great and fixed principles the questions which came before them respecting buying and selling of goods, respecting the affreightment of ships, respecting maritime assurances, bills of exchange, and promissory notes. The same undecidedness extended to all questions of colonial rights and transactions. `He saw,' says Lord Campbell,

> `the noble field that lay before him, and he resolved to reap the rich harvest of glory which it presented to him. Instead of proceeding by legislation, and attempting to codify, as the French had done very successfully in the "Coustumier de Paris," and the "Ordonnance de la Marine," he wisely thought it more according with the genius of our institutions to introduce his improvements gradually, by way of judicial decision.'

On all these great points, he laid down those principles which have become the practice of our time. He created a new judicial system, in fact, applicable to our new commercial and colonial requirements. 'Most of us,' says Chief Justice Buller,

> 'have heard these principles stated, reasoned upon, enlarged and explained, till we have been lost in admiration at the strength and stretch of understanding exerted. And I should be sorry to find myself under a necessity of differing from any case upon this subject which has been decided by Lord Mansfield, who may be truly said to be the founder of the commercial law of this country.'

This of itself would have been glory enough for any one man. In some cases, subsequent legislation has contravened his decisions, as in the case of the legality of Ransom Bills, and the right of impressment of seamen; but it has confirmed him in giving British subjects right of appeal against the arbitrary proceedings of the governors of any of its foreign and colonial possessions.

Lord Mansfield destroyed the right of wrecking. He laid it down, that whenever the owners of a wrecked vessel could prove their ownership, everything belonging to the wrecked vessel belonged sacredly to them, and to no one else; but he settled a far greater question - namely, that no man has a right of property in any human creature. He it was who in the case of James Somerset, a negro, decided that 'Slaves cannot breathe in England.' 'Villeinage,' he said,

> 'has ceased in England, and it cannot be revived. The air of England has long been too pure for a slave, and every man is free who breathes it. Every man who comes into England is entitled to the protection of English laws, whatever oppression he may heretofore have suffered, and whatever may be the colour of his skin -
>
> Quamvis ille niger, quamvis tu candidus esses.
>
> Let the negro be discharged.'

In those words Lord Mansfield shed a new and immortal splendour on his country, for which every Englishman for all time ought to be grateful to him. He further defended the honour and security of women in the case against Sir Francis Blake Delaval, and he established literary copyright in authors. As I have already said, he had a most perspicuous sense of justice, and exercised it nobly in all cases where his interests or his political prejudices did not interfere. In those cases he often lamentably failed, and Junius did not neglect to seize upon and drag these deficiencies before the public with merciless severity. In the case of Lord Grosvenor v. the Duke of Cumberland for the seduction of his wife, he laid it down to every one's astonishment, that it made no difference as to the amount of damages, whether the culprit were rich or poor, a peasant or a prince. Junius said,

> 'I shall not attempt to refute a doctrine which, if it were meant for law, carries falsehood and absurdity on the face of it; but if it were meant for a declaration of your political creed, is clear and consistent.'

From the time that his lordship became Lord Chancellor, and a member of the Cabinet, this leaning towards governmental interest became more conspicuous. 'He was,' says Lord Campbell, 'always ready as a champion of the Ministers.' In the early part of the reign of George III, when the great Lord Chatham was dismissed to make way for the weak favourite Lord Bute, Mansfield was in office and in close alliance with that favourite. After his speedy fall

Mansfield still remained a member of the Cabinet, and in this position was called upon to decide in the attacks of the Crown on the subject, and on members of Parliament in the case of the notorious John Wilkes; and in this he did himself honour by pronouncing against the validity of general warrants, and in reversing the outlawry of Wilkes; but he afterwards, though then no longer a member of the Cabinet, neutralised the credit thus obtained, by defending the House of Commons in its unconstitutional proceedings of returning Colonel Luttrell instead of John Wilkes for Middlesex, in spite of Wilkes's great majority, and although he himself had reversed Wilkes's outlawry. His reasons for this conduct he said were locked up in his breast and should die with him, which need not have been the case, were they just reasons.

In the unhappy quarrel with the North American colonies, he also took the now universally acknowledged unconstitutional course of asserting the right of the 'mother country to tax them without representation,' for which Chatham hurled his most indignant thunder at his head; and Lord Camden upbraided him in his more noble conceptions of constitutional right. Still further to injure the reputation of Lord Mansfield for impartiality where the Crown was concerned, now arose the grand and trenchant attacks of Junius on both ministers and monarch; and in the trials of Rex *v.* Woodfall, Lord Mansfield, presiding, endeavoured to persuade the jury that they had nothing to do with the law of the case, they had only to decide the facts of the publication of the letters, and leave the judges to decide whether they were libellous. All we can say on behalf of Lord Mansfield's conduct is, that judges before him had done the same; but it was due to his clear sound sense to have gone the other way. The jury, aware that if they left the law with the judges they surrendered absolutely the liberty of the subject and the freedom of the press, gave a verdict of 'Guilty of publishing only!' And in spite of the reasonings of Lord Mansfield, when the same point was tried at Guildhall, in the case of Miller, the publisher, the jury found a verdict of Not Guilty. At this time also, Mansfield was not only Lord Chief Justice, but he held the seals of the chancellorship or keeper, and received the emoluments of both; the other weakness of his character was for making money; and he did not escape the lash of Junius for this monopoly. He asks,

'Who is it who attacks the liberty of the press? Lord Mansfield! Who invades the constitutional powers of juries? Lord Mansfield! Who was that judge who, to save the King's brother, affirmed that a man of the first rank and quality, who obtains a verdict in a suit for criminal conversation, is entitled to no greater damages than the meanest mechanic? Lord Mansfield! Who is it makes Commissioners of the Great Seal? Lord Mansfield! Who is it who frames a decree for these Commissioners deciding against Lord Chatham? Lord Mansfield! Compared to these enormities, his original attachment to the Pretender, to whom his dearest brother was confidential secretary, is a virtue of the first magnitude.'

He added,

'Considering the situation and abilities of Lord Mansfield, I do not scruple to affirm, with the most solemn appeal to God for my sincerity, that, in my judgment, he is the worst and most dangerous man in the kingdom.'

'When political considerations mixed themselves with the trial,' Lord Brougham pronounces the same judgment on Lord Mansfield as Junius. On the occurrence of the sudden death of Lord Chatham when addressing the House of Lords, it is recorded, to the great discredit of Lord Mansfield, that, whilst all, friends or opponents, were greatly affected by this startling event, Lord Mansfield alone sat silent and unmoved by the spectacle of this final scene of his old antagonist. He would not vote one way or another for the pension to his widow and family; nor would he attend the funeral in Westminster Abbey. These circumstances betray a pettiness of feeling which prohibits our placing their possessor, amongst the truly magnanimous great.

After this period, however, Lord Mansfield displayed several instances of a liberal character beyond the prejudices of his age. Though he continued to urge those measures against the American colonies which lost them - which, however, must have been lost some time - he showed a great liberality in religious matters at home. He supported a Presbyterian minister in the demand of possession of his own chapel; he decided that Quakers might be admitted to make an affirmation instead of an oath in all civil cases, and avowed his opinion that a Quaker's affirmation ought to be accepted in all cases, as much as the oath of a Jew or Gentoo, or any other person who feels bound by the oath he takes. He decided against the Corporation of London, which sought to augment its revenues, and punish Dissenters, by electing them to the office of sheriff, and then heavily fining them for serving without conformity to the Established Church. For this decision Lord Mansfield in the city was cried down as little better than an infidel; and soon after, when he directed a jury to find a verdict of Not Guilty in the case of a Roman Catholic priest for celebrating mass, which Catholics did, though the law then forbade such celebration, he was denounced as not only a Papist, but a Jesuit in disguise. This, coming just before the riots, called the Lord George Gordon riots - in which Lord Mansfield directed an acquittal of Lord George on the charge of instigating the riots, although in those riots Lord Mansfield's house and invaluable law library were burnt, and his own life put in peril - no doubt, led in a great degree to those attacks on his person and property, although his arbitrary spirit towards the press, and some other unpopular things, had their share in the resentment against him. Erskine was the counsel for Lord George Gordon on this trial, and made the charges of his client having incited the mob to burn the house and library of such a man as Lord Mansfield, and to make war on the King, and to compass his death - the usual law jargon in cases of high treason - look supremely ridiculous.

No conduct could be nobler than that of Lord Mansfield on the burning of his house and library; and had his demeanour been such in the general events of his life, it would have placed him amongst the greatest, as he was one of the ablest of mankind.

'His library contained the collection of books which he had been making from the time that he was a boy at school at Perth, many of them the cherished memorials of early friendship; others rendered invaluable by remarks in the margin, in the handwriting of Pope or Bolingbroke, or some other of the deceased wits and statesmen with whom he had been familiar. Along with them perished the letters between himself, his family, and his friends, which he had been preserving for half a century, as materials for memoirs of his times.'

It is likewise believed that he had amused his leisure by writing for posthumous publication, several treatises on judicial subjects, and historical essays, filling up the outline of the admirable sketch he had given in his `Letters to the Duke of Portland.' All his manuscripts had remained in his town house, and they were consumed through the reckless fury of the illiterate wretches who could form no notion of the irreparable mischief they had done.

So then the Vandals of our isle,
Sworn foes to sense and law,
Have burnt to dust a nobler pile
Than ever Roman saw.

And Murray sighed o'er Pope and Swift,
And many a treasure more,
The well-judged purchase, and the gift
That graced his lettered store.

Their pages mangled, burnt and torn,
Their loss was his alone,
But ages yet to come shall mourn
The burning of his own.

- Cowper.

Who can estimate the poignancy of feeling over such a loss? Yet Mansfield bore it with an outward calm truly philosophical, and refused to ask any compensation for it. In private life Lord Mansfield is uniformly represented as being extremely amiable, as fond of having his young friends and relatives about him, and of promoting their interests in life. He was also fond of ornamenting his grounds, and some cedars in the plantations opposite to his house at Caen Wood were planted by him. He died on March 20, 1793, aged nearly eighty-nine years.

Such was Lord Mansfield, a most able man, without original genius; a great lawyer, but not a great patriot. Yet, with all his faults, he was a real benefactor to his country, by the general justice of his decisions, and his establishment of large and clear principles of judicature. These benefits must always be coupled with his memory.

One thing Lord Mansfield, in accordance with bis character, kept steadily in view: the acquisition of a title crowning the accumulation of a large fortune. He had to this end a fondly-cherished maxim: 'The funds give interest without principal, and land principal without interest, but mortgages both principal and interest.' Therefore, with the exception of Caen Wood, he purchased no land, and he did not invest in the funds; and at the time of his death the interest of his money on mortgages amounted to £30,000 a year. To swell these mortgages for years - in fact, for a longer time than had been known since the reign of William III, the seals of the chancellorship were held by him, along with his office of Chief Justice - indeed, till `Junius' frightened him out of his impudent monopoly. He was soon frightened, for his zealous biographer, Lord Campbell, confesses that he had as little moral courage as heart.

Let us close this article with an instance of generous strategy in a man of that humble rank which derives its lustre, not from estate or coronet, but from its own innate value. When the infuriated mob who had destroyed Lord Mansfield's house, books, pictures, everything, in Bloomsbury Square, were on their way to destroy his house at Caen Wood, Giles Thomas, the landlord of 'The Spaniards,' at the end of Hampstead Heath, learning their object, stood at his door and invited them to drink. He threw open his cellars to this hot and thirsty crew, already broiling from the fire in Bloomsbury, and whilst they caroused, he had a messenger speeding his way to the barracks for a detachment of the Horse Guards. By the time that the rioters had exhausted the barrels of `The Spaniards,' they found this troop drawn up across their way to Caen Wood. The steward and Mr. Wetherall, the medical man of the family, had also sent out ale in abundance from the cellars of Lord Mansfield; and thus, at once tottering under the fumes of beer and confronted by the soldiery, the mob fled, and left Caen Wood to stand peacefully through more peaceful times.

CROMWELL AND ANDREW MARVELL

In Highgate, Hampstead, and many another old suburb of London, we see capacious mansions of a former age standing in their walled enclosures of several acres, consisting of gardens and shrubberies, with their rustic summerhouses, old-fashioned conservatories, wide walks, and full-grown trees, most pleasant and ample retirements. These were, some of them, the abodes of the nobility, many more those of the merchants and wealthy citizens of London. We see at a glance, if we get a peep over their lofty walls, affluent of peach, nectarine, and apricot, in what lordly spaces they could indulge their expansive human nature; for it is a most elastic thing, this human nature, and can crouch almost into a nutshell, or dilate itself over the vastest palace. One sees how plentiful land was then, when the metropolis, thought so alarmingly great, was advancing but leisurely, according to our notions; and through what bowery lanes those sedate and worshipful citizens rode on sober steeds from their banks in Lombard Street, or their shops in Cheape, to these manor-like houses. These are fast being broken into by the builder, their walls prostrated, their quaint alcoves demolished, their quince trees, and mulberry trees, and broad-spreading cedars felled, and a whole town raised on the site of each of them. Where one warm merchant reposed of yore, a score or two of busy families elbow each other now in all compactness.

Such metamorphoses have taken place here, but yet not so extensively as elsewhere; and perhaps no part of the metropolitan suburbs can in the same space show so many of these old historic mansions as the descent of the hill out of Highgate towards Holloway. Here, on what is styled the Bank, I am about to make a call at several, and first at the house of Oliver Cromwell, and of that simpler and purer republican, Andrew Marvell. The residences of these Commonwealth's men stand scarcely a stone's throw from each other, but on opposite sides of the street. They are very different, as the men were; in their relative size and their general character, you see the different spirit and fortunes of the two men.

The one speaks of a builder who led conquering armies and trod on thrones and the necks of kings; the other of the poor, the unambitious, the uncorruptible patriot. Cromwell House, still so called, is a solid red brick mansion, capable of accommodating a successful general; Marvell's is a simple half-timbered cottage, where the honest member for Hull, who had occasionally to borrow a guinea, might retire to pen his parliamentary letters to his constituents, or a lyric in praise of the blind and then little regarded author of 'Paradise Lost;' or to scarify by his biting satire the great criminals of the time.

Cromwell House
(From a photograph taken expressly for this work)

But Cromwell House is rather called so because he built it than because he lived there. In fact, we can find no evidence of his having made it more than an occasional visit. It is said to have been built by him about the year 1630, for the residence of General Ireton, who had married one of his daughters. Prickett, in his 'History of Highgate,' says:

'Cromwell's house was evidently built and internally ornamented in accordance with the taste of its military occupant. The staircase, which is of handsome proportions, is richly decorated with oaken carved figures, supposed to be of persons in the General's army, in their costume, and the balustrades filled in with devices emblematical of warfare. On the ceiling of the drawing-room are the arms of General Ireton; this, and the other ceilings of the principal apartments, are enriched in conformity with the fashion of those days. The proportions of the noble rooms, as well as the brick-work in front, well deserve the notice and study of the antiquary and the architect. From the platform on the top of the mansion may be seen a perfect panorama of the surrounding country.'

The figures here mentioned stand on the posts of the staircase. They are each about a foot high, and were originally twelve in number. They are now ten, and really represent the different kinds of soldiers of the time.

In 1864, a fire broke out in Cromwell House, but did not injure the staircase, or anything of historical interest. It was thoroughly restored, and presents much the same appearance as before.

As for the front deserving the attention of the architect, that certainly is not on account of any architectural beauty, but it well deserves it from the excellence of the bricks and brickwork. The bricks and brickwork of our old mansions, as Hampton Court Palace, the part built by Wolsey, this old house, and hundreds of old mansions in town and country, show how far, in this hurrying and money-scraping age, we have gone backward in the quality of brick and bricklaying. And yet this is scarcely a correct expression, for we can go back to no period of our history in which the brick and bricklaying are not far superior to ours. Look at the fineness, the solid smoothness of the brick; at the nice and compact manner in which it is laid; and then turn to the coarse, often very unequally burnt brick of today, and the coarse mortar in which it is set, often in rude layers of nearly an inch thick, and the contrast is disgraceful to this age of boasted progress in the arts, but an age in which strength and beauty of building are sacrificed to the sordid calculations of the builder's profits. This was the case in the decline of Rome. No people in their best days built more magnificently than the Romans; none in their decline so shabbily and unsubstantially. Juvenal, describing the buildings of Rome, as well as its luxury and vices, astonishes us by his actual descriptions of London in Rome. In his third Satire he says, you were always having the houses tumbling about your ears, and hurrying to escape from fires:

> *- incendia, lapsus*
> *Tectorum assiduos, ac mille pericula sævæ*
> *Urbis.*

And again:

> *Nos urbem colimus tenui tibicine fultam*
> *Magna parte sui*, &c.

The builders ran up their slim walls and daubed them with stucco to make them look decent, as ours do. 'Hence,' says Juvenal,

'the greater part of the houses are kept standing by frail props, which the agent erects to prevent their instant fall. He stops up the old cracks, and assures you you may sleep in peace! But next, your neighbour shouts for water - he is running to save his moveables - the flames are already in the third storey, and woe to them who live in the garrets!'

The front of Cromwell's house is low, being only of two storeys finished by a parapet, so that the roof, which is thrown backwards, adds little to its elevation. It is distinguished for that solid and excellent masonry just noticed. It has a narrow cornice or entablature running the whole length of the front over each row of windows. Its doorway is arched and faced with a portal of painted wood, in good keeping with the building. In front is a gateway with solid, square pillars surmounted by stone globes. At the lower end a lofty porte-cochère admits to the rear of the building. The mass of the mansion running backwards is extensive, and behind lies a portion, at least, of its ancient gardens and pleasant grounds.

Ireton married Bridget, the eldest daughter of Cromwell, who, after his death, became the wife of General Fleetwood. Ireton was one of the stanchest, bravest, cleverest, and most unflinching of Cromwell's generals. He was born at Attenborough, a village a few miles from Nottingham. He received a first-rate education at Oxford, but was called away from the university by the outbreak of the civil war, being a most zealous admirer of the old Greek and

Roman republicanism. He married Bridget Cromwell in 1646, and was afterwards the very right-hand man of the great Oliver. The year before this, indeed, he commanded the left wing at the victorious battle of Naseby. He was constantly with Cromwell when he was in treaty with King Charles at Hampton Court, in 1647. He aided him in his struggle with the Adjutators and the Levellers; he sat on the trial of the King, and voted heartily for his death in 1648. The following year he accompanied the Protector to Ireland, and was left in command there, where he died of fever, November 26, 1651, being only forty one years of age.

Such was his able and determined character, that those who aimed at the life of Cromwell aimed at Ireton's too, not thinking themselves safe while he lived, even were Cromwell killed. Morrice, in his 'Life of Lord Orrery,' declares that Cromwell himself related that in 1647, at the time they were endeavouring to accommodate matters with the King, Ireton and he were informed that a scheme was laid for their destruction, and that they might convince themselves of it by intercepting a secret messenger of the King's, who would sleep that night at the 'Blue Boar' in Holborn, and who carried his despatches sewed up in the skirt of his saddle. Cromwell and Ireton, disguised as troopers, waited that evening, seized the saddle, and found letters of the King's to the Queen in France, confirming all that they had heard. From that hour, convinced of Charles's incurable treachery, they resolved on his death. Such was the son-in-law for whom was built Cromwell House.

Andrew Marvell

Andrew Marvell was one of the purest and noblest patriots that ever lived. Any one may see that by a single glance at his house. It is small and poor, just as an honest patriot's is sure to be. Over the way, as we have seen, is the house of a daring republican general and son-in-law of the equally daring Protector; men who in helping their country took care to help themselves. Just above it stood the house of the Earl of Arundel; and an earl has naturally a big house. Just below Marvell's, and on the same side, stood and stands the house of the Earl of Lauderdale, in Marvell's time one of the cruellest and most rapacious scoundrels that a debauched king could set to fleece his unfortunate subjects. This man, too, must have a great house and grounds; but Andrew Marvell was neither a revolutionary general nor a commonplace earl, nor a great Government harpy; he was only a patriot, and therefore he had only a little half-wooden tenement, such as - there it is below! You can look at it, and take note what sort of a house an honest man and a patriot may expect.

Andrew Marvell's House
(From a Photograph taken in 1848)

Andrew Marvell was the son of a clergyman at Hull, the master of the public grammar school there, who was drowned in crossing the Humber in 1640. He must have had the same noble nature as his son, for he crossed in a storm to assist in the passage of a young couple on their way to be married, though he had so little expectation of reaching the other bank in safety, that, on stepping into the boat, he threw his cane on shore, and cried, `Ho! ho! for heaven!' His son Andrew was a student at the time at Cambridge, and just twenty years of age. He inherited a small patrimony; travelled several years on the Continent; went as secretary of Earl Carlisle into Russia; became assistant Latin secretary with Milton to Cromwell; and in 1658 became member of Parliament for Hull. From the year of the Restoration of Charles II, 1660, we find Marvell writing a weekly letter to his constituents at Hull, till his death in 1678, having represented that town just twenty years. During this long period he was once about a year and a half in Holland, but, except on this occasion, was constantly at his post, and frequently received a barrel of ale from his constituents in sign of their goodwill.

The reason of Marvell writing a weekly letter was plainly the want of newspaper reports at that time, and of the slowness of the circulation of information, the post itself being slow enough. These letters of Marvell's are generally short, plain, matter-of-fact ones, such as an ordinary letter-sheet would contain, but giving the people of Hull to know exactly what Government and Parliament were doing. Besides his parliamentary duties, Marvell was industriously employed in writing poetry, satirical and religious, and the most slashing exposures of the corruptions and corruptors of Church and State. In a dissolute and dishonest reign like that of Charles II, we may imagine what such exposures would be. They fill three large quarto volumes. The chief of these are `An Account of the Growth of Popery and Arbitrary Government in England,' `The Rehearsal Transposed,' in which he most vigorously castigates Dr. Parker, Bishop of Oxford, for his base time-serving, and his fierce persecution of the Nonconformists. Such was Parker's fury, that he sent Marvell word, in an anonymous note: `If thou darest to print any lie or libel against Dr. Parker, by the eternal God I will cut thy throat.' But Marvell printed, and completely cowed the blustering bishop. Bishop Burnet says that Parker went on publishing his virulent books, till Marvell not only put down him, but his whole party. Dean Swift, noticing the short existence generally of the answers to books, accepts that of Marvell as the work of a 'great genius;' and says it continued to be read, though Parker's writings had sunk long ago. Marvell's wit was joyous, but unsparing, and had a deadly sting in it. In the same manner he disposed of Dr. Turner, Master of St. John's College, Cambridge, in an essay called, 'The Divine Mode,' and wrote a splendid treatise on General Councils, in which he handles ruthlessly the squabbles of bishops in all ages, saying that the very first council, that of Nice, had, according to Eusebius, nine creeds, and, in fact, that it had a dozen. He adds sarcastically, that as bishops grew worse and worse, bishoprics grew better and better.

'A Seasonable Argument to all the Grand Juries' following his essay on General Councils, the vicious Court and Church could stand it no longer. He had made free with the profligacy, the extravagance, and the mistresses of Charles II, and out came a royal proclamation, offering a high reward for the apprehension of Marvell. He thought it safest to retire to Hull for a while; but this did not protect him, for he died suddenly directly afterwards - namely, in August, 1678, in his fifty eighth year, as it was firmly believed, and as his biographer boldly asserts - by poison! His life had been repeatedly attempted before. In one of his letters, dated from Highgate, he states that his foes were implacable, and that he was frequently threatened with murder, and waylaid in his passing to and from Highgate, where he was fond of lodging. His only remark on this was that he was 'more afraid of killing than being killed.' The poetry of Marvell was much admired at the time, but has lost a little of its attraction now, though there are some pieces, such as 'The Bermuda Hymn,' that are very charming. This begins and ends thus:

> Where the remote Bermudas ride,
> In ocean's bosom unespied,
> From a small boat that rowed along
> The listening winds received this song:-
> 'What should we do but sing His praise
> That led us through the watery maze
> Unto an isle so long unknown,
> And yet far kinder than our own?'
> . . .
> Thus sung they in the English boat,
> A holy and a cheerful note;
> And all the way, to guide their chime,
> With falling oars they kept the time.

But if we are to accept as proved the statements of Captain Thompson, Marvell's biographer, the patriot had claims to poems universally admired, but attributed to others. Three of these are paraphrases of psalms, always attributed to Addison because they appeared in the 'Spectator,' just as scores of articles are now, and will be hereafter, attributed to Charles Dickens, because they appeared anonymously in `Household Words,' &c. These are the psalms, beginning -

> When Israel fled from Pharaoh's hand.

Secondly -

> The spacious firmament on high,
> With all the blue, ethereal sky.

And thirdly -

> When all thy mercies, O my God,
> My rising soul surveys.

Captain Thompson claims also the ballad of 'William and Margaret,' ascribed to Mallet, for Marvell, and on the ground that he finds these in the manuscript book of his unpublished poems, with his own corrections of them. The verses commencing, 'When Israel fled from Pharaoh's hand,' are, however, well known to be not Marvell's but that of Dr. Watts.

But my space fills: I must leave Marvell's poetry for his patriotism. The profligate King had often tried to win him over by offers of wealth and promotion. Here is one of these attempts:

The king sent the lord treasurer Danby to wait upon him with a particular message. His lordship with some difficulty found his elevated retreat, which was in a second floor in the Strand. Lord Danby, from the darkness and narrowness of the staircase, abruptly burst open the door, and suddenly entered the room, wherein he found Mr. Marvell writing. Astonished at the sight of so noble and unexpected a visitor, he asked his lordship with a smile if he had not mistaken his way. 'No,' replied my lord, with a bow, 'not since I have found Mr. Marvell;' continuing, that he came with a message from the king, who wished to do him some signal service, to testify his high opinion of his merits. He replied, with his usual pleasantry, that kings had not the power to serve him; he had no void left aching in his breast; but, becoming more serious, he assured his lordship that he was highly sensible of this mark of his Majesty's affection, but he knew too well the nature of Court favours, which were expected to bind a man in the chains of their interest, which his spirit of freedom and independence would not suffer him to embrace. These royal offers proving vain, Lord Danby began to assure him that the King had ordered him a thousand guineas, which he hoped he would receive till he could bring his mind to accept something better and more durable. `Surely,' said Marvell, with a smile,

> 'you do not, my lord, mean to treat me ludicrously by these munificent offers, which seem to imply a poverty on my part. Pray, my lord treasurer, do these apartments wear in the least an air of need? And as for my living, you shall hear of that from my servant.'

Calling his servant, he asked, `Pray, Jack, what had I to dinner yesterday?' 'A shoulder of mutton, sir.' 'And what do you allow me to-day?' 'The remainder, hashed.'

> 'And to-morrow, my lord Danby, I shall have the sweet blade-bone broiled; and when your lordship makes honourable mention of my cook and my diet, I am sure his Majesty will be too tender in future to attempt to bribe a man with golden apples who lives so well on the viands of his native country.'

The lord treasurer, unable to withstand this, withdrew with smiles, and Marvell sent to his bookseller for the loan of a guinea.

The Roman general who was tempted in a similar manner as he was supping on a dish of boiled turnip's, and who asked the tempter whether a man who supped on turnips was likely to sell his country, was not a more heroic patriot than Andrew Maxwell. It was a prophetic coincidence that named him a - Marvel. Rare are the men of this divine stamp! In a most debased and demoralised age Marvell stood poor - willingly, voluntarily poor and incorruptible. Like the angel Abdiel, he stood

> Among the faithless, faithful only he.

Witty beyond most of his age; the friend of Milton, and one of the first to discern and proclaim the magnificent genius of `Paradise Lost,' expressing his amazement at it in those fine lines, beginning

> When I beheld the poet blind, yet bold;

learned and accomplished by study and travel; having a wonderful influence in the House of Commons; capable by his talents and personal suavity of reaching the highest honours of the state, he preferred to be the unshaken friend of England, liberty, and Magna Charta; the advocate of justice and virtue, and the terror of the evil and corrupt, who never felt safe till, having missed him with the dagger of the assassin, they despatched him with poison. There is no spot on the hill of Highgate, few in England, that can boast the memory of such a man; and yet that little picturesque cottage of his, with its little slip of garden behind, with its raised walk, where the patriot no doubt often paced, and planned some onslaught on the enemies of his country, is, even as this page goes to press, being swept away. The property has lately fallen into the hands of Sir Sydney Waterlow; great alterations are contemplated, and already Marvell's house, being greatly dilapidated, has been condemned to fall, and the last trace of this God's true nobleman is wiped out from amongst us for ever.

His remains lie in St. Giles's Church, London, near those of Sir Roger L'Estrange.

ARABELLA STUART AND LORD BACON

A little higher up the hill, or Bank, as it is called, than Cromwell House, once stood Arundel House, the suburban residence of the Earls of Arundel. It has long been gone, but some remains of its garden walls still exist. Its site is now occupied by some modern houses, but its position may be known by its abutting on an old house called Exeter House, probably also from its being once the abode of the Earls of Exeter. Of this, however, there seems to be no record. It is not until towards the middle of the reign of James I that we hear of the Earl of Arundel having a house at Highgate. When Norden wrote his 'Survey of Middlesex' in 1596, the principal mansion was one thus mentioned:

> 'Upon this hill is most pleasant dwelling, yet not so pleasant as healthful, for the expert inhabitants there report that divers that have long been visited with sickness, not curable by physick, have in a short time repaired their health by that sweet salutarie aire. At this place Cornwalleys, Esquire, hath a very faire house, from which he may with great delight behold the stateley citie of London, Westminster, Greenwich, the famous river Thamyses and the country towards the south very farre.'

On the accession of James, the Spanish Ambassador, Gondemar, excused his absence, on account of his retreat to Highgate to take the fresh air. It was Gondemar who, on the departure of one of his suite to Spain, facetiously bade him recommend him to the sun, for he had not seen him here for a long time. Does the 'Spaniards' public house, at the entrance of Hampstead Heath from Highgate, date from the occasional retreats of the Spanish Ambassador to these hills? But the question here is, was the house of the Cornwallis family on what is called the Bank, that which became the property of the Earl of Arundel?

Lysons has remarked that there is in the Harleian Manuscripts, 6994, fol. 43, a letter of Sir Thomas Cornwallis, dated 'Hygat, 16 July 1587.' Sir Thomas, who was treasurer of Calais and Comptroller of the Household to Queen Mary, had been knighted as early as 1548, so that _____ Cornwalleys, Esq., mentioned by Norden in 1596, was, doubtless, his son William, who had taken up his residence there, whilst Sir Thomas had retired to his mansion at Brome, in Suffolk. It is said that this house at Highgate was visited by Queen Elizabeth in June 1589. The bellringers at St. Margaret's, Westminster, were paid 6d. on the 11th of June, when the Queen's Majesty came from Highgate.

It is certain, however, that James I, the year after his accession, visited the Cornwallises. On May 1, 1604, it was the scene of a splendid royal festival. Ben Jonson was employed to compose his dramatic interlude of 'The Penates' for a private entertainment of the King and Queen given on Mayday morning by Sir William Cornwallis, at his house at Highgate; and Sir Basil Brooke, of Madeley, in Shropshire, was knighted there at the same time.

At the end of the same year Sir Thomas Cornwallis died at his house at Brome - namely, on the 24th of December, aged eighty five; and a writer in the 'Gentleman's Magazine' for 1828, part i. p. 588, says that

> ` . . . it is most probable that Sir William then removed to reside in the Suffolk mansion,, as we hear no more of his family in Highgate. This residence, it is clear, from what has been already stated, had been the principal one in the place; and as we find the Earl of Arundel occupying one of a similar description a few years later, whilst we have no information of his having erected one for himself, there appears reason to presume that it was the same mansion.'

This might be so; but as there were several fine old houses at that period in Highgate, it is mere supposition. That which gives the most probability to the conjecture is that the prospect over London and the country accords well with the situation. The same writer continues:

> `The first mention I have found of the Earl of Arundel at Highgate, is of the date of 1617; and this is also connected with the history of the great Bacon. At that time the King was in Scotland, and Sir Francis, having been recently appointed Lord Keeper, was left at the head of the Privy Council in London, where, according to the satirical Weldon, he occupied the King's lodgings at Whitehall, and assumed the state of

royalty. During the absence of the Court, the lords were entertained by turns at each other's houses; and in Whitsun week, says Mr. Chamberlain, in a letter to Sir Dudley Carleton, the Countess of Arundel - the Earl being with the King in Scotland - made a grand feast at Highgate to the Lord Keeper, the two Lords Justices, the Master of the Rolls, and I know not whom else. It was after the Italian manner, with four courses, and four tablecloths one under another; and when the first course and tablecloth were taken away, the Master of the Rolls, Sir Julius Caesar, thinking all had been done, said grace, as his manner was when no divines were present, and was afterwards well laughed at for his labour.'

In 1624, we find the King sleeping at this mansion. He went on Sunday, June 2, towards evening, to Highgate, and lay at the Lord of Arundel's to hunt a stag early the next morning in St. John's Wood. 'The death of the Viscount St. Albans, in the year 1626, is the only subsequent event connected with the Earl of Arundel's house,' says this writer, 'that I have yet met with.'

Arundel House numbers amongst its chief historical associations two very different and yet very interesting ones - the flight from it of Arabella Stuart, in the reign of James I, and the death of the great Chancellor Bacon in the same reign, about fifteen years afterwards.

Arabella Stuart

Arabella Stuart was one of those charming women who might in private life have been happy themselves, and the source of much happiness to others, but whose lives were cursed by too near a proximity to a throne. Like Elizabeth of England and James I, she was descended from Henry VII, through Margaret, the daughter of that king, married to James IV of Scotland, and afterwards to Archibald Douglas, Earl of Angus. James I had the precedence in royalty of her by being the descendant by the English princess and the King of Scotland, whilst Arabella was only the offspring of Margaret Tudor's second marriage with the Earl of Angus. Had James had no children she would have been the next heir to the English throne. But though this was her exact position, and though she never showed the slightest ambition for reigning, she was too royal not to excite the fears of both Elizabeth and James. There were serious doubts of the legitimacy of Elizabeth, her father having married Anne Boleyn before the divorce from his queen, Catherine of Arragon. In fact, Henry VIII had by public acts declared her illegitimate. On this score Elizabeth was enormously jealous of Arabella Stuart, and did all in her power to prevent her marriage. Indeed, it was a system of Elizabeth's to keep everybody about her unmarried if she could; but as regarded Arabella Stuart it was a point of life and death with her. James himself during Elizabeth's reign, and when he had neither wife nor child, had proposed to marry her to Esme Stuart, Duke of Lennox, but Elizabeth immediately put Arabella in prison, and sent James a very cutting and insulting letter for daring to propose such a thing. Elizabeth thus watched her as a cat watches a mouse; yet, from all that we can learn, Arabella Stuart was much more disposed to enjoy a cheerful life amongst her friends than to incur the heavy cares of a crown. She was handsome, clever, fond of literature and poetry; very intellectual and witty, as letters of hers yet remaining show; and was of a particularly frank and generous character.

Having escaped from a miserable state of surveillance by the death of Elizabeth, she quickly found herself as completely in durance under her cousin James. Arrived himself at the English throne, though the father of several children, he became as fearful of Arabella Stuart marrying as Queen Bess had been. Cecil, his cold-blooded minister, took care to have her secured till James was settled in the kingdom, and then James resolved to keep her as cautiously as Elizabeth had done. There were various offers for her hand - one from the King of Poland; another from Count Maurice of Gueldres; but James peremptorily refused them all for her, and put her under the care of that virago, the Countess of Shrewsbury, who was always building and scolding.

Scarcely was James in England, however, before an alleged plot, in which Lord Cobham, Lord Grey, and the celebrated Sir Walter Raleigh, were charged with being concerned, made him more fearful of Lady Arabella than ever. It was said that they had planned to engage the King of Spain, the Archduke of Austria, and the Duke of Savoy, to place Arabella on the throne, on condition that she should tolerate Popery, and take as a husband whatever person they should choose. At the trial, in which Coke, the attorney-general, used the most violent and abusive language towards Sir Walter, the Lady Arabella was present in the gallery with a crowd of the nobility, and Lord Howard, afterwards of Effingham, said for her that she had no concern whatever in the matters alleged; and Cecil himself gave evidence that she had indeed received a letter from Lord Cobham on the subject of her claims to the throne, but that she had only laughed at it and sent it to the King. James contented himself with confiscating the property of the accused, banishing some and imprisoning others. Raleigh remained in the Tower on this charge twelve years, though he stoutly denied his guilt, and though nothing was really proved against him.

James might have permitted the Lady Arabella to marry, and dismissed his fears, but then, instead of a poor, pusillanimous creature, he must have been a magnanimous one. She was dependent on the Crown for fortune; and the pension allowed her was miserably paid. Under these circumstances she met with an admirer of her early youth, William Seymour, second son of Lord Beauchamp, the eldest son of the Earl of Hertford. Their juvenile attachment was renewed, and the news of it flew to James and greatly alarmed him. Seymour on his side was descended from Henry VII, and there were people who thought his claim better than James's, for Henry VIII had settled the descent, in case of failure of his own issue, on his youngest sister Mary and her line, which was that of the Seymours. James fiercely reprimanded Seymour for presuming to ally himself with royal blood, though Seymour's was as royal as his own, and forbade them on their allegiance to contract a marriage without his permission. But love laughed at James, as it is said to do at locksmiths, and in 1610 it was discovered that they were really married. James committed Seymour to the Tower, and Arabella to the custody of Sir Thomas Parry, in Lambeth, but not thinking her safe there, he determined to send her to Durham under the charge of the bishop of that see. Refusing to comply with this arbitrary and unjustifiable order, she was suddenly seized by officers in her bed, and was carried thus, shrieking and resisting, to the Thames, and rowed some distance up the river. She was then put into a carriage and conveyed forcibly as far as Barnet. But by this time her agitation of mind had brought on a fever, and a physician called in declared that her life must be sacrificed by any attempt to carry her further. After some demur James consented to her being brought back as far as

Highgate. The account says that she was conveyed to the house of a Mr. Conyers. Tradition asserts this house to be that now called Arundel House. Probably it belonged to a Mr. Conyers before it became the property of the Earl of Arundel, whose it was when Lord Bacon was its guest, fifteen years afterwards.

Lady Arabella had leave to stay here a month, and this term was extended to two months, which she made use of to establish a correspondence with her husband in the Tower, and to plan a scheme for their mutual escape. This plan was put into effect on June 3, 1611, the very day that the Bishop of Durham had set out northward to prepare for her reception. The following is the account of this romantic adventure, chiefly from Winwood's 'Memorials of the Reigns of Elizabeth and James I.':

Disguising herself by drawing a great pair of French fashioned hose over her petticoats, putting on a man's doublet, and a man-like peruke, with long locks over her hair, a black hat, black cloak, russet boots with red tops, and a rapier by her side, she walked forth between three and four of the clock in the afternoon with Mr. Markham. After they had gone afoot a mile and a half to a sorry inn where Crompton attended with horses, she grew very sick and faint, so that the ostler that held the stirrup said that the gentleman would hardly hold out to London. The mounting of the horse, however, brought blood into her face, and so she rode on towards Blackwall. There she found boats and attendants, who rowed her down the river to Gravesend, where a French boat lay in waiting for her. She expected to find her husband on board; but Seymour, though he had managed to get out of the Tower disguised as a physician, had not yet arrived. The French captain, conscious of the dangerous attempt in which he was engaged, grew impatient, and in spite of Lady Arabella's entreaties, fell down the river and put to sea. Seymour, finding the vessel gone on his arrival at the appointed place, engaged the captain of a collier to carry him over to Flanders for £40. The captain of the collier carried Seymour safe to Flanders, but poor Arabella was not so fortunate. No sooner was the escape of the two prisoners ascertained than there was a fearful alarm and bustle at Court. The Privy Council met, a proclamation was issued, setting forth that the fugitives were gone to the Spanish Netherlands to come back with an army to overthrow the Government and restore Popery. Letters were despatched to the

Archdukes, the King of France, and other Catholic sovereigns, warning them against harbouring the traitors, and demanding their surrender. A number of vessels of war dropped hastily down the Thames in pursuit, and another put out of the Downs. The latter intercepted the boat carrying Lady Arabella in the Calais roads; and after a sharp struggle the Frenchman struck, and gave up the fugitive. The poor distracted Arabella was carried back to London, and committed to the Tower, exclaiming that she could bear her fate could she but be sure of the safety of her husband. Her grief and despair soon deprived her of her senses, and after a captivity of four years she died in the Tower on September 27, 1615. No care seems to have been taken to ease her mind by the news of the safe escape of Seymour. In vain, whilst she retained her senses, did she plead for her liberty: in vain did the Queen endeavour to move the obdurate James in her favour. As for Seymour, he was permitted to return to England after the death of his wife, and lived to be a very old man. He became, in the course of inheritance, Marquis of Hertford, fought for the Crown in the civil war, though he had married the sister of the Earl of Essex, the parliamentary general. He lived to witness the Restoration; and Charles II restored to him the title of Duke of Somerset, which had been acquired and again forfeited by his great-grandfather, the Protector. He did not die till 1660, nearly half a century after this adventure; and he showed that he never forgot Lady Arabella, by naming one of his daughters by his second wife after her.

Lord Bacon

From Arundel House, in 1626, went forth another and more remarkable person, not on a flight to the Continent, but into eternity.

Francis Bacon, Baron Verulam, Viscount St. Albans, the man who had reached the highest legal honours attainable in England, who had sat in the seat of his father Sir Nicholas Bacon, Lord Keeper, as Lord High Chancellor; the man who had reached a far higher glory than any legal or state function could confer - who had revolutionised philosophy, and laid the foundation of all our modern progress in science, came here, unknowing of it, to die. The worldly glory of Bacon at this epoch had vanished. For five years he had been a fallen and disgraced man, banished from the court, made incapable of holding any public employment, and living at his house in Gorhambury, at St. Albans, or in Gray's Inn, a fallen, disappointed man: yet the greatest man, so far as intellect was concerned, that ages had produced. In the words of the poet:

> The greatest, wisest, meanest of mankind.

There have been attempts of late years to clear Bacon of the charges of accepting bribes as a judge, and to justify him. The attempt has only ended in whitewashing him. There is a craze now to whitewash the great delinquents of former ages. Richard III, Henry VIII, Queen Bess, Lord Bacon, have all found zealous men with their great buckets of whitewash and busy brushes to clean them, but the dirt still lies under, the rains of common sense fall, and it reappears. Froude, Basil Montagu, Hepworth Dixon, and others make us think of Pope's lines:

> Some in their choice of friends (nay, look not grave),
> Have still a secret bias to a knave:
> To find an honest man I beat about,
> And love him, court him, praise him, in or out.

Unfortunately, what can Bacon's distinguished advocates do, though they 'praise him, in or out,' seeing that he himself has fully admitted his crime?

Lord Bacon will always receive his just deserts. We owe him incalculable benefits for the publication of his 'Novum Organum,' which cut down the delusive syllogisms of Aristotle, and taught us to seek facts from nature, and to draw our deductions alone from them. For this he will always receive the gratitude and the intellectual homage of mankind; but mankind will not on that account declare him as morally as he was intellectually great. He showed himself weak where his interests and his ambition were concerned; he set a bad example - the more pernicious the greater the man; and for that he bore and must bear his punishment - the pity of mankind. We love him; but we cannot, therefore, pronounce him faultless. As the Lord Chancellor of England, he received presents from clients, knowing that such presents were given to do what Solomon says they do - 'blind the judge.' His great apologist, Basil Montagu, says that 'this had been done long before, and was commonly done by judges.' So much the worse! But this does not excuse a man of the clear understanding and high moral teaching of Bacon. Murder, robbery, adultery, were common in his day, and had been for thousands of years. The excuse for Bacon's failing would extend to every possible crime, and utterly put an end to the ten commandments, and make virtue a solemn humbug. Solomon, in his day, was the greatest genius, and the greatest fool. With all his knowledge, and all his proverbs, he was a monstrous sensualist; with all his praise of God he sunk into a miserable idolator. Will his talents or his philosophy excuse his crimes or heathenism? On the contrary, they stamp them as the more pitiful, and cry to us as an eternal warning to take heed how we stand. On these clear and indestructible distinctions stands the security of all morals, public and private.

The character of Bacon as drawn even by his own friends, in his own age, was one of personal ambition, vanity, and weakness in such a degree as to make him a marvel, considering his intellectual strength and eminence. In his office he assumed, especially during the King's absence in Scotland, a state and consequence more regal than judicial. Sir Anthony Weldon, in his 'Court of King James,' says that he bade the other privy councillors, if they took seats near him, keep their distance, so that Secretary Winwood rose, went away, and never would sit any more under his encroached state, but despatched a messenger to let the King know that he had better hasten back, as his seat was already usurped. He kept a state and household in rivalry of the greatest nobles. On the King's return, and the menace of his disgrace, Weldon says that he showed as much baseness; that Buckingham kept him two days waiting at his antechamber door amongst the lacqueys, and that when at length admitted, he fell down flat at the duke's foot, kissing it, and vowing never to rise till he had his pardon.

Basil Montagu himself tells us that his ostentation of liberality was most pitiful; that when the King sent him a buck he gave the keeper fifty pounds, when the man would, no doubt, have thought himself well treated by the present of one; that a worthy old gentleman going to him about a suit, to Gorhambury, saw two of his gentlemen, one after another, in Bacon's momentary absence from the room, open his money drawer and fill their pockets with both hands, and go away without a word. When he told Bacon of this he only shook his head and said that he could not help himself. Well might he say to his servants when, after his disgrace, on passing through the hall, they rose, 'Sit down, my masters. Your rise has been my fall!' Basil Montagu also tells us that the Prince (I suppose Prince Charles), coming to London after Bacon's fall, saw at a distance a coach followed by a train of horsemen, and hearing that it was Bacon, said: 'Well, do what we can, this man scorns to go out like a snuff.' And as to the bribery, Bacon does not attempt to deny it. In a letter to the King, dated May 1621, he says candidly that he had taken bribes. Nay, on his trial, he delivered in a list of twenty eight cases, the sums received amounting to £10,660 - an amount equal to £60,000 now. And these were only well-known cases. The sums ranged from £50 and £100 to £1,000 each. He gives all the names of the persons, and endeavours to excuse himself by saying that he in some cases, after all, decided against the bribers. What are we to think of such morality? These people openly, avowedly, paid him money to sell them an unjust advantage. He pocketed the money and then did not give it. Another excuse is that he received many of the sums *after* the decisions, as if this could not be by arrangement. In some cases, however, as in that of Lady Wharton, he directly sold her a judgment contrary to justice for £300 beforehand. In other cases, which he specifies, he sent after the trial to *borrow* money, £500 or £1,000 from the person to whom he had awarded the victory. This money he does not pretend was ever to be paid again. Such was the case of William Compton, to whom he sent for £500; of William Peacock, to whom he sent for £1,000, and so on. In plain terms, he levied blackmail as the price of his decisions.

Such was Francis Bacon - in his actions little, if anything, better than his contemporaries; in his philosophy great beyond any age; in his gift to mankind of his 'Novum Organum,' a benefactor of such magnitude that his moral weaknesses lie in the splendour of his intellectual glories like spots on the sun, which leave that luminary, in spite of its blemishes, the noblest visible object of our universe. The true greatness of Bacon is not demonstrated by endeavouring to conceal his faults, but by leaving them to sink into their proper insignificance by the side of his genuine grandeur.

This is the account of his death as given by Basil Montagu, John Aubrey, Wotton, and Rawley:

'In the spring of 1626 his strength and spirits revived after the weakness brought on him by the winter. He returned to his favourite seclusion in Gray's Inn, from whence, on April 2, either on his way to Gorhambury or when making an excursion into the country with Dr. Witherborne, the King's physician, it occurred to him as he approached Highgate, the snow lying on the ground, that it might be deserving consideration whether flesh might be preserved as well in snow as in salt; and he resolved immediately to try the experiment. They alighted from the coach, and went into a poor woman's house at the bottom of Highgate Hill, near the spot at which Hagbush Lane comes out into the Holloway Road, and bought a hen, and stuffed the body with snow, and my lord did help to do it himself. The snow chilled him, and he fell so extremely ill that he could not return to Gray's Inn, but was taken to tbe Earl of Arundel's bouse at Highgate, where be was put into a warm bed; but it was damp, and had not been slept in for a year before.'

Whether Sir Thomas Meautys, his most constant friend, or Dr. Rawley, could be found does not appear; but a messenger was immediately sent to his relation, the Master of the Rolls, the charitable Sir Julius Csesar, then grown so old that he was said to be kept alive beyond nature's course by the prayers of the many poor whom he daily relieved. He instantly attended his friend, who was confined to his bed, and so enfeebled that he was unable to hold a pen; yet he wrote to Lord Arundel by dictation:

`My very good Lord, I was likely to have had the fortune of Caius Plinius the elder, who lost his life by trying an experiment about the burning of the mountain Vesuvius. For I also was desirous to try an experiment or two touching the conservation and induration of bodies. For the experiment itself, it succeeded remarkably well; but in the journey between Highgate and London, I was taken with a fit of casting, as I know not whether it was the stone, or some surfeit, or cold, or, indeed, a touch of them all three. But when I came to your lordship's house, I was not able to go back, and therefore was forced to take up my lodging here, where your housekeeper is very careful and diligent about me, which I assure myself your lordship will not only pardon towards him, but think the better of him for it. For, indeed, your lordship's house was happy to me, and I kiss your noble hands for the welcome which I am sure you give me to it.'

This letter shows that at the moment he dictated it the great ex-chancellor did not suppose himself on his deathbed; but he died in the arms of Sir Julius Caesar on the morning of Easter Monday, April 9, 1626, in the sixty sixth year of his age. He was buried by direction of his will, in St. Michael's Church, St. Albans, near his mother, where a monument, exhibiting him as seated in his chair, supporting his head on his hand, was erected to his memory by his faithful friend, Sir Thomas Meautys.

LAUDERDALE HOUSE AND NELL GWYNNE

When Andrew Marvell sought retirement at Highgate he did not get out of the vicinity of bad company. Just below his modest house, on the same side of the road, stood the ample one of the Duke of Lauderdale. This house still remains. It has no architecture about it. It has two fronts, one facing the highway, and the other looking down south-eastward towards Holloway. It has on each front a very simple pediment, and has been stuccoed, probably, in very recent years. Some of the old gardens remain, but much altered, and in them stands an old-fashioned circular conservatory. The grounds appear to have been extensive, running pretty closely in the rear of Marvell's cottage. This mansion is said to have been built about the year 1660 - that is, coincident with the restoration of Charles II, one of whose most active and detestable ministers Lauderdale was from first to last. Nay, we are assured that he was a prominent man, even in the reign of Charles I, in Scotland, being then a Covenanter, and one of those who sold Charles I to the English army. He turned round completely under Charles II, and became one of the most frightful persecutors of the Covenanters that existed; he and Archbishop Sharpe going hand-in-hand in their diabolical cruelties. He was not only an English Minister, a leading one of the celebrated Cabal Administration, but Lord-Deputy of Scotland, where nothing could surpass his cruelty but his rapacity. Lord Macaulay draws this portrait of him:

'Lauderdale, the tyrant deputy of Scotland at this period, loud and coarse both in mirth and anger, was perhaps, under the outward show of boisterous frankness, the most dishonest man in the whole Cabal. He was accused of being deeply concerned in the sale of Charles I to the English Parliament, and was, therefore, in the estimation of good Cavaliers, a traitor of a worse description than those who sat in the High Court of Justice. He often talked with noisy jocularity of the days when he was a canter and a rebel. He was now the chief instrument employed by the court in the work of forcing episcopacy on his reluctant countrymen; nor did he in that cause shrink from the unsparing use of the sword, the halter, and the boot. Yet those who knew him knew that thirty years had made no change in his real sentiments; that he still hated the memory of Charles I, and that he still preferred the Presbyterian form of government to any other.'

If we add to this picture Carlyle's additional touch of 'his big red head,' we have a sufficient idea of this monster of a man, as he was at that time at work in Scotland, with his renegade comrade, Archbishop Sharpe, with their racks, thumbscrews, and iron boot in which they used to crush the legs of their victims with wedges, so vividly described by Sir Walter Scott, in 'Old Mortality' and in the 'Tales of a Grandfather;' whilst their general, Turner, was pursuing the flying Covenanters to the mountains and morasses with fire and sword.

Lauderdale House
(From an original drawing by J. W. Archer, in the
possession of W. Twopeny, Esq.)

Such was Andrew Marvell's near neighbour when Lauderdale was in England, during which time he was always an advocate for bringing down a huge Scottish army to crush the liberties of England. His master Charles had sold himself to the French King for an annuity of £200,000 a year and a promise of soldiers to re-establish Popery. To complete this military despotism, Lauderdale got an Act passed in Scotland for the raising of an army there which the King should have the right to march to any part of his dominions; and Bishop Burnet gave evidence at the bar of the English Commons that this wretch had told him that his design was to have an army of Scots to keep down the English, and an army of Irish to keep down the Scots. Not being able to carry out the whole of this diabolical scheme, he, however, managed to bring down the wild Highlanders on the Covenanters, and let them loose on the west of Scotland like a legion of desolating fiends. During all this time Lauderdale and his duchess sold honours and estates in Scotland, and seized on the property of the persecuted, so that they would have become enormously rich had they not been still more enormously ostentatious and lavish in their style of living. Yet the profligate Charles still protected this monster from the equal abhorrence of Scots and English.

When Lauderdale was in Scotland on this devil's business, no doubt his indulgent master used to borrow his house at Highgate for one of his troop of mistresses; and thus it was that we find pretty Nelly Gwynne flourishing directly under the nose of the indignant patriot Marvell. If Charles had picked his whole harem, however, he could not have found one of his ladies less obnoxious than poor Nelly. As for Lucy Waters, the mother of the Duke of Monmouth, she was dead. Lady Castlemaine, Duchess of Cleveland, the mother of the Dukes of Grafton, was a bold and fiery dame, who kept even the King in constant hot water. Madame Querouaille, made Duchess of Portland, mother of the Dukes of Richmond, was the spy of Louis XIV of France, sent expressly to keep Charles to his obedience, and for which service Louis gave her a French title and estate. Moll Davis, the rope-dancer, the mother of the Radclyffes, had lost her influence, and Miss Stewart had got married to the Duke of Richmond. Of all the tribe, Nelly was the best; and yet Marvell launched some very sharp arrows at her. Charles he describes as he might see him walking in the Lauderdale gardens, as

> Of a tall stature and of sable hue,
> Much like the son of Kish, that lofty grew;

and Nelly, as 'that wench of orange and oyster,' in allusion to her original calling.

On Charles he spent his wit continually; and his reckless yet timid character was never better hit off than in the following stanzas:

I'll have as fine bishops as were e'er made with hands,
With consciences flexible to my commands;
And if they displease me - I'll have all their lands.

I'll have a fine navy to conquer the seas,
And the Dutch shall give caution for their provinces;
And if they should beat me - I'll do what they please.

I'll have a fine court, with ne'er an old face,
And he who dare beard me shall have the next grace,
And I either will vacate or buy him a place.

I'll have a privy purse without a control,
I'll wink all the while my revenue is stole;
And if any is questioned - I'll answer the whole.

If this please not - I'll reign then on any condition;
Miss and I will learn to live on exhibition,
And I'll first put the Church, then the Crown, in commission.

Elinor, or Nell Gwynne, who was of the lowest extraction, commenced life by selling oysters about the streets, and then oranges at the theatres. According to her own account in 'Pepys,' vol. iii. p. 399, she 'was brought up in a brothel, to fill strong waters for the gentlemen.' Her beauty, wit, and extreme good-nature seem to have made her friends amongst the actors; and her figure and loveliness raised her to the stage. There she attracted the dissolute monarch's attention by a merely ludicrous circumstance. At another theatre an actor had been introduced as Pistol, in a hat of extravagant dimensions. As this caused much merriment, Dryden had Nelly to appear in a hat as large as a coach wheel. The audience was vastly diverted, and the King, who was present, taken at once by his fancy. But as she was already the mistress of Lord Buckhurst, Charles had to compound for the transfer of Nelly by an earldom, making him Earl of Middlesex. Nell soon won the ascendency amongst the mistresses of the King,

Who never said a foolish thing,
And never did a wise one.

Though extremely gay and witty, Nell Gwynne seems never to have shown any hauteur in her elevation, nor any avarice - a prominent vice in some of her rivals. On the contrary, she made no secret of condemning her peculiar position, and was always ready to do a good action. On one occasion, seeing a clergyman in the hands of constables, she inquired the cause, and hearing that they were taking him to prison for debt, she paid the demand, and let him return to his family.

Though often insulted, she never sought revenge, and no doubt kept the King from it; nay, there is reason to believe she induced him to show a magnanimity in some cases that was not in himself. Had the following incident happened to one of the other royal mistresses, there is little doubt that the result would have been very different: On a visit to Winchester, Charles wished one of the clergymen, the Rev. Thomas Ken, to allow Nell to lodge at his house; but Ken positively refused, however much it might offend the King. His friends thought there was an end to his preferment; but, some time after, on the death of the Bishop of Bath and Wells, Charles asked what was the name of that little man at Winchester who would not let little Nell lodge at his house, and on being told, to the astonishment of the whole court, conferred on him the bishopric. Charles never endowed Nelly with the wealth and titles that he lavished on his other women, probably because she did not worry him; but on his death-bed, his conscience pricked bim for his neglect, and he said, 'Don't let poor Nelly starve.' A frail security against starvation for a king's mistress in a new court.

The circumstance which connects her memory with Lauderdale House is the tradition that, as the King delayed to confer a title on her child, as he had done on the eldest son of others of his mistresses, she one day held the infant out of an upper window of Lauderdale House, and said, 'Unless you do something for him, here he goes!' On which Charles replied, `Save the Earl of Burford!' Whether this was exactly as related or not, it is very like one of Nell's lively sallies; and the child was created Earl of Burford, and afterwards Duke of St. Albans.

It is rather a curious coincidence, that, on the western ascent into Highgate, a few years ago, lived a Duchess of St. Albans, the wife of one of Nell's descendants, who had also begun life, like Nell, as an actress. I have often heard a lady speak of her as Miss Mellon, acting in a country theatre. Like Nelly, she had, whether actress or duchess, a noble nature; and the inhabitants of Highgate still hear in memory her deeds of charity, as well as her splendid fetes, in some of which, they say, she hired all the birds of the bird-dealers in London, and fixing their cages in the trees, made her grounds one great orchestra of nature's music. What a holiday for the birds!

THE WHITTINGTON STONE

Descending the hill from Lauderdale House towards Holloway, and not far before we come to the Archway Tavern, we arrive at a massive stone standing on the edge of the footpath, which seems to give reality to the tales of our nurseries. It bears this inscription:

WHITTINGTON STONE.

Sir Richard Whittington, Lord Mayor of London,

1397 Richard II.
1409 Henry IV.
1419 Henry V.

So Dick Whittington was a real man of flesh and blood, flourishing in a historic period, and not the creation of some old story-teller who delighted to amuse children. So, then, here he really sat and listened to Bow bells, which rung him back to be thrice Lord Mayor of London. Whatever of fable has wreathed itself like ivy round this old history, there was a *bona fide* substantial British oak for it to twine round. Here Dick sat on a stone (which appears to have been the base of an ancient cross) and listened to that agreeable recall. The stone, we are told, is not the actual one on which Dick sat. That had been thrown down, had become broken to pieces, and these fragments were removed years ago and placed as kerb-stones against the posts at the corner of Queen's Head Lane. But this stone was erected on or near the spot as a proper memorial of the fact that the hero of this story, no longer Dick, but Sir Richard Whittington, loved to ride out in this direction, and to dismount, in order to walk up the hill, at this stone, and by it to remount again - a very characteristic trait of Whittington's humanity, which many fine fellows would do well to imitate, who, instead of dismounting, often put spurs to their or their master's horses and gallop up the long and steep ascent. To various such wind-breakers I have presented the 'Little Horse Book' of the Royal Society for the Prevention of Cruelty to Animals, as a piece of instructive reading.

Whittington Stone and the Lazar House
(From an old print, by Chatelaine, in the possession of J. E. Gardner, Esq.)

Though other of the incidents of Dick Whittington's life may have been embellished, I should be sorry to cast a doubt on the cat story - that cat which Dick, in his sleeping-place in the scullery of Mr. Fitzwarren, the rich merchant, being wofully tormented with rats, bought for one penny of an old woman in the street, and which, so mightily pleasing the Dey of Algiers by clearing his table of the same vermin, made Dick's fortune. Yet there is a very ancient story in the Scandinavian Sagas something like it; but so there is, too, of the story of William Tell shooting the apple on his son's head. We will refuse to give up an atom of faith in Dick's cat. Cat or something made a wonderful man of him. History tells of his deeds with all sober and authentic gravity. Thrice was he in reality Lord Mayor of London. In the reign of Edward III he made the King a present of £10,000, a vast sum in those days, towards the expenses of his war with France. In the fifty second year of the reign of this Edward, Dick was knighted, and made Lord Mayor instead of Adam Staple, who would not raise the city poll-tax for the King, amounting to £4,000. In 1377, the first year of Richard II, he was made member of Parliament. Stow tells us that he was then a great merchant dealing in wool, leather, and pearls, which last were then much worn by the ladies. When near forty he married the daughter of his old master, Miss Fitzwarren, and served his first regular mayoralty in 1397. He was one of those who had the melancholy duty of guarding his captive monarch, Richard II, to the Tower. He assisted at the coronation of Henry IV, and figures on various occasions in that reign. In the time of the warlike Henry V, during his third mayoralty, in 1419, he entertained that monarch and his queen at Guildhall. On this occasion he performed an act of princely loyalty, if we may use such a phrase, which has only been equalled by the great weaver of Augsburg. In the noble building in that city, now the inn of the Three Moors, we are told that Count Fugger, the weaver-merchant, entertained Charles V, and afterwards consumed in a fire of cinnamon a bond of a million of florins due from the Emperor. No doubt Count Fugger had read the history of Dick Whittington - who has not? - and so determined to emulate the following noble deed:

'At this entertainment the King particularly praised the fire, which was made of choice woods, mixed with mace, cloves, and all other spices; on which Sir Richard said he would endeavour to make one still more agreeable to his Majesty, and immediately tore and threw into the fire the King's bond for 10,000 marks due to the Company of Mercers, 12,500 to the Chamber of London, 12,000 to the Grocers; to the Staplers, Goldsmiths, Haberdashers, Vintners, Brewers, and Bakers, 3,000 marks each. "All these," said Sir Richard, "with divers others lent for the payment of your soldiers in France, I have taken in and discharged, to the amount of £60,000 sterling. Can your Majesty desire to see such another sight?" The King and nobles were struck dumb with surprise.'

In the 'Gentleman's Magazine,' vol. lxvi. part ii. p. 545, is an engraving of the house, in London, said to be that of Dick Whittington, in which he lived, and which, with other property in London, he left to his college, or hospital for poor people. It was situated four houses from Mark Lane, in Hart Street, up a gateway, and was then (1796) occupied by a carpenter and basket-maker. It was described in the old leases as Whittington's Palace, and its appearance, especially the external, warranted a probability of the truth. It formed three sides of a square, but, from time and ill-usage, was much altered. Under the window of the first storey were carved, in basso-relievo, the arms of the twelve companies of London, except one, which was destroyed to make room for a cistern. The wings were supported by rude carved figures of satyrs; and from its situation near the church, it is probable that it had been a manor house. The principal room had the remains of grandeur. It was about 85 feet long, 15 broad, and 12 feet high. The ceiling was elaborately carved, over which was a continuation of Saxon arches in basso-relievo, and between each arch a human figure. The ante-room had nothing worth notice but the mantel-piece, which, however, was much more modern than the outside, as was that of the adjoining room, which belonged to the basket-maker. It was not quite so large as the principal room, but the ceiling was as superbly decorated with carving. On a tablet was the date 1600, and on another the initials

$$\frac{P}{M. \ M.}$$

This room appeared to have been fitted up long since the building of the house. In medallions on the above ceiling were several heads of the Caesars, and two coats of arms, a chevron between nine pallets; but no colours were expressed.

As this house must have been in perfection in the time of Stow's writing his 'History of London,' it is odd that he does not mention it, and equally so that it is passed over by Maitland, who neither noticed it nor the Walbrook House.

Numerous, besides those already mentioned, are the records of the munificence of Sir Richard. He built a church in Vintry Ward; almshouses and a college in the same ward; founded a noble library in the church of Grey Friars, near where Christ Church in Newgate now stands. He rebuilt Newgate, repaired Guildhall, and endowed Christ Church with a considerable sum. Some of his buildings perished in the Great Fire of London; his college was sold by the Mercers' Company, but they are said to still maintain the almshouses for thirteen poor men. But what concerns us on this occasion is, that the Mercers' Company, having £6,600 in hand from the estates of Sir Richard Whittington in 1822, commenced a set of almshouses for twenty four single women not having individually property to the amount of £30 a year. They receive a yearly stipend of £30 each, besides other gifts, with medical attendance and nurses in time of illness. The establishment was proposed to be erected in the main road, near to the Whittington Stone; but ground not being procurable, they built it in the Archway Road, nearly opposite to this stone. This is a much better situation, from its greater openness and retirement. The buildings are Gothic, of one storey, forming three sides of a quadrangle, having the area open towards the road. In the centre of the main building is a chapel or oratory for the reading of daily prayers. The establishment has its tutor or master, its matron, nurses, gardener, gatekeeper, &c. It is a remarkably pleasant object from the road, with its area embellished by shrubbery and sloping lawn.

Blessed be the memory of those good old times, when great-hearted men and women, who had much to leave, and few to leave it to; who remembered the hand which had made their own path through life easy and honourable, and desired to give Him an eternal testimony of their gratitude, by caring for the comfort of His poorer children. A miserable philosophy of late years, falsely called Utilitarian, has discouraged the leaving of money to the infirm and the poor, and of erecting almshouses for the aged and indigent, on the plea that it tends to destroy the spirit of enterprise and of self-dependence; as if in youth the heart of man calculated on an almshouse in old age, and therefore sat down on a dunghill and did nothing. No man in the fire and ardour of youth, nor woman either, thinks of almshouses; but in the rude shock of life, when all plans have been shattered, and age comes on without provision and without friends, then how cheering must be the prospect of a little quiet nook, where the last days of existence may be spent, secured from the butcher hand of starvation, and the vulture beak of despair. A higher philosophy than the Utilitarian - that of Him who said the poor shall never cease out of the land, and what ye do unto the least of these little ones, ye do unto me - guided the acts of our noble ancestors, and happily is again beginning to influence the best spirits of our time. It is delightful to see the snug homes which the guilds and trades have raised here and there for their aged veterans. It is delightful to see a Shaftesbury, a Southwood Smith, a Miss Coutts, and many others, raising good, healthy homes for the poor; and the noble banker, Peabody, setting splendid example to the wealthy of the application of their money to the necessary requirements of their less fortunate brethren. A genuine Utilitarianism is fortunately reviving - that of utilising money for general happiness; and it only requires that the higher moral sense, the higher conscientiousness of this age, shall prevent the harpies of selfishness again invading the sacred heritage of the poor and infirm, as they have formerly done, both in charities educational and philanthropic, in order to give us again benefactors as princely as the Whittingtons of old.

BLAKE'S ORPHANAGE

Towards the end of the seventeenth century, a William Blake, woollen draper, of Maiden Lane, Covent Garden, purchased Dorchester House, formerly the residence of the Marquises of Dorchester, and standing where part of the Grove Row now stands, with the most praiseworthy design of establishing it as a school or hospital, for the maintenance of forty fatherless boys and girls. The boys were to be taught the art of painting, gardening, casting accounts, and navigation, or put forth to some good handicraft trade. The girls were to learn to read, write, sew, starch, raise paste, and make dresses, so as to be fit for any good service. The system of education for both boys and girls was most rational, and anticipated the working schools of our own time.

Dorchester House
(From an old print in Prickett's 'History of Highgate.')

William Blake gave £5,000 for the property - his whole fortune - and hoped that the benevolence of the wealthy would furnish the necessary funds for its support. But, far from being so fortunate as Franke of Halle, the Curé d'Ars, or Muller of Bristol, he found charity much colder than he expected. Having exhausted his own resources, he made earnest appeals to the titled and city ladies of London, but in vain. For some time his generous establishment struggled on. In 1667 there were thirty six poor boys, in a costume of blue and yellow, maintained and educated in it. It still existed in 1675, but it does not seem to have continued longer than 1688, or about twenty years. Blake wrote a curious book, called 'Silver Drops, or Serious Things,' to describe and recommend the institution. It is written in a most eccentric style. He describes himself as being in a full trade when he commenced this undertaking, but that, from the liabilities into which it brought him, he was seized and imprisoned for about two years. He speaks of the place as 'at first only for a summer's recess from London, which, having that great and noble city, with its numerous childhood under view, gave first thought to him of so great a design.' His style is frequently unintelligible:

'The Title (the Ladyes, etc.) no Diminution, Honoured it witness Two Sacred Monuments in their Honour, The Praise of the Virtuous Lady by Solomon, Jedediah, or the Lord's Beloved; the Epistle to the Elect Lady by John, the beloved disciple.'

Speaking of the grounds, he says,

'All these dedicated by a solemn devotion to God, and cannot be Ananiaz'd and Sapphira'd, being so incontrovertible a good purpose without their sin.'

The style almost insane, the nobility of soul struggling through it, the piety and spirituality, the desire to have the boys taught the art of painting, and the name William Blake, strongly persuade me that this strange and yet good man must have been the grandfather or great-grandfather of William Blake, the eccentric but inspired writer and artist of that name. None of the biographers of Blake trace him beyond his father, who was a hosier, of 28 Broad Street,

Carnaby Market, London. It would be worth the while of the lovers of Blake to trace this out.

As a frontispiece to his 'Silver Drops,' there is a print of Dorchester House, which he had converted into this admirable institution. The margins of the print are full of notes, in which he complains that he is treated as a madman. He observes that if Sir Francis Pemberton, Sir William Ashurst, both residents at Highgate, and his own brother, F. Blake, would yet assist him, the school might be saved, and all yet be well. Blake's mansion, thus abortively devoted to an excellent purpose, is engraved in Lysons' 'Environs of London,' and also in the 'Gentleman's Magazine,' vol. lxx. part ii. p. 721.

RELIGIOUS COMMUNITIES IN HIGHGATE

Jewish Synagogue

Some years ago there was a Jewish academy in Highgate, conducted by Mr. Hyman Hurwitz. It was the only thing of the kind in the kingdom, except one on a small scale at Brighton. It had generally about a hundred pupils, sons of the chief families of the Jews; and there was a synagogue for their use. There was also a school for Jewish young ladies, established by Miss Hurwitz, the sister of Mr. Hurwitz.

Presbyterian Chapel, and New Independent Chapel

The chapel, standing in Southwood Lane, on the same side as the grammar school, and near to it, has since become the Independent Chapel, where the Rev. Josiah Viney preached before the handsome new chapel was built for him facing the open space where the old pond was. I may note, in passing, that Mr. Viney has been the first to set the excellent example of erecting model dwelling houses in Highgate for the poor, which, I am happy to hear, are not only very much appreciated by the working class, but profitable to the benevolent erector. Opposite to the old Presbyterian Chapel, now become the National school, stands another chapel, built for the Methodists, but now belonging to the Baptists.

The Presbyterian Chapel in Southwood Lane, it appears, was constantly attended by the father of the celebrated John Wilkes, in his latter years, and to the time of his death. The mother of Wilkes was a Dissenter; and in his youth, John Wilkes himself used to attend this chapel occasionally. A writer in the 'Gentleman's Magazine,' vol. lxviii. part i. p. 126, says that he learned these particulars from members of the Presbyterian congregation of the chapel when he was presbyter, and from the clerk, who had held that office for nearly forty years. He said that the father of John Wilkes used to come to the chapel in his coach-and-six. This writer gives the names of some of the ministers of this chapel:

The Rev. Dr. Sleigh.

The Rev. Mr. Hardy, minister for many years, and who died there.

Dr. Towers, who removed to the Presbyterian Chapel at Newington Green. He was a man well known by his writings, and was a popular leader amongst the Dissenters.

The Rev. David Williams, afterwards dignified with the name of the High Priest of Nature, and for many years the avowed champion of infidelity. Here he delivered those discourses on 'Religious Hypocrisy,' which he afterwards published in two volumes. In his farewell discourse he gave, what the writer thought, some wholesome advice to the Dissenters.

The Rev. Samuel Tice, stated to be highly respected by both Dissenters and Church people.

The Rev. John Baptist Pike, M.D., who introduced a short liturgy of his own.

The Rev. Alexander Crombie, LL.D., author of a 'Defence of Philosophical Necessity.'

Besides these, Mr. Rochemont Barbauld, who married the celebrated Miss Aikin, officiated for some time at this chapel, previous to settling at Hampstead.

During the ministry of Mr. David Williams, the meeting was numerously attended, and Highgate Old Chapel being shut up for repairs, the greater part of the members of the Establishment attended this chapel during the interim. Some time previous to the ministry of Mr. Tice, a separation in the congregation took place, and those who left erected the chapel opposite, now occupied by the Baptists.

Catholic Chapel

Of late years the Catholics have established a large chapel and house for priests on the hill descending towards Holloway, by the entrance to Maiden Lane, under the name of St. Joseph's Retreat. The greater part of the priests there being foreign, and with a predominance of Italians, speaks pretty plainly of its origin in the Propaganda, and it seems to have succeeded greatly, its chapel being generally crowded, especially by the Irish living in Upper Holloway. For many years, the Roman Catholic Church has instituted a system of perpetual prayer, which is carried on by priests and nuns, whose especial office it is, for the conversion of England; and the strange tendency evinced, especially amongst the established clergy, towards a reversal of the Reformation, looks as though the ceaseless prayers were in course of being answered.

DAVID WILLIAMS, FOUNDER OF THE LITERARY FUND

A somewhat more extended notice of this gentleman is worthy of a place here. He was born at a village near Cardigan in 1738, and received the chief portion of his education at a college of Dissenters at Carmarthen, where their young men were prepared for the ministry. In later years he attributed the revulsion which took place in his opinions and feelings concerning religious institutions to the harsh, cold, and oppressive manner in which the doctrines and duties of Christian faith were disguised in the stem and rigid habits of a Puritanical master. On leaving this seminary, he became the minister of a small congregation at Frome, in Somersetshire, but soon removed to a more important charge at Exeter. There his abilities and agreeable manners drew him into much notice, and into more social pleasures than some of the elder members of the society thought becoming in a minister; and reproof was conveyed in a manner more calculated to excite anger than produce reform. The young minister, however, unfortunately for his monitors, had knowledge of their own doings and private characters, which produced a stunning retort; and, to prevent a disagreeable exposure, these Nestors agreed to a compromise, by which Mr. Williams left Exeter and took the office of pastor at this chapel at Highgate. There he remained a year or two, and we have seen under what circumstances he left.

In 1770, he appeared as the defender of Mossop against David Garrick, in a letter to Garrick, which contained a masterly critique on the great actor, and at the same time an unsparing attack on his proceedings. The letter produced the intended effect; Mossop was liberated, and the letter withdrawn from further publication. Soon after followed his 'Philosopher, in three Conversations,' and this was soon followed by 'Essays on Public Worship, Patriotism, and Projects of Reformation.' The appendix to these essays gave a strong indication of his detestation of intolerance, bigotry, and hypocrisy, the seed of which had been sown in the ascetic Welsh school of Carmarthen, and which became the leading character of his subsequent life. His sermons, chiefly upon religious hypocrisy, marked the close of his connection with the body of Dissenters. He now settled in Chelsea and published, in 1773, 'A Treatise on Education,' recommending a method founded on the plans of Commenius and Rousseau, a system which he proposed to carry into effect. He married a young lady not distinguished either by fortune or connection, and soon found himself at the head of a lucrative and prosperous establishment; but this gleam of good fortune was speedily overcast by the death of his wife, which, with the anxious attendance upon her in her illness, gave such a shock to both his health and spirits, that he never surmounted it. He gave up his establishment, and quitted Chelsea.

During the residence of Mr. Williams at Chelsea, he for a time gave an asylum to Dr. Franklin in his house, at a period when there was a popular excitement against him in connection with American affairs. Franklin was a member of a club of literary men and politicians, of which club David Williams was also a member. In this club a scheme for universal uniformity of worship was drawn up, on principles supposed to be capable of uniting all parties; and Mr. Williams composed and published 'A Liturgy on the Universal Principles of Religion and Morality.' With this was combined a set of lectures illustrating these principles, delivered in the chapel in Margaret Street, Cavendish Square; forming two volumes, 1776. This service lasted about four years, but drew little attention, and involved the lecturers in serious difficulties. As the acknowledgment of the being of a God was the only tenet demanded of its members, this theistic church had nothing sufficiently binding in its composition to hold any great number of men together who had no other bond of union.

Mr. Williams now supported himself by preparing young gentlemen for the learned professions, and especially for political and diplomatic life, and in connection with this employment published 'Lectures on Political Principles,' and 'Lectures on Education.' At the same time he proved himself, by his constant readiness to assist his friends and others in moments of distress and difficulty, to possess a heart as generous as it was devoted to human liberty and progress. During the alarm in 1780 from the outburst of French revolutionary principles, he published a tract entitled 'A Plan of Association on Constitutional Principles,' and in 1782 'Letters on Political Liberty,' a work extensively read in both England and France. It was translated by Brissot, and procured Mr. Williams an invitation to Paris to assist in drawing up a constitution for France, one of the earliest of the numerous constitutions which appeared and perished in succession during the violent effervescence of the Revolution. He continued only about six months in Paris. He gave temperate and most excellent advice to the party of the Gironde, with which he was in communication, which had it been taken might have prevented the shedding of torrents of blood. But the tornado of excited human passion swept all reason before it, and Mr. Williams took his leave prognosticating the awful scenes which followed. He brought with him home a letter from the French Minister of War to Lord Grenville, intended to enable Mr. Williams to make known to the British Ministry the real sentiments and wishes of the French Administration; but Mr. Williams never was admitted to an audience of Lord Grenville. He left the letter in the hands of Mr. Aust, Under Secretary of State, and nothing more was heard of it. A mention of this circumstance is made in Bisset's 'History of George III.' In fact, his going to France had ruined him with the Ministry here, and he found liimself denounced in England as a democrat, and in France as a royalist. Before leaving England he had removed to Brompton, for the purpose of executing an engagement which he had made with Mr. Bowyer, to superintend a fine edition of Hume's `History of England,' and to write a continuation of it; but he found this engagement now cancelled in consequence of some intimation on the part of Government. Such was the jealousy of French revolutionary ideas by the British Government, that Mr. Williams might have foreseen that his intercourse with political leaders in Paris would evoke the deepest suspicions of him here. Still, undaunted by this rebuff, he published his `Letters to a Young Prince,' and engaged in and com- pleted in one volume quarto, `History of Monmouthshire,' with plates by his friend the Bev. John Gardner.

The work, however, on which he laboured with the most benevolent enthusiasm, and for which he will always be held in grateful remembrance by thousands who have derived from it comfort and support in the seasons of deepest distress, was that of the establishment of the 'Royal Literary Fund.' On this philanthropic achievement he built the dearest hopes of his fame, and he built them not in vain. In connection with this noble institution the name of David Williams will always be held in honour. An excellent bust of him, executed by Richard Westmacott, and presented by him to the Institution, stands in the house of the Fund. During his residence at Chelsea, Mr. Williams had conceived the plan of this society for the assistance of deserving authors, and in 1788 and 1789, he succeeded in establishing it; and devoted all his talents and energies, and much of his time, to the advancement of its interests. He had the satisfaction of seeing it continually rise in public estimation. The Prince of Wales honoured it with his patronage, and conferred on it an annual donation for the purpose of purchasing a house for the use of the Society, and expressly desired that Mr. Williams should reside in it. A work entitled the 'Claims of Literature,' explanatory of the nature, promotion, and purposes of the Society, was published by Mr. Williams and several of his zealous and able coadjutors, each putting his name to his own portion of it. Thus launched, this benevolent Institution never looked hack, but has gone on from year to year, for eighty years, diffusing substantial blessings amongst those for whom it was designed.

During the peace of Amiens, Mr. Williams again visited Paris, but this time, it is believed, on a private commission from our Government to the First Consul, as he was seen repeatedly entering the Government offices before his departure. He still continued to write for the promotion of his views of political progress, and produced 'Egeria, or Elementary Studies on the Progress of Nations in Political Economy, Education and Government,' and 'Preparatory Studies for Political Reformers.' He died on June 29, 1816. The whole of Mr. Williams's proceedings evince an enthusiastic love of liberty and a generous regard for the good of his fellow men. His weakness was the abandonment of faith in the Christian religion, the result of the unloveable form in which he had seen in his youth the doctrines of what was called Christianity, presented in the practices of those who mistook harshness and severity for the life of that religion which, on the contrary, is gentleness and love.

HIGHGATE IN THE FORMER TIMES OF RITUALISM

On June 30, 1637, one of the most atrocious pieces of political and priestly cruelty was perpetrated on the celebrated William Prynne and his coadjutors, Dr. Bastwick, and the Rev. Henry Burton, who had formerly been chaplain to Charles I. The same popish infatuation about ritualism was rife in the Established Church as at the present time. Archbishop Laud, backed by the King, was at the head of this movement, and stopped at no tyrannous audacity or cruelty to carry his point. Prynne, for his stern opposition to these attempts, had already had his ears cut off in the pillory. He had now the stumps of them gouged out, and his friends had theirs cut off. They were each, besides being fined £5,000, branded on both cheeks with the letters S. L. for 'seditious libeller,' kept in the pillory for two hours in the face of a burning sun, and condemned to separate prisons for life. It was in carrying out the latter part of this diabolical sentence, that of conveying them to their prisons, that, soon after this odious exhibition, Highgate witnessed one of the most extraordinary scenes in its history. It was that of a vast crowd, said to be a hundred thousand in number, accompanying Mr. Burton for two miles beyond that village on his way. They cheered and applauded him enthusiastically, as an undaunted champion of religious and political liberty, and threw money into the coach to his wife as she drove along. Similar scenes were enacted on the conveyance of Prynne and Bastwick out of London, giving the great champion of Ritualism an example of British feeling which, had he had the wisdom to take warning by, would have saved his head. The present ritualistic mania is but a very mild and feeble repetition of the desperate game played by the daring and unscrupulous Anglo-Papist, Laud. The King and his archbishop, by cutting off ears, had roused a spirit in the people which would be satisfied with nothing short of heads.

HIGHGATE CEMETERY

Highgate has its Père-la-Chaise, a cemetery lying on the slope of the hill southward, commanding a fine view over London. In fact, in situation and in tasteful laying-out, it is one of the most attractive cemeteries in the kingdom. The vicinity to London has in a few years densely crowded it with graves and enormous loads of monumental marble, so that a great extension of it has been necessary. Such a cemetery in a popular suburb is but a questionable institution for the deposit of the London dead, which, continually carried thither in hearses, is neither a very cheerful object, nor would it be very satisfactory in a sanitary point of view, were it not that the ground is a deep stiff clay, which must effectually prevent any exhalations from the mountain of decaying mortality accumulated there.

Many names, familiar to London ears, present themselves on the tombs as you wander through this city of decomposition; and some of considerable distinction. The French have found their Montmartre or Père-la-Chaise here; Germans, their Friedhof, and natives of countries still more distant lie scattered here and there. Perhaps no tomb has ever attracted so many thousand visitors as that of Tom Sayers, bearing on it his own portrait and that of his dog, Wombwell. With his lion standing over him as if to say, 'Well, he kept me cramped up for many years in his vans, but I have got him safe under my paw at last,' was, in its newness, a thing of much note; but never had a charm for the pugnacious populace of London like the tomb of the great boxer.

Artists Interred in Highgate Cemetery

Alfred Edward Chalon, brother of the more celebrated John James Chalon, was buried in this cemetery in October 1860. He was a native of Geneva, and a Royal Academician of London. His chief reputation is for portrait painting, and that mostly in water colours.

Charles Joseph Hullmandel was buried there in November 1850. Hullmandel was of German extraction. He was one of the greatest improvers of lithography, and extended its use in various directions. He introduced tinting and colours into this department of printing, in which style splendid folio works by Stanfield, Harding, Nash, Roberts, Haghe, &c. have been produced. In the more highly coloured style, Cattermole's 'Portfolio,' and Mr. S. C. Hall's 'Baronial Halls,' are specimens. Mr. Hullmandel afterwards invented modes of putting on and multiplying patterns on rollers for calico-printing by machinery, and for producing patterns of all kinds of coloured marbles on earthenware, extraordinary specimens of which were executed by Messrs. Copeland, of Old Bond Street. Perhaps to no one man has lithography owed so much of its present status.

William Henry Hunt, the pre-eminent painter of country scenes and objects, was buried in this cemetery in February 1864, in the presence of many artists of note. Everyone knows his rustic boys, as familiarly as they know such boys in the real life of the country. Whatever Hunt undertook, whether a single object, a bird's nest, a flower, a living object, or a landscape at large, it stood forth like life itself, and life in one of its most piquant aspects.

Sir William Ross, the fashionable and truly excellent miniature painter, died on January 20, 1860, and his remains were deposited here. Sir William's pencil had been employed on the portraiture of many royal personages, including those of the English, French, Belgian, and Portuguese royal families, besides of great numbers of the aristocracy. Sir Thomas Lawrence declared him the first miniature painter of his day.

Near the upper entrance gate lie the remains of Mrs. Bartholomew, the artist and wife of the celebrated flower painter, Mr. Valentine Bartholomew.

Amongst men of literary note whose remains are interred in this cemetery we observe, on the high terrace near the church, the tomb of Alaric A. Watts, Esq., whose poetry, strictly of a lyrical kind, has touched, by its tender and domestic tone, the holiest chords in the hearts of thousands, and whose services, as editor of the 'Literary Souvenir,' in the refinement and advancement of English art, deserve a permanent and grateful remembrance. As an active and energetic member of the periodical and newspaper press, Mr. Watts also discharged an honourable life's labour. Near him also lie the remains of the wife and of one of the daughters of Dr. Robert Chambers, of `Chambers's Journal,' and author of much sterling literature of his own.

HIGHGATE ARCHWAY

The Archway Road, which avoids the steep hill by which Highgate is entered on the north, east, and west, and which leaves the village on its south-west, was made by Act of Parliament, conferred on a company in the year 1809. The archway was built by Mr. Robert Vazie, engineer. It consists of one large arch, forming a bridge 36 feet high, with a handsome stone balustrade. It is 300 feet in length. The company was empowered to borrow £60,000 for the formation of the bridge and road. A tunnel was first completed, but tunnelling being then but imperfectly understood, it fell in on April 13, 1812, with a tremendous crash, and the labour of several months was, in a few minutes, converted into a heap of ruins. Some of the workmen, who were going to resume their tasks - for luckily it was between four and five o'clock in the morning - described the noise that succeeded it as like distant thunder. It was the crown arch, near Hornsey Lane, which first gave way, and the lane in consequence fell some feet deep, and became impassable. The houses in the vicinity felt the shock like that of an earthquake. The falling in had been anticipated by the workmen for nearly a fortnight, and is considered to have originated in a too economical use of brick in the arch, and in the quality of the cement for uniting them having been deteriorated by too great a proportion of sand and lime. The interest in the work had, on the Sunday (that is, the day before), attracted 800 persons; but providentially the fall was reserved for a moment when nobody was there.

This catastrophe resulted in the formation of an open cutting, and the erection of the present fine arch. In the excavation of the road, a variety of curious fossils was discovered, amongst them fossil teeth, commonly called shark's teeth, sometimes sword-fish teeth, but unlike either; petrified fish; nuts resembling the palm nut, and a great variety of shells; nautili much larger than those generally found in a fossil state; petrified wood, very abundant; a peculiar resinous substance, not yet described by any naturalist, but resembling amber. Close to this Archway now runs a railway line.

Highgate Archway from the North Side
(From a photograph)

A considerable extent of woods belonging to the See of London, and called Bishop's Woods and Hornsey Woods, are yet standing on this side of Highgate; but the church lands lying betwixt Highgate and Crouch End are already in the hands of the Ecclesiastical Commissioners, and offered by them for building land. Gas is carried from Muswell Hill to Highgate, in anticipation of what, in a very short time, will make its appearance - a populous town all over the ground which formerly constituted Harringay Park; a wonderful contrast to the state of things seen at the making of the Archway Road, when old prints show the country all about to have lain open.

It is worth noting, that on the making of the Archway Road it was found impossible, from springs and boggy spots, to make the road solid; and Telford was called in, who laid in those places a solid pavement of stone, which conquered the difficulty.

As a proof of the slowness of ideas, even in this active country, we may state that in 1781 a road was projected to turn to the right hand of Highgate from the Great North Road, coming from Finchley, near the North Hill, and proceeding by Caen Wood, down the valley by the ponds, to come out on the level below Millfield Lane, somewhere near the present St. Alban's public house. This was nearly thirty years before the Archway Road was made. The object of this road, says a writer in the 'Gentleman's Magazine' of that date, was to decrease the cruelties to horses, suffered daily by them in dragging heavy loads up West Hill. He says,

> 'Amongst the numerous useful improvements, made of late years in
> roads and communications in the environs of this great metropolis, it is
> annoying that nothing should have been thought of to divert the Great
> North Road so as to avoid the passing over Highgate Hill, which has
> ever been the dread of all passengers and carriers, and, indeed, a re-
> proach to the community. Not a day passes, nor has probably ever
> passed, but some accident has happened on this hill; and I will venture
> to say that the injuries sustained upon it, could they be ascertained, are
> enormous, not to mention the delay it occasions to the traveller, and the
> labour to the horses, at which every humane heart must bleed, who are
> witnesses to their passage up or down in loaded carriages. I mean that
> side of the hill that leads from Kentish Town.'

This statement the writer accompanied by a plan and figures,
showing the advantages of the route, which would, undoubtedly,
have been a very good one; but there can be as little doubt the
influence of Lords Mansfield and Southampton defeated its
accomplishment. In 1809, the Archway Road was made, affording
relief to the traffic up the Holloway Road; but 'this horrible hill' -
that is, West Hill - has continued to the present time a daily scene
of agony to horses, in vain attempts to draw up it the ponderous
loads of coal and beer. Living on this hill, and the windows of my
study looking out upon it, I was tortured for nine years by the
cruelties which it occasions. I have often seen men flogging,
shouting and swearing at their overtasked horses for three and six
hours together. My repeated attempts through the 'Times' and
'Morning Star' to induce the authorities to even adopt the roller, to
abate the annual aggravation of the deluges of loose stones with
which it was mended, proved in vain; and it was only in the
humane oversight which the Royal Society for the Prevention of
Cruelty to Animals, in response to my repeated suggestions, that I
at length saw some little abatement of these horrors. From 1781,
the date of the article in the 'Gentleman's Magazine,' to 1869, are
eighty eight years, during which, since the humane project of the
writer in that magazine, these daily cruelties have been tolerated
under the eye of the public with apparent indifference.

West Hill

In the house and grounds of the late Duchess of St. Alban's now resides Miss Burdett Coutts, famous for her wealth, her extensive benevolence, her erection of dwelling-houses for the poor, churches for church-goers, and bishoprics for the colonies. A daughter of Sir Francis Burdett, she has not appeared ambitious to follow in his democratic steps, but rather to become a nursing-mother to the Church of England. She has founded the bishoprics of Adelaide, of Natal, of Columbia in the north-west of America, and built churches in Westminster and Carlisle. I suppose no other woman under the rank of a queen ever did so much for the Established Church; had she done it for the Catholic Church she would undoubtedly be canonized as St. Angela. But, perhaps, the noblest and most enduring of her works is seen in the clean and smiling hearths of hitherto too much neglected and ill-housed poverty.

The Hermitage on West Hill

On West Hill, a little above the entrance to Millfield Lane, stood inclosed in tall trees a small house called the Hermitage. Adjoining it was a still smaller tenement, which was said to be the real and original Hermitage. It consisted only of one small low room, with a chamber over it, reached by an outside rustic gallery. The whole of this Hermitage was covered with ivy, evidently of a very ancient growth, as shown by the largeness of its stems and boughs, and the prodigality of its foliage. In fact, it looked like one great mass of ivy. What was the origin of the place, or why it acquired the name of Hermitage, does not appear; but being its last tenant, I found that its succession of inhabitants had been numerous, and that it was connected with some curious histories. Some dark tragedies had occurred there. One of its tenants was a Sir Wallis Porter, who was an associate of the Prince Regent. Here the Prince of Wales used to come frequently to gamble with Sir Wallis. This Hermitage, hidden by the tall surrounding trees, chiefly umbrageous elms, and by the huge ivy-tod, seemed a place well concealed for the orgies carried on there. The ceiling of the room they used was painted with naked figures in the French style, and there they could both play as deeply as they pleased, and carouse as jovially. But the end of Sir Wallis was that of many another gamester and wassailer. Probably his princely companion, and *his* companions, both drained the purse as well as the cellar of Sir Wallis, for he put an end to his existence there, as reported, by shooting himself.

The Hermitage, Highgate Rise
(From a photograph in the possession of the Author)

There was a pleasanter legend of Lord Nelson, when a boy, being once there, and climbing a very tall ash tree by the roadside, which therefore went by the name of 'Nelson's Tree,' till it went the way of all trees, to the timber yard.

It was reported, too, that Fauntleroy, when the officers of justice were in quest of him, concealed himself for a time at this Hermitage. The account of Fauntleroy's crime and fate are thus recorded in the 'Gentleman's Magazine' for 1824, part ii. p. 461:

'October 30, 1824.—The trial for forgery of Mr. Henry Fauntleroy, acting partner of the banking-house of Marsh and Co., Berners Street, took place. The case, on account of the vast extent of the forgeries committed, and the high respectability of the firm, has caused an unusual degree of public interest. In the years 1814 and 1815, Mr. Fauntleroy, it appears, disposed of Bank of England stock, by forged powers of attorney, to the amount of 170,000*l*. The prosecution was instituted by the Bank. At seven o'clock the doors leading to the court-house of the Old Bailey were beset. Pounds were offered for seats in the gallery, and the court was excessively crowded in every part. The jury being sworn, the clerk read the first indictment, which charged Henry Fauntleroy with forging a deed with intent to defraud Frances Young of 5,000*l* stock, and with forging a power of attorney with intent to defraud the Bank. The Attorney-General, in his address to the jury, described the prisoner as the acting partner in the house of Marsh and Co., in Berners Street. Mr. Fauntleroy, the father of the prisoner, became a partner at its establishment, and continued such till his death in 1807. At that period the prisoner was admitted into tlie concern, and became the most active member of it. In 1815 Frances Young, of Chichester, a customer of the house, lodged in their hands a power of attorney to receive the dividends on 5,450*l* Three per Cent. Consols. The dividends were regularly received; but soon afterwards another power of attorney, authorising the prisoner to sell that stock, was presented to the Bank, and the sale was effected by him. To this power the prisoner had forged the name of Frances Young and of two witnesses to it. But the most extraordinary part of the case was, that amongst the prisoner's private papers, contained in a tin box, there had been found one in which he acknowledged his guilt, and adduced a reason for his conduct.

The Attorney-General read the paper, which presented the following items:—De la Place, 11,150*l* Three per Cent. Consols; E. W. Young, 5,000*l* Consols; General Young, 6,000*l* Consols; Frances Young, 5000*l* Consols; H. Kelly, 6,000*l* Consols; Lady Nelson, 11,995*l* Consols; Earl of Ossory, 7,000*l* Four per Cents.; — Perkins, 4,000*l*. Consols. Sums were also placed in the names of Mrs. Pelham, Lady Aboyne, W. R. and H. Fauntleroy, and Elizabeth Fauntleroy, and the learned gentleman observed, that all the sums were added together, and the sum totals 120,000*l*, appeared at the foot of this list in the prisoner's handwriting. The statement was followed by this declaration:—

"In order to keep up the credit of our house, I have forged

powers of attorney for the above sums and parties, and sold out the amount here stated, and without the knowledge of my partners. I kept up the payment of the dividends, but made no notice of such payments in our books. The Bank began first to refuse to discount our acceptances, and to destroy the credit of our house; the Bank shall smart for it."

The Attorney-General then called his witnesses, who confirmed in every point his statement of the case. The prisoner, on being asked what he had to say in his defence, read a paper stating that, on his joining the firm in 1807, he found it deeply involved, in consequence of building specu-lations. The house remained in embarrassment till 1810, and then it experienced an overwhelming loss from the failure of Brickwood and Co., for which concern they had accepted and discounted bills to the amount of 170,000*l*. In 1814, 15 and 16, the firm was called upon, in consequence of the speculations in building, to produce 100,000*l*. In the year 1819 the most responsible of the partners died, and the embarrassments of the house were increased by being called upon to refund his capital. During all this time the house was without resources, except those for which he was now responsible. He received no relief from his partners. He had overdrawn 100,000*l*. He kept two establishments on a very moderate scale. He never embezzled one shilling. Having finished reading the paper, he sate down, and wept with much agitation.

Sir Charles Forbes, and fifteen other respectable witnesses, attested their high opinion of the prisoner's honour, integrity, and goodness of disposition. The Jury, after ten minutes' consideration, returned a verdict, Guilty of uttering —.'

Every exertion was made by Mr. Fauntleroy's counsel, his case having been twice argued before the judges; first, before Mr. Baron Garrow, at the Old Bailey; and since before the Twelve Judges at Westminster, when both decisions were against him. Many petitions were presented to his Majesty, in favour of the unhappy man; but all in vain. He was executed on Tuesday, Nov. 30, 1824.

The crowd to witness the execution of Mr. Fauntleroy was

enormous; it was estimated at nearly 100,000. Ludgate Hill, Skinner Street, Newgate Street, from which it was impossible to catch a glimpse of the scaffold, were blocked up by dense masses of people. Every window or housetop which could command a view of the dreadful ceremony was likewise occupied. The execution took place soon after eight o'clock a.m. Mr. Fauntleroy was dressed in a black coat, waistcoat, and trousers, with silk stockings and shoes. The demeanour of the unhappy man was perfectly composed. His eyes continued closed, and he was led by the two sheriffs. He never turned his head to the right or the left. The moment he appeared on the scaffold, the vast crowd took off their hats. As Mr. Cotton was reading the usual service, the drop fell, and the awful scene closed.

The Hermitage, of which the author of this work and his family were the last occupants, with its quaint buildings, its secluded lawn, and its towering trees, ten years ago gave way to a terrace of suburban houses.

Residences of Charles Mathews, Senr., And John Ruskin

Charles Mathews's House
(From a drawing in Mr. Gardner's Collection)

A little way on the left hand, after entering Millfield Lane, stands the house formerly inhabited by Charles Mathews, but which has since been much enlarged by succeeding proprietors.

Mathews spent a large sum on the house and the gardens, which he made altogether a very charming retreat. The next house on the same side, a plain but comfortable cottage, called Millfield Cottage, is said to have, for a short time, been occupied by John Ruskin, the great art critic. Mr. Ruskin himself, however, recollects nothing further than that, as a child, he lived with his father and mother in a cottage at Highgate or Hampstead. Tradition, therefore, may take the liberty of saying Highgate.

Here, then, I close my gathering on this hill of a few historic waifs and strays. They are snatched from the engulfing ruin of the advancing tide of population. What the last generation saw we see only in isolated fragments - a stump, a piece of ancient wall here and there. What we see our children a very few years hence will see no more. There are men, not very old, living, who remember the wide commons of Finchley and Highgate which lay around in airy expanse. In 1812, or thereabout, they passed into enclosure. Even the little open strips of land peeping into the village were imprisoned within garden hedges and walls. Not a foot of such folks land can now be discerned. But about fifty years ago, the people of Highgate made their visits to town in a stage-coach, which performed the journey in between two and three hours; fare half-a-crown; and such was the arduous undertaking, that the passengers regularly stopped to take tea on their return at the Assembly House, Kentish Town. A very little beyond this Assembly House, now a tavern, is the Old Farm House. You will readily find it by that name; but don't look for poultry and geese in its yard, cattle in its fields, or milk and butter in its dairy. The only cattle are the human kind densely crowded all round it in their close-packed houses; the only geese those who haunt its spirit tap - for it is a gin-shop public house. But the other day all in front of this strange Old Farm House, as far as Camden Town, were green fields; they are now houses and shops. Hampstead, a generation or two ago, was considered so remote and obscure a place, that in that once most popular story, 'Henry, Earl of Moreland,' its hero having been stolen away from his father by his uncle, the wealthy London merchant, was taken there to be unheard of. The uncle lived in great splendour in a great house, and young Moreland rode and drove about openly, but nobody found him out; and the uncle having at length to go to London on important business, he did not find himself able to get back again under a fortnight, during which time, so unvisited was Hampstead by the post, that little could be heard of him. In less than another fifty years we may safely prophesy that all these suburbs will be engulfed in London, and that it will be in vain to look for historical associations in Highgate.

The ground where Bacon died, and Marvell lived, where no doubt Milton sometimes visited Marvell; where of late years Coleridge philosophised; where the genial Leigh Hunt loved to walk; where Keats learned in its green lanes that

A thing of beauty is a joy for ever;

and Shelley, that so-called atheist, who had more love to his neighbour in his soul than a thousand nominal Christians, who, under the divine opal arch of heaven, learnt to denounce the despotisms of earth - which are

Tyrants to the weak and cowards to the strong;

It is something to have seen all this as they saw it. To have seen through long summers the artists in its Poet's Lane, sketching lovingly every tree and sylvan view; and swarming Londoners traversing its glades, and drinking in their sunshine and their freshness a life for the coming week of cribbed and cabined labour in town - to have seen and enjoyed all this in peace, on the very edge of the great roaring vortex of Mammon, is to have this privilege in its latest period. Every day descends this hill towards the great mart of trade and speculation, a multitude of heavy-browed men, whose every third word, if listened to, is *shares*. As in New York the air is said to be alive with the sound of 'dollar,' the air around London is resonant of 'shares, shares' - a certain proof that these will, ere long, conglomerate into one share, a ploughshare of destruction to every green thing, and leave in their place only a mere monotonous region of dusty streets and incrustation of brick. These papers may then bear witness that in 1869 there were really fields, lanes, and woods round Highgate, and within it historic traces of long past times. Meanwhile, *Dum vivimus vivamus.*

KENTISH TOWN AND CAMDEN TOWN

These places do not lie within the limits of this work; but as bordering on Hampstead, and still closer on Highgate, the following statements, as showing the wonderful rapidity with which they have grown up, are not uninteresting in connection with our subject.

In a 'History of Kentish Town,' published by J. Bennett in 1821, it is stated that in the middle of the last century, Kentish Town was a retired hamlet, of about 100 houses, detached from each other on the roadside. Between 1775 and 1795, it had increased in buildings one half; and in 1821 it contained 504 houses and 100 cottages below the rate of houses. There were also 48 houses on the Marquis of Camden's estate, where Camden Town now stands. In 1251, there were only 40 houses in the whole parish of St. Pancras. In May, 1821, these had increased to 9,405 houses, with 71,838 inhabitants.

MUSWELL HILL

Of this place, being a continuation of the ridge of hill running north of London, from Hampstead to this spot, little seems to have been recorded by the topographers. It is a fine easy walk from Highgate thither, with extensive views over town and country. It is about five and a half miles from London, with the advantage of the Great Northern Railway running just below it through Hornsey. Norden says, that at Muswell Hill, called also Pinsenall Hill, there was some time a chapel, dedicated to Our Lady of Muswell, of whom, of course, there had been an image, and a great resort of pilgrims. This arose from a miraculous cure said to have been performed on a King of Scots, who in some early time had been divinely directed to Muswell Hill, and healed by the waters of a well there. This well was called Mouse-well, or Muswell, probably originally Moss-well, on the spot where the chapel stood. The fame of the well, however, departed at the Reformation, and in the reign of Queen Elizabeth, when Norden wrote, its supernatural virtues had all evaporated. Norden says that on the site of the well, and farmhouse adjoining, in his time, 'Alderman Roe had a proper house.'

The chapel had been an appendage to the Priory of Clerkenwell, having, it is supposed, been built on land granted to that convent by Richard de Beauvois, Bishop of London, in the year 1112. To whom this property was granted on the fall of the Papal Church does not appear; but William Cowper, and his wife Cecily, alienated it in 1546, in the reign of Edward VI, to Thomas Goldynge, and by various transfers it passed successively into the possession of the families of Goodwyn, Wighell, Rowe, Muffett, and Pulteney, to the Earl of Darlington.

At the top of the hill, a building called the Exhibition Building, in rivalry of the Crystal Palace, has been erected on land named Alexandra Park, after the Princess of Wales. Many handsome villas of London merchants and other men of wealth, amongst them that of the great librarian, Mr. Mudie, are now scattered over the hill; and at its foot, in a secluded spot, there is a cottage called Lalla Rookh Cottage, because it was occupied by Thomas Moore during the time that he was putting 'Lalla Rookh' through the press. This Eastern poem had been written during three years, from 1813 to 1816, that he had lived in the Peak of Derbyshire, at Mayfield Cottage, near Ashbourne. The cottage at Muswell Hill stands in very secluded grounds. There he and his wife, and their two daughters, spent the summer of 1817; and his wife stayed there while he made a trip to Paris, where he collected materials for that humorous production, 'The Fudge Family in Paris.' From Paris he was hastily recalled by the illness of his eldest daughter, who died soon after he reached home, and was buried in Hornsey churchyard. From Lalla Rookh Cottage, Moore removed to Sloperton Cottage, near the village of Bromham, in Wiltshire, and near the residence of the Marquis of Lansdowne, Bowood, where he lived for the rest of his life.

Dr. Jackson, the present Bishop of London, was, in his early days, incumbent of Muswell Hill, being at the same time headmaster of Islington Proprietary School.

Whilst this passes through the press, I have received the following particulars from H. F. Church, Esq.:

`The inhabitants of Muswell Hill have enjoyed from time immemorial the use of the ancient well, commonly known as the Mus-Well. In December, 1861, these rights were threatened by one of the owners of the estate on which the well is situate, and the mouth of it was closed. It was a serious privation for the poorer inhabitants, for the supply of water at that time was very bad. Wells could not, except at a great expense, be sunk on the southern side of the hill, on account of the immense depth of the London clay; while on the northern side, the wells were situate on the premises of the better classes only; and the water of these wells proved on analysis to be much inferior to that of the Mus-Well. A few public-spirited inhabitants resolved to maintain the public rights. A subscription was raised, and the well opened, but only to be again closed. After fruitless negotiations, an action was commenced to establish the right. It was defended with much spirit; but after the evidence of some very old inhabitants had been taken, the defendants submitted, and judgment was signed in the action (Howell v. Rhodes, Q.B.), April 26, 1862.

Since that time, not only have the public rights been undisturbed, but, on the occasion of the passing, by the Legislature, of the Muswell Hill Estate Act, two or three years ago, for the Alexandra Park Company, clauses were inserted which protected for the future the inhabitants in the fullest enjoyment of the now public well (St. Dunstan's), in the neighbourhood, which is of the greatest antiquity, and possesses a reputation for medicinal virtues.

The well, some eighty years ago arched over with brick, is at this time supplied by the company with a pump,'

HORNSEY

The parish of Hornsey includes the hamlets of Muswell Hill, Crouch End, Stroud Green, formerly the seat of the Stapletons, and nearly two-thirds of Highgate. The name was written previous to the sixteenth century, Haringee, Haringhee, or Haringey; and Lysons thinks if anything is to be learned of the etymology of the names it must he sought for in its ancient appellation. Har-inge, the meadow of hares, is not very wide of its original orthography. It appears to have been shortened into Harnsey, and then gradually changed to Hornsey.

Hornsey Church
(From an original Sketch, by O. Jewitt)

The manor of Hornsey has belonged to the See of London from a period beyond the reach of any record that has yet been discovered. The bishops had a palace on this manor, from which are dated several acts previous to the fourteenth century. The more ancient building, occasionally occupied by the prelates, is supposed to have stood on Lodge Hill, which is situated at the eastern extremity of Lord Mansfield's wood, and the remains of a moat are still to be seen in a contiguous field. Norden, in the reign of Elizabeth, describes this elevation as

'a hill or fort in Hornsey Part, which is called Lodge Hill, for that thereon, sometime, stood a lodge, when the park was replenished with deer; but it seemeth by the foundations, that it was rather a castle than a lodge, for the hill is at this day trenched with two deep ditches, now old and overgrown with bushes. The rubble thereof, as brick, tile, and Cornish slate, are in heaps yet to be seen, which ruins are of great antiquity, as may appear by the oaks at this day standing, above a hundred years in growth, upon the very foundations of the building.'

A succeeding palace was burnt down in Bishop Aylmer's time, who was elevated to the see in 1576. This house Strype supposes to have stood at Hornsey.

In the great park at Haringay, or Hornsey, the nobles in Richard II's time assembled to oppose his extreme favouritism towards Robert de Vere, Earl of Oxford, whom he had created Duke of Ireland, and towards the Earl of Suffolk. Amongst these were the Duke of Gloucester, the Earls of Arundel, Warwick, Derby and Nottingham, and several others. This formidable demonstration alarmed the King, who requested a meeting at Westminster, where he received them kindly, gave them fair words, took them into his chamber, and make them drink together. He agreed to send the favourites from court, but it was not for long. Richard could not so easily lay aside the weaknesses which ultimately discrowned him.

Another curious circumstance took place in Hornsey Park at a later date - 1441 - in the reign of Henry VI. The Duchess of Gloucester was tried for practising by sorcery against the King's life. And amongst her alleged accomplices were Thomas Southwell, a canon of St. Stephen's, and Roger Bolingbroke, an astrologer. It was affirmed in court that Bolingbroke had devised necromantic means for wasting and destroying the King's person, and that Southwell had said masses in the Lodge of Hornsey Park over the instruments which were to be used for that purpose. The story of this strange charge will be familiar to the reader both in the reign of Henry VI and in Shakspeare's drama of the same

King.

In those times of fierce factions and very slender moral principle, with a weak monarch on the throne, scenes were continually transacting amongst the powerful nobles or princes of the blood, which would make the hair of moderns stand on end. The two great kinsmen of Henry VI, the Cardinal Beaufort, the same whom Shakespeare represents to us as dying and 'making no sign,' and his uncle, Humphrey, Duke of Gloucester, had, during the King's minority, kept around him a fierce contest for pre-eminence. Gloucester was warm-tempered but generous, and greatly beloved by the people, who called him 'the good Duke Humphrey.' He is said to have been better educated than most princes of his time; to have been fond of men of talent, and to have founded one of the first public libraries in England. The Cardinal was a very different man - cold, calculating and unscrupulous in his ambition. He was intriguing for the Papal tiara, and was not a man to be particular as to the means by which to remove any one who stood in any manner in his path. The Duke of Gloucester was his rival for the possession of the person of the young King; and thus there is every reason to believe he set on foot the intrigue for the destruction of the Duke of Gloucester's influence, and even of himself, which catastrophe indeed soon followed.

The first object was to strike at his domestic happiness, and at the same time, at his esteem with the King. The Duke had married Eleanor Cobham, the daughter of Lord Reginald Cobham, who had in the first place been his mistress. Though he had made her his wife, her enemies never forgot her original connection with the Duke, and instead of her legitimate title, persisted in calling her Dame Eleanor Cobham. She is represented as a bold, ambitious, dissolute and avaricious woman. That is the portrait drawn by her enemies, and they did not stop there. The last attack of the Duke on the Cardinal, which seemed to aim at once at his life and honour, roused the crafty churchman to a deadly scheme of revenge. He called in that ecclesiastical machinery which in those ages could so readily be brought to bear as an object of coercion. His emissaries, whom he had everywhere, and especially in the Duke's household, reported that the Duchess had private meetings with one Roger Bolingbroke, a priest, who was a reputed necromancer, and with Margery Jourdemain, the celebrated witch of Eye. On this fact,

Beaufort resolved to found a charge, which should strike a fatal blow at the domestic peace and at the public favour of Gloucester.

The fact was that Bolingbroke was the Duke's chaplain, a man of great science, and especially addicted to astronomy, and its then common accompaniment, astrology, with the casting of nativities and the like. The Duke was extremely fond of the society of learned men, and held frequent discourses with the chaplain on the arts then popular. Suddenly, and immediately following his accusation of the Cardinal, he found his wife, to whom he was greatly attached, accused of high treason, 'for that she by sorcery and enchantment, intended to destroy the King, to the intent to advance and to promote her husband to the crown.'

Bolingbroke was arrested, and being accused of necromancy, was exhibited on a platform in St. Paul's Churchyard, with the instruments of his art; for he is declared by a writer of his time to have been the most celebrated astronomer and necromancer in the world. He was dressed in a wondrous robe, pretended to be that in which he practised his art, bearing in his right hand a sword, and in his left a sceptre, and seated on a chair, on the four corners of which were fixed four swords, and on the points of the swords four images of copper.

On the arrest of Bolingbroke, the Duchess of Gloucester, aware of the real direction of the intended blow, took refuge in the sanctuary at Westminster. Here she was brought face to face with Bolingbroke, who is made to say that it was at her instigation that he first applied to the study of magic; a very improbable circumstance, the more natural one being that his knowledge of astrology had tempted the Duchess to make dangerous inquiries, namely, whether the King or the Duke would be the longer liver, and whether there appeared any chance of the envied and maligned Dame Eleanor Cobham wearing a crown.

Besides the Duchess and Bolingbroke, there were arrested as accomplices, Thomas Southwell, a canon of St. Paul's, Hum, a priest, and Margery Jourdemain, the witch. The Duchess was examined in St. Stephen's Chapel, Westminster, by the Archbishop of Canterbury, and charged with having obtained love-philters, to secure the affection of her husband. But a much more terrible and absurd charge was that she had procured from Southwell and Bolingbroke a wax figure, which was so moulded by art, that when placed before the fire, as it melted away, the King's marrow would dry up and his life fade away. It was at the bishop's lodge, in Hornsey Park, that the necromantic ceremonies were performed by Bolingbroke for the preparation of the fatal waxen figures, and where Southwell said mass over them, to give them a greater potency.

Eight-and-twenty such charges were preferred against the Duchess of Gloucester and her alleged associates, some of which she is said to have admitted, but the majority and the worst to have denied; and on such ridiculous pleas, she was condemned, on three days of the week, to walk bareheaded, and bearing a lighted taper in her hand, through the streets of London, and afterwards to be confined for life in the Isle of Man, in the custody of Sir John Stanley. The unfortunate men of science were condemned to be hanged, drawn and quartered at Tyburn. Bolingbroke suffered the sentence, stoutly protesting his innocence; Southwell died in prison; and Hum received a royal pardon. Margery Jourdemain was burnt as a witch in Smithfield. As for the Duchess, the people, who attributed the whole of this atrocious proceeding to the Cardinal, and the other enemies of the Duke, instead of insulting her in her penance, followed her with deep sympathy and respect, and only the more attached themselves to the Duke as the victim of so ruthless a conspiracy. Gloucester himself, prostrated, as it were, by this stunning blow, said little, let it take its course, and brooded over it in silent grief. Shakespeare makes the weak and helpless King Henry thus express his knowledge that it was a base faction which thus pursued Gloucester:

> Ah, uncle Humphrey! in thy face I see
> The map of honour, truth, and loyalty;
> And yet, good Humphrey, is the hour to come,
> That e'er I proved thee false, or fear'd thy faith.
>
> What low'ring star now envies thy estate,
> That these great lords, and Margaret our queen,
> Do seek subversion of thy harmless life?
> Thou never didst them wrong, nor no man wrong.

The fortunes of our ill-fated monarchs seem to have been curiously connected with this park of Hornsey; amongst them, the poor smothered boy, King Edward V. His uncle, Richard of Gloucester, afterwards Richard III, had kidnapped him at Stoney-Stratford from his nearest relatives, and was conducting him to London, in order to murder him in the Tower with his brother Richard, the infant Duke of York. The monster uncle was conducting the young King with a strong force towards London, and at Hornsey Park he was met by the Lord Mayor of London and Corporation, in scarlet, and attended by 500 citizens, all in violet, who joined the royal procession. The Duke, habited, like all his followers, in mourning for the brother whose children he had determined in his heart to destroy, rode before the King, cap in hand, bowing low to the people, and pointing out the King to their notice, who rode in a mantle of purple velvet. Yet, with all this pretended devotion to his nephew, Richard had already sent the executioner to behead some of his nearest relatives and friends - Lord Gray, Sir Richard Vaughan, and Sir Richard Hawse, without warrant or trial, in that blood-stained den, Pontefract Castle. Scarcely did he arrive in London, when, with equally little ceremony, he struck off the heads of his uncle, Lord Rivers, and his chief supporter, Lord Hastings. It was a fine morning, May 4, 1483, when the young and doomed King rode through Highgate, thus attended by all the pomp of treachery. All nature looked happy and beautiful, but a cold dread lay on the hearts of the loyal people who had come out to meet and welcome him, only too soon to prove that the dread was not in vain.

A very different monarch, Henry VII, was also met here by the citizens of London, on his return from a successful Scottish war.

Amongst the monuments in Hornsey Church to men and women of station and name in their time, now pretty well forgotten, is that of Samuel Buckley, the editor of 'Thuanus,' who died in 1741. Amongst the tombs in the churchyard is that of the poet Samuel Rogers. He is buried in the family vault, and an inscription upon it records the date of birth and death of the poet, adding that he was 'author of the "Pleasures of Memory," ' but not specifying to what class of literature the work belongs. The following are the inscriptions on the face of the tomb:

'In this vault lie the remains of Henry Rogers, Esq., of Highbury Terrace; died December 25, 1832, aged 58. Also of Sarah Rogers, of the Regent's Park, sister of the above; died January 29, 1855, aged 82. Also of Samuel Rogers, author of the 'Pleasures of Memory,' brother of the above-named Henry and Sarah Rogers, born at Newington Green, July 30, 1763, died at St. James's Place, Westminster, December 18, 1855.'

Amongst the rectors of Hornsey was Thomas Westfield, who resigned the living in 1637, afterwards Bishop of Bristol, the most nervous of men. His biographer says that

'he never, though almost fifty years a preacher, went up into the pulpit but he trembled; and never preached before the King but once, and then he fainted.'

Yet he was held in such esteem by all parties, that on May 13, 1643, the committee for sequestrating the estates of delinquents, being informed that his tenants refused to pay his rents as Bishop of Bristol, speedily compelled them, and granted him a safe conduct for his journey to Bristol with his family, being a man of great learning and merit, and advanced in years. His successor at Hornsey, Thomas Lant, did not meet with quite such agreeable treatment. He was turned out of his living and house by the Puritans with great cruelty, they not allowing him even to procure a place of retirement. Samuel Bendy, rector in 1659, petitioned the Committee, setting forth that his income was only £92, out of which he had to pay £16 to the wife and children of the late incumbent. The committee made him recompense.

Dr. Lewis Atterbury, brother of Bishop Atterbury, whom we have mentioned at Highgate, was collated to the rectory of Hornsey in 1719. William Cole, the Cambridge antiquary, was rector of Hornsey, and died in 1782. He held the rectory only one year, 1749.

Amongst eminent persons who have lived or died at Hornsey, Reginald Gray, of Ruthin, Earl of Kent, died there March 17, 1573.

John Lightfoot, the learned commentator and Hebraist, went to reside at Hornsey in the year 1628, for the purpose of being near London, where he might have access to the library at Sion College.

One of his works is dated from his study at Hornsey. As John Lightfoot is stated to have been born in 1602, and to have published his first work, entitled 'Erubbim; or, Miscellanies Christian and Judaical,' in 1629, he could be only 27 at the time, and went to live at Hornsey when only 28 years of age. He was a zealous promoter of the Polyglott Bible, and at the Restoration was appointed one of the assistants at the Savoy Conference. In 1675 he became Vice-chancellor of Cambridge. For biblical learning he is said to have had few equals.

The Parish Church of Hornsey, dedicated to St. Mary, appears by the arms of Savage and Warham, two succeeding bishops of London, which are carved on the tower, to have been built about the year 1500.

William Howitt

PART III: ISLINGTON

ISLINGTON

Old Church
(From Nelson's 'History of Islington')

Many names and many derivations of name have been assigned to Islington. Isendune, Isendone, Iseltone, Hisselton, Hyseldone, Yseldon and Eyseldon, are the various forms of the name which present themselves for Islington at various periods. Of these, Isendune, Isendone, and Iseltone occur in 'Domesday Book,' and Isendone in the most ancient records of the church of St. Paul's. Lysons, and others, think that this means the Hill of Iron, because various chalybeate springs are found in this neighbourhood. The name, however, of Iseldon occurring in 'Domesday Book' induces Sharon Turner to derive it from Ysseldune, or the down of the Yssel, supposed to be the original name of the River of Wells, which fell into the Fleet River. Mr. Tomlins, in his 'Antiquarian Perambulation of Islington,' thinks that Ysel, or Eysel, is the same as Ousel, the diminutive of Ouse or Eyse, the British for either a river or water, and, therefore, means the town of the river. Skinner prefers to derive it from Gisel, a hostage, in Anglo-Saxon; but though there are entries in the Great Pipe Roll of Henry II and of John, of sending hostages from London to Lichfield, there is no known direct authority for asserting Islington to have been a fort for the retention of hostages.

Strype, in his edition of 'Stow's Surrey, 1755,' calls the parish that of 'Iseldon, corruptly, or commonly called, Islington.' Stow himself, in his 'Survey of London, 1598,' calls it Isledon. Yet, as early as the reign of Edward IV, in the Year-book Mich. 21, Ed. IV, fol. 73, it is called Islington. Houghton suggests a derivation from the British word Ishel, lower, and don from *twyn*, a fortified enclosure, indicating a tower or fort lower than others; a suggestion made feasible by the higher position of Hampstead and Highgate beyond it. Again, in the 'Turnament of Tottenham,' Hisselton is the name given it, plainly a corruption of Iseldon or Yseldon:

> Hither came all the men of that contray,
> Of Hisselton, of Highgate, and of Hacknay.

Whichever of these derivations be the correct one, I leave the reader to decide, for nothing is so uncertain as derivations, which so frequently are plausible, but as frequently uncertain. Of all things derivations are the most pliable.

Islington, till almost a recent period, was a village standing isolated in open fields. Lysons says the parish is three miles one furlong in length, two miles one furlong in breadth, ten miles and one half in circumference, and contains, exclusive of houses, gardens and wastes, 2,699 acres 37 perches of land, of which 22 acres only were arable, and about 10 nursery-grounds. When 'Domesday Book' was compiled, part of the parish was arable, part common pasture, and the rest consisted of woodland, oak, and beech, affording pannage for 60 swine. The population then consisted of only twenty seven persons and their families, who were chiefly shepherds, herdsmen, and tillers of the ground.

From earliest times Islington seems to have stood amidst extensive open fields, the resort of shepherds and graziers. The church stood in a field on the highest part of the town, and not far from the woods. It was dedicated to St. Mary, and was considered to be of very ancient date; some imagining that there had been a church there from the Saxon times. When the old structure was pulled down to erect the present one, in 1751, it was in a very ruinous state, but the tower was so strongly cemented as to require gunpowder to rend it to pieces. Of the church more anon - our present concern is with the open fields.

'Such was the jealousy of the inhabitants of London of encroachments, and being couped up in inclosures, that in 1514, finding themselves grieved with the inclosures of the common fields about Islington, Hoxton, Shoreditch, and other places near the city, whereby they could not be at liberty to exercise their bows, nor other pastimes in those fields, as aforetime they had been accustomed, they assembled themselves one morning, and went with spades and shovels unto the same fields, and there, like diligent workmen, so bestirred themselves, that within a short space all the hedges about those towns were cut down, and the ditches filled. The King's Counsail coming to the Grey Friars to understand what was meant by this, were so answered by the Mayor and Counsail of the citie, that the matter was dismissed; and so when the workmen had done their work, they came home in quiet manner, and the fields were never after hedged.'

Down to Charles II's time, little enclosure round London and especially on its north side, seems to have taken place. Lord Macaulay says:

'Whoever examines the maps of London which were published towards the close of the reign of Charles II, will see, that only the enclosure of the present capital still existed. The town did, just as now, fade by imperceptible degrees into the country. On the north cattle fed, and sportsmen wandered with dogs and guns over the site of the borough of Marylebone, and over far the greater part of the space now covered by the boroughs of Finsbury and of the Tower Hamlets. Islington was almost a solitude; and poets loved to contrast its silence and repose with the din and turmoil of the monster London.'

The word *monster* shows that Macaulay had Cowley in his mind on this occasion:

Methinks I see
The monster London laugh at me;
I should at thee too, foolish city,
But let thy wicked ones from out thee go,
And all the fools that court thee so,
E'en thou, who dost thy millions boast,
A village less than Islington will grow,
A solitude almost.

We find, by an Order in Council, of Sept. 6, 1666, issued immediately after the great fire in this same reign, that the fields about Islington were crowded with the thousands of people who had fled out of the burning city with what of their effects they could save. John Evelyn, in his `Diary,' on Sept. 5, says:

'The poore inhabitants were dispersed about St. George's Fields and Moor Fields, as far as Highgate, and several miles in circle, some under tents, some under miserable huts and hovells, many without a rag, or any necessary utensils, bed or board, who from delicatenesse, riches, and early accommodations in stately and well-furnished houses, were now reduced to extremest misery and poverty.'

The next day, he visited this awful scene again, and says:

'I then went towards Islington and Highgate, where one might have seene 200,000 people of all ranks and degrees, dispersed and lying along by their heapes of what they could save from the fire, deploring their losses, and though ready to perish for hunger and destitution, yet not asking one penny for relief, which to me appeared a stranger sight than any I had yet beheld. His Majesty and Council indeede tooke all imaginable care for their reliefe by proclamation for the country to come in and refresh them with provisions. In the midst of all this calamity and confusion, there was, I know not how, an alarme begun, that the French and Dutch, with whom we were now in hostility, were not only landed, but even entering the citty. There was in truth some days before great suspicion of those two nations joining; and now, that they had been the occasion of firing the toune. This report did so terrifie, that on a suddaine, there was such an uproare and tumult, that they ran from their goods, and taking what weapons they could come at, they could not be stopped from falling on some of those nations whom they casually met, without sense or reason. The clamour and peril grew so excessive, that it made the whole Court agonized, and they did with infinite pains and great difficulty reduce and appease the people, sending troopes and soldiers and guards to cause them to retire into the fields again, where they were watched all this night. I left them pretty quiet, and came home sufficiently weary and broken. Their spirits thus a little calmed, and the affright abated, they now began to repair into the suburbs about the citty, where such as had friends or opportunity got shelter.'

Wild as were these scenes, there were much ruder ones at an earlier day in the same locality, where those found there did not hesitate to 'ask for a penny,' nor for any number of pennies. The liberty offered by these open lands induced persons travelling with an equipage, often to turn aside from the deep and miry highways, and take the nearest route across the fields to their point of destination. Thus we read that in July, 1561, Queen Elizabeth went from the Tower through Houndsditch to the Spittle, and down Hog Lane, over the fields to the Charterhouse. From thence, in a few days, she took her way, 'over the fields,' to the Savoy; and shortly after, she came from Enfield to St. James's. On this occasion, the hedges and ditches between Islington and the Palace were cut down to make the next way for her.

Strype relates a curious occurrence on a similar cross-country trip of Elizabeth's, just twenty years later in the same neighbourhood:

'Beyond Aldersgate Bars, leaving the Charter House on the left hand, stretches up towards Iseldon, commonly called Islington; a country town hard by, which in the former age was esteemed to be so pleasantly seated, that, in 1581, Queen Elizabeth, in one of the 12 days, on an airing, will that way to take the air, where near the town she was environed with a number of begging rogues, as beggars usually haunt such places, which gave the Queen much disturbance. Whereupon Mr. Stone, one of the footmen, came in all haste to the Lord Mayor, and to Fleetwood, the Recorder, and told them the same. That same night did the Recorder send out warrants into the same quarter, and into Westminster and the Duchy, and in the morning he went out himself and took that day seventy-four rogues, whereof some were blind, and yet great usurers and very rich. Upon Twelfth Day, the Recorder met the Governor of Bridewell, and they examined together all the above said seventy-four rogues, and gave them substantial payment; and the strongest they bestowed in the Milne and the Lighters; the rest were dismissed with a promise of double payment if they were met with again.'

In the reign of Elizabeth, Gerard, the herbalist, used to frequent those fields to collect the herbs and flowers that he needed. He speaks of three kinds of orchises growing in those fields, where there was a bowling green under a few old shabby oaks. The fields to which he refers are supposed to be those called the Commandry Mantels, and other mantels lying between Islington, Barnsbury, and Clerkenwell. At this time there was a shepherd's hut and sheep-pens near the spot on which the Angel Inn now stands.

Old Angel Inn
(From a print in Mr. Gardner's Collection)

In an indenture of 1700, the Angel Inn is represented as standing in the fields, not far from this shipcote, or sheep-house. There is said to have been an Angel Inn on the spot for more than 200 years.

In the fields between Islington and Finsbury, and between Islington and Newington Green, the archers used to exercise their craft, and practise with their bow from time immemorial, of which much information may be found in Highmore's 'History of the Artillery Company,' Davies Barrington's 'Practice of Archery,' and Nichol's 'History and Antiquities of Canonbury House at Islington.'

In fact, the fields all to the north of London, especially about Islington, have from the earliest times been a favourite resort of the Londoners for open-air exercise and sport. Fitzstephen, who wrote in the time of Henry II, tells us that in the afternoons the youth of the city were accustomed to go out into the fields, with their teachers, to play at ball, the scholars of every school having their particular balls; whilst 'the ancient and wealthy citizens came on horseback to see these youngsters contending at their sport;' that exercises on horseback, to qualify them for military life, were practised every Friday in Lent, and that on these occasions the youth of the city came out in great numbers. He adds that they were fond of exercising their hawks there, and their dogs in the sports of the field; so there must have been plenty of game so near London as that. Stow says the fields of the northern environs of London were 'commodious for the citizens therein to walke, shoote, and otherwise to recreate and refresh their dulled spirits, in the sweete and wholesome ayre.' That the officers of the city, sheriffs, the porters of the King's beame or weighing-house, and others of the city, were in the habit of challenging 'all men in the suburbs to wrestle, shoot the standard, broad arrow, and flight, for games at Clerkenwell and Finsbury Fields.'

Archer of the Time of Charles I
(From a woodcut in Gervase Markham's
'Art of Archerie, 1634,' in the British Museum)

The Londoners claimed the fields betwixt Shoreditch, Hoxton, and Islington, known as Finsbury Fields, especially for the practice with the long-bow. The importance of maintaining the supremacy of the English bowmen was duly appreciated by all the Norman kings, as repeated enactments from the Conquest downward amply show. In 1365, Edward III made proclamation that the citizens on all occasions of leisure, or on holidays, should practise with bows and arrows, pellets and bolts, and forbidding them to waste their time 'in throwing of stones, handball, football, bandyball, lambuck, or cock-fighting, or other such vain plays, which have no profit in them.' In 1392, an Act was passed to oblige servants to shoot with bows and arrows on Sundays and holidays: knowing, as expressed by Sir John Fortescue, an eminent lawyer of Henry VI's reign, 'that the mighte of the realme of England standyth upon archers.'

Henry VIII was a zealous practiser of the long-bow, as of most other athletic sports. In the twenty ninth year of his reign, he granted a patent to Sir Christopher Morris, Master of the Ordnance, and others, that they should be overseers of the science of artillery, 'to wit, long-bowes, cross-bowes, and hand gonnes;' with liberty for them and their fraternity to exercise shooting at all manner of marks and butts, and at the game of the popinjay, and other games, as at fowl and fowls, as well in the city and suburbs as in all other places. This patent appears to be the origin of the City Artillery Company. In it was a remarkable clause - namely, that when anyone was shooting at a known and accustomed mark, and before discharging his arrow, pronounced the archer's usual word, 'Fast,' anyone passing shall be wounded or slain, the archer shall not be impeached or troubled for such mischance. Henry compelled every man to furnish his son at the age of seven with a bow and two arrows; and an Act of the sixth year of his reign obliges every man, except clergy and judges, to shoot at butts. Arthur, the eldest brother of Henry, had been equally fond of archery, whence an expert bowman was styled Prince Arthur. Kingsland and King Henry's Walk, between Newington Green and Ball's Pond, testify to the resort of Bluff Harry to these favourite haunts and amusements of the Londoners.

In a shooting match at Windsor, King Henry, near the close of the combat, observing one of his guard, named Barlo, preparing to shoot, said to him, 'Beat them all, and thou shalt be Duke of Archers.' Barlo succeeded, and Henry named him Duke of Shoreditch, the place that he came from. The Duke of Shoreditch descended for several generations with the captainship of the London Archers. Other distinguished archers won the titles of

Marquises of Islington, Hoxton, and Shacklewell, Earl of Pancras, &c.

Hall, in his 'Chronicle,' says,

' . . . that about the sixth of Henry VIII, the inhabitants of the towns about London, as Iseldon, Hoxton, Shoreditch, and others, had so enclosed the common fields by hedges and ditches, that neither the young men of the city might shoote, nor the ancient persons walke, for their pleasure in those fields, but that either their bowes and arrows were taken away or broken, or the honest persons arrested or indicted, saying that no Londoner ought to go out of the city but in the highways. This saying so grieved the Londoners, that suddainly this yeere a great number of the city assembled themselves in a morning; and a turner, in a foole's coate came crying thorow the city,— "Shovels and Spades! Shovel and Spades!" So many of the people followed that it was wonder to behold; and within a short space all the hedges about the city were cut down, and the ditches filled up, and everything made plaine, such was the diligence of these workmen.'

The rioters having thus effected their purpose, returned quietly to their respective homes; 'after which,' says Hall, 'those fields were never hedged.'

A grand shooting-match was celebrated in Smithfield in 1583, under the direction of the Duke of Shoreditch, Captain of the London Archers, assisted by his several officers, Marquises of Clerkenwell, Islington, Hoxton, Shacklewell, &c., which was attended by 3,000 archers, and lasted two days. On the second day the victors were mounted on horseback, and conducted away in triumph, escorted by 200 torch-bearers.

Paul Hentzer, in his travels in England in the reign of Elizabeth, observes that the English still made great use of bows and arrows, though other authorities show that the art had much declined; the bowyers, fletchers, stringers, and arrowhead makers complained to Government of the decay of their trade; and Stow informs us that through the enclosing of the fields, the archers had to creep into bowling-alleys and ordinary dicing-houses nearer home, where they found room enough to hazard them at unlawful games. James I endeavoured to revive archery, and issued letters patent to the Lord Mayor of London, the Lord Chancellor, and other distinguished persons, amongst whom was Sir Thomas

Fowler of Islington, to survey the open grounds within two miles around the city, formerly appropriated to such exercises, and to see them put in proper order as in the reign of Henry VIII. Charles I issued a like order, commanding the enclosure of the grounds to be prevented, and the mounds to be levelled wherever they obstructed the view from one mark to another. The marks, of which there were in the Finsbury Fields no fewer than 160, were placed at varying and uncertain distances, and they were called rovers, from the practice of roving and ranging across the fields and shooting at these marks, a practice much preferred by ancient archers to pricking, or shooting at a given mark from a certain distance. A print of an archer on the frontispiece of a rare tract in the British Museum - Gervase Markham's `Art of Archerie,' London, 1634, has been generally regarded as a representation of Charles I. This, and another woodcut of an archer in full costume, which adorns the Finsbury Archers' ticket of admission to the meeting of the Society of Archerie at Drapers' Hall, Throgmorton Street, July 24, 1676, are given by Nelson in his `History of Islington.' The members on receiving this ticket from Mr. William Wood, a celebrated archer, author of the tract entitled the 'Bowman's Glory; or, Archery Revived,' and Marshal of the Regiment of Archers, were each to pay him two and sixpence.

During the Rebellion the practice of archery had been neglected. Charles II again patronised it, and in 1682 there was a grand meeting of the Finsbury archers, at which the King was present, and the old titles of Duke of Shoreditch, Marquis of Islington, &c., were again bestowed on the most skilful.

Pepys, in his 'Diary,' May 12,1667, says:

'I walked over the fields to Kingsland and back again; a walk, I think, I had not taken these twenty years; but puts me in mind of my boy's time, when I boarded at Kingsland, and came to shoot with my bow and arrow in these fields. A very pretty place it is.'

Sir William Davenant, in his poem, `The Long Vacation,' describes the lawyers and proctors having their shooting matches in the suburban fields:

Each with solemn oath agree
To meet in fields of Finsburie.
With loynes in canvas bow-case tied,
Where arrows stick in mickle pride;
With hats turned up and bow in hand,
All day most fiercely there they stand,
Like ghosts of Adam Bell and Clymme -
Sol sets for fear they'll shoot at him.

But the Robin Hood ballads bring Clymme of the Clough, Adam Bell, and William of Cloudesley bodily on the scene with their great leader -

The King is into Finsbury Field
Marching in battle array,
And after follows Robin Hood,
And all his yeomen gay.

So jealous were the chartered company of archers, which to a late period formed a division of the Artillery Company, that they never omitted to knock down and destroy every fence or mound raised within the limits of their several practising grounds. Hatton says,

`They do by prescription march over all the ground from the artillery-ground to Islington and Sir George Whitmore's, levelling down gates, etc., that obstruct them in their marches.'

In Henry VIII's time, their privileges extended from Perelow's Pool, now called Peerless Pool, to Islington Common. Other places had similar rights, as Tothill Fields, St. James's Fields, Hyde Park, Mile End, Clerkenwell Fields, Hogsden, or Hoxton Fields; and those places which have the words Butts affixed, as Newington Butts, Lambeth Butts, were noted for the practice of the long-bow, and had shooting marks, or butts.

Highmore, in his `History of the Artillery Company,' gives us repeated accounts of the marches of the company to destroy the obstructions which were continually rising in their chartered grounds. Such he describes as taking place in 1782 and 1784, 1786 and 1791, and overturning all opposition, or compelling the encroachers to compound and pay for the accommodations they had usurped.

The distance at which a skilful archer could hit a mark is something wonderful. The longest distances between the marks in these fields were nineteen score, or 380 yards; the shortest nine score, or 180 yards. A curious fact is related of Topham, 'the strong man of Islington,' who could bend a stout poker round his neck, and do greater feats. He ridiculed the long-bow in a public house amongst archers as a plaything only fit for children. The archers laid him a bowl of punch that he could not draw the arrow two-thirds of its length, and on trial he lamentably failed. Such are the marvels of practice.

These privileges have, for the most part, long been lost, from the decay of archery, and the spread of bricks and mortar. Stow in his time lamented over the uncouth, but most persevering, encroachments of the citizens:

'Afterwards wee saw the thing in worse case than ever, by means of inclosure for gardens, wherein are builded many faire summer-houses; and, as in other places of the suburbs, some of them like Midsummer pageants, with towers, turrets and chimney-tops, not so much for use or profit, as for show and pleasure of men's minds.'

He ridicules their names as -

Kirbie's Castle, and Fisher's Folly,
Spinila's Pleasure, and Megse's Glory.

Though archery died out, pleasure continued to live, and sought its aliment at Islington. The spas, the wells, and the public houses, with their refreshments, music, and dancing, were the attractions. Full pictures of these are to be found in such productions as 'The Walks of Islington and Hogsden, with the Humours of Wood Street Couples: a Comedy, by Thomas Jordan, gent.,' 1641; 'Drunken Barnaby's Four Journeys to the North of England,' in the middle of the seventeenth century; 'The Merry Milkmaid of Islington, or the Rambling Gallants defeated,' acted at Newmarket; Ned Ward's 'Walk to Islington, with a description of the New Tunbridge Wells and Sadler's Music-house,' and George Colman's 'Spleen, or Islington Spa,' acted at Drury Lane in 1756. In this satirical piece, Colman's description of the citizen's country house at Islington, and the bustle occasioned by packing up the neats' tongues and cold chicken, preparatory to his wife's journey thither, by the coach-and-three, from the end of Cheapside, is amusing.

Old Sadler's Wells
(From a scarce print in Mr. Gardner's Collection)

We have already spoken of this class of amusements when speaking of the Wells of Islington. Bonnel Thornton, in several papers in the `Connoisseur,' has described the Sunday excursions of the citizens to this village, to drink ale and smoke their pipes; and Goldsmith has celebrated the tea parties, and the hot rolls and butter at White Conduit House. Nobody enjoyed such holiday trips into the country near London more than Goldsmith. In what he called his 'Shoemaker's Holidays,' he often turned his steps towards Islington. Three or four of his intimate friends, says the 'European Magazine,' rendezvoused at his chambers to breakfast about ten o'clock in the morning; at eleven they proceeded up the City Road, and through the fields to Highbury Barn to dinner. About six in the evening they adjourned to White Conduit House to drink tea, and concluded the evening by supping at the Grecian or Temple Exchange Coffee House, or at the Globe in Fleet Street. There was a very good ordinary of two dishes and pastry kept at Highbury Barn at this time, at 10d. per head, including a penny to the waiter; and the company generally consisted of literary characters, a few Templars, and some citizens who had left off trade. The whole expense of this day's fete never exceeded a crown, and oftener from 3s. 6d. to 4s., for which the party obtained good air and exercise, good living, the example of simple manners, and good conversation.

Let us conclude these Islington *villeggiaturas* of the Londoners by Sir William Davenant's mention of them in his 'Long Vacation':

> Now, damsel young, that dwells in Cheap,
> For very joy begins to leap;
> Her elbow small she oft doth rub,
> Tickled with hope of syllabub;
> For mother, who does gold maintaine
> On thumb, and keys in silver chaine,
> In snow-white clout wrapt nook of pye,
> Fat capon's wing, and rabbit's thigh:
> And said to hackney coachman, Go,
> Take shillings six - say, Aye or no;
> Whither? says he - quoth she, Thy teame
> Shall drive to place where groweth creame.
> But husband gray now comes to stall,
> For 'prentice notched he strait doth call. -
> Where's dame? quoth he - quoth son of shop,
> She's gone her cake in milke to sop.
> Ho! ho! - to Islington, enough,
> Fetch Job, my son, and our dog Ruffe;
> For there in pond, through mire and muck,
> We'll cry, 'hay, duck - there Ruffe - hay, duck!'

Islington was always famed for dairies, and it was a great treat for the citizens and their children to see cows actually grazing in the fields, and actual milk-maids milking them, and to have the luxuries of new milk from the cow; creams, custards, syllabubs, and the like rural dainties. The openness of the neighbourhood, and its elevation, gave them a great idea of its healthiness, and great numbers not only resorted there for a day's rural enjoyment, but for lodgings. From the great number of such visitors, Islington was familiarly called the 'London Hospital,' and Dr. Hunter relates an amusing anecdote in connection with this subject:

'A lady in advanced age, and declining state of health, went by the advice of her physician to take lodgings in Islington. She agreed for a suite of rooms; and coming down stairs, observed that the banisters were much out of repair. "These," she said, "must be mended before I can think of coming to live here." "Madam," answered the landlady, "that will answer no purpose, as the undertaker's men, in bringing down the coffins, are continually breaking the banisters." The old lady had heard enough: she hastily declined the apartments.'

The open fields of merry Islington, and of the country round it, are now dense and populous districts of the 'monster London.' It is not many years since I used to walk from Highgate to Ball's Pond, chiefly through open fields, where the new Cattle Market stands, on the ancient site of Copenhagen Fields, if not of Copenhagen House itself, thence by the site of the present City Prison, near Upper Holloway, and onwards by Canonbury House, still through green fields, where now Beauvoir Town presents its densely serried streets. The open fields and all their citizen pleasures and healthy exercises are gone, and cricket is the only athletic practice now witnessed where a few patches of free space permit it.

Not only the open-air games, but many traces of past history, are obliterated by the spread of houses. Where should we now find any remains of the entrenchments referred to in the following curious statement? During the Civil War, especially in 1642 and 1643, the London Militia marched out, and made entrenched camps at the different roads leading from the north towards the City, to defend the metropolis from the invasion of the King and his Cavaliers. The 'Perfect Diurnal' of the day states:

'October, 1642, the Militia made trenches and ramparts near all the highways beyond Islington, Mile End, St. Pancras, &c. — May 8, 1643, the work in the fields and trenches round the city goes on amain. Many thousands of men, women, and servants go out daily to work; and this day there went out a great number of the Common Council, and divers other chief men of the city, with the greatest part of the trained bands, with spades, shovels, pickaxes, &c. — May 9, this day many thousands of citizens, their wives and families, went out to dig, and all the porters in and about the city, to the number of 2,000. — May 23, 5,000 feltmakers and cappers went to work at the trenches; near 3,000 porters, and a great company of men, women, and children.

— May 24, four or five thousand shoemakers. — June 6, 6,000 tailors.'

Probably some of these trenches, before they were obliterated by the progress of building, were imagined to be traces of much more ancient camps.

PONDS, CONDUITS, AND RIVERS

From these elevated lands drained springs and watercourses, which were assisted by art to furnish water to the metropolis. Of the various wells which became noted as places of resort, I have already spoken; but a word more may be added regarding the ponds and conduits, and the New River.

Various neighbourhoods of London had their ducking- ponds - *i.e.*, ponds where the Londoners went with dogs, and hunted down unfortunate ducks that were procured for the purpose. In Henry VIII's time there were ducking-ponds in St. Botolph Without, Aldgate. The author of 'Merrie England' speaks of a ducking-pond in Mayfair in 1748; and there was one at Limehouse, &c. The ducking- ponds at Islington lay chiefly at the back of Islington, and are described as descending in succession (as do the ponds at present at Highgate and Hampstead) almost from Liverpool Road to Lady Huntingdon's Chapel, Exmouth Street, Spa Fields. On the site of this chapel stood, more than a century ago, a house of entertainment, called Ducking-Pond House; and the present burial-ground was, at that time, the actual pond. In a field lying between Islington and Holloway, whereon Felix Terrace has been built, was a ducking-pond. Where Cloudesley Terrace stands were deep ponds; where Albert Street now stands, that is, on the north side of the old site of White Conduit House, and again, at the north end of Claremont Place, were ponds. One of these, called Wheel, or Wheal Pond, was a very dangerous one, and the parish registers record the names of numerous people who were drowned in it. Howell, Ben Jonson, Davenant, and Pepys have all celebrated these ponds. Howell, in his 'Londonopolis,' in 1657, speaking of the out-of-door exercises of the Londoners, says:

`For healthful corporeal recreations, and harmless pastimes, London may go in the van to any place that I ever saw yet. Go and walk in the fields, you shall see some shooting at long marks, some at butts; some bowling upon dainty pleasant greens; some upon bares; some wrestling, some throwing the barre, some the stone; some jumping, some running;

some with their dogs at ducking-ponds.'

Ben Jonson makes one of his characters say:

> `Because I dwell at Hogsden (Hoxton), I shall keep company with none but the archers of Finsbury, or the citizens that come a-ducking to Islington ponds; a fine jest i'faith!'

There are old prints representing these ducking sports. Pepys, in his 'Diary,' March 27, 1664, says:

> `I walked through the ducking-pond fields, but they are so altered since my father used to carry us to Islington to the old man's at the King's Head, to eat cakes and ale, that I did not know where was the ducking-pond, nor where I was.'

The water from these ponds was conveyed to the Priory of St. John's, Clerkenwell, and the Charter-House. Various other parts of London were supplied from these springs, and from Highbury - as Aldermanbury, St. Giles's-without-Cripplegate, Shoreditch, Cold Bath Fields, and Clerkenwell. Much of the waste water passed into the Fleet Ditch; but since the cutting of the Regent's Canal, commenced in 1812, most of these sources must have been absorbed by it. The great event in the matter of water supply, which superseded the ponds and old conduits, was, however, the cutting of the New River.

The New River

For this grand scheme, by which all the north of London is supplied with fine pure water, we are indebted to the enterprise and mechanical genius of Sir Hugh Middleton. Sir Hugh, originally simple Hugh Middleton, was a native of Denbigh, in North Wales. His father was the governor of Denbigh Castle during the reign of Edward VI, Mary, and Elizabeth. Hugh was the sixth son, and had to make his way in the world.

The date of his birth is unknown, and very little is preserved regarding his early years. We find him established as a goldsmith in London, and yet he had continued his connection with Wales, and had acquired a large property by the working of copper mines there. It is supposed that his experience in mining, levelling, draining, and embanking, had qualified him for carrying out his great work, the formation of the New River. London had, up to his time, been very inadequately supplied with good water; but the eye of Hugh Middleton perceived how the springs of the Chadwell and the Amwell, near Ware in Hertfordshire, might be conducted to the metropolis, and he made an offer to effect this to the citizens of London. The offer was accepted, and, on April 20, 1608, he commenced this great work - much greater than it would be if done at the present time, with all our acquired knowledge of civil engineering. The distance from London by the road was about twenty miles, but the route which he found it necessary to take, for the proper level of his river, was upwards of thirty eight miles. He had in some places to make cuttings for his channel thirty or forty feet deep, and the porous nature of the strata through which these cuttings passed caused him many difficulties, but perhaps the crossing of valleys below his level caused him more. Over these the river had to he carried in wooden aqueducts, supported by wooden bearers, twenty feet high; and the construction of these, as well as the numerous bridges, about 200, which had to be erected for the accommodation of the proprietors of lands through which the stream was carried, occasioned an expenditure of time and money beyond the constructor's calculation. The part of the New River, about half way between Highbury and Hornsey, carried in one of these wooden aqueducts, was thence called the Boarded River. This was destroyed in 1776, and the river was then carried over an earthen embankment, and through a channel lined with clay. Besides the obstacles which nature interposed, there were still more thrown in his way by the selfish interests of influential individuals. Hugh Middleton had stipulated to complete the work in four years, but these causes compelled him to solicit an extension of the time, which was granted. But these vexatious delays had not only consumed his time, but his funds. His large property was exhausted by the undertaking, and he applied to the people of London, who were to reap the great benefit of his enterprise, but he found no response. In his difficulty, Middleton applied to James I, who agreed to advance money to the amount of half the total expenditure, on condition of half the shares being made over to him. The agreement for this purpose was signed on May 2, 1612, and by this assistance the work was brought to

---

completion on September 29, 1613, or in five years and five months from the commencement of the undertaking. On that day, which also saw the brother of Hugh, Sir Thomas Middleton, elected Lord Mayor for the ensuing year, the stream was admitted into the reservoir prepared for it at Sadler's Wells, near Pentonville. The total cost of the work was about £500,000. Middleton was knighted in honour of his great achievement; but it was a costly honour, for this noble gift to the great city for a long time did not seem to be appreciated. During eighteen years after its completion it produced no dividend, and the dividend of the nineteenth year was but £11 19s. 6d. on each share. To Sir Hugh, his success became, in reality, his ruin. He was compelled to sell most of his shares, and support himself as an engineer.

The New River was not the only great work of Sir Hugh Middleton. In 1622 he was created a baronet, and the motives for conferring this honour are enumerated in the patent. First, for the construction of this New River, and the inestimable benefit to London; second, for the gaining of a great quantity of land from the sea at Brading Haven, in the Isle of Wight - a work represented as one of stupendous labour; and, thirdly, for the discovery and profitable working of a rich silver mine in the county of Cardigan. King James, with a very commendable liberality, remitted the usual fine on the creation of a baronetcy, namely, £1,095; and, in 1636, Charles I regranted to Sir Hugh the whole of King James's shares, for an annual rent of £500. Notwithstanding this, Sir Hugh Middleton, with the too-common fate of public benefactors, died poor, and left a numerous family in difficult circumstances.

The original cost of the formation of the New River being about £500,000, each of the seventy two original shares must have been at the commencement of the nominal value of nearly £7,000 each; but so long was it before the concern paid, that the shares are said to have fallen almost to nil. Yet, long ago, the Company reputed their capital at upwards of £1,000,000 sterling, or £14,426 per share. Since then, shares have been selling at upwards of £20,000. Of course, in the progress of years, the Company has made many improvements in the bed and management of the river, in the augmented supply of water, by borrowing from the river Lea, and in the purification and distribution of the water. In consequence of the resistance of the proprietors of the river Lea to the abstraction of part of their water, and the litigation ensuing, the claims of the New River Company to a certain amount of water were settled in the year 1738 by an Act of Parliament, on the payment of a certain annuity. Since then, the Company has obtained unrestricted use of the Lea River water.

The moiety of the shares originally reserved by Sir Hugh Middleton for himself, and afterwards sold to different individuals, are called the Adventurers' Shares, and are those to which the government of the Company is attached. The other moiety, which was sold to the King, was excluded from any share in the management, to prevent the influence of courtiers. The £500 per annum stipulated by Charles II to be paid for ever to the Royal Treasury on the return of the thirty six shares to the Company is still paid; and, as some of those shares have been sold in fractional parts, Lord Chancellor Cowper, in 1711, decreed that the possessors of two or more fractional parts of a share may jointly depute a person to represent them in the government of the Company; whereupon every person so deputed becomes capable of being elected as one of the twenty nine representatives of the whole; the twenty nine governing shares representing the original number of proprietors, namely, Sir Hugh Middleton and the twenty eight persons to whom he sold so many of his shares.

Lewis, in his 'History of Islington,' denies that Sir Hugh Middleton was at his death in the state of indigence commonly represented, as he bequeathed several large sums of money, and thirteen New River shares, besides other property. The family, however, became pensioners on the Goldsmiths' Company. Lady Middleton, the wife of one of the descendants of Sir Hugh, had a pension of £20 from the company, which was continued to her son, Sir Hugh, who was the last direct male heir of the family, and with whom the title expired. This man was a low drunkard, and was boarded by a Mr. Harvey, of Chigwell, at a farmhouse there, where he died. Yet, in 1808, the sum of £50 was granted by the Corporation of London to a male descendant of the family in distressed circumstances. Another descendant, Jabez Middleton, had a pension of £52 per annum from the same body till his death, March 27, 1828; and in July of the same year, Mrs. Jane Middleton Bowyers had £30 a year allotted her, which annuity was reduced to 7s. per week in September, when Mrs. Plummer, another of the family, had also an allowance of 7s. per week. After that, the Corporation passed a resolution not to grant any more relief to Middleton descendants. Nelson says that some of the family had solicited the New River Company for assistance, but with what result he does not state.

Certainly, neither London nor the New River Company make a very splendid figure in their treatment of Sir Hugh Middleton and his family. The city, with all its wealthy merchants, left him in the midst of his great undertaking, so far as it was concerned, to perish with his half-executed enterprise. They were deaf to all his entreaties for help, and his representations of the vast benefits to result from his labour. King James stepped in, and saved both the New River and its creator - one of the wisest and most liberal things which the Scottish Solomon ever did. But the river completed, and become as profitable to the Company as invaluable to the metropolis, we have the above poor boons conferred on the family of the maker of the river, then fallen into decay; and a resolution on the part of the Goldsmiths' Company to be troubled no more with the necessities of these unhappy descendants of the great benefactor of London. True, the Goldsmiths' Company was not the only one on which the real claims lay, but the New River Company, of whose benefactions we have no account. It is not a very splendid story.

Lately the Company has greatly extended its resources of water, as well as its water sale. It has purchased the property of the Highgate and Hampstead Ponds Company, and that of the Artesian Well Company, which proved a failure, and having thus monopolised the water supply of nearly all North London, the public has complained of its being inclined to exercise its power somewhat despotically.

It may be well for all concerned to look back to the scene of the opening of this beneficent stream, when the joyous anticipations, long since so fully realised, were not so much for private gain as public benefit. Stow gives the following account:

'Being brought to the intended cisterne, but the water not as yet admitted entrance thereinto, on Michaelmasse day, in anno 1613, being the day when Sir Thomas Middleton, brother to the said Sir Hugh Middleton, was elected Lord Maior of London for the yeere ensuing; in the afternoone of the same daye, Sir John Swinnerton, Knt., and Lord Maior of London, accompanied with the said Sir Thomas, Sir Henry Montague, Knt., Recorder of London, and many of the worthy Aldermen, rode to see the cisterne, and first issuing of the water thereinto, which was performed in this manner:

A troope of labourers, to the number of sixty or more, well apparelled, and wearing green Monmouth caps, all alike, carrying spades, shovels, pickaxes, and such like instruments of laborious imployment, marching after drummes twice or thrice about the cisterne, presented themselves before the mount, where the Lord Maior, Aldermen, and a worthy company beside, stood to behold them: and one man, on behalf of the rest, delivered this speech:

> Long have we laboured, long desired and prayed
> For this great work's perfection; and by th' aid
> Of Heaven and good men's wishes, 'tis at length
> Happily conquered by cost, art, and strength.
> And after five yeeres' deare expence, in dayes,
> Travaile and paines, beside the infinite wayes
> Of malice, envy, false suggestions,
> Able to daunt the spirits of mighty ones
> In wealth and courage, this a work so rare,
> Only by one man's industry, cost and care,
> Is brought to blest effect; so much withstood,
> His only aime the citie's general good.
> And where before many unjust complaints,
> Enviously seated, caused oft restraints,
> Stops and great crosses, to our master's charge,
> And the work's hindrance; Favour now at large
> Spreads herself open to him, and commends
> To admiration, both his paines and ends -
> The King's most gracious love. Perfection draws
> Favour from Princes, and from all applause.
> Then, worthy Magistrates, to whose content,
> Next to the State's, all this great care was bent;
> And for the public good, which grace requires,
> Your loves and furtherance chiefly he desires,
> To cherish these proceedings, which may give
> Courage to some that may hereafter live,
> To practice deedes of goodness, and of fame,
> And gladly light their actions by his name.

At which words the flood-gates flew open, the stream ran gallantly into the cisterne, drummes and trumpets sounding in triumphal manner, and a brave peale of chambers gave full issue to the intended entertainment.'

In Goldsmiths' Hall there is a portrait of Sir Hugh Middleton, to which company he belonged, and to which he bequeathed a share in the New River towards *the relief of its poor members*; so that the small sum of money which this company doled out to Sir Hugh's descendants, when they fell into poverty, was drawn from funds which he himself had endowed them with. Under these circumstances, the paucity of the relief, and the passing of a resolution to give his descendants no more, are much to be regretted.

REMARKABLE BUILDINGS AND INSTITUTIONS

The parish of Islington contains six districts, or liberties, named from the manner in which they are situated, namely:

St. John of Jerusalem
Upper Barnsbury
Lower Barnsbury
Canonbury
The Prebend
Highbury, or Newington Barrow

It contains also the hamlets of Upper and Lower Holloway, Ball's Pond, Battle-bridge, the City Gardens, Kingsland Green, and the greater part of Newington Green. It is also divided into eight ecclesiastical districts, namely:

St. Mary's
St. John's
St. Paul's
Holy Trinity
St. Peter's
St. James's
All Saints
St. Stephen's

Without concerning myself very much with the topography of these different divisions, I shall endeavour to collect out of them an account of their most ancient or remarkable buildings, institutions, historical facts and historical characters.

One of the oldest establishments at the foot of Highgate Hill, just above Holloway, and near to where Whittington's Stone is placed, was a Lazar House, or hospital for lepers. This was one of four such hospitals erected at some distance out of London for the reception of people afflicted with the leprosy, or, as it was called, 'the linenless disease.' This phrase denotes the cause of leprosy -

the wearing of woollen garments next the skin, so that, not having these garments regularly changed and washed, but wearing them on till they were saturated with perspiration and dirt, the skin became diseased. On the introduction of linen and frequent washing, this loathsome disease rapidly disappeared. One William Pole, yeoman of the Crown to King Edward IV, being afflicted with leprosy, the King gave him a piece of land to build the hospital upon in 1473. The chapel attached to it was dedicated to St. Anthony, and the hospital is supposed to have been chiefly supported by offerings of votaries at the chapel. After the Reformation, the house appears to have become a poor-house. In an appointment of a keeper of this house by Elizabeth, in 1589, it is called an alms-house, and is described as having 'orchards, gardens, lands, tenements, meadows, pastures,' &c. The orchard and garden attached were described as very well planted. The place was broken up and the property sold by Cromwell's government, in the same year in which he became Protector - 1658. Further particulars of this institution may be found in Tomlin's 'Perambulation of Islington.'

Mr. Tomlin thinks that the old Whittington Stone was merely the basement of a cross once standing there, of which he gives a woodcut, and that this part of the story of Whittington is a myth. But why so? The basement of a cross by the wayside, from which the cross itself was broken, is just the sort of seat which a wayfarer would avail himself of.

Cromwell's House at Upper Holloway

In Nelson's time there were some old houses which appeared to have belonged to persons of eminence on the north side of the road at Upper Holloway. In one of them, which became the Crown public house, and which has long-since disappeared, there was a tradition that Cromwell had lived. Nelson doubts Cromwell ever having a house here, but thinks he might visit his friend, Sir Arthur Haselrigge, who, undoubtedly, had a residence in Islington, as appears by the following entry in the journals of the House of Commons, May 21, 1664-5:

'Sir Arthur Hesilrigge, by command of the House, related the circumstance of an assault made on him by the Earl of Stamford, and

Henry Polton and Matthew Patsall, his servants, in the highway leading from Perpoole Lane, Clerkenwell, as he was peaceably riding from the House of Commons to his house in Islington, by striking him with a drawn sword, and other offensive instruments, and was enjoined to keep the peace, and not to send or receive any challenge.'

The dangers of the road between London and such suburban villages as Islington were extraordinary in those and later times. Nelson says that as late as 1770, and later, the roads were so dangerous betwixt Islington and London, that few ventured back to London in the evening, but stayed in the village all night at the Angel, the Lion, or the Pied Bull. Even in the heart of the villages robberies were committed; both carriages and foot passengers were frequently stopped in the most daring manner; and it was usual for people walking from the city in the evening to wait at the end of St. John Street till a sufficient party were collected, who were escorted to Islington by an armed patrol appointed for that purpose. The annals of the Old Bailey abound with instances of delinquents who were apprehended for robberies and murders committed in that neighbourhood. A quarto sheet, published in 1674, bore the title, 'Four great and horrible murders; or, *Bloody News from Islington*: being a full and true relation how a woman's brains were knocked out by her own father, robbed, and her throat cut, on Tuesday the 5th of February; a man beaten to death the 8th of the same month,' &c.

This is not, however, more extraordinary than that murder and personal robberies are of nightly and almost daily occurrence in the most frequented streets of London at the present day. The Hornsey Road was formerly called Devil's or Du Val's Lane, and there used to be a moated house in it, called the Devil's House. It has been supposed the old name of Devil's Lane was changed into Du Val's Lane, in consequence of Du Val, a famous highwayman, frequenting that locality. The 'Memoirs of Du Val' state that this worthy was executed at Tyburn January 21, 1669, in his 27th year. That he lay in state in Tangier Tavern, St. Giles's, and was buried in the middle aisle of Covent Garden Church. That his funeral was attended with many flambeaux, and a numerous train of mourners, 'whereof most were of the beautiful sex.' Such hero-worshippers deserved to be robbed. Butler, author of 'Hudibras,' wrote 'A

Pindaric Ode to the happy memory of the most renowned Du Val,' in which he says:

> He, like a lord o' the manor, seized upon
> Whatever happened in his way,
> As lawful weft and stray,
> And after, by the custom, kept it as his own;

and says that had he gone on a little longer, he 'would have starved the mighty town, by cutting off its supplies through the wagoners, drovers, &c.' Dick Turpin, too, practised on coaches and chaises at Holloway and in the back lanes of Islington in May 1737.

At Upper Holloway, in those times, the 'Mother Red Cap,' celebrated by Drunken Barnaby, was a great resort of pleasure-seekers. The 'Mother Red Cap' was a favourite sign in those days. 'Red Cap,' says Tomlin, 'appears in old road-books about four miles beyond Coleshill, Warwickshire;' and John Buncle pathetically recurs to 'the merry dancings we had at "Mother Red Cap's," in Back Lane, Dublin.' Also in the play of the 'Merry Milkmaid of Islington,' enter Artezim as Mother Red Cap. There is also the well-known 'Mother Red Cap' at Camden Town, by the junction of the roads to Highgate and Hampstead. Drunken Barnaby, at 'Mother Red Cap' at Holloway, found very bad company:

> Veni Holloway, Pileum rubrum
> In cohortem muliebrem;
> Me Adonidem vocant omnes
> Meretrices Babylonis:
> Pangunt, tingunt, molliunt, mulcent,
> Et egentem foris pulsant, &e.

At Upper Holloway, the 'Half Moon' was also a noted public house. These houses were noted for cheese-cakes, as noticed in a 'Journey to Nottingham,' printed in the 'Gentleman's Magazine' of September, 1743: 'Through Holloway, famous for cakes, we onward tend.'

'Holloway cheese-cakes' was one of the London cries; they were sold by a man on horseback: and in 'Jack Drum's Entertainment,' (1601), in a random song, the festive character of these suburbs is denoted:

> Let us be seene on Hygate greene
> To dance to the honour of Holloway.
> Since we are come hither, let's spare no leather,
> To dance for the honour of Holloway.

Holloway was tlie suburban residence of the Blount family, already mentioned under the head of Highgate. Their country seat was at Tittenhanger, in Hertfordshire. They lived here for the greater part of the seventeenth century, and Sir Henry and his two sons, Sir Thomas and Charles, were all distinguished both as public men and writers. Charles Blount, the author of 'Anima Mundi,' and various other works full of the spirit of liberty and free-thinking, as well as translator of the first two books of 'The Life of Apollonius Tyanæus' by Philostratus, committed suicide in consequence of his deceased wife's sister refusing to marry him, after an adverse opinion as to the legality of such a union had been pronounced by the Archbishop of Canterbury and other divines. The old Manor House, their residence, was standing till within a few years.

Highbury House

Highbury, famous for springs and conduits which used to supply part of the city before the making of the New River, has always been famous for its elevated situation, and its fine views over Stamford Hill, Epping Forest, Hornsey Wood, Muswell Hill, Crouch End, Highgate, Caen Wood, Hampstead, and Primrose Hill. The water from the Highbury springs was conveyed as far as the White Conduit and St. Giles's, Cripplegate, and carried from the conduit to the private houses by men called water-bearers, in vessels called tankards holding about three gallons each. Ben Jonson, in his comedy of 'Every Man in his Humour,' introduces one Cob as a water-bearer. Women also were water-bearers, who carried it in pails. The Corporation of London were fond of making a day to visit the springs, on the 18th of September, when, according to Strype, they went attended by dogs, and hunted a hare or a fox, sometimes both, before dinner, at the head of the conduit.

Gerard, the English botanist of the sixteenth century, as before remarked, ranged the woods of Highbury, Islington, and Hornsey in search of plants. In his 'Herbal, or General History of Plants,' a work which contributed to diffuse a taste for botany, he says:

'Saw-wort groweth in woods and shadowy places, and sometimes in meadows. Likewise I have seen it grow in great abundance in the wood adjoining to Islington, within half a mile from the further end of the town.'

'The alder tree (Alnus nigra sive frangula) groweth in moist woods and copses; I have found great plenty of it in a wood a mile from Islington, in the way thence towards a small village called Harnsey.'

No doubt there were before the year 1607, in which Gerard died, a vast variety of plants and trees growing all over the districts of Islington, Highbury, Hornsey, and Highgate, where now only houses stand. At a comparatively recent period Hampstead Heath produced rare plants, of which Park presents us with a catalogue, but for which you must now go to a much greater distance.

The Manor of Highbury, formerly called Tollenton, was granted by the Conqueror to one Ranulf, when the manorial rights were valued in the Domesday Book at 40s. per annum. On the east side of Du Val's Lane was a moated site, supposed to have been that of the original Manor House, called Tollenton House or Lower Place, before the Manor House was removed to higher ground, thence called Highbury. The spot on which the Manor House was re-erected was supposed to be the site of a Roman camp. It acquired the additional name of Newington Barrow, antiquaries being divided in opinion as to whether the word Barrow came from Burgus, a camp, or from Alice de Barowe, who was lady of the manor in the thirteenth century, and in the year 1271 made it over with the whole lordship to the Priory of St. John of Jerusalem. The antiquaries do not seem to have had an idea that the word might come from the British, who might have raised a barrow there on the site of some battle before the Roman epoch.

The Manor House of Highbury appears to have been the favourite summer retreat of the Priors of St. John. Jack Straw, however, demolished it for them in Wat Tyler's rebellion. According to Stow, the haughtiness and ambition of the Knights Hospitallers, and the excessive riches they had accumulated, gave such offence to the common people at this period, that, in the insurrection under Wat Tyler, in the year 1381, after totally consuming with fire their magnificent priory in St. John Street, near Smithfield, 'causing it to burne by the space of seven dayes together, not suffering any to quench it,' a detachment of the insurgents proceeded with the same intention to the Prior's country house at Highbury. Jack Straw is stated to have headed this detachment, the number, according to Hollinshed, being 20,000, who 'tooke in hand to ruinate that house;' from which circumstance, and from his probably having made it a temporary station for himself and his followers, it was ever afterwards called Jack Straw's Castle.

The rebels found the house so substantially built of stone, that it was a tough job for them, after the fire had done its work, to pull the walls to pieces by main force. They seem, however, to have gone to work with right good will; and, having finished the house, they resolved to finish the Prior too. They marched to the Tower of London, in which he had taken refuge, and, no doubt, thought himself pretty safe; but the rebels surrounded the Tower, took it, and brought out the Prior, together with Simon Sudbury, Archbishop of Canterbury, John Legg, one of the King's sergeants-at-arms, and William Appledore, the King's Confessor, and beheaded them on Tower Hill. After William Walworth had killed Wat Tyler, and the rebels were dispersed, the King knighted Walworth and three other citizens; and

'upon the sand-hills towards Iseldone were created the Earls Marshall and Pembroke; and shortly afterwards, Nicholas Twyford and Adam Francis, Aldermen, were made Knights.'

The dagger with which Walworth stabbed Wat Tyler, Lewis says, was in the possession of Mr. Aldworth, a vintner at Islington, in 1730.

After the dissolution of the religious houses by Henry VIII, he granted the Manor of Highbury to Thomas, Lord Cromwell, on whose attainder it returned to the crown. Edward VI settled it on his sister, afterwards Queen Mary. James I settled it on his son Henry, Prince of Wales. It was on the death of the Prince of Wales that it settled on Prince Charles, who, on becoming Charles I, sold it to Sir Allan Apsley, in 1629. From that time the manor passed by sale to a number of successive proprietors.

One of the most noted and frequented places in this neighbourhood for some generations past is Highbury Barn.

Highbury Barn

On the ancient site of Highbury Barn, or Farm belonging to the Manor House, originally rose a small ale and cake house. Barn, it seems, amongst milk-dealers, was synonymous with farm or dairy, whence the term barn-measure as applied to milk in contradistinction to that by which it is retailed to the public. At some little distance northward was another dairy farm, called Cream Hall. To these places the Londoners, as we have stated, flocked to drink milk warm from the cow, and to eat cakes dipped in cream, custards, syllabubs, &c. All about Islington were localities celebrated for these rural dainties. From an ale and cake house Highbury Barn grew into a tavern with tea gardens. As the trade increased, Nelson says that the extensive barn belonging to the farm was added to the premises, and, being fitted up handsomely, became the principal room of the tavern. There the Court Baron for the manor was held. A Mr. Willoughby, who died in 1785, made a wonderful increase in the trade of the place. His son added a bowling green, trap-ball grounds, and tea gardens. He added a hop plantation and brewery, and prepared public dinners for corporate bodies, public charities, clubs, and other societies; so that it had a greater number of visitors than any similar place in London or its environs. It could accommodate from 1,500 to 2,000 persons at once; 800 people were known to sit down to a hot dinner together, on which occasion seventy geese were seen roasting at one fire. The Ancient Freemasons in 1808 sat down 500 in number to dinner there.

One of the most singular societies which used to dine annually at this tavern for many years was one of Protestant Dissenters, who took the name of `The Highbury Society.' On the day when a Bill, called the Schism Bill, was to have been passed, which aimed at the privileges of all religious denominations not in conformity with the Established Church, Queen Anne died, and there was an end of it. To commemorate this fortunate event, the Society was formed, and used first to hold its meetings at Copenhagen House. So far back, however, as 1740, Highbury Barn was the place of their rendezvous, and their mode of proceeding there was in a style singularly simple and even juvenile. They used to meet in Moorfields at one o'clock, and walk on to Dettingen Bridge, where the house called the 'Shepherd and Shepherdess' was afterwards built. Here they chalked the initials of their names on a post for the information of such as might follow. They then proceeded to Highbury, and to beguile the way, it was their custom in turn to bowl a ball of ivory at objects in their path. This ball was presented to the Society by Mr. William Field. After a light refreshment - and it must have been very light, for it only cost eightpence, and was accompanied by neither wine, punch, nor tea - they proceeded to the field to practise a peculiar game, called Hop-ball, which has been the great amusement of the Society from time immemorial at their meetings. This game is not used elsewhere in the neighbourhood of London, but one resembling it is practised in the west of England, whence it was probably introduced by members, natives of that quarter of the kingdom. In fact, there were numbers of West-of-England men among these Dissenters. The ball used on these occasions was worsted stitched over with silk or packthread, and was gratuitously furnished by some member of the Society.

In the report of a committee on the rise and progress of this Society, printed in 1808, it is stated that

'the following toast is always given at their anniversary dinner in August, viz.: The glorious First of August, with the immortal memory of King William and his good Queen Mary, not forgetting Corporal John, and a fig for the Bishop of Cork, that bottle-stopper.'

Corporal John was intended for John, Duke of Marlborough, the great friend of the Protestant and Whig interest. 'The Society,' adds Nelson, 'dine together weekly, on Saturday, from November to March, and consists at this time of between forty and fifty members.' An engraving from an original portrait by Thomas Stevens was published of Mr. Stephen Ponder, the treasurer of the Society, usually called Father Ponder, who died May 8, 1816, aged 71 years.

This Society appears to have ceased to exist for some years. An authority on such subjects thinks it was dissolved about the year 1833.

Highbury Barn, the scene of these and many other festive celebrations, is still a great place of public entertainment, combining a hotel, public gardens, and a regularly licensed theatre, as well as a dancing saloon. A ticket to the theatre, it seems, entitles the possessor to admittance to the dancing saloon, where all persons so introduced can join in the dances from ten to twelve o'clock p.m. In fact, the sober inhabitants of the neighbourhood regard this section of the Highbury Barn entertainments, with its musical band, and the occasional fireworks in the gardens, as a grand source of demoralization to the neighbourhood, as well as of disturbance to the families of regular houses.

The Sluice House, Eel Pie House, and Hornsey Wood House

Hornsey Wood House
(From an original drawing in the possession of J. E. Gardner, Esq.)

The Sluice House, Eel Pie House, and Hornsey Wood House, those ancient haunts of fishermen and lovers of rurality, are now gone or going. These places were formerly, and so late as the time of William Hone, great places of attraction to anglers and pleasure-takers, especially on Palm Sunday, when Hornsey Wood was ravaged for palms. It was a pleasant walk from Highbury Barn by the river to these places. Not a trace of Hornsey Wood House remains; the Sluice House is about to disappear, and great alterations are making in the river in the formation of the new place of public recreation, called Finsbury Park. In fact, the whole neighbourhood has undergone, or is undergoing, the same process of modernizing metamorphosis as the greater part of the vicinity of London for scores of miles round. Of Highbury Place, Highbury Terrace and College we shall have occasion to mention distinguished inhabitants.

Highbury College

Many of the early Dissenters being connected with the City of London by business, settled about Islington, Highbury, Hackney, and Stoke Newington. Their schools would plant themselves in the same localities. Consequently, we find that one of their earliest academies for theological students was at Islington, conducted by Theophilus Gale, an eminent minister and writer, and Mr. Rowe, who during the Commonwealth was a preacher at Westminster Abbey. The son of this Mr. Rowe, the Rev. Thomas Rowe, minister of the Independent Meeting House in Haberdashers' Hall, afterwards, in conjunction with Mr. John Eames, conducted a more celebrated theological academy in London, in which Dr. Watts was educated. At Islington also the Rev. Thomas Dolittle, minister of the Monkwell Street Chapel, had at one time a similar academy, and amongst his pupils was the celebrated Matthew Henry, the Bible commentator. At Newington, Daniel Defoe finished his education in another Dissenting academy, conducted by a Mr. Morton.

Congregationalist College

The Congregationalist College at Highbury, an offshoot from the one at Homerton, was built in 1825, and opened in September 1826, under the superintendence of Drs. Harris, Burder, and Halley, for the education of ministers of that persuasion. Amongst the distinguished men whom this college produced, are the popular minister of Rowland Hill's Chapel, Blackfriars Road, the Rev. Newman Hall, and Mr. George MacDonald, the distinguished poet, lecturer, and novelist. Mr. MacDonald, however, had previously graduated at the University of Aberdeen, and had there taken his degree of M.A. In 1850 the buildings and property of the College of Highbury were disposed of to the Metropolitan Church of

England Training Institution, and the business of the College transferred to New College, St. John's Wood, into which the three Dissenting Colleges of Homerton, Coward, and Highbury were consolidated.

CANONBURY

Canonbury Tower
(From a print in Mr. Gardner's Collection)

The spot in Canonbury round which the chief historical interest gathers is Canonbury House, or Tower, as it is now frequently called, from its square tower, the principal part of which yet remains. The manor, which used often to be printed Canbury and Cambray or Chambray, was early in possession of the Berners family, after whom Barnsbury takes its name. By them it was granted to the Priory of St. Bartholomew in West Smithfield. On the dissolution of the monasteries it was granted by Henry VIII to Lord Cromwell along with Highbury. On his death Anne of Cleves, whose ill-starred wedding with Henry had been Cromwell's work, and became his ruin, was dowered out of the wreck of his fortunes, and had an annuity of £20 a year out of this manor. Edward VI granted the manor for certain considerations to John Dudley, Earl of Warwick, a branch of whose family had a lease of the neighbouring manor of Stoke Newington. Dudley, who became Duke of Northumberland, aiming at securing the crown for his son, Lord Guildford Dudley, by a marriage with Lady Jane Grey, lost his head, and the manor reverting to the crown, was conferred by Queen Mary on Thomas, Lord Wentworth, who

411

alienated it to Sir John Spencer, an alderman and cloth-worker of London, who was Lord Mayor in 1594. Sir John was reputed the richest commoner of his time, and during his mayoralty showed himself on several occasions bold in resisting interferences of the crown in City affairs. For one such resistance he received a menacing message from Lord Treasurer Burleigh, which, however, did by no means daunt him.

The town residence of Sir John Spencer was Crosby Hall, the line old house on the east side of Bishopsgate Street, which had been built by Sir John Crosby, and was some time the residence of the Duke of Gloucester, afterwards Richard III. Sir John held his mayoralty there, and lodged and splendidly entertained the French Ambassador there in 1603, then Marquis de Rosny, afterwards the celebrated Duke of Sully, who arrived with a superb train soon after the accession of James I.

Sir John's country house, however, was this Canonbury House. It was a very fine and extensive house, as shown by a scarce print published by Boydell about 1760, from which, I suppose, is copied the engraving in Nelson's 'Islington,' facing p. 244. The site is one amongst the multitudinous proofs of the ecclesiastical eye for situation. It was built on this spot for the Prior of the Canons of St. Bartholomew, and rebuilt by William Bolton, the last Prior but one, who had scarcely finished it at his death in 1532. The tower of brick still remaining was part of his work, as was shown by his rebus, a bolt in a tun, visible in several parts of the building some years ago. About the house at that time were extensive gardens, a fine old park, and beyond open country. From the top of the tower a most extensive view was obtained over London, to Highgate and Hampstead in one direction, over Greenwich and the winding Thames in another. Sir John Spencer altered, enlarged, and beautified this place greatly.

The greatness of Sir John drew upon him dangerous eyes, and a plot was laid to kidnap him as he rode daily from his place of business in Bishopsgate Street over the moors to Canonbury. We have the fact related in a curious pamphlet, entitled 'The Vanity of the Lives and Passions of Men,' by D. Papillon, gent., 1651. It is as follows:

'In Queen Elizabeth's days, a pirate of Dunkirk laid a plot with twelve of his mates to carry away Sir John Spencer; which if he had done, fifty thousand pounds would not have redeemed him. He came over the seas in a shallop with twelve musketiers, and in the night came into Barking Creek, and left the shallop in the custody of six of his men, and with the other six came as far as Islington, and there hid them in ditches, near the path in which Sir John always came to his house; but, by the providence of God, Sir John, upon some extraordinary occasion, was forced to stay in London that night, otherwise they had taken him away; and they, fearing they should be discovered, in the night time came to their shallop, and so came safe to Dunkirk again.'

But a more successful pirate than the man of Dunkirk appeared in the person of Lord William Compton, Lord President of Wales, and the second of the title. Sir John Spencer had but one child, a daughter, heiress to all his wealth, said by some to amount to as much as £800,000 - a stupendous sum in those days. This bold young spark managed to win the goodwill of Miss Spencer, and smuggled her away in a baker's basket. The truth of this fact is attested by a painting of the elopement in this manner, preserved at Castle Ashby, the seat of the Marquis of Northampton, the descendant of this marriage, and possessor, in consequence, of the manor of Canonbury.

For some time, however, it appeared probable that Lord Compton was more sure of the lady than of the fortune. Sir John Spencer was so incensed at the elopement, that he discarded his daughter, and vowed that he would cut her off with a shilling. In this strait, Queen Elizabeth, who was no favourer of marriages in general, came to the rescue and invited Sir John to stand sponsor with her to the first child of a young couple abandoned by their father. Sir John accepted the office, and declared that as he had renounced his own daughter for her disobedience, he would adopt this boy, her Majesty's protégé, in her stead. The Queen took him at his word, and on meeting the young parents, he found that he had adopted his own grandson.

Sir John died in 1609, and Lord Compton was so overwhelmed by the immensity of the wealth falling to him, that he lost his senses. In a letter of March 22, 1609, given in Winwood's 'State Papers,' vol. iii. p. 136, a Mr. Beaulieu tells Mr. Trumbull that

'the poor lord is not like, if God do not help him, to carry it away for
nothing; or to grow very rich thereby, being in great danger to lose his
witts for the same; whereof, being at the very first newes, either
through the vehement apprehension of joy for such a plentiful succession, or of carefulness how to take it up and dispose it, somewhat
distracted, and afterwards naturally well restored, he is now of late
fallen again, but more deeply, into the same frenzy; so that there
seemeth little hope of such a recovery. And what shall these thousands
and millions avail him, if he come to lose, if not his soul, at least his
witts and reason? It is a faire and ample subject for a divine to course
riches, and a notable example to the world not to wooe or trust too
much in them.'

In another letter, the same gentleman says that he was become
so frantic that it was necessary to keep him bound; and that the
administration of his goods and lands was committed to the Lord
Chamberlain, Privy Seal, and Worcester. Lord Compton, however,
did eventually recover his senses; and certainly the following letter
addressed to him by his wife, no longer crumpled up in the baker's
basket, but assuming her full height and dignity, was admirably
adapted to act as a sedative. Who shall not say that his lordship
owed the return of his sober senses to it, and to a continued course
of the same cooling regimen? The letter has no date, but appears to
have been written pretty soon after the great windfall. It was first
printed in the 'European Magazine' for June, 1782:

'My Sweet Life,—Now I have declared to you my mind for the settling
of your state, I suppose it were best for me to bethink or consider with
myself, what allowance were meetest for me. For considering what care
I have had of your estate, and how respectfully I dealt with those
which, by the laws of God, of nature, and of civil polity, wit, religion,
government, and honesty, you, my dear, are bound to, I pray and
beseech you to grant me 1,600*l* per annum, quarterly to be paid.
Also, I would, besides that allowance for my apparel, have 600*l* added
yearly, quarterly to be paid, for the performance of charitable works;
and for these things I would not, neither will be, accountable for.
Also, I will have three horses for my own saddle, that none shall dare to
lend or borrow; none lend but I, none borrow but you.
Also, I will have two gentlewomen, lest one should be sick, or have
some other lett; also believe that it is an undecent thing for a

gentlewoman to stand mumping alone, when God hath blessed their lord and lady with a great estate.

Also, when I will a-hunting, or hawking, or travel from one house to another, I will have them attending me; so, for either of those said women, I must and will have for either of them a horse.

Also, I will have six or eight gentlemen. And I will have my two coaches, one lined with velvet to myself, with four very fair horses; and a coach for my women, lined with sweet cloth; one laced with gold, the other with scarlet, and laced with watchet lace and silver, with four good horses.

Also, I will have two coachmen, one for my own coach, the other for my women.

Also, at any time when I travel, I will be allowed not only carroches and spare horses for me and my women, but I will have such carriages as shall be fitting for all, orderly, not pestering my things with my women's, nor theirs with chambermaids, nor theirs with wash-maids.

Also for laundresses, when I travel, I will have them sent away before with the carriages, to see all safe; and the chambermaids I will have to go before with the greens, that the chambers may be ready, sweet and clean.

Also, for that it is indecent to crowd up myself with my gentleman-usher in my coach: I will have him to have a decent horse to attend me either in city or country; and I must have two footmen; and my desire is, that you defray all the charges for me.

And for myself, besides my yearly allowance, I would have twenty gowns of apparel, six of them excellent good ones, eight of them for the country, and six other of them very excellent good ones.

Also, I would have to put in my purse 2,000*l* and 200*l*; and so for you to pay my debts.

Also, I would have 6,000*l* to buy me jewels, and 4,000*l* to buy me a pearl chain.

Now, seeing I am so reasonable unto you, I pray you to find my children apparel, and their schooling, and also my servants - men and women - their wages.

Also, I will have my houses furnished, and all my lodging-chambers to he suited with all such furniture as is fit, as beds, stools, chairs, suitable cushions, carpets, silver warming-pans, cupboards of plate, fair hangings and such like: so for my drawing-chambers in all houses, I will have them delicately furnished, both with hangings, couch, canopy, glass, carpet, chair-cushions, and all things thereunto belonging.

Also, my desire is, that you shall pay all my debts, build Ashley-house, and purchase lands; and lend no money - as you love God - to the Lord Chamberlain, who would have all, perhaps your life, from you. Remember his son, my Lord Warden, what entertainment he gave me when you were at Tiltyard. If you were dead, he said, he would be a husband, a father, a brother: and he said he would marry me. I protest, I grieve to see the poor man have so little wit and honesty to use his friend so vilely. Also he fed me with untruths concerning the Charter-house; but that is the least: he wished me much harm. You know him. God keep you and me from such as he is!

So now that I have declared to you what I would have, and what that is that I would not have, when you be an earl, I pray you to allow 1,000*l* more than I now desire, and double attendance.

Your loving wife,
Eliza Compton.'

A glorious letter! A grand, managing, and stately lady! who, if she inherited a million of money, knew how to spend it in a princely manner; and to have everything in order and in keeping with her dignity, not forgetting that of her husband, and of the whole family. Lord Compton, on the digestion of this letter, continued in his senses ever afterwards. His loving wife had ballasted his boat so effectually, that it could not fail to ride steadily. He became an earl, as she expected, being created Earl of Northampton in 1618, and, no doubt, she got her extra £1,000 per annum and double attendance.

As London, under the names of Canonbury and Islington, came crowding up about this house and its ample gardens and fair lakes, the proprietors began to desert it for more distant ones; it became the house of the steward, and the chambers were let as lodgings to gentlemen from London who sought suburban quiet. Newbery, the publisher, had rooms in it, and Goldsmith used to visit him there. As difficulties pressed on Goldsmith, he would remain hidden there for weeks, giving out that he was away in Yorkshire, or elsewhere. He came to like Canonbury House so much that he had summer lodgings in it, and his literary friends used to visit him there. Sam Johnson, no doubt, showed his ponderous figure there frequently. He and his associates would adjourn to the Crown Tavern in the Lower Road, and be very jolly. It is said that he wrote the 'Deserted Village,' the 'Traveller,' and part of the 'Vicar of Wakefield,' in Canonbury Tower.

Washington Irving visited Canonbury Tower because Goldsmith had inhabited it. He says:

'I was shown the very apartment. It was a relic of the original style of the castle, with panelled wainscot and Gothic windows. I was pleased with its air of antiquity and its having been the residence of poor Goldy.'

Irving located his 'Poor Devil Author' there, and described what he himself, no doubt, saw:

'Sunday came, and with it the whole city world, swarming about Canonbury Castle. I could not open my window but I was stunned with shouts and noises from the cricket-ground; the late quiet road beneath my window was alive with the tread of feet and the clack of tongues; and to complete my misery, I found that my quiet retreat was absolutely a show-house, being shown to strangers at sixpence a head. There was a perpetual tramping upstairs of citizens and their families to look about the country from the top of the tower, and to take a peep at the city through the telescope, to try if they could discern their own chimnies.'

Besides Goldsmith, other literary men had lodgings occasionally in the tower: Smart, the poet; Chambers, author of the 'Cyclopædia;' Humphreys, author of 'Canons,' a poem, 'Ulysses,' an opera, and translator of 'Spectacle de la Nature.'

Here Humphreys breathed his last, the Muse's friend,
And Chambers found his mighty labours end.

See on the distant plain, majestic shows
Old Canonbury's tower, an ancient pile,
To various fates assigned; and where by turns
Meanness and grandeur have alternate reigned.
Thither in latter days hath genius fled
From yonder city to repine and die.
There the sweet bard of Auburn sate, and tuned
The plaintive moanings of his village dirge.
There learned Chambers treasured lore for *man*,
And Newbery there his A B C for *babes*.

William Hone was fond of a stroll to Canonbury Tower, and has left us in his 'Everyday Book' a very good woodcut of it.

At an earlier date, 1600, Sir Arthur Atye, public orator to the University of Oxford, lived there. Lord Chancellor Egerton, afterwards Lord Ellesmere, and Viscount Brackley resided there from and after 1605. Sir Francis Bacon, Lord Verulam, when Attorney-General, in 1616, became lessee from Lord and Lady Compton. And in 1625 Lord Keeper Coventry made Canonbury House his residence for several years, that is, to 1635. Lord Derby visited Lord Coventry at Canonbury House in the last-named year, and was 'detained by the greatest snow he ever saw in England.' William Fielding, Earl of Denbigh, died at Canonbury House in 1688. Arthur Onslow, the Speaker of the House of Commons in 1761, sought for health at the tower. Many distinguished and historical characters have inhabited this old house since Queen Elizabeth used to visit it and hunt there. Where are the woods and heaths which lay around it now? Cut down, fenced in, and covered with a dense town, one mass with Islington, and Islington with London. The old tower itself is hemmed in and shut up amidst houses.

NEWINGTON GREEN

Newington Green is one of the old places of the parish, and has had ancient houses and distinguished inhabitants. It had till of late years a still out-of-the-way look, surrounded in most parts by large old trees, and green lanes led to it from most sides. Population and houses have now crowded up to it on all sides. On the south side used to stand the large mansion of the Mildmay family, now altered and converted into two or three dwellings. Sir Henry Mildmay in the reign of Charles I obtained this house with its park, gardens, &c., of more than forty acres, and extending nearly to Ball's Pond, with his wife, the daughter of Alderman Halliday, who had lived there. Sir Henry Mildmay was one of the judges of King Charles, and his property was, therefore, forfeited at the Restoration, except this of Newington Green, which had been settled by the careful alderman on his daughter, Lady Mildmay, and descended to her posterity. Sir Henry's brother, Anthony, was on the opposite side in the civil war, and was so much attached to Charles that he attended him on the scaffold, as one of his confidential servants, and was one of the number who superintended the interment of his remains at Windsor. In this house were, and probably still are, handsomely wainscotted rooms, carved chimney-pieces, and stuccoed ceilings, one of these having the initials J. R., those of King James, very likely commemorating a visit of his to the family of Sir William Halliday, who, besides the daughter married to Sir Henry Mildmay, had another, married to Sir Edward Hungerford.

There used to be a very old house at the north-east corner of the Green, which has long ago given way to some modern ones, which tradition says used to be occupied by Henry VIII; or, when he came there with many attendants, these occupied this old house, and he himself the large one afterwards belonging to the Mildmays. That Henry was fond of this neighbourhood, no doubt on account of the hunting which it afforded, as well as of witnessing archery, bull-baiting, and bear-baiting, is well known, and the walk proceeding from the south-east comer of the Green to the turnpike road by Ball's Pond still bears the name of 'King Henry's Walk,' though now a street.

Here also lived the unfortunate Henry Algernon Percy, Earl of Northumberland, who incurred the monarch's displeasure by being attached to Anne Boleyn before Henry ever saw her. He was the lamb that had muddied the stream to this brutal despot by drinking out of it below him. There is a letter extant, dated from Newington Green, May 13, in the twenty eighth year of Henry's reign, in which the Earl of Northumberland wishes damnation on himself if ever there were any contract or promise of marriage betwixt Anne Boleyn and himself. Nevertheless, whatever formal contract there might or might not have been between them, there was undoubtedly a warm attachment, and, no doubt, mutual promises. Henry Percy was in attendance on Cardinal Wolsey, and the lion-hearted and lion-taloned monarch soon became aware of this attachment, and severely snubbed Wolsey for permitting it, and sent him to break off all hopes on the part of the young lord. He in his turn was severely snubbed by Wolsey, and as Wolsey had got a great fright, he gave young Percy a great fright, and the poor young fellow had to write this letter to Thomas, Lord Cromwell, disavowing, on pain of damnation, the sacred affection and hope of his life. Harry Tudor, however, was not to be satisfied with any pro-testations, however solemn or awful. He made Wolsey send for the Earl, and they forced him into a marriage with Lady Mary Talbot, daughter of the Earl of Shrewsbury, for whom he had no affection. Little did Wolsey imagine that this evil deed would in the end work his own ruin; but Anne Boleyn, who seems to have had a devoted love for Henry Percy, never forgot the Cardinal's part in it. From her, there is no doubt, came the damning whispers against Wolsey which raised the deadly malice of the King against him. We are told that she and her father worked incessantly for his ruin; and he had a significant reminder of the fact when Henry sent for him from his palace of Cawood, in Yorkshire, to complete his destruction. The person sent to execute this office was Henry Percy, Earl of Northumberland. Wolsey at first hoped that, as the Earl had been brought up amongst his retainers, his presence was a sign of the King's returning favour. The Earl's salutation, 'My Lord, I arrest you of high treason!' struck him dumb, and must have shown him the finger of Anne Boleyn in his fate. In this

Newington Green at that day, there must have been a sad heart, which, amidst all the insignia of station, felt the heavy remembrance of a rudely torn-up happiness. And he was doomed to feel still the diabolical malice of the greatest monster of lust, ferocity, and ruffianism that ever sate upon a throne. The Tudor who revelled in the blood of wives and nobles, had the consummate barbarity to appoint the Earl of Northumberland one of Anne's judges. Not content with having torn her from him, he resolved that he should sit to destroy her; but the trial was too much for Percy's feelings. He was seized with such agitation and illness in the court, that he was obliged to quit it, before the arraignment of Lord Rochford, Anne Boleyn's brother, and died a few months afterwards.

Northumberland is said 'prodigally to have given away a great part of his lands and inheritance to the King and others.' Under what pressure was this done? Probably something of the same kind as that under which he gave to the King the woman of his heart! The King, no doubt, wanted these lands, and in Henry VIII, to want anything was to have it.

A gold ring, set with diamonds, was found nearly fifty years ago behind Mildmay House, two feet deep in the earth, supposed to have belonged to some lady of Henry VIII's court.

The Presbyterian Chapel

The Presbyterian Chapel at Newington Green, which dates from 1708, has a history of considerable interest. Like most other Presbyterian chapels in England, it found its congregation go over at a particular crisis to Unitarianism, to which it still adheres. It has had a succession of able ministers, some of whom are of world notoriety, and to whom we shall return in the notices of our great men. Amongst these were Dr. Price and Mr. Rochemont Barbauld. To Dr. Price there is an inscription tablet in the chapel, as follows:

'To the memory of Richard Price, D.D., F.R.S., born at Tynton, Glamorganshire, Feb. 23rd, 1723; died at Hackney, Middlesex, April 19th, 1791. Theologian, philosopher, mathematician; friend to freedom, as to virtue; brother of man; lover of truth, as of God. His eminent talents were matched by his integrity, simplicity, and goodness of heart; his moral dignity by his profound humility. Few have been more useful in their generation, or more valued by the wise and good: none more pure and disinterested. Honoured be his name: imitated his example.'

This inscription was written by the Rev. Thomas Cromwell, a descendant of Oliver Cromwell, and his biographer, till recently minister of this chapel. There is also a commemorative tablet:

'In memory of Anna Lætitia Barbauld, daughter of John Aikin, M.D., and wife of the Rev. Rochemont Barbauld, formerly the respected minister of this congregation. She was horn at Kibworth, in Leicestershire, 20th of June, 1743, and died at Stoke Newington, 9th of March, 1825.'

A just and well-deserved eulogism follows.

ISLINGTON GREEN

The Green, which once had its watch-house, its cage, its engine-house and pair of stocks, and was the refuge of dust heaps and rubbish, now presents the appearance of an enclosed shrubbery. Since the passing of the Reform Bill, it has been made the place of election. There are, or were, several houses of note and antiquity in the vicinity of the Green. In the Lower Street, opposite the end of Cross Street, was a house called The Fisher House.

The Fisher House

This had been the residence of Sir Thomas Fisher about the commencement of the seventeenth century. The arms of Fisher and Fowler were over opposite doors on the landing-place of the grand staircase. Anthony Wood says that Ezekiel Tongue, author of several tracts against the Papists, kept an academy there, teaching young ladies Latin and Greek in the large gallery of the house. Since then it became occupied as a lunatic asylum.

The Fowlers, lords of the manor of Barnsbury, had a house nearly opposite to Fisher House.

The Fowler House

The family of Fowler was a very considerable one in the reigns of Elizabeth and James I. Sir Thomas Fowler, Knt., was deputy-lieutenant of the county of Middlesex, and one of the jurors on the trial of Sir Walter Raleigh in 1603. His son Thomas was created a baronet in 1628; and on his death, his brother Edmund Fowler succeeded to the title, which in him became extinct, and the family name and property passed to Sir Thomas Fisher, who married the daughter of the second Sir Thomas Fowler, which explains the union of the arms on the Fisher House. On a ceiling of this house were the arms and initials of Queen Elizabeth and the date 1595. There were also the arms of Sir Thomas Fowler, and of Jane, his wife. Little of these, however, if anything, according to Tomlin, now remains; a Dissenting chapel [is now] standing on the site of the Fowler House. The memory of these ancient houses is still perpetuated by prints, of which good ones exist in the first edition of Nelson's 'Islington.'

What has survived is a small building in a small street called Allen Street, and which bears the traditional name of Queen Elizabeth's Lodge. This is not more than fifteen feet square, and therefore has puzzled people by such a name. It formerly stood at the extremity of the garden belonging to the Fowler House, and probably being at that time the lodge of Sir Thomas Fowler's house, Elizabeth passed through it on visiting there; or she might occupy the house some time on her sojourn in Islington.

The Old Queen's Head

Old Queen's Head
(From a print in Mr. Gardner's Collection)

The 'Queen's Head' in the Lower Street, at the corner of Queen's Head Lane, is supposed to have been originally a gentleman's house, and Mr. Ellis, in his 'Campagna of London,' p. 96, says that, according to tradition, it was the residence of Lord Treasurer Burleigh, when the Queen was here. Tradition adds that not only Essex, her favourite, resided occasionally here, but that the Queen herself did. Ellis says that there were formerly in a yard of a neighbouring tenement two lions carved in wood, the supporters of the Cecil arms, confirming the belief of the Cecil family having possessed the place. It has been supposed that Sir Walter Raleigh converted this house into an inn when he obtained his licence from Queen Elizabeth 'for keeping taverns and retailing wine throughout England,' and that he gave it the name of the 'Queen's Head,' in honour of his royal mistress. Possibly, the house had fallen into decay, for, at one time, Queen Elizabeth's saddler is stated to have lived in it.

When Brewer compiled his 'Beauties of England and Wales,' in 1816, the 'Queen's Head' was one of the most perfect specimens of ancient domestic architecture remaining in the environs of London. It was a strong wood and plaster building of three stories, projecting over each other, and forming bay windows in front, supported by brackets and carved figures.. The centre protruded several feet beyond the rest of the front, and formed a commodious porch, to which there was a descent of several steps. The superstructure was supported by caryatides of carved oak, crowned with Ionic scrolls, standing on each side of the entrance. The interior was in the ancient style of oak panelled wainscot, stuccoed ceilings, and carved chimney-pieces. The stone slab over the fire-place of a front room on the ground floor had a classical design of Diana and Actæon in relief, with mutilated figures of Bacchus, Venus, &c. This ancient building was pulled down in 1829, and a new house, still called the *old* 'Queen's Head,' erected on the site.

The Pied Bull

Not far from the Green also stands an old house strongly affirmed to have been the residence of Sir Walter Raleigh. It is, and has been for a great many years, a public house, called the 'Pied Bull.' It has undergone many alterations, and the last time I saw it it was still undergoing such. There are no arms or direct indications of Sir Walter's possession of this house. The arms emblazoned on a window were those of Sir John Miller, impaling those of Gregg of Suffolk; but it is supposed that those of Sir Walter may have occupied the same place, and have been erased for Miller's; for the border enclosing the arms consisted of two mermaids, each crested with a globe, and as many sea-horses supporting a bunch of green leaves over the shield; and the lower part contained a green and grey parrot. These representations of maritime and tropical emblems seem allusive to Sir Walter's transatlantic adventures, and the green leaves were imagined to be those of tobacco, which he introduced. But these really seem to be the arms of Sir Francis Drake.

Pied Bull
(From Nelson's 'History of Islington')

There was a chimney-piece in the 'Pied Bull' ornamented with a representation of Faith, Hope, and Charity, with their usual insignia, in niches, surrounded by a border of cherubim, fruit, and foliage. Above the figure of Charity, which occupied the centre, were two Cupids suspending a crown, and beneath were the supporters of the royal arms in a couchant position. This was a conceit of the artist in compliment to the maiden Queen. The ceiling also contained a personification of the five senses in stucco, with the name of each in Latin underneath. In the window were also arms of Porter and Pennythorne. In the 'Life of Sir Walter Raleigh,' by Oldys and Birch, it is stated that the tenant, at that time, affirmed that his landlord possessed old account-books which put it beyond all doubt that the house did belong to Sir Walter, with fourteen acres of land. There can, therefore, remain no question as to its having been the residence of Sir Walter Raleigh. At what time it became an inn does not appear. Good views of the 'Pied Bull ' exist in Nelson's 'Islington.'

Ward's Place

The buildings bearing this name, between Lower Chapel Street and Paradise Place, occupy the site of an old house which was pulled down in 1800. There was a tradition that it had been called Hunsden House, from having been the residence of Henry Carey, cousin of Queen Elizabeth, created by her Lord Hunsden. On the front of the old house, abutting on Lower Street, was inscribed King John's Place, and tradition asserted it to have been an occasional residence of that monarch, for which nothing conld be more natural, for John was fond of hunting and had hunting-lodges in various parts of the kingdom, either as Prince or King. It appears that Sir Thomas Lovell, Knt., rebuilt the house, which remained till 1800; and from armorial bearings of Dudley executed in the stained glass of one of the windows, there is little doubt that it belonged at one time to Robert, Earl of Leicester, Queen Elizabeth's unprincipled favourite, and is another proof of how much that Queen frequented this neighbourhood, thus necessitating her courtiers to have houses here too. It afterwards became the property of Sir Robert Ducy, Bart., the banker to Charles I. The house was distinguished for its stained-glass windows illustrating the Scripture subjects of the 'Faithful Steward,' the 'Prodigal Son,' Apostles and Saints. It had also a splendid chimney-piece, containing the arms of the City of London with those of Lovell quartering Muswell, or Mosell; the arms of the Priory of St. John of Jerusalem; of Gardeners of London, Grocers; and of the Company of Merchant Adventurers.

THE OLD AND NEW PARISH CHURCH

Amongst the dozen or more churches and chapels of ease in different parts of Islington, four of which, St. Paul's near Ball's Pond, St. Peter's, Trinity, and St. John's, were erected by Charles Barry, Esq., architect of the New Houses of Parliament, we must devote a few words to the old and new church of St. Mary, because they are matters of history. The old church is supposed to have been built about 1483, from an inscription on the steeple discovered when pulling it down in 1751. The remains of many people of note who had lived in the place lay in the interior. Amongst these were the ashes of Lady Alice Owen, who erected the school and almshouses in St. John Street Road, Clerkenwell; various members of the Fowler family; of Sir Nicholas Kempe, member of the High Commission Court under Charles I, and a son of Sir Harbottle Grimston, a leading politician of Cromwell's time, and speaker of what was called the 'Healing Parliament.'

In the churchyard lay the dust of Richard Cloudesley, who, out of an uneasy conscience, as Purlet in 'De Miraculis Haturæ' suggests, 'on ye score of some sinue by him peradventure committed,' left various bequests to this and other churches, for masses, requiems, and great wax candles to 'burn at the sacryng of the mass.' The most valuable of these bequests was that of the Stoney Field of fourteen acres, or, as stated later, sixteen acres, and something more. This land in Henry VIII's time was valued at £4 per annum; in 1809, upon an application from the Corporation of London, to purchase it as an eligible spot for a cattle market, it was valued at £22,893 15s. Its rental has been employed in repairing the parish church and the three new ones. It is now worth vastly more, being covered with streets and squares, including Cloudesley Square, Cloudesley Terrace, Stonefield Street, &c.

Within the present parish church, amongst the numerous remains of many eminent citizens and their wives, lie those of the only daughter of Lord Delamere, who died in 1717. In the south aisle is a marble tablet in memory of Dr. Hawes, the founder of the Humane Society, which says that he was 'buried near these walls,' meaning, doubtless, outside of them. There is a cross against the wall of the north aisle in memory of Margaret Saville, one of the Fowlers of Islington, and wife of Sir Henry Saville of Yorkshire, supposed to be the father of the more celebrated Sir George Saville.

In the churchyard there are inscriptions to the memory of Sir John Mordaunt, late of Tangier, knight banneret, who died in 1723. There is an inscription on a vault, recording the burial there of John Nichols the printer, author of the 'History of Leicestershire,' and editor for nearly half a century of the 'Gentleman's Magazine.' His two wives and several children, as well as other members of his family, occupy the same tomb, or have a record upon it.

In the Register are some curious entries. We find that, in 1593, 106 persons died of the plague in Islington; and in 1665, 593 persons, 94 dying in one week.

Sir William Perriam, Lord Chief Baron of the Exchequer in the reign of Elizabeth, was married at this church to Margery Huchyson, April 6, 1562.

Sir Henry Yelverton, Solicitor and Attorney-General to King James, was as a child baptised in this church in 1566.

Lady Worcester, the daughter of Sir Anthony Browne, standard-bearer to Henry VII, and ancestor of the Lords Browne and Montagu, was buried here in 1584. She was widow of the Earl of Worcester, who died in 1549.

Many members of the families of Fowler and Fisher lie buried in this church.

Richard, a son of Sir Thomas Holte, of Aston, in Warwickshire, was baptised October 2, 1604; Katharine, his daughter, was buried August 3, 1605.

Ann Compton, daughter of Lord William Compton, and wife of Ulick Burgh, Marquis of Clanricard, baptised Sept. 6, 1605.

Several of the family of Sir James Stonehouse were married or buried here. The Stonehouse family were for many years impropriators of the rectory.

Sir Henry Ascough, Knt., and Mary Southwell, married Feb. 9, 1608.

John, son of Sir Henry Dymock, baptised April 28, 1625.

Sir George Wharton, son of Lord Wharton, and James Stewart, godson to James I, and eldest son of Lord Blantyre, Lord

Treasurer of Scotland, quarrelled and ran one another through. James ordered them to be buried in one grave. There was published at the time 'A lamentable Ballad of a Combate lately fought near London, between Sir James Stewart and Sir George Wharton, Knights, who were both slaine at that time.' This may be found in Lewis's 'History of Islington,' as well as the challenge and reply. They were buried November 10, 1609.

In the following year another duel took place here betwixt John, son of Sir John Egerton, and one Edward Morgan, in which Egerton was killed, and Morgan nearly so. Egerton was buried here April 22, 1610.

Many other people of title were interred or married, buried or baptised, at this church. Amongst these was a son of the Lord Keeper Coventry, baptised, and a daughter of Sir Simon Dewes, also baptised. Sir Simon was a great antiquary, the author of the 'Journals of Parliament during the reign of Elizabeth.' His 'Letters,' two of which are dated from Islington, are preserved in the Harleian Manuscripts. He professed, in his 'Historical Inquiries,' to have been able to correct Camden's 'Britannia' in almost every page.

William, son of Benjamin Hewling, baptised Oct. 28, 1665. This unfortunate youth, and his brother Benjamin, were both condemned by Judge Jeffreys, and executed for being concerned in Monmouth's rebellion.

Playford, the celebrated writer on music, lived at Islington, and his son John, afterwards a printer of music, was baptised in this church Oct. 6, 1665.

Susanna Creed, and her daughter Hester, hilled by a elap of thunder (*sic*) in their beds, buried Aug. 10, 1690.

The celebrated John Blackburn, a nonjuring bishop, and editor of 'Bale's Chronycle concerning Sjr Johan Olde-castell,' and of an edition of Lord Bacon's works, buried Nov. 19, 1741.

Dr. Robert Poole, buried June 3, 1752. Dr. Poole was author of 'Travels in France;' of the 'Physical Vade Mecum,' and was the institutor of the Small Pox Hospital.

Here lie the remains of Osborne the bookseller, who used to boast that he was worth £40,000, and whom Dr. Johnson knocked down with a folio, in Johnson's own lodgings, and put his foot upon his neck, 'Because,' said Johnson, 'he was impertinent, and I beat him.'

The Rev. John Lindsay, an intimate friend of Blackburn, and, like him, a nonjuring divine, buried July 2, 1768. Mr. Lindsay was fifty years a minister in Aldersgate Street, and author of `A Short History of the Regal Succession,' and other works.

John Hyacinth de Magelhaens, buried February 13, 1790. This remarkable Portuguese was great-grandson of the celebrated Ferdinando Magelhaens, the discoverer of Magelhaens' Straits. He was also a relative of the Jesuit Magelhaens, who travelled in China from 1640 to 1648, and continued to reside at Pekin till his death in 1677. John Hyacinth Magelhaens was an acute chemist and natural philosopher. He had been a monk at Lisbon, but renounced the Roman faith, and came to live in England, where he was F.R.S. and member of various foreign societies. He translated Cronstedt's `Essay towards a System of Mineralogy.' He was author of various works of a chemical character, on impregnating common water with fixed air, and on imitating Pyrmont, Bath, Spa, Tunbridge, and other waters. He was well known in the Netherlands, where he had been a canon, and was master of Portuguese, Spanish, Italian, English, French, Latin, and some Dutch. He lived in lodgings in Islington, and desired to be buried very privately.

Thomas Cooke, buried August 30, 1811, aged eighty five. He was called the Miser of Pentonville, and died with the reputation of never having helped a single individual, or done any single act of good through his whole life. But he bequeathed £127,205, and that chiefly to charitable institutions. There is a life of him by W. Chamberlaine.

The Rev. John Pridden, buried April 12, 1825. Mr. Pridden was son-in-law to Nichols, editor and proprietor of the `Gentleman's Magazine,' and assisted him in his topographical pursuits. He spent thirty years of his life in making an epitome of the six volumes of the rolls of Parliament; but what he deserves a notice here for especially, is that he surveyed the ground betwixt Snow Hill and Holborn, and submitted to the Corporation the plan of a handsome bridge to connect them. The Corporation highly commended the plan, but left it to the citizens of the present day to carry out.

We now come to the most extraordinary entry of all, that of

the baptism of Olive, *soi-disant* Duchess of Cumberland.

Mrs. Olivia Serres

The present generation has seen Mrs. Ryves, the daughter of Olivia Serres, spending her life in endeavouring to establish the claims which her mother advanced to be the grand-daughter of the Duke of Cumberland, brother of George III. Mrs. Ryves has brought her case before the Courts of Justice repeatedly, and finally in 1866(?), with very little satisfaction. It has long been quite clear that Mrs. Serres was an impostor of the first rank. She was an indefatigable forger of documents to prove her successive claims; and in contemplating these claims, no one can fail to see their emptiness and their contradictory nature. In the course of her adventures in this pursuit, she suddenly appeared at St. Mary's, Islington, in her forty ninth year, and was baptised as the daughter of the Duke of Cumberland, having in her infancy been baptised at Warwick as the daughter of Robert Wilmot, a house painter. In the 'Traveller' newspaper, September 12, 1821, appeared this paragraph:

'Royal Christening.—The public will be surprised and amused at the following relation, which we have from a correspondent, of the baptism of a full-grown princess, which took place at Islington Church a few days ago. About eleven o'clock in the forenoon, on Thursday last, the carriage, apparently of a person of rank, was observed standing at the door of the curate, which was soon afterwards driven to the gate of the churchyard. The curiosity of the neighbouring inhabitants was much excited on seeing a portly, well-dressed dame, apparently about fifty, handed out of the coach by a dashing young fellow of not more than half her age, and on whom it was now concluded the lady was about to bestow her fair hand at the altar. The parson, the lady, and her friend, were some time in the church, the party not having thought it necessary even to send for the parish clerk to record the proceedings. The curiosity excited by this mystery remained ungratified till the secret became known to those whose prying inquisitiveness led them the day after to peep into the parish register, where the matter stands clearly developed in the following terms:—"1821, Sept. 6, baptised Olive, only daughter of the late Henry Frederick, Duke of Cumberland, by his first duchess." '

Mrs. Serres figures in the 'Gentleman's Magazine' in 1814, vol. lxxxiv. part 1, as the advocate of her grandfather, Dr. Wilmot, being Junius, but there is no claim in these letters of her being the daughter of the Duke of Cumberland. But in 1820, six years afterwards, she had pondered out a new phase of her story, and presented a petition to the House of Commons, July 11, as Princess of Cumberland.

In October, 1821, she placarded the walls of London with a statement, that not being able to get a payment of £15,000 left her by George III - a fact which, she said, had been proved by law - she was then under arrest for debt. She dated from 45 King Street, Soho, signing 'Olive.'

We now see the object of the baptism in the preceding month at Islington. In June 1822, her claims were argued by Dr. Dodson and Dr. Haggard in the Prerogative Court, and they were replied to by Dr. Lushington, and the Court decided that the application did not come within its jurisdiction. In court with Mrs. Serres appeared a gentleman calling himself Captain Fitz-Stratherne, cousin of the Princess Olive.

In the 'Gentleman's Magazine' for 1822, part ii. p. 34, Mrs. Serres relates that in the beginning of June of that year the late Earl of Warwick appeared to her with a large sealed packet in his hand. Whether he left this packet or not, she does not say; but we may infer that the packet contained the documents of which she afterwards made so much use.

In an article following this extraordinary letter, it is stated that she had recently issued, from her apartments on Ludgate Hill, a proposal to publish by subscription two volumes of poems, in which she repeats the story of the £15,000 left by George III, and the refusal on the part of Government to pay it her. This article then goes on to show the contradictory statements which, from time to time, she had made. First, of Dr. Wilmot being the author of Junius, and never married. Then of her being herself the daughter of his brother, Robert Wilmot, of Warwick. Then, in the 'British Luminary,' of 1821, that Dr. Wilmot was privately married to the Princess Poniatowski, sister of Stanislaus, King of Poland; and that she herself was the daughter of this marriage, and, of course, had claims on the throne of Poland. That she was brought up by Mrs. Payne, wife of Captain Payne, and sister of Dr. Wilmot, who himself bestowed great care on her education. That both the Earl of Warwick and the Duke of Cumberland sought her hand of her mother, but of course the Duke of Cumberland prevailed. That, on the 4th of March, 1767, they were married by Dr. Wilmot at the house of Lord Archer, in the presence of Lord Brooke, afterwards Lord Warwick, and a Mr. Addez. This marriage was known only to a few persons about the Court. The Princess Poniatowski, wife of Dr. Wilmot, in 1771 suffered from some dreadful transaction which is not explained, gave birth to Olive the Pretender, and was conveyed to France in a state not to be described, and died in a convent of a broken heart.

It is remarked in the article, according to. her own account, that the Earl of Warwick in 1815 revealed the secret of her illustrious birth. She swore positively to this, and that it was thus made known that she was not the niece of Dr. Wilmot, but his daughter, and the Duke of Cumberland her grandfather, Yet, notwithstanding her knowledge of this grand secret, we find her publicly stating in 1817, two years after, that Dr. Wilmot was her uncle, and was never married! Thus, admitting that she knew her royal birth, she must have been deceiving the public in 1817 respecting the presumed author of Junius. George III died in January, 1820, and Mrs. Serres made her claims on his will in the ensuing session of Parliament.

The 'Leeds Mercury' published an article given in the above account, most convincingly exposing the contradictions of her statements at different times. It gives the baptismal registry of Olive's birth at the parish church of St. Nicholas, Warwick: 'April 15, 1772, baptised, Olive, daughter of Robert and Anna Maria Wilmot.' Yet Olive asserted that she was baptised in London in 1821, as daughter of the Duke of Cumberland. We have just seen how this was done. Well does the 'Leeds Mercury' say:

'The lady was famed for dealing in documentary evidence; but, unfortunately for herself, the writers of all her documents always happen to die before their letters and certificates are produced.'

The pretended will of George III was not his acknowledged will, or a codicil to it; but, like all Mrs. Serres's documents, was written on an odd scrap of paper, which seemed to have been carried in the pocket till the edges were worn off, and which she had pasted on another paper. It was as follows:

'George R.

St. James's.

In case of our Royal demise, we give and bequeath to Olive, our brother of Cumberland's daughter, the sum of Fifteen Thousand Pounds, commanding our heir and successor to pay the sum privately to our said niece, for her use, as a recompense for the misfortunes she may have known through her father. June 2, 1774.

Witness—J. Dunning.   Chatham. Warwick.'

Mrs. Serres managed to impose on the Duke of Kent, who allowed to her and to her daughter, Mrs. Ryves, £400 a year, which was paid to them by the late Robert Owen, of Lanark. At his death three years' payments were found to have been made by Robert Owen which had not been refunded, owing to the death of the Duke of Kent. His son, the present Hon. Robert Dale Owen, received this money from the Crown when in England in 1860, on agreeing to give up all letters and other documents connected with these payments, which he did.

On June 18, 1823, Sir Gerard Noel, in the House of Commons, moved that the petition of Mrs. Serres for the granting of her claims on the will of George III should be taken into consideration. This motion was seconded by Joseph Hume, when Sir Robert Peel, amid the laughter of the House, stripped away all the pretence of the *soi-disant* Princess of Cumberland, by the most convincing facts and dates, and the motion was withdrawn. Before this time Mrs. Serres had set up her carriage, assumed the royal arms and livery, and with these paraded boldly before the public. The result of the discussion in the House of Commons was to lop the Olive-branch from the royal tree on which she had endeavoured to engraft herself. But her daughter, Mrs. Ryves, being educated in a belief of these papers by her mother, and confirmed in the assurance of their truth by the annuity from the Duke of Kent, has prosecuted her supposed claims only to make them the misery of her life, leaving her in a poverty the more hard to bear after the indulgence of such splendid hopes. The schemes of her mother, undoubtedly, constituted one of the most daring and persevering attempts at public imposition in history.

THE ANGEL INN

The ancient house, which was pulled down in 1819 to make way for the present one, exhibited the usual features of a large old country inn, having a long front, with an overhanging tiled roof, and two rows of windows, twelve in each row, independent of those in the basement story. The principal entrance was beneath a projection, which extended along a portion of the front, and had a wooden gallery at the top. The inn yard, approached by a gateway in the centre, was nearly a quadrangle, having double galleries, supported by plain columns and carved pilasters, with caryatides and other figures. These galleries had, doubtless, been often thronged with spectators of dramatic entertainments, at the period.when inn-yards were customarily employed for such purposes.

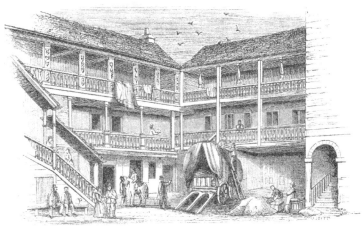

Old Angel Inn
(From a print in Mr. Gardner's Collection)

PRIORY OF ST. JOHN OF JERUSALEM

In Clerkenwell there are two reminders of the past that crave a brief notice: the Priory of St. John of Jerusalem and Dame Alice Owen's Hospital. As we approach the old archway at St. John's Square, Clerkenwell, we are not only reminded of Edward Cave and his 'Gentleman's Magazine,' of his great contributor, Dr. Johnson, and of those times, but of a far earlier age, when the Knights Hospitallers were living in their magnificent house there, of which this single Gothic archway is the sole remains. That archway is a standing monitor of the inevitable tendency of institutions which in their hour of prime seem to bid defiance to time and opinion. The Knights Hospitallers rose from the smallest beginnings, and under the humblest pretences. After the taking of Jerusalem in 1099 by Godfrey of Bouillon, they offered themselves as 'servants of the poor, servants of the Hospital of Jerusalem.' Their professed object was merely to nurse the wounded; then they advanced to the assumed duty of keeping open the highways to the Holy Sepulchre, and so must he armed and mounted; but so poor were they, in reality or pretence, that they adopted for their seal the representation of two men riding on one horse. They made a solemn vow of poverty, chastity, celibacy, and mortification of the flesh. But as the superstition of the times soon offered them wealth and lands, they readily accepted them, and became one of the most haughty, cruel, and domineering bodies in Christendom. They appear to have been instituted in Jerusalem in 1048, and were not long in reaching England. One John Briset is said to have been the founder of the Priory in Clerkenwell, about 1100. They were not long in acquiring a considerable part of the manor of Barnsbury; a knight's fee in Islington, supposed to be the lands constituting part of the manor betwixt Tollington Lane and the western extremity of the parish; and the Manor of Highbury, reaching from Smithfield to the parish of Hornsey, and including the whole of the parish of St. John and part of that of St. James, Clerkenwell; a tract of land contiguous to their house, upwards of twelve miles in circumference, and which they continued to possess till the time of the Dissolution. In a record of the possessions of this order, in the year 1373, the following occurs: West Smithfield, Finchley, Islington, Kentish Town, and Canonbury Manor. The Lord Prior had precedence of all the lay barons in Parliament, and chief power over all the preceptors and lesser barons of the order throughout England.

Who could have believed that so stately, powerful, and rich a body could ever be overturned, and only a single arch of their magnificent house remain to tell the tale? Yet the insolent pride and villanies of this order had given them some rubs, both at home and abroad. At the dissolution of the religions houses, they were found to have lands in England of the yearly value of £2,385 12s. 8d., and about the year 1240 they are said to have possessed 19,000 lordships or manors in different parts of Christendom. Such a holy corporation must have felt persuaded that it should last for ever. But its end, like that of every spiritual corporation, must come when it has first ripened and then rotted in men's opinions. King Henry came, and with him their end. Henry VIII turned the noble Priory into a coach house for 'his toyles and tents for hunting and for war;' and Somerset, the Protector in the reign of Edward VI., blew up the church with gunpowder, together with its 'great bell-tower, a most curious piece of workmanship, graven, gilt, and enameled, to the great beautifying of the city;' and Somerset carried away the stone thereof to build his palace in the Strand.

Such are the lessons of history; and they should teach the members of institutions founded on human opinion merely, that however mighty and flourishing they may appear at a given time, a breath can, and some day will, overthrow them, as it overthrew the Church of Rome when it seemed fixed for ever in this country.

Islington seems to have been a very land of Goshen for conventual institutions. Formerly the following monastic bodies had estates in this parish:

The Nunnery of Clerkenwell.
The Knights of St. John of Jerusalem.
The Priory of St. Bartholomew, London.
The Abbey of Vale Royal, Cheshire.
The Priory of St. Mary Spital, or New Hospital of our Lady
    without Bishopsgate, London.

DAME OWEN'S HOSPITAL AND SCHOOLS

Formerly, on the east side of St. John's Street, Clerkenwell, stood a low range of brick buildings; they were the Free School and Almshouses of Lady Owen. The almshouses accommodated ten poor women, each having a single apartment and a small garden behind. The school accommodated thirty boys. Over the entrance gate was a stone bearing an inscription, stating that the six Almshouses and Free Grammar School were built and endowed by Lady Alice Owen in 1613, under the government of the Worshipful Company of Brewers of the City of London.

In 1840-41, these buildings having become dilapidated, the trustees pulled them down and erected new ones in Owen Street, the School and Master's House on one side of the street, the Almshouses on the other. The buildings are of red brick with stone coping, and are handsome, light, and airy. There are twelve almshouses of two rooms each, with a centre accommodating two inmates, so that fourteen instead of the original ten poor women are provided for: seven from Islington, seven from Clerkenwell. Each of them, besides her house, receives 8s. per week, and at Christmas 10s. 6d. to purchase coals. They have each a gown every two years. The school accommodates eighty five boys, who are taught reading, writing, and accounts; of whom four-fifths are from Islington and one-fifth from Clerkenwell.

And what induced Dame Owen to leave this excellent endowment? The story is well worth telling, for it belongs to the simple times when people believed in a special Providence. This Alice Owen was a native of Islington, and some accounts state her to have been a poor girl, who went to milk her master's cows in the open fields. Other accounts have it that she was a Miss Wilks, a daughter of a gentleman of considerable landed property. The most prevailing version is the following:

'In the reign of Queen Mary it was an exercise for archers to shoot with their bows and arrows at butts. This part of Islington was at that time all open fields and pasture land; and on the same spot of ground where the school (the old one) now stands, was a woman milking a cow. The Lady Owen, then a maiden gentlewoman, walking by with her maid servant, observed the woman a-milking, and had a mind to try the cow's paps, whether she could milk, which she did, and at her withdrawing from the cow an arrow was shot through the crown of her hat (at which time high-crowned hats were in fashion), which so startled her that she then declared, that if she lived to be a lady, she would erect something on that very spot of ground, in commemoration of the great mercy shown by the Almighty in that astonishing deliverance. This passed on till she became a widow lady; her servant at the time this accident happened, being still with the lady, reminded her of her former words; her answer was, she remembered the affair, and would fulfil her promise; upon which she purchased the land from the "Welsh Harp" to the "Turk's Head," Islington Road, and built thereupon, as appears with the arrows fixed on the top.'

The foundress, it seems, was thrice married, her last husband being Sir Thomas Owen, one of the Justices of the Court of Common Pleas, whence her title. She founded the school and hospital three years before her death, which latter event took place in 1613, and she was buried in Islington Church, where there is a monument to her memory. On pulling down the old almshouses, two of the original arrows that she had fixed on the top of her building, showing the truth of the story, were found in the wall, and are now in the Master's care. When that archer in Islington Fields 'drew a bow at a venture,' little did he think that his arrow was winged with a livelihood for fourteen poor women, and education for nearly a hundred boys of his neighbourhood, for all time to come.

HISTORICAL FACTS CONNECTED WITH ISLINGTON

Queen Boadicea

The earliest historical event of any importance connected with the parish of Islington, is that of a great battle fought betwixt the Romans and the British under Queen Boadicea. That such a battle was fought somewhere near London is attested by Tacitus. Tradition locates the event at Battle-bridge, thence so named. Some critics have endeavoured to remove the site of the battle from this neighbourhood to Epping Forest, for which there is no authority whatever, and nothing, indeed, as a plea for such a supposition, but the description of the ground which they cannot make agree with that of the Roman historian: 'Locum arctis faucibus et à tergo silva clausum;' and 'Angustias loci pro munimento.' ('A place with a narrow approach, and with a wood at its back;') ('having the narrow boundaries of the situation as a defence'). A critic in the 'Gentleman's Magazine' for May 1824, thinks that the valley at Battle-bridge was not so narrow as thus described, but we prefer following a fixed tradition on such occasions to critical fancies indulged in more than 1,800 years after the event. The character of ground in that length of time, near a large and ever-growing city, changes wonderfully. Roman London itself is some fifteen or twenty feet under the present city, and the valleys on the northern side of it must have greatly changed their appearance from the washing down of soil from the hills, and the accumulation of debris in them. Here tradition places this great and decisive battle, one which rivetted the Roman yoke for ages on the nation, and here we have no doubt it occurred. It was in the year of Christianity 61 that it took place; so that for more than 1,800 years the fame of that fierce and bloody conflict has hovered over the spot, whilst fields, trees, streams and green nature have been gradually overturned and extirpated by the ever-extending metropolis. The bridge over the River Fleet, whence the name, has also disappeared, giving way to a great underground sewer, and the Fleet itself becoming a hidden Styx, rolling its dark tide to the Thames beneath the feet of the unconscious city population. What none of these mighty changes have been able to remove, nor all of them together, the pen of the critic tries to remove in vain. That is Battle-bridge, and there Queen Boadicea, 'bleeding from the Roman rods,' made a stupendous, unsuccessful, but never-to-be-forgotten attempt to avenge her own wrongs, and the wrongs of her daughters and her country.

The causes and consequences of this battle, according to Tacitus, in the fourteenth book of his 'Annals,' are these: Suetonius Paulinus, the commander of the Roman forces in Britain, under Nero, attributing the persevering resistance of the Britons to the instigation of the Druids, determined to pursue these powerful priests to their last retreat in the Island of Anglesea. Crossing over in flat-bottomed boats, he attacked the infuriated Britons, and destroyed them and the Druids amid their burning groves. Whilst he was, however, taking measures to fix a garrison, and to secure the retention of the island, news was brought him that the tribe of the Iceni had revolted, and were joined by the Trinobantes. Catus Decianus, the procurator of the province, had seized on the government and property of Boadicea, the widowed queen; and when she resented his conduct, had her beaten with rods, and her two daughters dishonoured. Burning for vengeance, Boadicea had roused her subjects, and called in the aid of the Trinobantes. The other neighbouring States promised secretly to support her. They attacked the Roman town and garrison of Camelodunum (Colchester), took and burnt it, laying the country all round in ashes. They engaged and defeated Petilius Cerealis, at the head of the ninth legion, putting the infantry to the sword. Catus Decianus, sensible that he was the cause of the revolt, fled to the Continent, pursued by the curses of both Britons and his own countrymen.

In this crisis Suetonius hastened by forced marches to London, where he proposed to fortify himself; but owing to the flight of Decianus, and the defeat of Cerealis, he felt his few remaining forces incompetent to defend it. He selected a position narrow in its approach, and surrounded by woods and hills, and there, with only 10,000 men, he resolved to await the Britons. These had now swelled to an incredible number, had marched to Verulamium (St. Alban's), seized and sacked it. They carried fire and sword in all directions where Romans were to be found, and sacrificed 70,000 of them to their vengeance. The enemy could only approach Suetonius in front. He posted his infantry in the centre, the cavalry on each wing, and his light-armed troops as a reserve. The Britons came on in confused masses, shouting and exulting as in certainty of victory, and a full revenge for all past injuries and oppressions. They posted their wagons, loaded with their wives and families, in a semicircle in front of the Romans, on the plain, that they might witness their triumph.

Boadicea in her chariot, attended by her two daughters, rode along the ranks, animating them to the onset by the recital of the wrongs of herself, her daughters, and her people. Suetonius, on his side, harangued his troops on their past glory, on the alternative being to conquer or die, and on the grand fact that the greatest victories had been frequently won by the smallest numbers. He gave the charge, and his battalions advanced in the form of a wedge, cutting through the immense multitude before them, and dividing them into two bodies. The cavalry advanced on each side, bearing down all before them with their spears, and the light troops followed, killing all that came in their way. The Britons, at first furious and determined, were soon thrown into confusion by the steady and murderous advance of the Roman host, and gave way and fled. But their wagons stopped their way, and driven one on another in hopeless chaos, the Romans made a terrible and promiscuous havoc of them. The cattle mixed with the frantic mob, fell with their drivers, and added to the heaps of the slain. Neither sex nor age was spared. According to the Roman writers, 80,000 Britons were put to the sword, whilst of the Romans only about 400 were slain, and as many wounded. Boadicea, seeing that all was lost, ended her unhappy existence by poison. Such was the bloody struggle which through so many centuries has left its name on Battle-bridge. An evidence of the presence of the Romans on this spot was found some years ago in the skeleton of an elephant. Elephants were used by the Romans in their war in Britain, and Polyænus mentions the effect one of them had in forcing the passage of the Thames by Julius Cæsar.

Llewellyn Prince of Wales at Islington

The following curious note relative to the causes of the disturbances in Wales during the reign of Edward I occurs in the

Mostyn Papers concerning that period, and is quoted by Carte, in his 'History of England.' The Snowdon barons had accompanied Llewellyn to London, and joined their homage with that of their prince. These with their numerous trains were quartered at Islington, and well entertained. Unhappily they could not drink the wine and ale of London; the English bread they slighted; and the environs afforded not milk enough for their party. Their pride, too, was disgusted at the continual staring of the Londoners, who followed them in crowds to stare at their uncommon garb. 'No!' chorused the indignant Britons, 'we will never again visit Islington except as conquerors.' And from that instant they resolved to take up arms.

Arrest of Henry VI at Islington

In 1465 the unfortunate Henry VI, into whose fate Shakespeare has thrown so much poetry, was brought through Islington a captive, on his way to the Tower. For twelve months after the battle of Hexham, where he suffered a thorough defeat, and whence his queen, Margaret of Anjou, managed to escape to France, Henry had wandered from place to place amongst the friends of the House of Lancaster in Westmoreland, Lancashire, and Yorkshire. At the various halls and castles where he sojourned, tradition has to this day retained the memory of his presence. There are 'King Henry's Chamber' and 'King Henry's Parlour' still pointed out, the bath that he used, and the boot, spoon, and glove that he left with his host, Sir Hugh Pudsay, at Bolton Hall, Yorkshire. He was at length betrayed by Cantlow, a monk of Abingdon, and was taken by the servants of Sir John Harrington, as he sat at dinner at Waddington Hall. He was treated with the utmost indignity on his way to London. He was mounted on a miserable hack, his legs being tied in his stirrups, and an insulting placard fixed on his back. At Islington Warwick met the fallen King, and disgraced himself by commanding the thronging spectators to show no respect to him. To enforce his command by his example, he had his gilt spurs taken from his feet, and then led the unhappy man three times round the pillory, as if he had been a common felon, crying 'Treason! Treason! Behold a traitor!' Enduring all this ignominy with the utmost meekness, he was, however, roused by the blow of a rude churl to the expression,

'Forsooth and forsooth, ye do foully to smite the Lord's anointed!' He was accompanied by Dr. Manning, Dean of Windsor, Dr. Bedle, and young Ellerton, who had their feet tied under their horses' bellies, and thus was conducted to the Tower.

Edward IV

The conqueror of Henry VI was met soon after between Eyseldon and Shoreditch, by the Lord Mayor and Aldermen of the City, who offered him an address of congratulation on his good fortune, and were rewarded with the honour of knighthood.

Henry VII

On his return to London, after the defeat of Lambert Simnel and his adherents, Henry VII was met in Hornsey Park by the mayor, aldermen, sheriffs, and principal commoners of the city of London, all on horseback, and in one livery, to attend on him, when he dubbed Sir William Horne, mayor of London, knight; and between Islington and London, he dubbed Sir John Percivall, alderman, knight.

Henry VIII

Henry VIII frequently visited Islington, in which parish and its immediate vicinity several of the principal nobility of his court resided. Among these were Dudley, Earl of Warwick, who held the manor of Stoke Newington; and Algernon Percy, Earl of Northumberland, who, as we have stated, had an ancient mansion at Newington Green, whence he wrote the letter regarding Anne Boleyn which we have quoted.

Queen Mary - Burning of Protestants

In 1557 Queen Mary sent her pensioners in grand procession to meet the ambassador of the King of Muscovy at Islington.

In the same year several Protestants, who had assembled for religious worship at the 'Saracen's Head,' at Islington, under pretence of seeing a play acted there, on the third Sunday in Advent, were arrested by the Vice-Chamberlain of the Queen's household, and committed to prison. Of these persons John Rough, who had been a preacher among the Black Friars at Stirling, and afterwards chaplain to the Earl of Arran, and an intimate friend of

John Knox, was burnt at the stake in Smithfield, and four of the others were burnt in one fire at Islington. Fox, in his 'Acts and Monuments,' says these four others were Richard Roth, Ralph Allerton, James Austoo, and Margery Austoo. They were burnt on the 15th of September of that year. The infamous Bishop Bonner charged them with the heinous offence of reading the Communion Book, and using the fashion of the latter days of Edward VI. Fox relates the treacherous manner in which about forty persons were apprehended for Protestant worship:

'June 27, 1558, secretly in a back close, in a field by the town of Islington, were collected and assembled together a certain company of godly and innocent persons, to the number of forty men and women; who, there sitting together at prayer, and virtuously occupied in the meditation of God's holy word, first cometh a certain man to them unknown, who, looking over unto them, so stayed and saluted them, saying they looked like men who meant no hurt. Then one of the said company asked the man if he could tell whose close that was, and whether they might be so bold there to sit. "Yea," said he, "for ye seem to me such persons as intend no harme," and so departed. Within a quarter of an hour after cometh the constable of Islington, named King, warded with six or seven others, accompanying him on the same business; one with a long bow, another with a bill, and others with their weapons likewise. The which six or seven persons the said constable left a little behind him, in a close place, there to be ready if need should be, while he, with one with him, should go view them before; who, so doing, came through them, looking and finding what they were doing, and what bookes they had; and so going a little forward, and returning back againe, bade them deliver their bookes. They understanding that he was constable, refused not so to do; with that cometh forth the residue of his fellows above touched, who bade them stand and not depart. They answered again they would be obedient, and ready to go whithersoever they would have them. And so they were first carried to a brew-house but a little way off, while that some of the said soldiers ran to the justice next at hand; but that justice not being at home, they were had to Sir Roger Cholmley. In the meantime some of the women, being of the same number of the aforesaid forty persons, escaped away from them, some in the close, some before they came to the brewhouse; for so they were carried, ten with one man, eight with another, and with some more, with some less, in such sort that it was not hard for them to escape that would. In fine, they that were carried to Sir Roger Cholmley were twenty-seven; which Sir Roger Cholmley and the recorder taking their names in a bill, and calling them one by one, so

447

many as answered their names he sent to Newgate; in the which number of them that answered and that were sent to Newgate were twenty-two.

These two-and-twenty were in the said prison of Newgate seven weeks before they were examined, to whom word was sent by Alexander the keeper, that if they would hear mass they should all be delivered. Of these foresaid twenty-two were burned thirteen; in Smithfield, seven; at Brainford, six.'

One is sorry to find Sir Roger Cholmeley, the founder of the Highgate Grammar School, engaged in such a terrible business as this: a tool of the bloody bigotry of the time.

Queen Elizabeth

We have made mention of the visits of Elizabeth to Islington and Canonbury; her having the hedges cut down for the passage of her coach across the fields; her besetment with a troop of sturdy beggars; and of the association of her name with various places in this neighbourhood. To keep the district rural she forbade the erection of any further buildings within a distance of three miles from the City gates.

The Earl of Essex

Queen Elizabeth's unfortunate favourite, when he set out to occupy the post of Lord Lieutenant of Ireland, passed through Islington, attended by a splendid retinue of noblemen and gentlemen on horseback. Hume says,

'Essex left London in the month of March, attended with the acclamations of the populace; and what did him more honour, accompanied by a numerous train of nobility and gentry, who, from affection to his person, had attached themselves to his fortunes, and sought fame and military experience under so renowned a commander.'

To see a Lord Lieutenant of Ireland now setting out for his government with his suite on horseback, would be as astonishing as to see him come speedily hack to have his head taken off at the will of the monarch. There is some difference betwixt now and then, betwixt Tudor and Guelph.

James I

When James approached London to take the crown in 1603, he was met at Stamford Hill by the Lord Mayor and Aldermen of the City in their robes of state, accompanied by five hundred of the principal citizens on horseback, gorgeously apparelled, who hailed his arrival, and escorted him through the fields of Islington to the Charter House. John Saville, who delivered a congratulatory address to the King at Theobalds, which he soon after published, with some particulars of the King's entry into London, states as follows:

'After his Majestie was come from Kingsland there begun a division among the people which way his Highness would take when he came at Islington, but in fine he came the higher way by the west end of the church; which streete hath ever since been, and I gesse ever will be, called King's Street, by the inhabitants of the same. When his Highness had passed Islington and another place called New Rents, and entered into a close called Wood's Close, by a way that was cut of purpose through the bancke, for his Majestie's more convenient passage into the Charterhouse Garden; the people that were there assembled I compare to nothing more conveniently than to imagine every grasse to have been metamorphosed into a man, in a moment, the multitude was so marvellous, amongste whome were the children of the Hospital singing, orderly placed for his Majestie's coming along through them, but all displaced by reason of the rudeness of such a multitude.'

Charles I

On his return from Scotland in 1641, where he had been endeavouring to conciliate the discontent, which had arisen among his Scottish subjects, on his route towards the capital, Charles I passed through Islington, accompanied by the Queen, the Prince of Wales, and the Duke of York, and, attended by a splendid cavalcade, entered the City by Moorgate. It was the last time that he ever did enter London except as a prisoner. Matters were fast coming to a crisis with this stiff-necked and slippery king. His right-hand champion of despotism, the Earl of Strafford, had paid on the block for his treason to the nation. Laud the great ritualist, and as great a tyrant, was awaiting the same fate. By the following summer Charles had consummated his offences against the liberties of the people. He had entered the House of Commons and endeavoured to seize five of the most patriotic members that ever sat there: John Hampden, Pym, Hollis, Haselrigge, and Strode. Failing in this attempt, Charles had stolen away northward, hoping to receive an army from Scotland, to put down his indignant subjects. He set up a military court at York, coquetted with the fleet, and hung like a thunder-cloud over the districts north of the capital. In May and June the people of London, animated by the spirit and proclamations of Parliament, set about to fortify every line of approach to the City. We have already noticed how men, women, and children, all works and trades, turned out with spades and picks, and cast up embankments, and made trenches by every highway from the north. The train-bands; the porters, with their wives and children, 3,000 in number; 5,000 feltmakers and cappers; 5,000 shoemakers; 6,000 tailors, all digging and delving as one man, to preserve their freedom from the myrmidons of a king gluttonous of power and of a monstrous self-will. Besides numerous defences thrown up round Islington, they made a battery and breastwork at Mount Hill in Goswell Street Road; another at St. John's; a large fort, with four half bulwarks, at the New River Upper Pond, and a small redoubt near Islington Pound. This evidence of the spirit of London firing up made the melancholy desperado retire to Nottingham, and set up his standard, which the winds of a warning heaven blew down speedily and vainly, for the Stuart soul was in every generation warning-proof.

Oliver Cromwell Connections

Oliver Cromwell's fate was not unconnected with Islington. Here lived, in his unambitious days, one of his most highly-favoured officers as a drayman, and afterwards as stoker at the brewery of Islington. Having joined the parliamentary army, he soon rose in Cromwell's favour, who made him a colonel of dragoons, and put much trust in him. 'Colonel Okey,' says the *Magna Britannia*, 'was a person of more bulk than brains, and more strength than wit,' just the sort of man for a brewer's drayman. The man, however, had sense and honesty enough to perceive and despise the aim of Cromwell at the regal power which he had himself put down as an offence. On the trial of the King, Cromwell, without consulting Okey, put his name down as one of the judges, and compelled him to act, which cost him his head. The execution of the King over, however, Okey determined to have no more to do with the Protector, but fled to Holland, where he lived till the Restoration, when he was seized by Sir George Downing, Minister of Charles II at the Hague, and, with Miles Corbet and John Banksteap, sent to London and there executed. This bit of grace, however, was accorded to his remains by Charles the Dissolute: his body was not quartered and hung on different city gates, as those of the others were, but given to his relatives for burial, 'because in his last speech he had spoken dutifully of his Majesty.'

Sir Arthur Haselrigge, member of parliament for the county of Leicester, and a great friend of Cromwell's, was an inhabitant of this parish, as we shall more fully mention in another place.

The parliamentary general Skippon, who was desperately wounded at the battle of Naseby, had a critical adventure in passing through Islington, on his way to London. Vicar, in his 'England's Worthies,' gives this quaint account of the affair:

'After this renowned commander had lyen a while at Northampton town, or thereabout, for the dressing of his wounds, and it being held fit by the parliament, who took tender care of him, to remove him thence to London, for the more hopeful care, this brave gentleman being, with all easiest convenience, put into a horse-litter to be brought to London, and coming to Islington, a toun little more than a mile from London; it pleased the Lord that it should so fall out, to the greater setting forth of his power and providence, that in the said toun a great mastiffe dog, on a suddain, ran most fiercely out of a house, fell furiously upon one of the horses that carried the litter, seized him behind, and made the horse fling and fly about, and beat and shake the litter up and down, too and fro, in a most dangerous manner, shaking the gentleman's sorely wounded body thereby, and ready continually to overthrow the litter, and greatly endanger the noble gentleman's life; all which while there being no possible means to beat off the dog, or make him leave his hold of the horse, till they ran him through with a sword and killed him; which as soon as they could, they did, and so brought this noble gentleman to his house in Bartholomew the Great.'

The author adds, that notwithstanding 'this terrible brunt,' the general suffered very little, and prayers being put up in all the churches in London, and Mr. Trapham, a famous surgeon, employed, he was completely cured, 'thus making it manifest that God had reserved him graciously unto yet more glorious works.'

But this was not the last connection of Cromwell's fortunes with Islington. His assumption of the supreme power had deeply exasperated the friends of the monarchy, and various conspiracies were set on foot against his life. At the head of one of these was a Major Henshaw, who came over from Paris in 1654, and proposed to assassinate Cromwell at Hampton Court. His plan was to get thirty stout men for the purpose. A young enthusiastic gentleman, named Gerard, undertook to procure twenty five of them, and Colonel Finch and Henshaw were to bring the other five. Vowell, a schoolmaster of Islington, was very zealous in the plot, and engaged in procuring arms, and Billingsley, a butcher of Smithfield, engaged to seize the troopers' horses grazing in Islington Fields. The soldiers were to be then fallen upon at the mews; Charles II proclaimed; Rupert was to appear with a large force of royalists, English, Irish, and Scots, and there was to be a general rising. Saturday, May 20 was fixed for Cromwell's assassination; but before this wild scheme could be accomplished, forty of the conspirators were seized, some of them in their beds. Vowell was hanged, and Gerard, on his own request, as a gentleman, was beheaded on July 10.

Private and Public Meetings

We have already described the strange scene of the burnt-out inhabitants of London, congregated with their effects in the fields of Islington. Since then political meetings have at times drawn great numbers of Londoners into the fields about Islington. Copenhagen House, and the fields about it called Copenhagen Fields, have borne that name, according to tradition, since the King of Denmark paid his visit to his brother-in-law, James I. The house is said to have been opened by a Dane, and to have been much frequented by his countrymen living in London on account of business, or otherwise. 'Coopen-Hagen' is the name given to the place in the map in Camden's 'Britannia,' published in 1695. It became a great tea-house and resort of the Londoners to play at skittles and Dutch-pins. It commanded a splendid view over the metropolis and the immense western suburb, the heights of Highgate and Hampstead, and the rich intervening meadows. In 1826, the landlady told William Hone, that at the time of the London riots in 1780, the mob, on its way to burn down Lord Mansfield's house at Caen Wood, passed by her house, and so alarmed her that she applied to Justice Hyde, who sent a party of soldiers to protect her till the riots were over. On one occasion, this landlady, Mrs. Harrington, had a most daring burglary perpetrated on the house, the interest of which, however, brought an increase of visitors; her landlord enlarged the premises, and it became a great fives-playing place.

Copenhagen House
(From an old print in Mr. Gardner's collection)

Copenhagen House became still more noted for the meetings of the London Corresponding Society, an association of the full-length reformers of the day, who hoped to reap great benefit from the examples of the French revolutionists. On October 26, 1795, no fewer than 40,000 people are said to have been collected there, and various speakers addressed them from their different platforms. Some of these called on their hearers to note the circumstance of the King's going to the House of Parliament on the 29th. On that day an immense crowd assembled in the park; the King was shot at, and was very rudely treated, but escaped unhurt. It would appear from this that there were persons present at this meeting who were in the secret of this plot, but some of the speakers must have been men of a different stamp, for we have a speech of John Thelwall, well known for his trial on a charge of treason with Hardy and Horne Tooke, made at this great meeting in Copenhagen Fields, in which he asserts peaceful discussion, and not tumultuary violence, to be the means for redressing public grievances. Thelwall seems to have been a frequent speaker at these meetings. They were continued till the volunteers were called out to disperse them.

In April, 1834, the Trades' Unions selected Copenhagen Fields for their great meeting, in order to form a procession to Whitehall, to present an address to His Majesty, signed by 260,000 Unionists, on behalf of their fellows at Dorchester, convicted of administering unlawful oaths. Conspicuous amongst the leaders of this meeting, which mustered 40,000 strong, were Robert Owen, of Lanark, and the Rev. Dr. Wade - the latter clad in full canonicals, having his sacred robe of black silk with a crimson collar round his neck. In this style the monster procession marched through London, but Lord Melbourne refused to receive the address.

Cattle Markets

A large section of these Copenhagen Fields, where the Londoners sought amusement and the graver exercise of political agitation, is now occupied by the New Cattle Market. The enormous inconvenience, cruelty, and public danger occasioned by driving the weekly hosts of cattle and sheep through the crowded streets of the metropolis had long been a subject of discussion and serious reflection amongst the metropolitan public. A Mr. Perkins, of Bletchingley, in Surrey, seized the opportunity to remove the public difficulty by a bold speculation. He projected and built a new cattle market near Ball's Pond, at a cost of £100,000. It was commenced in 1833, by sanction of an Act of Parliament, and completed in 1836. The object of Mr. Perkins was good, but it was destined not to be profitable, for he received determined opposition from the City authorities, and the site was too near London to obviate, for any considerable period, the mischief it was intended to remedy. It was soon surrounded by a dense population. It was extinguished by an Act of Parliament, to make way for the city scheme of a market in Copenhagen Fields. For this purpose,

Copenhagen House and Fields, to the extent of seventy five acres, were purchased by the Corporation of London, and converted into the present New Cattle Market, which was opened June 13, 1855. Commodious as is this site, it has the fault of being too near London. It is already environed by houses, and must become more and more so. Eventually, the London abattoirs must be placed away in the country, and the meat sent up by railway.

New Prisons Built

Pentonville Prison was commenced in 1840, as an experiment of a model prison, in which an improved discipline could be carried out. The first stone was laid on April 10 of that year by Lord Lansdowne, attended by several members of Parliament, and other gentlemen interested in the improvement of prison discipline. He also laid the foundation stone of the New City Prison, which superseded the Compter, at Holloway, and which was opened October 6, 1832.

REMARKABLE PERSONS WHO HAVE LIVED
IN THE PARISH OF ISLINGTON

Owing to the vicinity of London, a considerable number of men and women of distinction for their talents, or otherwise, have at one time or another lived in and around Islington. I shall give a few brief notices of the most remarkable of them.

John, Second Baron Berners

This nobleman was the descendant of the Berners family, who were for many generations proprietors of the manor of Bernersbury - or, as now called, Barnsbury - of Canonbury, and some parts of that of St. John of Jerusalem. These possessions, or part of them, they held in the reign of Richard II. The aunt of Lord John Bouchier Berners, the translator of 'Froissart,' was the celebrated Dame Juliana Berners, author of the famous 'Treatise on Hawking,' printed in 1481, and who is, therefore, one of the earliest female authors of England. Dame Julia is reported to have been Prioress of Sopewell Nunnery, in Hertfordshire, and is stated to have been living in 1460. Holingshed places her at the close of the reign of Edward IV, and calls her

> 'Julian Bemes, a gentlewoman endued with excellent giftes bothe of body and minde, who wrote certain treatises of hawking and hunting, delighting greatly hirself in those exercises and pastimes. She wrote also a book of the laws of armes and knowledge apperteyning to heraldes.'

Wynkyn de Worde calls these

> 'Treatyses perteynyng to Hawkynge, Huntynge, and Fyshyne with an Angle; and also a right noble Treatyse of the Lygnage of Cot Armours, endynge with a Treatyse which specyfyeth of Blasynge of Armys.'

In the treatise on heraldry, Dame Juliana professes to teach 'how gentylmen shall be knowen from ungentylmen.' These works were printed at the Abbey of St. Alban's, on which the nunnery of

Sopewell was dependent. In 1810, a facsimile edition of that of Wynkyn de Worde was printed by Mr. Hazlewood, consisting of 150 copies.

Lord Berners, the translator of Froissart, is ranked by Fuller as the fourth literary nobleman of England; his predecessors being Lord Cobham, Tiptoft Earl of Worcester, and Lord Rivers. Lord Berners was a great traveller, as well as an accomplished scholar. He sate in the eleventh Parliament of Henry VII, and accompanied that monarch to the siege of Boulogne in 1492. He took an active part in suppressing an insurrection in Cornwall, headed by Michael Joseph, a blacksmith, and Flammock, a lawyer, and afterwards supported by Lord Audley. He was high in favour with Henry VIII; was captain of pioneers at the siege of Terrouenne, in 1513; two years afterwards he was made Chancellor of the Exchequer for life; and in 1514 was one of the splendid train appointed to attend Princess Mary, the King's sister, to Abbeville, on her way to be married to Louis XII of France. He afterwards accompanied John Kite, Archbishop of Armagh, in an embassy to Spain, to congratulate King Charles on his accession.

His great work, the translation of the 'Chronicles of Froissart,' was undertaken by command of the King, and was the first historical work of magnitude in the English language. It became the most popular book of that and the next age, and was only superseded in ordinary use by the translation of Mr. Johnes. A reprint of Lord Berners' translation was published by Mr. Utterson in 1812.

Besides Froissart, Lord Berners translated from the French the 'History of Arthur Little Britain;' the 'History of Huon of Bourdeux;' and the 'Golden Boke of Marcus Aurelius.' From the Spanish, 'The Castle of Love.' He also wrote a work on the 'Duties of the Inhabitants of Calais,' of which town he was governor in his later years; and a comedy called 'Ite in vineam meam,' which was usually acted in the great church of Calais after vespers.

Lord Berners died in 1532, when his title became extinct, and his property passed to his sole surviving daughter, who was married to Edmund Knyvet, Esq., of Ashwellthorpe, in Norfolk. The manor of Barnsbury passed to the Fowler family, but the title of Lord Berners was revived in the descendant of Lord Berners, the translator, in 1832, but again in the female line, and under the name of Wilson. How few, in hearing the familiar name of Barnsbury, connect its possession with the noble translator of the 'Chronicles of Froissart.'

Sir Henry Yelverton

Sir Henry Yelverton was a judge of much note under King James I. He was baptised at St. Mary's Church, in Islington, July 7, 1566, and most probably was born there, though said to have been born at Easton Mauduit, in Northamptonshire, his father's estate. He was successively solicitor and attorney-general, and a judge of the Court of Common Pleas under James. He did not, before arriving at the bench, escape some trouble and imprisonment in the Tower, through, in some manner, crossing the interests of the Duke of Buckingham; but made his apology, and escaped with a fine of £4,000, and regained his liberty. He died in 1629-30, and was buried at Easton Mauduit.

Robert Brown

Amongst the earliest lecturers of the parish of Islington stands the name of this clergyman, who founded the sect of the Brownists, out of which developed the numerous and influential body of the Independents. He is said to have commenced his campaign against the principle and practices of an endowed church about 1580, and having preached to a Dutch congregation in Norwich, he made many converts to his views. Persecution compelled him to flee to Holland, where, at Middleburgh, he had a body of proselytes. On his return to England he renewed his preaching against the Establishment, and was excommunicated by the Bishop of Peterborough; but, remarkable enough, he renounced the principle of separation in or about the year 1590, and accepted the living of Achurch, in Northamptonshire. Fuller says that he kept a curate to do the work of the parish, and that though he opposed his parishioners in judgment, he was willing to take their tithes. In fact, Fuller says that he led an idle and dissolute life, had a wife with whom he did not live for many years, and a church in which he never preached. Neither Neal nor Mosheim give him a good character. He was nearly related to the Lord Treasurer Cecil, and his advice and persuasion may have induced him to take a church living so contrary to his principles, and endeavour to be quiet; but as Byron says,

Quiet to quick spirits is a hell.

And so Brown found it. He quarrelled with his parishioners, struck the constable for demanding a rate from him, was summoned before the magistrate, and committed to Northampton Gaol. He was at the time so decrepid, that he was carried thither on a feather-bed in a cart; where, boasting that he had been put into thirty two prisons, in some of which he could not see his hand at noonday, he died, in the year 1636, and in the eighty first year of his age.

According to Adams, in his 'Dictionary of All Religions,' the principles of Brown were common to Nonconformists long before his time. That he only by his vehement style of preaching, and by his works, 'The Life and Manners of True Christians,' and 'A Treatise of Reformation without Tarrying for Any,' made them more known. To the principles already proclaimed, rather than to Brown, the Independents owe their origin.

Bishop Stillingfleet

This celebrated prelate was a prebendary of Islington, but does not seem ever to have resided there.

John Bagford

This antiquary, and great collector of old English books, prints, &c., whose collections are in the British Museum, died at Islington, May 15, 1716.

Addison

Addison is said to have resided, or lodged rather, at Islington, on the strength of an asserted date from this place of his paper in the 'Spectator,' No. 393, to which, on reference, I find no date at all.

De Foe

De Foe undoubtedly was educated there, at the Nonconformist seminary. Four years under the Rev. Mr. Morton there appears to be all the education that he received. His father, a butcher in St.

Giles, was not rich, and being a dissenter, educated his son as such. De Foe was, therefore, a dissenter in religion, a radical in politics, and a violent opponent of the Stuarts and of Queen Anne's government. These principles paved his way through life with continual martyrdoms. He narrowly escaped being hanged by Jeffreys for engaging in the rebellion of Monmouth. For his satirical pamphlet, 'The Shortest Way with the Dissenters,' which was treated by the dissenters as serious advice to the Government to make away with them, whilst it really was a satire on their treatment by the Government and the Church, he was imprisoned for seditious libel, put in the pillory, and fined. He declared it robbed him of £3,500. After more than a year's imprisonment, and the reduction of his family to destitution, he was still watched, after being set at large, and a scheme set on foot to kidnap him, and compel him into the ranks of the army. He had one short glimpse of political favour, when he was sent as a Commissioner to Scotland to promote the Union, and again he was fined and imprisoned for two pamphlets: 'What if the Queen should Die?' and 'What if the Pretender should Come?' Never was there a more busy, scrambling, wrestling life than that of De Foe. Writing political pamphlets, tracts on political economy, manufacturing of bricks and pantiles, editing a newspaper; writing novels and a history of the Plague in London, he struck upon one conception, that of his 'Robinson Crusoe,' which of itself made him immortal, and the fountain of wonderful delight to all young and adventurous minds for all ages. De Foe kept up his fight for freedom and truth for seventy years, and died in the parish of St. Giles's, Cripplegate.

Edmund Halley, the Astronomer

Halley, the celebrated astronomer-royal, went to reside in Islington in 1682, on his marriage with Mary, daughter of Mr. Tooke, auditor of the Exchequer, and fitted up an observatory there for astronomical purposes; and he continued to reside there till 1696. Halley has been ranked next to Newton. He rendered essential services in the department of astronomy; and amongst these was a voyage to St. Helena in 1676, where he made a catalogue and map of 350 stars of the southern hemisphere, besides adding an observation of the transit of Mercury over the sun's disc, and other valuable items of knowledge. He afterwards went to

Dantzic, and to France, and other parts of the Continent on errands of a like kind. On his road to Paris he was the first to witness the return of the celebrated comet of 1680 from perihelion, after its disappearance in the preceding month. From his observations on this event, Newton verified his deductions in his 'Principia' of a comet's orbit from the theory of gravitation. He stimulated Newton to the publication of the 'Principia,' and superintended the printing of it. In 1698 he was sent out by William III to observe the variations of the compass, to settle the latitude and longitude of various places of the American settlements, and to discover land south of the Western Ocean. He continued his voyage till September, 1700. He visited, in the course of this voyage, the Canaries, Madeira, Cape de Verd Islands, St. Helena, Barbadoes, and Brazils. He afterwards was sent twice to the coast of the Adriatic to assist in the formation and repair of harbours.

A still greater feat is attributed to him by Dr. Sykes, the then Hebrew Professor at Cambridge - that of completing a translation of a rare tract of Apollonius Pergæus from the Arabic, of which he was entirely ignorant, and of making two important corrections in the text. If this be true, he must have been more clairvoyant than the celebrated Swedenborg. In November, 1703, he became Professor of Geometry at Oxford. About 1713 he removed to London, and became Secretary to the Royal Society. The 'Society's Transactions,' from 1686 to 1692, had already been superintended by him as assistant secretary. In this connection, Halley, in alliance with Newton, unfortunately for both their reputations, became concerned in the arbitrary and dishonest conduct towards Flamsteed, the then astronomer-royal, which all lovers of science must for ever deplore. Their breaking open the seal of his catalogue of the fixed stars, and appropriating them, and printing them under the name of Halley, with the title of 'Historia Cœlestis,' the unacknowledged use of his extensive lunar observations, and their rude and insolent conduct to Flamsteed, furnished one of the most melancholy stories in the history of science, and one fully proved by Mr. Francis Baily in his 'Account of the Rev. John Flamsteed.'

Halley is also accused of equal unfairness towards Leibnitz. Not less disgraceful is his recorded conduct towards Robert Hook, in removing his name from observations on a comet in his

'Synopsis Cometica,' and substituting that of Auzout; Hook, it is supposed, having offended him after the first correct publication of the fact.

Halley was the son of a soap-boiler, of Winchester Street, London; but he was born at Haggerston, October 29, 1656. His contributions to the science of astronomy are: 1. The discovery and the detection of the amount of what is called the long inequality of Jupiter and Saturn, which he confidently expected would be shown to be a consequence of the law of gravitation, as was afterwards done. 2. The detection, by comparison of ancient and modern observations of eclipses, of the slow acceleration of the moon's mean motion. 3. The first prediction of the return of a comet, that called after him, 'Halley's Comet.' 4. The explanation of the appearance of Venus at particular seasons, arising out of the now well-known method of estimating the brilliancy of the planet. 5. The recommendation to observe the transit of Venus for the determination of the sun's parallax. Halley died at Greenwich Observatory, in January, 1741-42, in his 86th year.

Topham, the Strong Man

At the south-east corner of Gadd's Row, now St. Alban's Place, formerly lived a man whose feats of strength are only exceeded by those of a Samson or a Hercules. This Thomas Topham was the son of a carpenter, and followed his father's trade till he was of age. At the age of twenty four he became the host of the 'Red Lion,' near the old Hospital of St. Luke. This location he had no doubt chosen because, as Pennant observes, 'Moorfields was the gymnasium of our Capital;' and the famous ring, over which Old Vinegar presided, was the great resort of cudgellers, wrestlers, back-sword players, and boxers, from all parts of the metropolis. Here he gave the first exhibition of his amazing strength, by lying on his back and, placing his feet against the low wall which divided Upper from Lower Moorfields, pulled against a horse. He afterwards pulled against two horses; but his legs being placed horizontally, instead of rising parallel to the traces of the horses, he was jerked from his position, and had one of his knees much hurt. Dr. Desaguliers, who was considered, from his knowledge of mechanics, a good authority, says, that had he been in a proper position, he might have kept his position against the pulling of four horses without the least inconvenience.

On another occasion he proved his strength against a horse, to the great amusement of a crowd. A race being run on the Hackney Road, a fellow with a horse and cart interrupted the pleasures of the spectators by keeping close to the contending parties. Topham suddenly stepped into the road, seized the tail of the cart, and in spite of all the fellow's exertions in whipping his horse to get forward, drew it back. The man was in a towering rage, but dared not apply his lash to a person of such prodigious strength, and the crowd were in the highest delight at the spectacle.

Dr. Desaguliers says he himself saw him perform the following feats: By the strength of his fingers he rolled up a very strong and huge pewter dish of the hardest metal. He broke seven or eight pieces of a tobacco-pipe by the force of his middle finger, having laid them on his first and third finger. Having thrust the bowl of a strong tobacco-pipe under his garter, his legs being bent, he broke it to pieces by the mere action of his muscles, without altering the position of his legs. Another bowl of this kind he broke between his first and second finger, by pressing them together sideways. He took an iron poker, about a yard long and three inches round, and struck upon his left arm, between the elbow and the wrist, as though he had no feeling, till he bent the poker to nearly a right angle. With such another poker, holding the ends of it in his hands, and the middle of it at the hack of his neck, he brought both ends of it together before him; and, what was yet more difficult, he pulled it almost straight again. He broke a rope of two inches circumference, though, in consequence of his awkward manner, he was obliged to exert four times the strength that was necessary. He lifted a rolling-stone of 800 pounds weight with his hands only, standing in a frame above it, and taking hold of a chain that was fastened to it.

Probably the exercise of these feats drew his attention from his business, for he failed at the 'Red Lion,' and afterwards took the 'Duke's Head' at Islington. A print in Kirby's 'Wonderful Museum,' (1803), represents Topham performing the amazing feat of lifting three hogsheads of water, weighing 1,831 pounds, by means of a wooden stage on which he stood over the hogsheads. This he performed publicly in Cold Bath Fields, on May 28, 1741, before Admiral Vernon and thousands of spectators, in commemoration of the taking of Portobello.

Topham not only travelled to exhibit his marvellous powers, but he was fond of an *extempore* lark. On his way home one night, finding a watchman asleep in his box, he lifted man, box, and all upon his shoulders, and carried his load with the greatest ease into Bunhill Fields burying-ground, where he set it down, to the great amazement of the watchman on awaking. On another occasion, sitting at the open window of a public-house, a butcher happened to pass with half an ox on his back. Suddenly stretching out his arm, Topham lifted the load from the butcher's back into the room, to the man's infinite amazement.

Going once on board a vessel lying in the river from the West Indies, he picked up a cocoa-nut and cracked it at the ear of a sailor, just as one might crack an egg-shell, giving the sailor a great fright. That shrewd observer, William Hutton, the historian of Derby, saw Topham there, and relates many marvels of his performances. Alderman Cooper, on his application for a permission to exhibit at a shilling a head, requested him to strip that he might see whether he exhibited muscular development corresponding to the fame of his doings, and he was astonished at the sight of his arms and thighs. He appeared nearly five feet ten inches high, and walked with a slight limp, the consequence of his hurt when pulling against the two horses. Hutton says he could lift two hundredweight with his little finger, and move it gently over his head. He lifted an oak table six feet long with his teeth, though half a hundredweight was hung to the extremity. He broke a rope fastened to the floor that would sustain twenty hundredweight; took up Mr. Chambers, Vicar of All Saints, who weighed twenty seven stone, and raised him with one hand. His head being laid on one chair and his feet on another, four people, fourteen stone each, sate upon his body, whom he heaved at pleasure. Mr. Hutton adds,

> 'Being a master of music, he entertained the company with *Mad Tom*. I heard him sing a solo to the organ in St. Warburgh's Church, then the only organ in Derby; but though he might perform with judgment, the voice was more terrible than sweet, and scarcely seemed human. Though of a pacific temper, and having the appearance of a gentleman, he was liable to the insults of the rude. The ostler at the Virgin's Inn, where he stayed, having offended him, he took one of the kitchen spits from the mantel-piece, and bent it round the fellow's neck like a

handkerchief, but as he did not choose to tuck the ends into the ostler's bosom, the cumbrous ornament excited the laughter of the company, till he condescended to untie his iron cravat.'

In 'The Eccentric Minor,' preceding the account of Topham, there is an engraving of this scene. Hutton says, that Topham had lifted his own horse over a turnpike gate, through which the keeper would not let him pass without an exorbitant toll; and that he carried away the beam of a house, as a soldier carries his firelock.

Two quarrelsome fellows who came to his house would insist on fighting him. Topham, weary of their bravadoes, took each by the neck and knocked their heads together as he would have done those of two boys, till they very humbly begged his pardon, and prayed him to cease.

It is a curious coincidence that this modern Samson had also his Delilah, in the person of a faithless wife, whose infidelities drove him to desperation, in a fit of which he beat her unmercifully, stabbed her in the breast, and then inflicted several wounds upon himself with the same weapon, of which he died in a few days, in the prime of life, on August 10, 1749. This occurred at a public house in Hog Lane, Shoreditch, which he kept, having left Islington.

Unquestionably Thomas Topham, the strong man of Islington, was one of the most powerful men that ever lived.

John Banks
This bookseller and writer of some eminence died at Islington, April 9, 1751. The work he is best known by is 'The Critical Review of the Life of Oliver Cromwell,' which has often been reprinted.

Mrs. Forster, Granddaughter of Milton
Mrs. Forster kept a chandler's shop at Lower Holloway for some years, and died at Islington, May 9, 1754, in the sixty sixth year of her age. In her the family of the author of 'Paradise Lost' became extinct. She had lived many years in indigence, and at last sank under the weight of poverty and the infirmities of age. It does not appear that her grandfather's admirers took any notice of her till 1750, when on April 5 of that year 'Comus' was represented at

Drury Lane Theatre with a new prologue by Dr. Johnson, spoken by Garrick, for her benefit, which produced her £130. Dr. Johnson says she had so little acquaintance with diversion or gaiety, that she did not know what was intended when a benefit was offered her. She knew little of her grandfather, and that little was not good. She told of his harshness to his daughters, and his refusal to have them taught to write; but in opposition to other accounts, represented him as delicate, though temperate in his diet.

This is a fine specimen of how nobility is acquired and rewarded in this country. If a man adds a grand enlargement to the perpetual fame of his country by an achievement of literary powers, he gets ten pounds for his work, and his posterity are suffered to sink into poverty, ignorance, and extinction. If he kills men enough, or sells himself sufficiently to the ministers of the day, or talks loud enough in the courts of law, he is put into the peerage, an estate is frequently bought for him at the national cost, and his posterity continue to revel in affluence and distinction. What numbers of such nobility have we on the benches of our House of Lords; but the descendants of our greatest geniuses, the founders of the brightest and most universal glory of the nation - where are they? But the tree produces fruit of its own kind; the spirit and sentiment of a nation are seen in its rewards. What it really values it recognises; what it does not value, however it may profess to own it, it does not reward.

Collins, the Poet

Collins, the Poet, whose lot fell in evil times, those called, as if in exquisite ridicule, the Augustan Age of England, spent some time at Islington. His noble Odes were pronounced by no mean critic 'only inferior to the divine lyrics of Milton.' Dr. Johnson says, 'Poor dear Collins! I have often been near his state, and have it, therefore, in great commiseration.'

Collins died at Chichester, June 12, 1759. He had lived for some years there in the Cloisters with his sister. Sometimes he was so insane as to 'run howling about the aisles of the cathedral like a houseless dog.' Yet there he wrote his splendid 'Ode on the Superstitions of Scotland,' which, with his other odes, will ever keep their charmed hold on the English mind. Perhaps no lyrical poet has ever combined so much imagination, so much delicate feeling, and so much music in a dozen lines as Collins in his

ODE WRITTEN IN THE YEAR 1746

How sleep the brave, who sink to rest,
By all their country's wishes blest!
When Spring, with dewy fingers cold,
Returns to deck their hallowed mould;
She there shall dress a sweeter sod,
Than Fancy's feet have ever trod.

By fairy hands their knell is rung;
By forms unseen their dirge is sung;
There Honour comes, a pilgrim gray,
To bless the turf that wraps their clay;
And Freedom shall awhile repair,
To dwell, a weeping hermit, there.

His Odes had fallen almost dead from the press, and in his indignation he had burnt all the unsold copies. This neglect was telling awfully on his sensitive nerves, and insanity was waiting for him. To soothe and raise his spirits, he made a tour in France, and on his return settled down in Islington. There Dr. Johnson found him, waiting, he said, for his sister, who had promised to join him. He had but one book! Johnson, curious to know what book was the chosen companion of a man of letters, asked a sight of it. It was an English Testament, such as children carry to school. 'I have but one book,' said Collins, 'but it is the best.' Nothing soothed him so much as the reading of the Bible to him. Afterwards, at Chichester, a servant read to him, but so miserably ill that he was constantly correcting his mistakes.

Johnson never saw Collins after he left Islington, but he continued warmly to sympathise with him, as he had done at an earlier period, when he rescued him from the bailiff, as he also did Goldsmith. Johnson often wrote to Joseph Warton about him. Both the Wartons used to visit him at Chichester, where he finished his days. To Joseph Warton Johnson says,

'How little can we venture to exult in any intellectual powers or literary attainments, when we consider the fate of poor Collins! I knew him a few years ago full of hopes and projects - versed in many languages, high in fancy, and strong in retention. This busy and forcible mind is now under the government of those who lately would not have been able to comprehend the least and most narrow of its designs. Poor dear Collins!'

Colley Cibber

Colley Cibber, one of our most prolific and successful dramatic authors, and Poet Laureate to George II, lived and died in Islington, next to the 'Castle' public house and tea-gardens, mentioned in the twenty sixth paper of the 'Connoisseur.' Besides tragedies and comedies to the number of twenty five, some of which still continue to be played as stock pieces, Cibber adapted Molière's 'Tartuffe' to the English stage, under the name of 'The Nonjuror,' which has again been remodelled as the 'Hypocrite.' Cibber was one of those on whom Pope fell foul in the 'Dunciad,' and on whom many others vented their envy on his becoming Poet Laureate; but he had the sense to take it all in good part. He wrote an 'Apology' for his own life; and two extraordinary epistles to his lampooner, Pope. He died in 1757. His son Theophilus, who followed in his father's dramatic career, but at a great distance as to merit, was drowned on his passage to Ireland in the year of his father's death.

Lewis tells us that Charlotte Charke, the youngest daughter of Cibber, kept a public house at Islington, where she died in 1760; that is only three years after her father. The education that she had received was more suitable to a boy than a girl; and as she grew up she followed the same plan, being found more generally in the stable than the parlour, and a more perfect mistress of the currycomb than the needle. She had a splendid equipage, and numerous servants at her command; yet, unmindful of her advantages and extravagant in her habits, her life was passed in the extremest distress. After her marriage with Mr. Richard Charke, an eminent violin player, of dissolute character, from whom she shortly separated, she applied to the stage, apparently from inclination as well as necessity, and experienced miseries of a kind of which no one who knows anything of the character of a strolling company of actors can he ignorant. In 1755 she came to London, where she published the 'Narrative of her own Life.' By her conduct she seems to have incurred the lasting alienation of her father's regard.

Alexander Cruden, author of the `Concordance'

At a house in Camden Passage, near the west end of Camden Street, and, at an earlier period, Upper Street, Old Paradise Row, lived Alexander Cruden, the author of the 'Concordance of the Old and New Testaments.' In this gentleman we have a curious proof of how much of insanity and sound practical sense can exist in the same person. That Mr. Cruden was actually insane, but with a harmless though sometimes rather intrusive insanity, there can he no doubt. Eccentricity is the mild term for his idiosyncrasy, but does not reach to the full extent of his condition. He was the second son of Mr. William Cruden, a merchant, and chief magistrate of Aberdeen, where he was born, in 1701. He commenced his education at the Grammar School of Aberdeen, where he had for schoolfellows the Earl Marischal and his brother, the celebrated Field-Marshal Keith. He afterwards entered the Marischal College with a view to the ministry. At the age of eighteen, he became attached to the daughter of a clergyman of Aberdeen, who refused him, and this at once brought out the latent excitability of his temperament. He became outrageous, forced his way into her father's house to see her, and the father ordered his doors to be closed against him. This had such an irritating effect upon him, that he was obliged to be kept in confinement for a considerable time. The conduct of the lady soon showed that he had had an excellent escape in her rejection of him, but he never lost the sense of injury he had received. He now gave up all intention of entering the pulpit, and proceeded to London, where he became a private tutor, attending several families, and preparing youths for University. He went as tutor for some time to the Isle of Man, and in 1732 returned to London, and commenced as a corrector of the press and as a bookseller. His shop was under the Royal Exchange, and whilst living there, he met with a severe shock on calling at the house of a gentleman, where the door was opened by the woman of his love, now a woman in peculiar circumstances of disgrace.

In 1733 he began his great work, the 'Concordance of the Scriptures,' a work of immense labour, and which bears all the evidence of clear and wise exercise of his faculties. All his eccentricities were exhibited in his life; in his grand work he manifested nothing but sober intelligence and steady exertion. The amount of labour and care which his persevering research has opened to all Biblical enquirers is beyond calculation. He had expectation of patronage from Queen Caroline, and dedicated the work to her; but she died a few days before the publication, and he suffered a severe loss and disappointment. He had pursued his labour upon it with such ardour, instead of continuing his teaching and employing his leisure hours on his compilation, that through the queen's death, and the slow sale at first, he became involved in debt, and was compelled to close his shop. He was now without employment, without friends, and without hope. He had conferred an immense benefit on the world, and the world yet knew nothing of it. The effect upon his mind was such that it was necessary to send him to a private madhouse at Bethnal Green. His conduct in the asylum was harmless, but singular. On regaining his liberty he published a pamphlet entitled,

'The London Citizen extremely injured: giving an Account of his Adventures during the time of his severe and long Campaign at Bethnal-Green for Nine Weeks and Six Days; the Citizen being sent there in March 1738, by Robert Wightman, a notoriously conceited, whimsical Man; where he was chained, handcuffed, strait-waistcoated, and imprisoned, etc: etc.'

He also commenced an action against Dr. Munro and other defendants, which was tried at Westminster in 1738, but the verdict was given against him. He published an account of this at the time, with remarks on the management of private madhouses, which certainly needed great reforms, but Cruden's reputation was not likely to give proper force to his statements. He dedicated the work to the King.

After this, Mr. Cruden, who certainly never appeared insane in the eyes of his employer, returned to correcting the press, and superintended the publication of several editions of the Greek and Roman classics, which were executed with great accuracy. In this employment he spent several years, making himself of great use to the booksellers in all departments where scholarship was needed. His manners were inoffensive; he was found to be trustworthy, and was most punctual in the fulfilment of his engagements. Again, however, his old attack of insanity came upon him, and he was for the third time shut up in an asylum. On his release, he again published a statement of his case under the title of 'The Adventures of Alexander the Corrector, in three Parts.' Maitland, in his 'History of London,' vol. i. p. 712, says that 'Alexander Cruden, citizen and stationer, much disordered in mind, and lately patient in a madhouse, insisted on being put in nomination at the election for city representatives in the year 1754;' but adds in a note,

'In order to efface any ill impressions which may be made of this gentleman, it is an act of justice to acquaint the world that, upon the strictest enquiry, we find him to be a person of sound morals, unaffected piety, and a sincere well-wisher to all good men, and the useful author of the best Concordance in any language of the Bible.'

Says Nelson:

'The only circumstances by which he was convicted of lunacy in the general opinion, were those which might have in former ages convicted persons of higher distinction. These were an extraordinary zeal for doing good in ways not generally adopted by mankind. He seems to have considered himself appointed as a general reformer; and in his attempts to reform, he departed from accustomed rules, and was sometimes irregular in invading the province of the Divine and the Legislator. But in the manner of doing even these things real insanity may evince itself. No sound person could expect to accomplish what he now attempted. On coming out of the asylum in 1753, he insisted that those who had been the means of his confinement should submit to be imprisoned in Newgate, in compensation of the injuries they had brought upon him. To his sister he proposed what he thought very mild terms - namely, the choice of four prisons - Newgate, Reading, and Aylesbury Gaols, and the prison in Windsor Castle. This as a good-humoured joke might look like a clear idea of intimating poetical justice, but Cruden was perfectly serious in the matter; and as his relatives did not show any disposition to incarcerate themselves in penance, he commenced actions against his sister and three others, which were tried in February, 1754. He laid his damages at £10,000. None but a madman, however innocent, could hope for success in such an attempt. When the verdict was against him, as it was sure to be, he again published the account of their trial in a sixpenny pamphlet, dedicated once more to the King, and went to Windsor to present it, but was refused admittance. Not discouraged by these repeated rebuffs, he solicited the honour of knighthood, and, of course, with the same result. His madness now took the form of endeavouring to induce or oblige people to keep the Sabbath according to his own notions. He went to exhort all whom he found walking in the streets on Sundays to go home and keep the day holy. He took a violent aversion to John Wilkes, then in the height of his popularity, and used to traverse the streets with a piece of wet sponge to wipe from walls and shutters the celebrated No. 45 wherever he found it chalked up. Not content with this, he wrote a pamphlet against Wilkes. All words and phrases injurious to good morals he also expunged from the public walls; and he would enter any mob or tumultuous assembly of people, without the authority of a magistrate, and in a solemn and commanding manner desire the contending parties to depart quietly to their homes, which, from his venerable appearance, and the mildness of his address, would often produce the desired effect.'

During all this time Mr. Cruden was pursuing his profession as a corrector of the press, and in enlarging and improving his 'Concordance' with the most sane and exemplary propriety. He was fortunate enough to be allowed to present a copy of his second edition of the 'Concordance' to the King in person, though he did not get knighted for it, as probably he hoped. He was at this time corrector of the press to the 'Public Advertiser,' the newspaper of Mr. Henry Woodfall, in which the stinging epistles of Junius appeared. His mania of philanthropy, for such it was, however commendable, had now also a great triumph, and it was a wonderful one in that age. He managed by incessant and undaunted applications to the Earl of Halifax, then Secretary of State, to get the sentence of one Richard Potter, who was tried and convicted for uttering, knowing it to be forged, a seaman's will, commuted to transportation. Such a success was amazing, for no crime was more inflexibly expiated on the gallows at that period. But Cruden represented Potter as a poor ignorant creature, who knew no better, and was in reality the tool of another; and he exerted himself with the man to instruct him in the principles of religion, and convert him to a good member of society. He prayed with him, conversed with him on the true ends of life, and to all appearance with much success. He completed his Christian benevolence to this man by clothing and feeding him, and preparing him for his new life in another hemisphere. In token of his gratitude, Mr. Cruden presented to the Earl of Halifax a copy of the second edition of his 'Concordance,' to which was prefixed an elegant Latin dedication to his lordship.

Delighted with his success, Cruden continued his labours amongst the prisoners in Newgate. He visited them every day, gave them New Testaments, catechisms, &c., instructed them, and bestowed small pecuniary rewards on the most persevering. He was doomed to disappointment, for he found his books exchanged for money, and the money expended in drink; and he abandoned his noble design in despair. But his example was not lost. At a later day, Mrs. Fry, and the ladies of the Society of Friends, took up the good work, and brought it at the same time under the influence of men of political influence; so that out of this humble beginning, reform of our prisons has developed.

Mr. Cruden, to extend the knowledge of what might be done amongst convicts, published 'The History of Richard Potter.' He also, in returning one Sunday evening from a place of worship, cast his eye on the face of a man in which, to his quick glance, misery and despair were profoundly scored. He immediately fell into conversation with him, and in the end drew from him the confession that the deep destitution of his family had driven him to the contemplation of suicide. He expostulated with him on the wickedness of his intentions, and did not rest till he had afforded him such assistance as restored him to peace and comfort.

In 1769, Mr. Cruden returned to his native city, Aberdeen. There he set himself with great ardour to reform his townspeople. He gave a lecture in a public hall, and exhorted all of every rank to mend their ways. He had the fourth commandment printed in the form of a handbill, and distributed to all persons that he met in the streets on Sunday. For young people he had his pockets full of tracts, and some of them of considerable price, which he gave to all who promised to read them. He was very winning in his manner with children, but to some persons his simply presenting a tract was an act of satire. To a conceited young clergyman he gave the little catechism used by children in Scotland, called the 'Mother's Catechism, dedicated to the young and ignorant.'

After a year's labour of this kind at Aberdeen, he returned to London, and resumed his lodgings in Camden Street, where he died, November 1, 1770, in the sixty ninth year of his age. He left £5 per annum to assist in educating a student at the Marischal College.

In the heart of Alexander Cruden there was no insanity. It was animated by a zealous love of mankind, but his head had that touch of disorder which gave an odd character to his proceedings, and he had that indomitable tenacity of purpose which is generally a symptom of lunacy. In his later years, he suddenly stepped up to a young lady who was walking with a gentleman in the street, and made her an offer. Such absurd outbreaks of fancy are decisive of disorder of mind. The miracle is, that in his great work, 'The Concordance,' not a trace of his malady appeared. He compiled also a Concordance of Milton's works - a labour of scarcely less extent than that of his 'Concordance.' He compiled, moreover, 'An Account of the History and Excellency of the Scriptures,' and a Scriptural dictionary, or 'Guide to the Holy Scriptures.' He was an Independent, and for the greater part of his life attended Dr. Guise's meetings; but after Dr. Guise became superannuated, he attended Dr. Conder's chapel, on the Pavement, Moorfields, going to Dr. Guise's old chapel on the first Sunday in every month, when the Sacrament was administered. Undoubtedly, Alexander Cruden was one of the most extraordinary men who ever lived in Islington.

James Burgh, John Allingham, Dr. Nicholas Robinson and Isaac Ritson

James Burgh, author of 'Dignity of Human Nature,' 'Political Disquisitions,' and other works, lived in Colebrooke Row, Islington. In the same row lived John Allingham, a wine merchant and dramatic writer; Dr. Nicholas Robinson, a celebrated physician and medical writer, died at Islington. Isaac Ritson, a young man who died at the age of twenty seven, who translated 'Homer's Hymn to Venus,' Hesiod's 'Theogony,' and was author of various productions, also lived in Islington; and many other men of about the same literary rank.

Joseph and Mrs. Collyer

Joseph Collyer was the translator of Klopstock's 'Messiah,' and of 'Noah,' another work from the German. Mrs. Mary Collyer, his wife, had also the reputation of having translated Gesner's popular romance, 'The Death of Abel,' from the same language; but Nelson, in his second edition of the 'History of Islington,' says that it was not done by her, but by a Mr. Mackay, who gave it to Mr. Collyer, who was a printer, of Plough Court, Fetter Lane, who affixed the dedication to Queen Charlotte, just then arrived in England, as translated by Mary Collyer, a widow, to provide by its sale for her children. A copy was sent to the Queen, and graciously received; but the Queen expressing a desire to see the widow, Mrs. Collyer, who knew no language but her own, took care not to appear.

This Mr. and Mrs. Collyer resided in Islington. Their son Joseph was a celebrated engraver in the stippled style. He was senior associate engraver of the Royal Academy, and his works are conceived in his own peculiar style of art.

Oliver Goldsmith

We have already noticed that Goldsmith was fond of making holiday visits to Islington and Highbury, and that he had also lodgings occasionally in Canonbury Tower, where he was near his publisher, Mr. Newbery, and where he is said to have written part of his 'Vicar of Wakefield,' the whole of his 'Deserted Village,' and probably his 'Traveller.' Having in my 'Homes and Haunts of the Poets' related the incidents of Goldsmith's residence here, I now merely transcribe those passages:

'In 1762 Goldsmith quitted Wine-office Court, and took lodgings in the house of a Mrs. Elizabeth Fleming, in Islington. This was to be near his friend, Mr. Newbery. Here he continued till 1764, chiefly employed upon job-work for Newbery; of which the most important was, "Letters of a Nobleman to his Son," and the "History of England." He used to relieve the monotony of his life by weekly visits to the Literary Club, of which Johnson, Burke, and Sir Joshua Reynolds were principal members, and which was held at the Turk's Head, Gerrard Street, Soho. Here, there is every reason to believe, occurred the event already alluded to,—the threat of arrest, and the sale of the [manuscript] of the "Vicar pf Wakefield" by Johnson to liberate him. Of this story there have been various versions. Mrs. Piozzi, Sir John Hawkins, Cumberland, and Boswell, all relate it; all profess to have heard it from Johnson, and yet each tells it very differently. In all these stories, however, there is a landlady demanding arrears of rent, and bailiffs waiting to arrest if the money were not forthcoming. All agree that Goldsmith was drinking, most of them say Madeira, to drown his vexation; and Cumberland adds, that the landlady proposed the alternative of payment or marriage. Whether the latter point were really included in the demand, is not ever likely to be known; but that Mrs. Fleming, who went by the name of Goldsmith's hostess, and is thus painted by Hogarth, was the woman in question I think there can be little doubt; though Prior, the biographer, would fain exempt her from the charge, and suppose the scene to occur in some temporary lodging. There does not appear the smallest ground for such a supposition. All facts point to this place and person. Goldsmith had been here for a year and a half; for Prior himself gives the particulars of this landlady's bill reaching to June 22. As it occurred in this year, and about this time; for it is expressly stated that the "Vicar of Wakefield" was kept about two years by the bookseller unpublished - and it was not published till the end of March, 1766 - it could not possibly happen anywhere else. He could not have left Mrs. Fleming, or if he had, he could not have been away long enough to accumulate any alarming score. Here, on the contrary, everything indicates that he was in debt and difficulty. He bad been at least a year and a half here, and might, and probably had run a good way into his landlady's books. Tbe biographer states expressly that Goldsmith was in great difficulties, and for some months invisible - said to have made a trip into Yorkshire. The biographer also shows that Newbery, the bookseller, generally paid the landlady for Goldsmith; but it came out that Goldsmith was now also very far behind with Newbery, owing him no less than £111; and next comes an obvious dislocation with Newbery himself. It is a fact which does not seem to have struck the biographer, that when Johnson sold the [manuscript] of the "Vicar of Wakefield," he did not sell it to Newbery, though Newbery was not only Goldsmith's publisher, but his own. He went and sold it to a nephew of Newbery's, Mr. Francis Newbery, of Paternoster Row. Now there must have been a reason for this; and what so likely as that Goldsmith, having run too deeply into debt, had alarmed Newbery - publishers are careful men - that he not only had refused to advance more, but had withdrawn his guarantee to the landlady. This being the case, Goldsmith would be at his wit's end. With long arrears of rent and board, for Mrs. Fleming found that too, and the security withdrawn by Newbery, she would be alarmed, and insist on Goldsmith's paying. To Newbery he could not fly, and in his despair he sent for Johnson. Johnson sold the novel, but not to Newbery. With him it would only have gone to reduce the standing claim; with another, it would bring what was wanted, instant cash. What confirms this view of the case is, the fact, that immediately after this Goldsmith did quit his old landlady and returned to London.

Canonbury Tower, or Canonbury House, as it is indifferently called, is often said to have been a residence of Goldsmith, and the room is shown which he used to occupy, and where it is said he wrote the "Deserted Village." The reason, besides, that it was near Newbery, given for Goldsmith going to live at Islington, is, that it was a pleasant village. When Goldsmith's difficulties increased, probably he found it convenient to hide from his creditors in the tower, where he lay concealed for days and weeks. Very probably he was there all the time he was said to be in Yorkshire. He is supposed to have made a visit to the tower in 1767, when his permanent abode was in the Temple; but he had apartments for the summer in Canonbury Tower, and was visited there by most of his literary friends. On many of these occasions they adjourned to a social dinner at the "Crown" in the Lower Road, where tradition states them to have been very jolly. These periods admit of part of the "Vicar of Wakefield," and of the whole of the "Deserted Village" being written here.'

Dr. Richard Price

On the western side of Newington Green, in the Parish of Islington, lived at one time this distinguished Nonconformist minister, who made so prominent a figure during the periods of the American War and the French Revolution, by the ardour of his spirit of liberty, and at the same time by his profound skill in financial calculations.

Dr. Price, as stated, was born at Tynton, in Glamorganshire, February 23, 1723, a son of a second marriage, with his living to make in the world. On arriving in London he obtained, through the influence of a paternal uncle, admission to a Dissenting academy, where he pursued his studies in mathematics, philosophy, and theology. In 1743 he engaged himself as chaplain and companion of the family of Mr. Sheathfield, of Stoke Newington. In this family he continued thirteen years, and soon after the death of his patron became morning preacher at the chapel on Newington Green. He married in 1757, and in the following year acquired a great reputation by the publication of his first work, 'Review of the Principal Questions and Difficulties of Morals.' In 1767 a number of gentlemen of the legal profession consulted him on a plan for securing annuities to their widows. This turned his attention to such plans, and led him to the discovery of the generally defective system on which life assurance societies and the like were based. His treatise on 'Reversionary Payments,' 1769, quickly destroyed a number of the most rotten of them, and produced a reform of the rest. On such subjects Dr. Price became the great authority, publishing 'Short and Easy Theories for finding in all cases the difference between the Value of Annuities payable yearly, half-yearly, quarterly, and monthly;' and 'On the Proper Method of calculating the Value of Reversions depending on Survivorship.' His 'Northampton Tables' were, till recently, the common basis of calculations of life assurance companies, and were superseded only by an actual alteration in the ratio of mortality, owing to the more healthy modes of life, which he himself was one of the first to bring about by his remarks on the different effects on population and longevity betwixt town and country; on the insalubrity of marshy situations, etc.

The American War aroused him to the defence of human liberties, and his 'Observations on Civil Liberty, and the Justice and Policy of the War with America,' placed him in the foremost ranks of liberal philosophers. The French Revolution strengthened these principles in him, but did not, as in many other cases, shake his deeply-seated religious convictions. He had vigorous but friendly contests with Dr. Priestley on materialism, necessity, etc., and ably vindicated the immortality of the soul, and the doctrines of revealed religion. He was the friend of Howard the Philanthropist, Priestley, Franklin, and most of the prominent reformers of the time. Pitt consulted him on the best mode of liquidating the National Debt, the result of which is said to have been the adoption of the Sinking Fund. Dr. Price died in 1791, having passed through an active existence and an amount of usefulness rarely accomplished by one man. His works are numerous. In the Presbyterian Chapel at Stoke Newington there is an inscription to his memory, designating him justly, as 'Theologian, Philosopher, Mathematician; Friend to Freedom as to Virtue; Brother of Man; Lover of Truth as of God.'

Rev. George Marriott

The Rev. George Marriott, rector of Twinstead, in Essex, and lecturer of St. Luke's, Old Street, died at Islington in 1798. He had been chaplain to the British Factory, in Sweden, and was the author of several poems.

Rev. John Palmer

The Rev. John Palmer lived at Islington some years, and died there in 1790. He was author of a 'Defence of the Liberty of Man as a Moral Agent,' in reply to Priestley, and various other works of a religious character.

Mary Woolstonecraft

Mary Woolstonecraft taught a day-school at Newington Green when she was twenty four years of age, and there made the acquaintance of Dr. Richard Price, in whom she must have found a congenial soul, so far as freedom and human progress were concerned. As authoress of the 'Rights of Woman,' the wife of William Godwin, the author of 'Caleb Williams' and of 'Political Justice,' the mother of Mrs. Shelley, this remarkable woman has a host of titles to immortality. Though much and severely criticised for her opinions in her own day, every year since has been bringing her theories nearer and nearer to practical realities; and we now see such men as John Stuart Mill, John Ruskin, and a multitude of profoundly enlightened men, calling on the nation to concede to woman those rights which Mary Godwin so eloquently advocated. She died in August, 1797, and her remains lie in Old St. Pancras churchyard.

Baron D'Aguilar

Baron D'Aguilar, One of the most extraordinary, and at the same time most cruel and revolting wretches who ever lived anywhere, resided at No. 21 in Camden Street, Islington. This was a Portuguese Jew, named Baron Ephraim Lopez Pereira D'Aguilar. He had also a small yard and barn for many years on the west bank of the New River, at the place where it emerges from beneath the road near the south end of Colebrooke Row. The subject of our present notice was the son of Baron Diego D'Aguilar, a Portuguese Jew, who died in England in 1759. He was born at Vienna, about the year 1740, and on the death of his father succeeded to his title and estates. In 1757 he was naturalised, and about the same time married the daughter of Moses Mendez Da Costa, Esq., a rich merchant, of London. Miss Da Costa's large fortune was luckily settled on herself previous to their marriage. He had two daughters by this lady, who, on their mother's death, which occurred in 1763, inherited her property.

In the year 1767 Baron D'Aguilar married his second wife, the widow of Benjamin Da Costa, Esq., a merchant. During his first, and a short portion of his second marriage, the Baron lived in great splendour in the house built by his father-in-law, Mendez da Costa, in Broad Street Buildings. He kept an elegant establishment of carriages, horses, and, as he often boasted, of between twenty and thirty servants. All at once, however, he began to change his mode of living. The plea was the loss of a considerable estate in America, through the war; but this loss demanded no such extra-ordinary retrenchment. Perhaps the real cause was his dissatisfaction with his second wife. She is reported to have been a good and accomplished woman, and probably was much too refined for so base and sordid a wretch as he eventually proved to be. His wife's large fortune was, with Jewish care, also settled securely on herself. Whatever was the cause, however, he threw up his house in Broad Street, withdrew from his family connections and the gay world, and assumed an air of poverty. With this change came also a change in his habits. He grew rapidly mean, penurious, dirty, and disgusting in his manners. He treated his wife with the utmost brutality; locked her up in a hayloft, starved and insulted her. For this conduct he was successfully prosecuted in the Court of King's Bench. During the trial he appeared with the utmost unconcern in open court; and when the verdict was against him, impudently petitioned the Bench to cause his wife to pay half the expenses, on account of his poverty. He was in reality extremely rich.

The Baroness D'Aguilar died six or seven years before her miserable husband. Whilst she was living, he took a house in Shaftesbury Place, Aldersgate Street, as well as the one in Camden Street, Islington. In these houses he kept a number of women whom he had seduced, and by whom he had numerous illegitimate children. These women and their families all lived together in these abodes of infamy. Besides these houses he had two at Bethnal Green, crammed with the costly furniture which he removed from Broad Street Buildings, and which he never used afterwards. He had also a mansion at Twickenham, which he used to call his country house; but this, too, was shut up, and a man, on a small monthly pittance, kept an eye over it. Besides these he had another shut-up house at Sydenham, with a few cattle on the premises; but these he suffered to be really starved to death, the man who had care of them, a poor shoemaker, having kept them alive as long as he could, but as he could neither get to see nor hear from the baron, they all perished.

ut the perfection of his cruelty to animals was seen on a farm which he had at Islington, and which acquired the name of 'Starvation Farm.' The baron carefully apportioned the food which his cattle was allowed, and frequently gave it them with his own hands; but it was so miserably deficient, that the poor creatures perished piecemeal. Their stalls and yard were never cleaned out, and were literally one great dung hill. When any of them died, he ordered the man who had charge of them to bury them in the heap of manure, and at his death it is reported that the remains of nearly forty carcases of such starved-to-death creatures were found in the accumulated refuse heap of years. On one occasion the man sold the body of a starved calf to a vendor of dog's meat; but he summoned the man before a magistrate for embezzling his property, had 1s. 10d. deducted from his wages - the amount received for the dead calf - and then he turned him away.

Such was the ravenous famine amongst his stock on this 'Starvation Farm,' that the animals attacked and devoured each other. The pigs chased and devoured the famished and skeleton fowls. There was no society then for the protection of animals, or the baron would have been arrested in his detestable career; but the populace in their indignation hooted and pelted the miserable baron whenever they could get a sight of him on the premises, which was in a squalid dress, covered with filth. In Granger's 'Wonderful Museum' there are portraits of Baron D'Aguilar, and a view of 'Starvation Farm.'

On one occasion he villainously had the carcase of one of his starved cattle slyly thrown into the New River, and narrowly escaped a prosecution for it. At this farm he kept locked up his old favourite coach, a cumbrous machine drawn in his gala days by four horses, which now passed a miserable hungry existence on 'Starvation Farm.' Nelson says:

> `Having totally forsaken all genteel society, and given himself up to the most wretched and abandoned pursuits, he never cared to see any of his

family, or his former respectable connections. He would sarcastically tell his sons-in-law that they were gentlemen, and not fit associates for him; and his daughters that they were too fine to sit in his company. The large estate which he lost in America he never attempted to recover; nor would he suffer any person to interfere in the business, though with a probability of success. He is said to have been an excellent scholar; to have written with great elegance and facility; and he had some of his natural children educated under the first masters, and behaved towards them with the greatest paternal kindness.

In his last illness, notwithstanding the severity of the weather, and the dangerous nature of his complaint, he would not allow a fire in his house, nor admit a doctor into his presence; but he followed the prescriptions of a medical man, to whom he sent every day a fee of one guinea, with a statement of his symptoms. His youngest daughter affectionately sent several times in his last moments, begging permission to see him, but with dreadful imprecations, to which he was much addicted, he declared she should never enter his presence. He died at his house in Shaftesbury Place, on March 16, 1802, at the age of sixty-two. His body was removed to Islington, and thence carried to the Jews' Burial-ground at Mile-End.

Thus lived and died the Baron D'Aguilar, who possessed both the means and the ability for the exercise of virtuous and munificent actions; but whose life was, for the most part, absorbed in habits the most unnatural, inhuman, and degrading. He left two legitimate daughters, who, by his dying intestate, administered, and came into possession of all his property, while a number of poor objects, who had natural claims on his protection, and who had been supported by him in his lifetime, were left altogether destitute.

The Baron's effects at Islington were sold by auction, which lasted two days; his stock of lean cattle sold for 128*l*, and his favourite coach, which was almost dropping to pieces, was bought for 7*l*, for the sake of the springs. He had a valuable library in Shaftesbury Place, consisting of Hebrew, English, and foreign literature, which was also sold. His diamonds, jewels, &c., were reported to be worth 30,000*l*; and his plate consisted of seven hundredweight, in articles of various descriptions. He had, moreover, a stock of about forty bags of cochineal, and twelve bags of fine indigo, probably worth near 10,000*l*. These articles he had purchased many years before his death on speculation, resolving never to part with them until he had a desirable profit. The total bulk of his property is supposed to have been upwards of 200,000*l*.'

On what system, social, physical or metaphysical, are we to explain these enigmas of the human race? Is it a peculiar species of insanity which takes a pleasure in whatever is low, vile, degrading, and cruel? Are such persons possessed by unclean spirits? or is it avarice, which, overcoming the early fondness for social station and display, brings to light the really preponderating elements of their character? Avarice, filth, and cruelty usually hold together by a primæval and powerful affinity. Baron D'Aguilar was not only cruel to animals, but still more so to human beings, and pre-eminently to his own mistresses and children. He was kind and affectionate, we are told, to his natural children; but after educating them highly, and rendering them the more sensitive to the impressions of poverty and neglect, he left them to these miseries at his death with the most heartless indifference. The real causes which go to the production of these revolting characters seem to defy the profoundest powers of intellectual analysis. We are compelled to content ourselves with the assertion of the inspired Hebrew: `The human heart is deceitful above all things, and desperately wicked.'

Alexander Aubert

Mr. Alexander Aubert, a merchant of London, lived in Islington many years, and was buried there in 1805. Mr. Aubert appears to have been a very accomplished man, and very influential amongst his neighbours. He was wealthy, and was made Lieutenant-Colonel of the Islington Volunteers in 1792. He was on friendly terms with William Pitt, Lord Melville, George Rose, and the leading Conservatives of his time, and occasionally entertained them at his house at Highbury, where he had an observatory. But the circumstance which will longest preserve his memory, is that he was a zealous friend and patron of Smeaton, the engineer. Under his directions chiefly, Smeaton enlarged and improved the harbour of Ramsgate. He revised and corrected for publication Smeaton's account of the building of Eddystone Lighthouse, and promoted his interests in every possible way.

Abraham Newland

Abraham Newland, the celebrated manager of the Bank of England, resided at Highbury many years. This gentleman, whose name for so many years figured on the notes of the Bank of England of a value, taken altogether, almost incalculable, was the son of a baker in Castle Street, in Southwark. He was educated for the counting-house, and in his eighteenth year took his seat as a clerk in the Bank of England, whose chief cashier he was destined to become. Abraham Newland was a bachelor, and of careful habits. Of course, therefore, he became very rich; but he continued to lead a citizen sort of life, which would greatly astonish gentlemen of his class and affluence now. At fifteen minutes past nine o'clock in the morning Mr. Newland was constantly seen at his desk in the Bank, and was never absent from his duty until three in the afternoon. Though he possessed a handsome house in a fine situation, with ample grounds, and though the surrounding country was most pleasant and inviting, he never enjoyed the pleasures it afforded for many hours at a time; for while he retained his situation at the Bank, he constantly kept his apartments in that building. His usual practice was to repair to Highbury in his carriage after dinner, drink tea with his housekeeper, and afterwards perambulate the path along the front of the houses, or take a walk on the gravel-way leading to Highbury Barn, returning invariably to London to sleep!

This extraordinary specimen of a plodding citizen, who preferred the air of London to that of the country, who balanced his household books every evening before he went to bed, and who, with a property of £130,000, spent only a few hundreds a year, did contemplate, ever and anon, organising an establishment of a more commanding character, and actually on the scale of £6,000 per annum. But it was merely a dream - he never did it; but he did prevail on himself to retire from business, and resign his situation, on September 17, 1807, whereupon, like many another old plodder, with no other interest or passion in the world but business, he immediately collapsed - died out and disappeared - on November 21 of the same year, or in two months and three days from his renouncing the habits of a life of nearly sixty years! His actual age was seventy-seven years.

It is scarcely necessary to say that this bank automaton was in politics what is called a King's man; that is, that he worshipped the government by whose business he grew rich, but that he had forgotten to worship anything higher, being, says his biographer, in this respect only like too many more who are so devoted to manufacturing wealth, that they even forget there is a God, and therefore but dimly believe in Him. The witty song of Charles

Dibdin, junr., sung at Sadler's Wells Theatre, will always perpetuate the name of this curiosity of Threadneedle Street:

> There ne'er was a name so bandied by Fame,
> Through air, through ocean, and thro' land,
> As one that is wrote on every bank-note:
> You must all know *Abraham Newland!*
> Oh! Abraham Newland,
> Notified Abraham Newland!
> I've heard people say, 'sham Abraham' you may,
> But you musn't sham Abraham Newland.

Dr. William Hawes

Dr. William Hawes was Founder of the Royal Humane Society. If the Royal Literary Fund owes its origin to a Dissenting minister of Highgate, Islington possesses as great an honour in being the birthplace of the founder of the Royal Humane Society. William Hawes, M.D., who first projected, and was from its establishment to the termination of his life the chief supporter of this excellent Society, was born in this place in 1736. His father for many years kept the house formerly called 'Job's House,' but better known as 'The Old Thatched House Tavern,' during whose time it was burnt down and rebuilt on the same site, and again was pulled down on the formation of Halton Street. He received the early part of his education in the seminary of honest John Shield, in Islington, and completed it at St. Paul's School. On the expiration of his apprenticeship to Mr. Cansan at Vauxhall, he became assistant to Mr. Dicks in the Strand, whom he succeeded in business. In 1773 he began to attract public notice by his incessant endeavours to awake a general attention to the resuscitation of drowned persons. With the usual slowness of the English people to receive new ideas, no effect had been produced by the many zealous articles during the preceding thirty years which had appeared in the 'Gentleman's Magazine,' recommending this practice. With all this preparation for his humane labours, Dr. Hawes found his endeavours to save the lives of his countrymen who had the misfortune to drown, not merely received with indifference, but with ridicule, animosity, and opposition. He was treated, as such enlightened innovators always are, as a silly enthusiast, as a man seeking notoriety by attempting extraordinary and absurd achievements. The recovery of people apparently drowned was declared, even by medical men, an impossibility. Dr. Hawes, however, was made of the true stuff; one of those men whom Providence raises up and maintains by his omnipotent spirit to do the so-called impossible in defiance of prejudice and persecution. He took the surest measures of obtaining opportunity to prove the practicability of resuscitation, by advertising rewards to persons who, between Westminster and London Bridges, should, within a certain time after the accident, rescue drowned persons from the water, and bring them ashore to places appointed for their reception, notice being immediately given to him, and prompt means used for their recovery. For twelve months Dr. Hawes continued to pay these rewards himself, and case after case of successful recovery being effected and made known, the public mind was at length effectually aroused to the reality of such recovery, and to the immense good to be done by its regular practice. Dr. Cogan, the well-known translator of the works of Camper, and author of religious and philosophical works, remonstrated with Dr. Hawes on the ruin to his private fortune which the continuance of his rewards for the recovery of drowned persons would bring upon him, recommending that they should form a society for this special purpose. Dr. Hawes accepted the idea. They agreed each to bring forward fifteen friends to a meeting at the 'Chapter Coffee House,' in 1774, and there and then The Humane Society was established. In the following year an excellent sermon, preached at St. Bride's Church by the Rev. R. Harrison, excited a considerable interest in its behalf. The personal exertions of Dr. Hawes were, however, still constantly demanded to sustain and extend the sympathy with the Society's labours, without which there would probably at this moment be none of those kindred institutions now planted in India, America, and throughout Europe, wherever, indeed, there are great rivers or other waters.

The mind of Dr. Hawes was incessantly at work to prevent loss of life in various ways. In 1774 he published 'An Account of Dr. Goldsmith's last Illness,' whose death he ascribed to the improper administration of a popular medicine, and pointed out the danger of using powerful drugs. In 1777 appeared his 'Address on Premature Death and Premature Interment,' which he distributed extensively, to awaken a salutary caution in the public mind against the interment of persons supposed to be dead before it had been clearly ascertained that they were so. This was a subject which had long dwelt in his mind, even before that of the resuscitation from drowning. Still, at this time, we are as a people too careless on this subject. The Germans in many places have houses appointed for the reception of persons who, though apparently dead, show no signs of decomposition. The dead are not buried so soon in England as in many other countries, but in all cases where there is not an absolute certainty of death having taken place, the body should be kept till signs of decomposition appear.

At the General Court of the Directors of the Humane Society in 1776, Dr. Towers presiding, the Society had to congratulate itself on the number of successful and astonishing cases of recovery from drowning, and high encomiums were pronounced on the invaluable labours of Dr. Hawes and his colleague, Dr. Cogan. In 1780 'An Examination of the Rev. John Wesley's Primitive Physic,' by Dr. Hawes, had reached a third edition. In the recommendation of popular remedies by the venerable founder of the Methodist Society, Dr. Hawes saw much danger to those who put great faith in him, and exposed with much irony, as well as serious argument, the absurdity of many of the nostra recommended by him to popular use. In 1781 he removed to Palgrave Place, and commenced practice there as a physician, having long possessed a diploma of M.D. In this year he presented an address to the Legislature on the importance of the Humane Society; and an address to the King and Parliament with observations on the General Bills of Mortality. These publications greatly raised his reputation both as a man of science and benevolence. In that year, too, he was elected Physician to the Surrey Dispensary, and immediately commenced a series of lectures on everything connected with suspended animation, being the first person who ever introduced the subject into medical education. These lectures extended to the following topics: The causes of suspended animation, and the most effective modes of recovery. The sundry derangements which suspend the action of the principal vital organs, the brain, the lungs, and the heart, with the best means of reviving their functions. An enquiry into the effects of animal, vegetable, and mineral poisons; their power of suddenly destroying the vital functions, and the most approved methods of preventing or neutralising their action. On modes of recovering people from syncope, inebriation, drowning, suffocation, cold or lightning. Remarks on still-born infants, and the most efficacious modes of restoring vital action. The various symptoms of apparent death occasionally occurring in acute diseases; measures for surmounting these; and, lastly, signs of death which are real and those which are dubious. In short, Dr. Hawes devoted his whole intellectual energies to counteracting the approach of death, through various channels. He closed his lectures by proposing prize medals, gold and silver, to be awarded to those who most effectively promoted these objects. In October 1782 the first gold medal was conferred on Dr. Richard Pearson, of Birmingham, and the silver medal on a writer under the name of 'Humanitas.' Since then, similar medals bestowed by the Medical Society have given rise to the invaluable works of Pearson, Goodwin, Coleman, Kite, Fothergill, &c.

In 1793, when the cotton manufactures had superseded those of silk, and the artisans of Spitalfields were reduced to starvation, chiefly through his exertions, and a letter which he published on the occasion, 1,200 families were snatched from ruin. In 1796 he published the 'Transactions of the Royal Humane Society from 1774 to 1784,' with a dedication to the King. Dr. Hawes had the satisfaction of not only seeing the most successful operations of the Society in London, but of assisting to found others in Edinburgh, Manchester, Bath, &c., and of corresponding with the founders of that of Massachusetts in the United States of America, and in almost every quarter of the globe. In the midst of these philanthropic labours he died, on December 5, 1808, in Spital Square, in his seventy third year. His remains were deposited in the new cemetery attached to the churchyard at Islington. His funeral was attended by the leading members of the Royal Humane Society, amongst whom were Dr. Lettsom and other eminent medical men. The Society erected a marble tablet to his memory in the church. Few are the men who have left the earth having more nobly discharged their duty to mankind.

Benjamin Hawes

This youngest brother of Dr. Hawes was also a native of

Islington, and scarcely less meritorious. He acquired a large fortune in the indigo trade in Thames Street, and bestowed his wealth with a liberal hand in relieving the distresses of his fellow-creatures. Many deserving men struggling with adversity received considerable transfers of bank-stock from him, but without being able to discover their benefactor. He took a zealous interest in the suppression of the slave trade, and in a letter to Mr. Wilberforce he offered to sacrifice several thousands a year towards a plan for compelling the Powers of Europe to abandon that detestable traffic. In all these cases he stipulated for the concealment of his name. He was for forty eight years a liberal subscriber to the Humane Society founded by his brother. He died at Worthing suddenly, when out walking, in 1822; and bequeathed, after the death of his niece, £24,000 to twenty different benevolent institutions - £1,000 to each [*sic*].

James Elphinston

James Elphinston, a critic and author of philological works, was the uncle of Dr. Strahan, vicar of Islington, by the marriage of his sister with Mr. Strahan, the great printer. He accompanied Carte, the historian, in a tour through Holland and Brabant to Paris. He was a great admirer of Dr. Johnson, and zealously promoted the circulation of 'The Rambler' in Edinburgh. In 1753 he left Scotland and settled at Brompton, and afterwards at Kensington, where he kept a large school. He translated Racine, the younger's, poem on 'Religion,' and wrote poems of his own; but his great distinction was the anticipation of the present system of phonography, or spelling of words according to their pronunciation. In later life he lived at Islington, but died at Hammersmith in 1809, aged eighty seven.

Joseph White

Joseph White, a collector of Saxon coins, and a naturalist, died at Islington in 1810.

Sir Brook Boothby

Sir Brook Boothby, the translator of 'Sappho,' and author of some poems, resided at Islington about this time [1810], though his ancestral estate was at Ashbourne, in Derbyshire.

William Huntington

William Huntington, one of the most extraordinary men of his time, lived at a house called 'Hermes Hill,' which had been the residence of a Dr. Valangin, a noted Swiss physician. This house was near the White Conduit spring, which passed by White Conduit House to the Priory of St. John, Clerkenwell, and to the Charter House. Huntington was originally a coalheaver, and gloried in the name. He has related his story in his book called 'The Bank of Faith.' He was born of peasant parents, in Kent, in 1744, and in his youth worked as a labourer and became a coalheaver. At one period of his life he fell into infidelity and wickedness, but becoming converted, he joined the Calvinistic Methodists, and became a very powerful and original preacher amongst them. He preached at one time at Margaret Street, in London; at Richmond, at Ditton, at Cobham, at Woking, at Warplesdon, and at Farnham, in Surrey, and used to walk to all these places; but feeling it at last too much for his strength, he acquired a horse. He had the most profound faith in the efficacy of prayer, calling it 'the Almighty Power of the Prayer of Faith,' and he records the most extraordinary instances of his being rescued from utter distress by the answers to his prayers. Whilst living at Hermes Hill, in 1811, the spring of the conduit having become choked, he attempted to clear it for the use of the neighbouring inhabitants, but the low mob, who disliked his homely and honest appeals to them to mend their ways, came in the night and flung whole loads of earth and rubbish into it, and again choked it and rendered it otherwise unfit for use. Huntington, after the death of his first wife, who had passed through the deepest depths of poverty and tribulation with him, married the wealthy relict of Sir James Sanderson, a London alderman, and passed the latter part of his life in affluence. He died in 1813, and was buried at Lewes; and, no doubt, remembering such attacks on him as that for endeavouring to clear the conduit spring at Islington, he dictated, a few days before his death, the following epitaph for himself, which appears on his gravestone:

'Here lies the Coalheaver, who departed this life July 1, 1813, in the 60th year of his age, beloved of his God, but abhorred by men. The Omniscient Judge, at the Grand Assize, shall ratify and confirm this to the confusion of many thousands; for England and its metropolis shall know that there has been a prophet among them.—W. H. S. S.'

The Rev. Timothy Priestley

The Rev. Timothy Priestley resided and died at his daughter's house in Lower Street. Timothy Priestley is distinguished as the brother of the celebrated Dr. Priestley rather than for anything else. He was first minister of Kipping, in Yorkshire, and afterwards of the Independent congregation in Cannon Street, Manchester; and, lastly, of the Independent Chapel in Jewin Street, London. He died in April, 1814, aged eighty years.

Thomas Skinner Surr

Thomas Skinner Surr, a somewhat voluminous novelist, was, for some years, an inhabitant of Islington. He wrote 'Christ's Hospital,' a poem; 'George Barnwell,' 'Splendid Misery,' 'A Winter in London,' and the 'Magic of Wealth,' novels. He was a clerk in the Bank of England, and married a Miss Griffiths, a sister-in-law of Sir Richard Phillips.

John Thurston and Robert Branston

These distinguished engravers lived at Holloway, near Lorraine Place. Mr. Thurston was a native of Scarborough, and originally a copper-plate engraver. Under the late James Heath, he engraved the two celebrated plates of the 'Death of Major Pierson,' and the 'Dead Soldier.' He turned his attention to designing on wood, and became one of the best wood-engravers of his time. Being of a retiring disposition, he was personally little known beyond the circle of his family and immediate friends. He was of a delicate constitution, and close application to his art is supposed to have shortened his days. He died at Holloway, in 1821, aged forty eight, and was buried in Islington churchyard.

Robert Branston also commenced as a copper-plate engraver, besides which he was a heraldic painter. He was a native of Lynn, in Norfolk. In 1802 he came to London and adopted the profession of a wood-engraver. His style of engraving was peculiarly his own. He engraved human figures and indoor scenes with great precision and clearness, but in trees and natural scenery he was not so successful. Some of his productions are to be found in the 'History of England,' published by Scholey; in Bloomfield's `Wild Flowers,' and other literary works; but the finest specimen of his skill is a large cut of the `Cave of Despair' in Savage's `Hints on Decorative Painting.'

Thomas Davison

Thomas Davison, the excellent printer of Whitefriars, Fleet Street, had his printer's ink and lamp-black manufactory in the Hornsey Boad, near Mount Pleasant; still, we believe, conducted by Messrs. Shackell and Co.

Mr. and Mrs. Barbauld

Mr. and Mrs. Barbauld have been already noticed as residents of this parish, by Mr. Barbauld's connection as minister with the Unitarian Chapel at Newington Green, and by a memorial tablet to Mrs. Barbauld in that chapel.

John Nichols

John Nichols, Printer and Proprietor of the `Gentleman's Magazine,' is one of the most distinguished men which Islington has produced, for there he was born on February 2, 1744. He was educated at the academy of Mr. John Shield, who seems not only to have been the chief keeper of a school at Islington, but meritoriously anxious to promote the talents of such amongst his pupils as showed any. Mr. Nichols was intended for the navy, but the death of his maternal uncle, Lieutenant Wilmot, put an end to this design, and he was apprenticed to the celebrated printer William Bowyer, whose renown as a topographer he was destined widely to diffuse. Mr. Bowyer early conceived a great regard for young Nichols, cultivated his literary talents, and in 1766 took him into partnership, and destined him for his successor. Previous to this he had published poems, amongst them one on Islington. From the period of his becoming partner of Mr. Bowyer to his death, he continued to produce elaborate historical, biographical, topographical and antiquarian books, with unremitting energy and astounding industry. In 1755 he published a valuable supplementary volume to Dr. Hawksworth's edition of Dean Swift's 'Works,' and in the following year, the `Original Works, in Prose and Verse, of William King, LL.D.' In 1778 he became a shareholder in the 'Gentleman's Magazine,' which he continued to edit for nearly half a century. In 1779, in connection with Dr. Ducarel, he published the 'History of the Abbey of Bee, near Rouen,' and 'Some Account of the Alien Priories.' Another coadjutor in these works, Richard Gough, the celebrated antiquary, became a close and life-long friend of Mr. Nichols. In 1780 he published a very curious 'Collection of Royal Wills,' aided by the same friends. Whilst compiling these great works, he also made and published a 'Collection of Miscellaneous Poems,' to which, in 1782, he added four other volumes. On the suggestion, and with the assistance of Mr. Gough, he began in 1780 to publish the 'Bibliotheca Topographica Britannica,' a work which grew into eight large quarto volumes, including many articles of British topography, manuscript or printed, which were in danger of becoming lost or were grown scarce.

In 1781 appeared 'Biographical Anecdotes of William Hogarth,' of which four editions were published between that date and 1817; and, in the latter year, he published the 'Biographical Memoirs of William Ged, including a particular account of his Progress in the Art of Block-printing.' In 1782 he produced the first volume of his 'Anecdotes of Bowyer and his Literary Friends,' which, under the name of 'Literary Anecdotes of the Eighteenth Century,' gradually grew to ten volumes; to which he afterwards added six more, under the title of 'Illustrations of the Literary History of the Eighteenth Century.' This may be considered the great work of Mr. Nichols' life. It contains accounts of all the principal works of the great authors of the time which Mr. Bowyer printed; but those who expect a collection of chatty anecdotes of the men of that period will find themselves disappointed. Then followed his work, ranking in bulk and reputation next to his 'Literary Anecdotes,' the 'History of Leicestershire,' which, from 1782 to 1815, grew to four large volumes. During the period in which he was producing the 'History of Leicestershire,' he wrote or edited no fewer than forty seven other works, including 'Bowyer's Greek Testament,' 'Bishop Atterbury's Correspondence,' the 'History and Antiquities of Lambeth Palace,' the 'Progresses and Royal Processions of Queen Elizabeth,' 3 vols., the 'Progresses of James the First,' 4 vols. Besides these were the 'History and Antiquities of

Canonbury, with some account of the parish of Islington,' and 'Illustrations of the Manners and Expenses of Antient Times in England.' He also edited an edition of the 'Tatler,' with notes illustrative of biography and manners.

Amid all these vast labours Mr. Nichols found time to distinguish himself as a member of the Corporation of London, and declared it the height of his ambition to be elected Master of the Stationers' Company, which took place in 1804. In January 1807 he had a fall in his printing office in Red Lion Square, which fractured his thigh; and a far more momentous misfortune overtook him in February 1809, by the destruction of his printing office and warehouses by fire, with all their valuable contents. This grand disaster did not, however, break his spirits or his perseverance. He received the most cordial sympathy, and offers of unlimited assistance, from his friends, and went on actively with his 'History of Leicestershire' and 'Literary Anecdotes.' These were completed by 1822; and on November 26, 1826, as he was proceeding up stairs to bed, he suddenly sunk on his knees, and expired without a sigh or a groan, aged eighty two. He was interred in Islington Churchyard, only a few yards from the house where he was born. His funeral was attended by Sir Henry Ellis, of the British Museum, Alexander Chalmers, W. Tooke, and other men of note. A tomb in the churchyard records his interment and many other members of his family. John Nichols was certainly one of the chief Titans of solid literature and printing.

Daniel Wilson, M.A. and D.D.

Daniel Wilson, M.A., and in 1832 D.D., was a man much esteemed by his parishioners in Islington, where he was vicar of St. Mary's. Mr. Wilson had been Vice-principal of St. Edmund's Hall, Oxford, where he highly distinguished himself, and gained several prizes. On his ordination he became curate to Mr. Cecil, at Chobham and Bisley, in Surrey; then curate of Upper and Nether Worton, in Oxfordshire. On the retirement of Mr. Cecil from St. John's, Bedford Row, he succeeded him in 1809; and in 1829, on the decease of Dr. Strahan, he became vicar of Islington. In 1832 he succeeded Bishop Heber as Bishop of Calcutta, and his son, the Rev. Daniel Wilson, toot his place as vicar of Islington.

Bishop Wilson was an author of a somewhat voluminous

character. He published two volumes of Sermons: 'Substance of a Conversation with John Bellingham the day Previous to his Execution;' 'A Tour on the Continent;' 'Lectures on the Evidences of Christianity,' and an edition of 'Baxter's Reformed Pastor,' &c.

Various Eminent Dissenting Ministers

Islington and Highbury have been also the residence of various eminent Dissenting ministers. The names of **Burder**, **Bogue**, and **Clayton** have a familiar sound there within the present century. The **Rev. Rowland Hill** in his time used to hold large meetings in the open air in White Conduit Fields.

William Woodfall

This great parliamentary reporter, and brother of the printer of the 'Public Advertiser,' and of the 'Letters of Junius,' lived some time in a house at the back of Colebrook Row.

John Thomas Smith

John Thomas Smith, for many years keeper of the prints at the British Museum, lived at No. 8, Popham Terrace, near the 'Barley Mow' public house, Frog Lane. Mr. Smith had the singular fortune of being born in a hackney coach, on June 23, 1766. As a boy he was employed in the studio of Nollekens, the sculptor, where he continued three years. He became a student of the Royal Academy, and was celebrated for his fine imitations of Rembrandt and Ostade; and copied several of the small pictures of Gainsborough, who kindly noticed him. His chief reputation, however, rests on the publication of several topographical works: 'Antiquities of London and its Environs,' 'Remarks on Rural Scenery, with Etchings of Cottages,' 'Antiquities of Westminster,' 'Ancient Topography of London,' 'Vagabondiana; or, Anecdotes of Mendicant Wanderers through the Streets of London, with Portraits of the most Remarkable,' and 'Nollekens and his Times.' Some of the topographical works contain engravings of topographical objects which no longer exist; and 'Nollekens and his Times' includes memoirs of Roubiliac, Hogarth, Reynolds, Fuseli, Flaxman, Blake, &c. Mr. Smith died March 3, 1833.

Nelson, historian of Islington

Nelson, the historian of Islington, lived and died at the house at the corner of Cumberland Street, on Islington Green.

Joseph Grimaldi

Joseph Grimaldi, the inimitable pantomimic clown, lived at No. 33, Southampton Street, Pentonville. He was the son of Signor Grimaldi, an artiste noted for his humour and eccentricities, who by day followed the profession of a dentist, and by night that of ballet-master at Drury Lane. For a period of forty years Grimaldi, the clown, delighted the laughter-loving audiences of Drury Lane, Covent Garden, and Sadler's Wells with a rich buffoonery peculiarly his own. He died in 1827, and Charles Dickens became his genial biographer.

Samuel Rogers

We have already mentioned the interment of the poet Rogers in the family vault in Hornsey churchyard. We have here to note his birth and early youth, the scene of which was Newington Green. The house in which Samuel Rogers was born is the first old house that presents itself on the west side proceeding from Ball's Pond. The date of his birth is July 80, 1763. His father, Thomas Rogers, and his maternal grandfather, Daniel Radford, were trustees for the Newington Green Presbyterian Chapel, which trust devolved on the poet. The poet and his family were, it thus appears, closely connected with the Unitarian congregation meeting there. This Daniel Radford was grandson of the distinguished Philip Henry, one of the ejected ministers, and father of Matthew Henry - the celebrated author of the 'Exposition of the Bible,' and other theological and critical works - Nonconformist minister of Hackney. By this line, the mother of the poet was a direct descendant of Philip Henry. Mr. Rogers's father was from Worcestershire, a banker in London, which business Mr. Rogers retained, so that he was always independent of the barren heights of Parnassus, and could afford to bring out his works in fine style and beautifully illustrated. Besides, Mr. Rogers was celebrated for giving excellent dinners and breakfasts to literary men; and what critic would think of quarrelling with a good dinner or even breakfast? Yet someone in 'Griffiths' Monthly Review,' who had probably been overlooked in these invitations, on the first occasion of Rogers appearing in print, that is, on the publication of his 'Ode to Superstition, and other Poems,' said, 'Mr. Rogers writes very pretty prose, but he should never think of meddling with verse!' The result showed that this censor should never have thought of meddling with criticism.

Mr. Rogers's future works are too familiar to the public to require particular reference; his 'Pleasures of Memory,' 'An Epistle and other Poems,' 'The Voyage of Columbus,' 'Jacqueline,' 'Human Life,' and, lastly, in 1830, when sixty seven years of age, his 'Italy.' All his poems are distinguished not only by a calm flow of diction and of feeling, but by an exquisite perception of the beauties and amenities of nature. There is, however, a very marked difference of style betwixt his earlier and later productions. The earlier ones are formed on the model of Pope: the latter ones have rhythm more peculiarly his own.

On quitting Newington Green, Mr. Rogers took chambers in the Temple, where he continued to reside five years. In 1800 he removed to 22, St. James's Place, overlooking the Green Park, where he lived for more than half a century, and, indeed, till his decease. In this house he wrote all his poems, except the 'Pleasures of Memory,' the 'Epistle,' and 'Ode to Superstition;' and here he was visited by a vast number of the chief authors of the time, amongst them Byron, Scott, Moore, Crabbe, Fox, Campbell, Wordsworth, Southey, Coleridge, &c. There also the Queen occasionally made him a morning visit. There he died, December 18, 1855; and his sister, who had lived with him, preceded him only on January 29 of the same year. His collection of pictures, antiquities, marbles, works of art and *vertù* of different kinds, books, plate, &c., were disposed of by Messrs. Christie and Manson, in a sale of twenty two days, and produced the sum of £50,148 14s. 3d.

Charles Lamb

Lamb and his sister lived for some years at Islington, on the banks of the New River, where George Dyer visited him. Dyer was the editor of the 'Cambridge Edition of the Classics,' and, in fact, that of 'Valpy,' for he compiled all this vast work except the preface - a work of 141 volumes. Dyer became blind through his immense labours and over-use of his eyesight; and, whilst he was in a state of purblindness, walked one day, on leaving Lamb's cottage, right into the river, and narrowly escaped drowning. Lamb used to quiz Dyer's simple-mindedness, but had a great regard for him, and ranked him amongst the best-hearted of mankind. Lamb was born in London, and educated at Christ's Hospital, where Coleridge was at the same time; and from this date commenced the friendship of these two men of genius, and continued to the end.

Charles Lamb's House
(From an original drawing by J. W. Archer,
in the possession of W. Twopeny, Esq.)

Lamb in his youth was attached to a young lady of Islington, whom he commemorated in his early verses as 'the fair-haired maid.' It was his delight to visit her, and enjoy a stroll with her through the fields at Islington; but a hereditary taint of insanity showing itself in him, and his sister becoming, ever and anon, confirmedly insane, and unhappily killing her mother in one of her paroxysms, he magnanimously gave up all idea of marrying, and devoted his leisure hours to literature and to her care. Though a simple clerk in the India House, Lamb's genius, quaint humour, and bonhommie, made his society sought after by the greatest minds of his age. Besides Coleridge, Southey, Wordsworth, Hazlitt, Rogers, Godwin, Barry Cornwall, Crabbe, Robinson, Sir Thomas Talfourd, and Moxon, the poet and publisher of poets, were his most intimate friends, and many of them constant visitors at his house, on the genial evenings which were spent there. His 'Essays, by Elia' afford the best idea of the man and his character, as much as of his genius. There was a quaint and racy humour about both his conversation and his writing, which were perfectly his own. His curious answer to one of the heads of the India House, who delicately reminded him of his habit of going late to office, is an unsurpassable specimen of his wit: 'Yes, that is very true; but then you see how early I go away!'

Charles Lamb was one of the most distinguished of the contributors to the 'London Magazine,' in which Hazlitt, Bowring, Barry Cornwall, and other of the leading literary men of the day were writers; and amongst them that extraordinary literary fop and poisoner, Wainwright, who contributed under the name of James Weathercock. How such men as Lamb and Proctor could admire the flashy articles of this man is amazing; hut the rogue revealed his real character by poisoning his sister-in-law, and it is pretty certain his father and mother-in-law, for their property, or for sums for which he had insured their lives. He had insured the life of his sister-in-law, a fine healthy young woman, in different offices for £30,000, and immediately afterwards she died suddenly. It was then recollected that his father-in-law and mother-in-law had also, in full apparent health, died suddenly. The assurance offices refused to pay the sums insured on the life of his sister-in-law, and Wainwright, though the charge of murder could not be substantiated, the nature and mode of action of strychnine being then little known, was transported for life to Tasmania, where he died. Lord Lytton has worked Wainwright up in 'The Children of the Night,' and an account of him is given by Talfourd in his 'Life and Letters of Charles Lamb.'

Besides his 'Essays,' Lamb gained considerable reputation by his poetry and by his 'Tales from Shakespeare.' Amongst the old English authors he luxuriated. His sister Mary, the author of the beautiful stories of 'Mrs. Lester's School,' also is said to have assisted him in his 'Adventures of Ulysses' and other things. He wrote also 'Rosamond Gray,' 'John Woodville,' a tragedy, and

'Specimens of English Dramatic Writers, who lived about the time of Shakespeare, with Notes.' Amid the many sorrows and severe trials of Charles Lamb, aggravated by much poverty in early life, he had the satisfaction of growing into comparative ease, and thus of not being under the necessity of writing for support. From this cause we have probably fewer works by him, but better. On his retirement from the India House he received an annuity of £450 a year in lieu of his salary, which had risen to £700 a year. After leaving Islington, he removed to Edmonton, where he died in 1834.

Sir Richard Phillips

In one of the detached houses opposite to Lorraine Place once lived the well-known publisher and author, Sir Richard Phillips. Sir Richard had passed through many dangers and adventures before he arrived at the dignity of knighthood. As a boy, he was brought up by his uncle, a brewer in Oxford Street; but not liking the trade, he determined to seek out a new track for himself. One of the first places which he procured was that of usher in a school at Chester. We next find him at Leicester, installed as schoolmaster, and also keeping a small shop for the sale of hosiery. He was still, however, aiming at a literary life, and conceived the idea of establishing a newspaper. The 'Leicester Herald' was the result of this speculation, and his republican principles having introduced him to Dr. Priestley, that remarkable man became his chief writer. To his newspaper he added the business of a bookseller; in fact, at that time of day, the country newspaper generally issued from the bookseller's shop. But these were arbitrary times: the 'Rights of Man,' by Thomas Paine, had excited a strong feeling of radicalism, and in many towns domiciliary visits were made by the magistrates to hunt out this alarming book, and all copies of it that could he found were collected and publicly burnt. Mr. Phillips was convicted of selling this work, and was committed for twelve months to Leicester Gaol. There he fell under the surveillance of the famous fat gaoler, Daniel Lambert, who, as fat men usually are, was a mild-tempered individual, and treated him very kindly.

This treatment by his townsmen seems to have greatly disgusted Mr. Phillips; he felt that he was moving in too contracted a sphere for a person of his liberal ideas, and he betook himself to the great centre of activity - London. There he commenced the 'Monthly Magazine,' a journal which he continued to edit for many years. He was fortunate to secure the able assistance in its management of Dr. Aikin; and he numbered on his literary staff Dr. Walcot, Mr. Belsham, Capel Lofft, Dr. Mavor, editor of a popular collection of 'Voyages and Travels;' Sir John Carr, also author of 'Travels in Ireland, Scotland, &c.;' Pratt, the poet; and his brother-in-law, Mr. Surr. In 1807 he was elected one of the Sheriffs of London; and, on presenting a corporation address to the King, he was offered the honour of knighthood, and accepted it, much to the surprise of his republican friends and readers. Sir Richard, however, made a good sheriff, and exerted himself to introduce reforms into the city, and particularly into the prisons, where they were much needed. During this time of public office and popularity, the affairs of Sir Richard were not in a prosperous condition; and in the following year, 1809, they came to a crisis. His large publishing establishment was broken up, and his effects sold. He managed, however, to buy in, through a friend, the 'Monthly Magazine,' and some of his most valuable copyrights, and these became his chief support during the remainder of his life. He died at Brighton in his seventy third year.

Amongst the publications of Sir Richard were various school books: 'A Letter on the Duties of a Sheriff of London,' 'Treatise on the Powers and Duties of Juries,' 'Golden Rules for Jurymen,' 'On Stramonium as a Remedy for Asthma,' 'A Morning Walk from London to Kew,' and 'Twelve Essays on the Proximate Causes of the Phenomena of Nature, developing new principles of Universal Causation.' Sir Richard imagined that he had disproved the laws of nature as explained by Newton, and penetrated deeper into the system of the universe than former natural philosophers and theologians. Public opinion has not supported his theories. He is believed to have drawn his ideas on these subjects very much from the speculations of Euler, the German natural philosopher, especially as enunciated in his 'Lettres à une princesse d'Allemagne sur quelques sujets de Physique et de Philosophie.'

Sir Richard was also one of the earliest vegetarians. The only time that I ever saw him was one on which he called to obtain some information in furtherance of a work which he had in hand.

We were just sitting down to dinner, and invited him to partake; but no sooner had he seated himself, than, to our consternation, he informed us that he never ate meat. We expressed our apprehension that he would not be able to make a dinner, and ordered up the pudding as the only resource. 'Don't make any alteration in your arrangements for me,' said the vegetarian knight, 'I see a very good first course before me.' There was a roast goose on the table, and a sauce-tureen of apple sauce. With the greatest coolness in the world, Sir Richard took up the sauce, turned it all out upon his plate, and quickly dispatched it, pronouncing it very good. With equal appetite and equal disregard of the wants of others, he made a vigorous attack on the rest of the vegetables, and raised our wonder at the digestive capacity of a then, to us, new animal of the granivorous order. After dinner, Sir Richard preferred his literary inquiries, and on certain books being named as the best sources, he begged to know whether we had them, and then to borrow them. We saw one after another descend into capacious and ominously gaping outside pockets in his coat, destined never to reissue from those gulfs within our reach or range of vision. Such was our sole experience of Sir Richard Phillips. We discovered that as he had, *soi-disant*, discovered new laws of nature, he had equally discovered new laws of morals and social intercourse. Sir Richard was one of the 'Curiosities of Literature.'

Miss Hannah Lawrence

This lady, the author of 'London in the Olden Time;' of 'Memoirs of the Queens of England from the Twelfth to the Sixteenth Century;' and of 'History of Women in England,' still resides at 22, Albion Terrace, Barnsbury. Miss Lawrence has also been an extensive contributor to the periodical literature of the day, especially to the 'Athenæum' and 'British Quarterly Review,' in which her criticisms are as remarkable for their fair impartiality as for their historic research.

Dr. Jackson

The present Bishop of London is connected with Islington by having held as his first appointment the head-mastership of Islington Proprietary School.

POSTSCRIPT

Here we wind up our volume. We have reached the limit of the Northern Heights of London; and I think the reader will confess that, in ranging all these pleasant heights, we have found an extraordinary wealth of persons and things of great interest. The metropolis below has sent up a certain portion of its most prominent and peculiar people for our more particular observation. Historic events are scattered over these hills in considerable numbers. Authors, artists, actors, seekers of pleasure, and seekers of purses, on foot and on horseback, have exerted their varied talents and tastes on this elevated theatre. Men and women, too, whose eccentricities were curbed by the densely-thronged life below, have come hither and expanded their idiosyncracies, as peacocks and turkeys expand their tails before a select number of their own kind. Misers have counted their gold in still corners; Dick Turpin and Co. have counted other people's more openly; domestic tyrants have reigned in melancholy glory over impotent victims; poets have fled from noise and duns to perfect those flowers of the spirit which are trampled upon by the iron heels of landlords and their horny-fingered emissaries. Speculative engineers have worked out the good of London at the cost of their own fortunes; and great lawyers - a species of ant-eaters, which live by putting out long tongues and licking up all the silly contentious flies that settle on them - have sought quiet green retreats here, in which at ease to digest the gatherings of Westminster Hall. A Baron D'Aguilar; a simple, gentle, maniacal Alexander Cruden; a Sir Hugh Middleton; a quaint Charles Lamb; a poetic and sarcastic Sam Rogers; an Oliver Goldsmith in his tower, and a Hawes on the border of the New River, pondering on the means of resuscitating the drowned; and the earlier spectacles of rising or falling Kings; of Henry VIII, figuring amongst the bowmen of Finsbury Fields; Elizabeth with her Walsinghams, Burleighs and Raleighs about her; or George II fortifying his suburbs against the discrowned Stuarts - all these have contributed their parts to our entertainment; and having done so much for the present and very appreciative generation, we also have done our best to perpetuate their sayings and doings, their labours and their pastimes, their gifts and graces.

THE END

OTHER WORKS BY WILLIAM HOWITT

VISITS TO REMARKABLE PLACES

Old Halls, Battle-Fields, and Scenes Illustrative of Striking Passages in English History and Poetry. Second and Cheaper Edition; with upwards of 80 highly-finished Woodcuts. Two Volumes, square crown 8vo. price 25s. (Longmans & Co.)

'The second edition of William Howitt's Visits to Remarkable Places - one of the best things he ever did - appears in two handsome volumes, copiously illustrated, and well suited for a gift-book of the solid order. It is above all fit for the library of the gentleman farmer, or a country resident, who has a taste for the country, the remarkable places Old England contains, and the associations connected therewith.' - Spectator.

'Mr. Howitt's two elegant volumes on old halls, battle-fields, and scenes illustrative of striking passages in English history and poetry have reached a second edition. The work is illustrated by numerous sketches of scenes and places, most of them exceedingly well known and appreciated. Alnwick is one of the places visited, and the graceful and original pen of Mr. Howitt is well adapted to enhance the interest which recent discussions have excited in respect to this famous spot in England's history. But indeed the whole work displays a rich field of historical and archæological matter, as must be evident from the mere mention of such names as Lindisferne, Culloden, and Flodden, Stratford-on-Avon, Hampton Court, Raby Castle and Brancepeth, Winchester, Seaton Delaval, Berwick and the Borders, and many more that might be named with these. The book is beautifully got up, and full of the interest attached to our ancient architectural relics and ancestral homes.'
- Builder.

THE RURAL LIFE OF ENGLAND

New and Cheaper Edition, uniform with Visits to Remarkable Places; with numerous Wood Engravings by Bewick and Williams. Square crown 8vo. price 12s. 6d. (Longmans & Co.)

'To those who have read The Book of the Seasons we do not know how we can more emphatically, and at the same time honourably, recommend these volumes, than by saying that we consider them even to surpass that work in variety, the completeness of their form and method, their curious scrutiny into odd corners and old customs, their graphic descriptions, their wisdom

and mild philosophy, and the rich relishing spirit that runs throughout, colouring all with the glorious tints of love and enthusiasm. It is not merely a charming, but an ennobling work.'
- Atlas.

THE HOMES AND HAUNTS OF THE POETS
New and Cheaper Edition. Illustrated. Crown 8vo. 7s. 6d. (Routledge & Co.)

TWO YEARS IN VICTORIA
Cheaper Edition. One Volume, 6s. (Longmans & Co.).

'This remains the only true picture of Australia after all the books that have been written on it.'
- Mr. R. H. Horne's 'Notes on Australia.'

`A perfect mine of anecdotes and facts which illustrate the state of the country and society with great force.'
- Times.

THE HISTORY OF THE SUPERNATURAL
Two Volumes, post 8vo. price 18s. (Longmans & Co.)

'These volumes show extensive research and a very elaborate industry. Everything pertaining to the supernatural in any time and in any place is brought together in them in one view.'
- British Quarterly Review.

THE HISTORY OF AUSTRALIAN AND NEW ZEALAND DISCOVERY
The only Complete and Connected History of these Discoveries. Two Volumes, 8vo. price 20s. (Longmans & Co.)

'The best and most comprehensive work which has yet appeared on the countries it treats of.' - Morning Advertiser.
'A most complete and faithful summary of the various discoveries in Australia during the last 260 years.' - Observer.
'An account of all the voyages and journeys which have contributed towards our present knowledge of Australia and the islands.' - Athenæum.
`Mr. Howitt does all the justice in his power to every gallant explorer; enlivens his history with many anecdotes, and has enriched his work with excellent maps.' - Illustrated News.
'An old friend of the public, Mr. William Howitt, who has been himself to

Australia, and whose son has made a name for himself there, has written this for a labour of love. Such a book from his hands cannot fail to be attractive.' - Examiner.

'The whole work is distinguished by a fulness of information, coupled with minuteness of detail, which indicate great research. A delightful book.' - Daily News.

'For all sorts and conditions of men this work possesses attractions.' - Morning Post.

'Mr. Howitt, not only personally connected with these colonies, but also with the subject, for his son enjoys a conspicuous position in the illustrious phalanx of Australian explorers, deserves the best thanks of the public, both at home and in the colonies, for the manner in which he has executed his task.' - Australian and New Zealand Gazette.

WOODBURN GRANGE

A Story of English Country Life. 3 vols. post 8vo. 31s. 6d. (Charles Wood.)

'In power of narrative it equals the most striking passages of Mrs. Wood and Miss Braddon.' - Philadelphia Press.

'It is a novel as thoroughly English as any we have read for a long time. It is very real, very truthful, and every incident might have happened, every character in it have lived.' - The U. S. Boston Banner.

Preparing for publication:

GEORGE FOX AND HIS FRIENDS: CONSTITUTING A HISTORY OF THE RISE OF QUAKERISM, ON A NEW PLAN.
By William Howitt.

This work, in its variety of historic characters, Fox, Penn, Barclay, Ellwood, Charles and James II., Cromwell, Milton, Naylor, Judge, and Margaret Fell, &c. &c. and the extraordinary pictures of the life and social struggles of those times - scenes in prisons, palaces, courts of justice, and city streets, on moors and mountains, on seas and in foreign lands - will present sources of interest of no ordinary kind.

NOTES TO TEXT

PART ONE: HAMPSTEAD

Cotton Manuscripts: Jul. c. iii. f. 101 b.

Arrived again in England at the end of October: Hackluyt's *Voyages*, vol. ii.

Made This Note: Pepys' *Diary*, vol. iv. p. 152.

Fifty years before: See *Gentleman's Magazine*, vol. lvi. p. 438.

In the Tatler: vol. ii. No. 59, August 1709.

Gentleman's Magazine: Vol. lxxxiii. pt. ii. p. 553

History of Musick: Vol. iv. p. 380.

As a proceeding at law, this bill . . . is certainly unique: *Gentleman's Magazine*, vol. lxxxii. part i. p. 610.

Punch: A satirical and humorous magazine established in 1841 and which ceased publication in 2002.

Life and Letters of Keats: Vol. i. p. 243,

Leigh Hunt gives us this picture of him here at Hampstead: Autobiography, vol. ii. p. 195.

He then tells an anecdote very characteristic of Shelley: Autobiography, vol. ii. p. 198.

Note of Mrs. Barbauld's to the great potter: 'Wedgwood Papers.' Mayer Manuscripts.

This proposition of Wedderburn's was at first opposed by Pitt and Grenville: Malmesbury Diary, III. 6.

Lord Brougham's estimate of this splendid adventurer: Historical Sketches, I. 87.

Uttered some pithy remarks in Parliament on the Bill for raising money for the Civil List: Harleian Manuscript 6389, f. 64.

He was actually in this house on September 3, 1712: Steele's Letters, Vol. I. p. 92.

Pope, in one of his letters to Martha Blount, says: Bowles' Supplement to 'Pope's Works,' p. 377.

Know, thou art a servant of the charity: Anecdotes, Vol. I. p. 302.

Where James was fond of staying: See 'History of England.'

They were much esteemed by those who had the honour of their friendship: See 'Noble's Memoirs of the Cromwell Family,' 1784,

8vo. Vol. I. p. 295.

Characteristic of the man: 'Memoirs of R. L. Edgeworth,' p, 223.

PART II: HISTORICAL ASSOCIATIONS OF HIGHGATE

Provided that they are not contrary to the founder's statutes:
Pat. 7 Eliz, pt, 2, April 6.

At the discretion of the governors for the time being: Entry in the Register of the chapel.

Says Lord Chancellor Campbell: `Lives of the Chief Justices,' vol. ii. p. 306.

Says Lord Campbell: `Lives of the Chief Justices,' vol. ii p. 576.

Had as little moral courage as heart: `Lives of the Chief Justices,' vol. ii. p. 508.

When the Queen's Majesty came from Highgate:
Nichol's Progresses of Queen Elizabeth, vol. iii. p. 30.

Sir Basil Brooke, of Madeley, in Shropshire, was knighted there at the same time: Nichols's Progresses of King James vol. i. pp. 430-437.

Was afterwards well laughed at for his labour:
Nichols's *Progresses of King James I*, vol. ii. p. 344.

Hunt a stag early the next morning in St. John's Wood:
Ibid. vol. iii. p. 978.

PART III: ISLINGTON

The fields were never after hedged:
Holinshead's *Chronicle*, vol. iii. f. 1494.

Macaulay had Cowley in his mind on this occasion:
Cowley's *Poems*, p. 95.

Stow gives the following account: Stow's *Survey*, p. 13.

John Buncle pathetically recurs:
Life of Buncle, vol. i. p. 104. Ed. 1825.

Were made Knights: Howe's *Chronicle*.

Greens: Green rushes for the floors.

Lord Chamberlain: Thomas, Earl of Suffolk, Lord Treasurer; one of the Committee of Lord Compton's estate.

Lord Warden: Theophilus, Lord Howard of Walden, who succeeded his father as Earl of Suffolk.

Paraded boldly before the public:
See the `Gentleman's Magazine,' vol. xciii. part 1, p. 637.

Dr. Desaguliers says he himself saw him perform the following feats: See *A Course of Experimental Philosophy*, by J. T. Desaguliers, LL.D. F.R.S., (1763) vol. i. p. 289.

Printed in Great Britain
by Amazon

62465078R00312